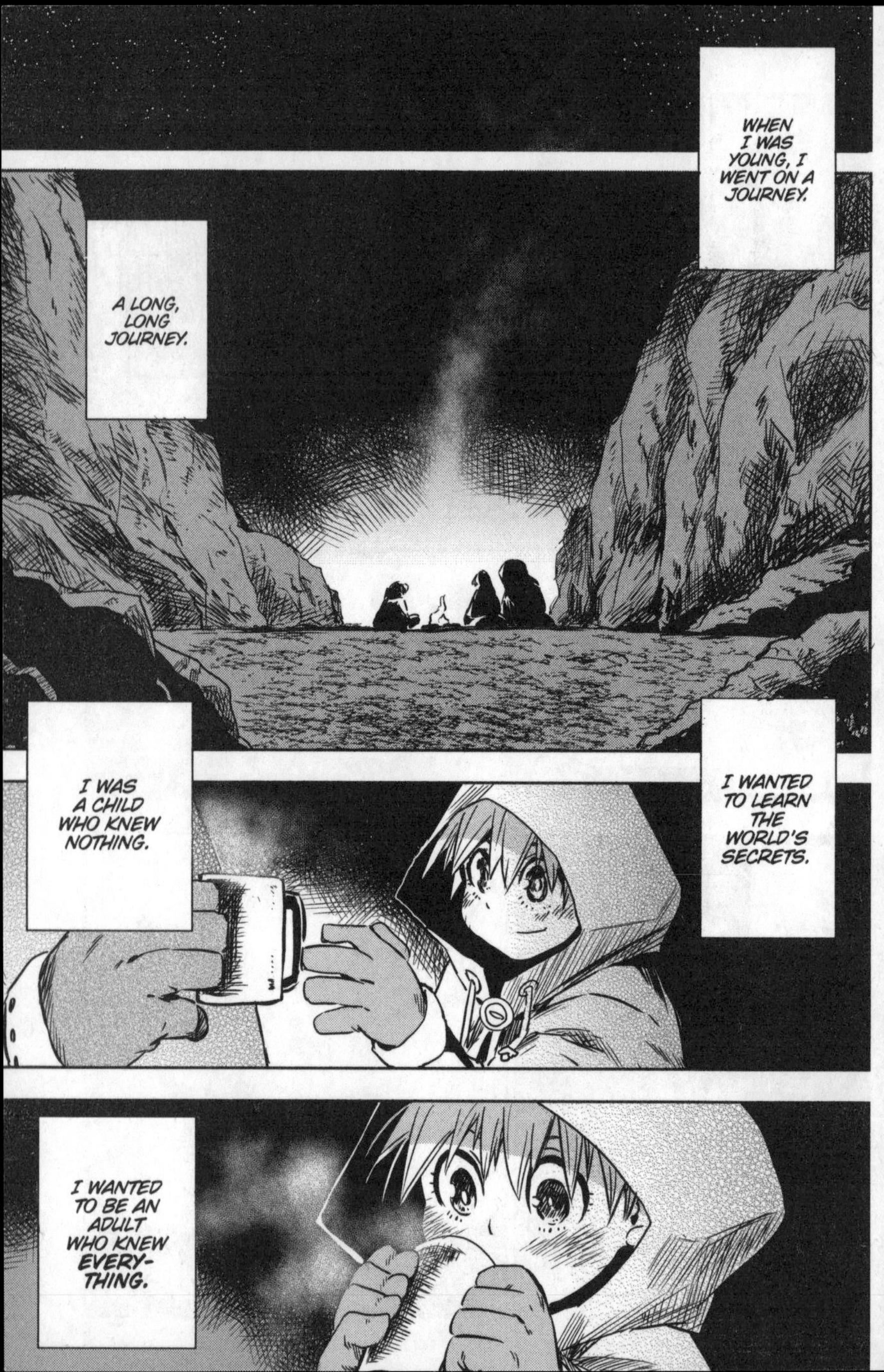
WHEN I WAS YOUNG, I WENT ON A JOURNEY.
A LONG, LONG JOURNEY.
I WANTED TO LEARN THE WORLD'S SECRETS.
I WAS A CHILD WHO KNEW NOTHING.
I WANTED TO BE AN ADULT WHO KNEW EVERY-THING.

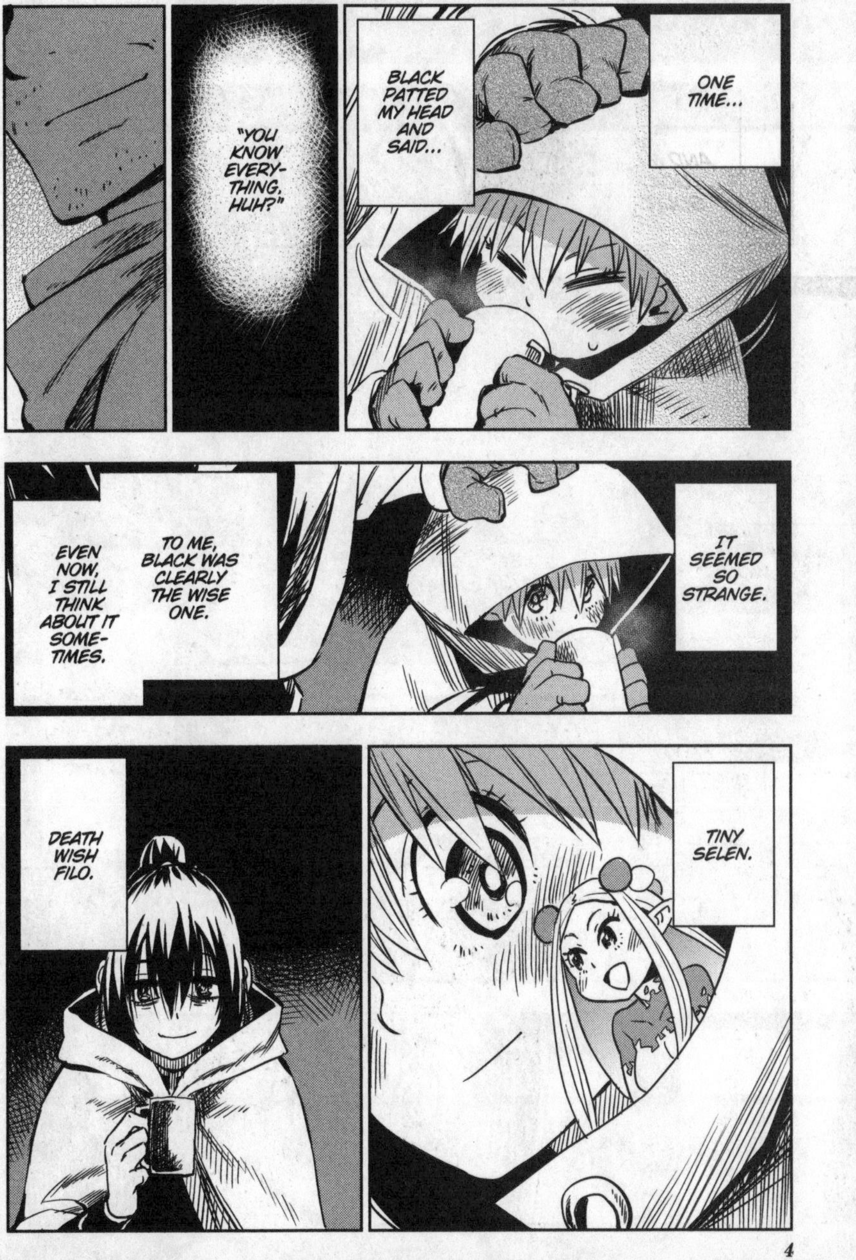
ONE TIME...
BLACK PATTED MY HEAD AND SAID...
"YOU KNOW EVERYTHING, HUH?"
IT SEEMED SO STRANGE.
TO ME, BLACK WAS CLEARLY THE WISE ONE.
EVEN NOW, I STILL THINK ABOUT IT SOMETIMES.
TINY SELEN.
DEATH WISH FILO.

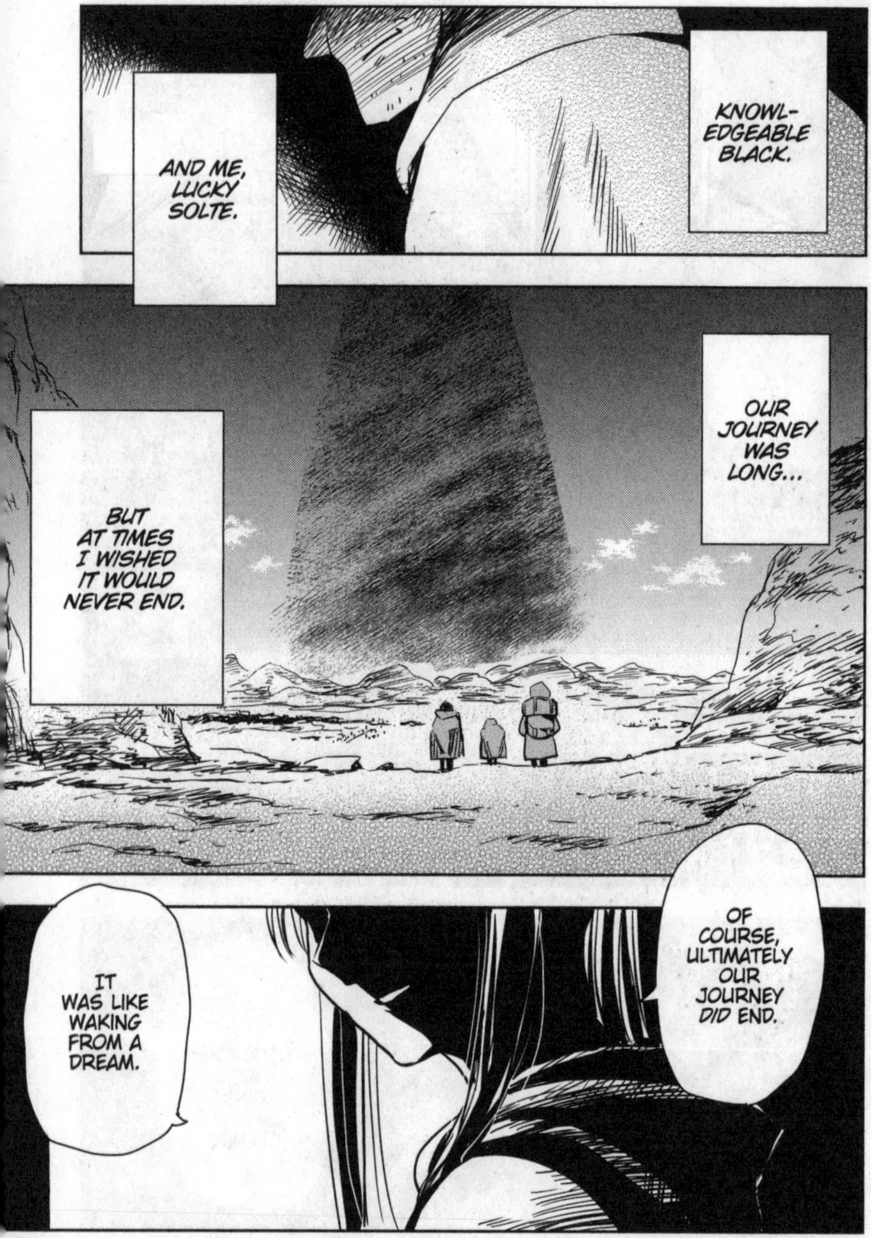
KNOWL-EDGEABLE BLACK.
AND ME, LUCKY SOLTE.
OUR JOURNEY WAS LONG...
BUT AT TIMES I WISHED IT WOULD NEVER END.
OF COURSE, ULTIMATELY OUR JOURNEY DID END.
IT WAS LIKE WAKING FROM A DREAM.

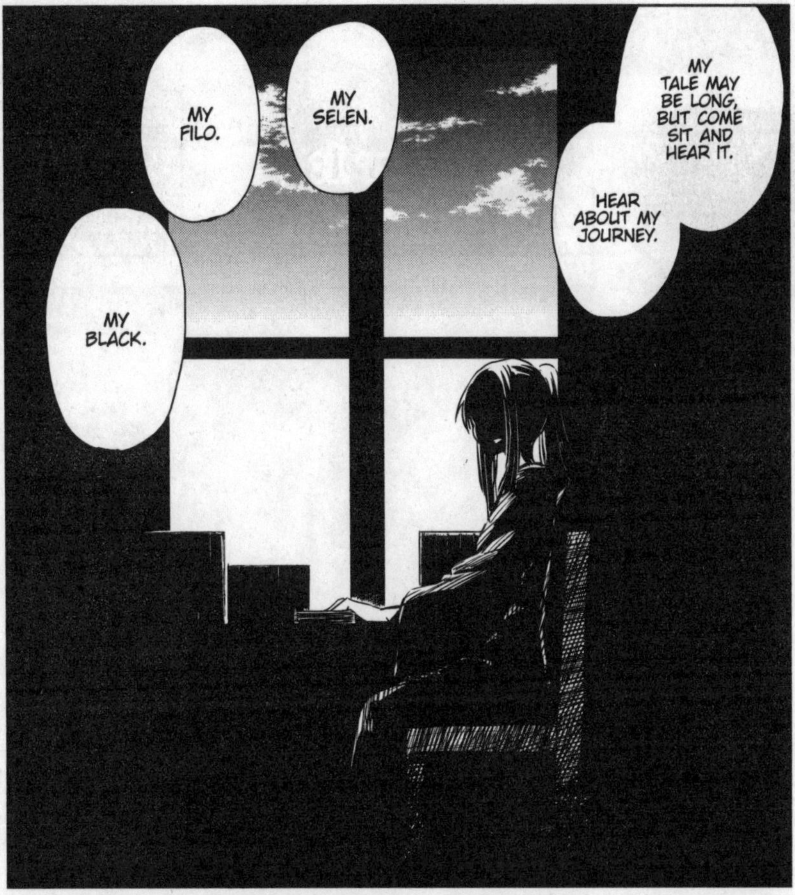
MY TALE MAY BE LONG, BUT COME SIT AND HEAR IT.
HEAR ABOUT MY JOURNEY.
MY SELEN.
MY FILO.
MY BLACK.

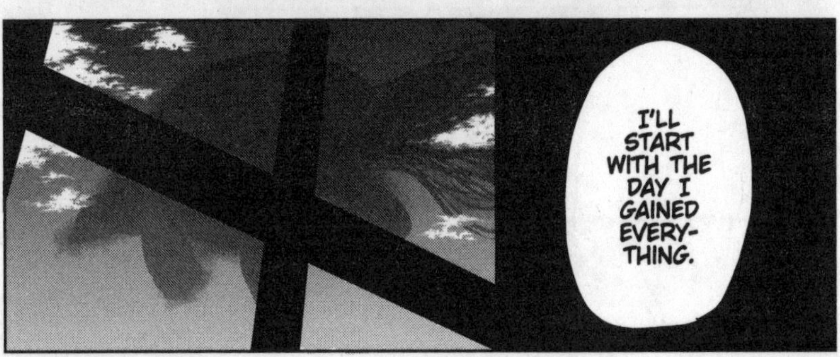
I'LL START WITH THE DAY I GAINED EVERY-THING.

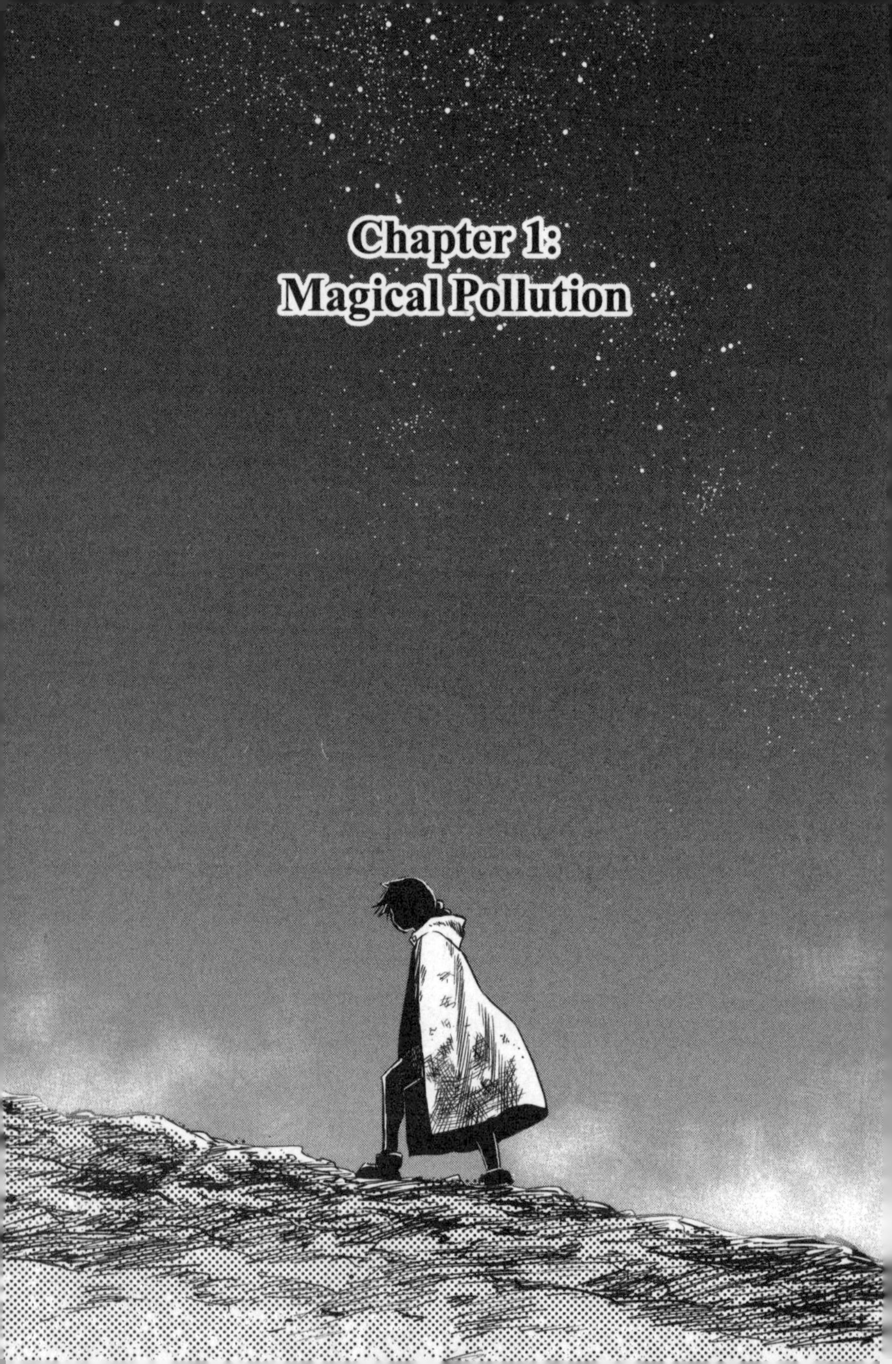
Chapter 1:
Magical Pollution

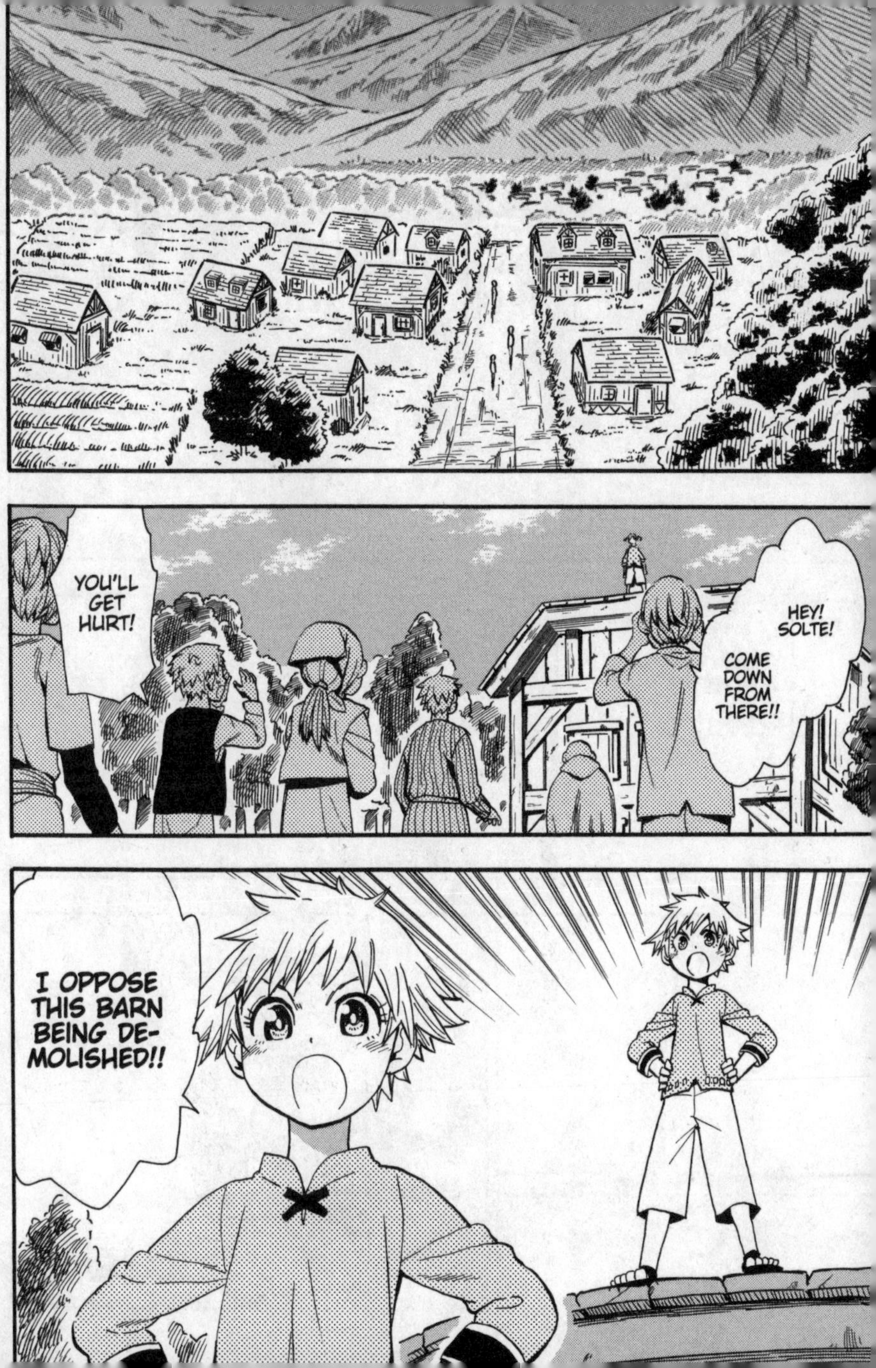
HEY! SOLTE!
COME DOWN FROM THERE!!
YOU'LL GET HURT!
I OPPOSE THIS BARN BEING DE-MOLISHED!!

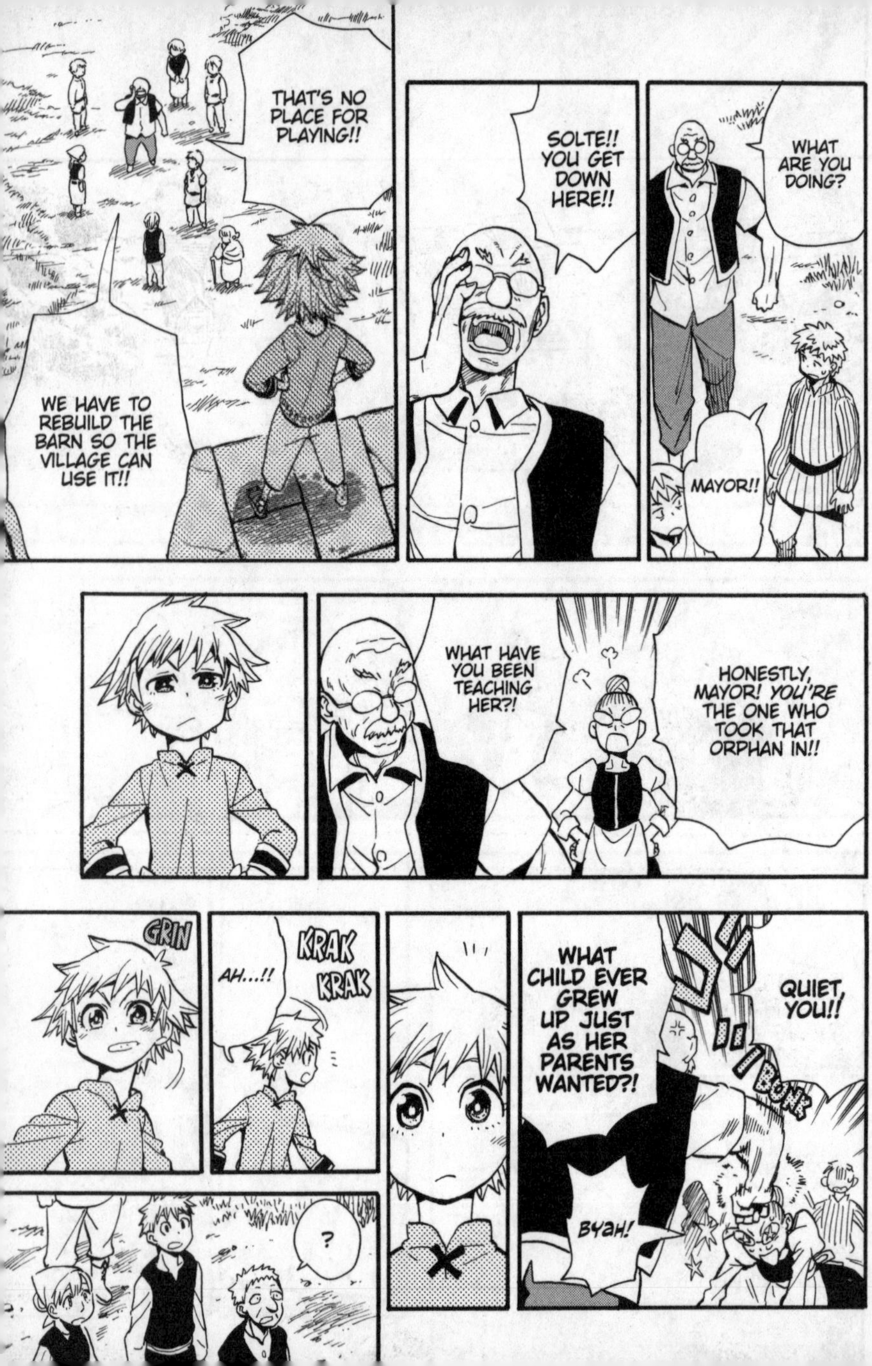
WHAT ARE YOU DOING?
MAYOR!!
SOLTE!! YOU GET DOWN HERE!!
THAT'S NO PLACE FOR PLAYING!!
WE HAVE TO REBUILD THE BARN SO THE VILLAGE CAN USE IT!!
HONESTLY, MAYOR! *YOU'RE* THE ONE WHO TOOK THAT ORPHAN IN!!
WHAT HAVE YOU BEEN TEACHING HER?!
QUIET, YOU!!
WHAT CHILD EVER GREW UP JUST AS HER PARENTS WANTED?!
DONK
BYAH!
KRAK
KRAK
AH...!!
GRIN
?

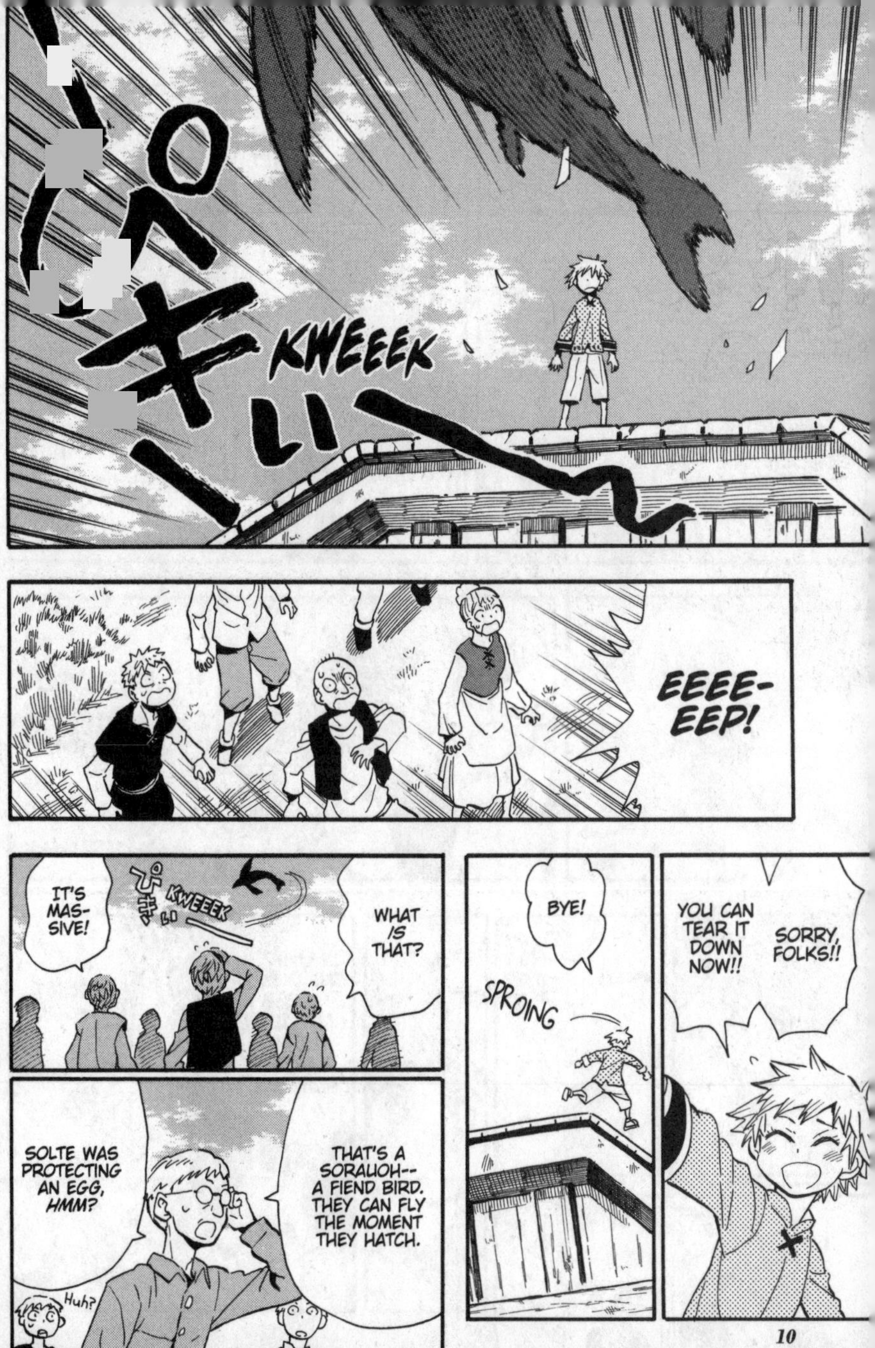
KWEEEK
EEEE-EEP!
SORRY, FOLKS!!
YOU CAN TEAR IT DOWN NOW!!
BYE!
SPROING
WHAT IS THAT?
KWEEEK
IT'S MAS-SIVE!
THAT'S A SORAUOH-- A FIEND BIRD. THEY CAN FLY THE MOMENT THEY HATCH.
SOLTE WAS PROTECTING AN EGG, HMM?
Huh?

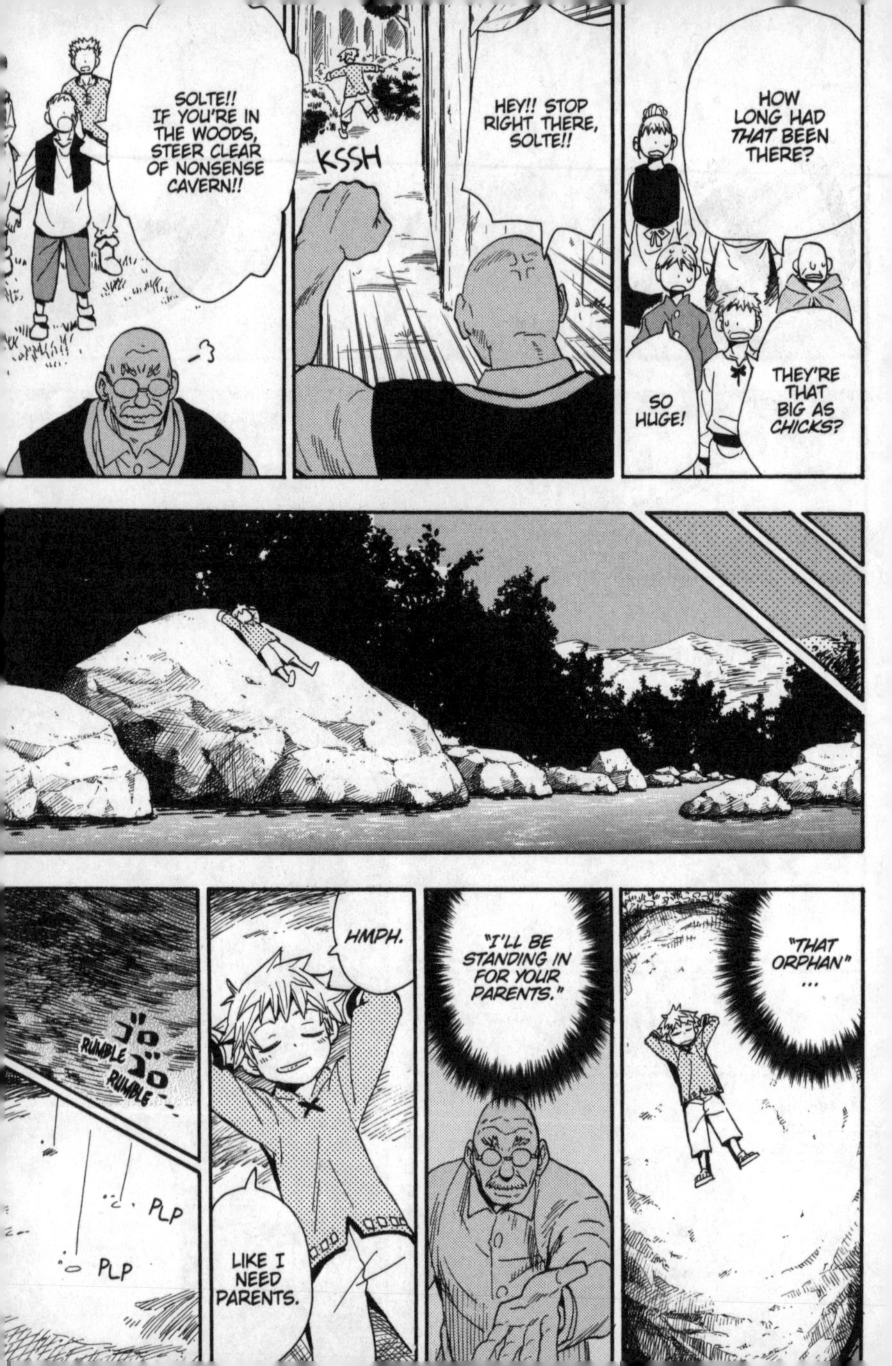
HOW LONG HAD *THAT* BEEN THERE?
THEY'RE THAT BIG AS *CHICKS?*
SO HUGE!
HEY!! STOP RIGHT THERE, SOLTE!!
KSSH
SOLTE!! IF YOU'RE IN THE WOODS, STEER CLEAR OF NONSENSE CAVERN!!
"THAT ORPHAN" ...
"I'LL BE STANDING IN FOR YOUR PARENTS."
HMPH.
LIKE I NEED PARENTS.
ゴロゴロ
RUMBLE RUMBLE
PLP
PLP

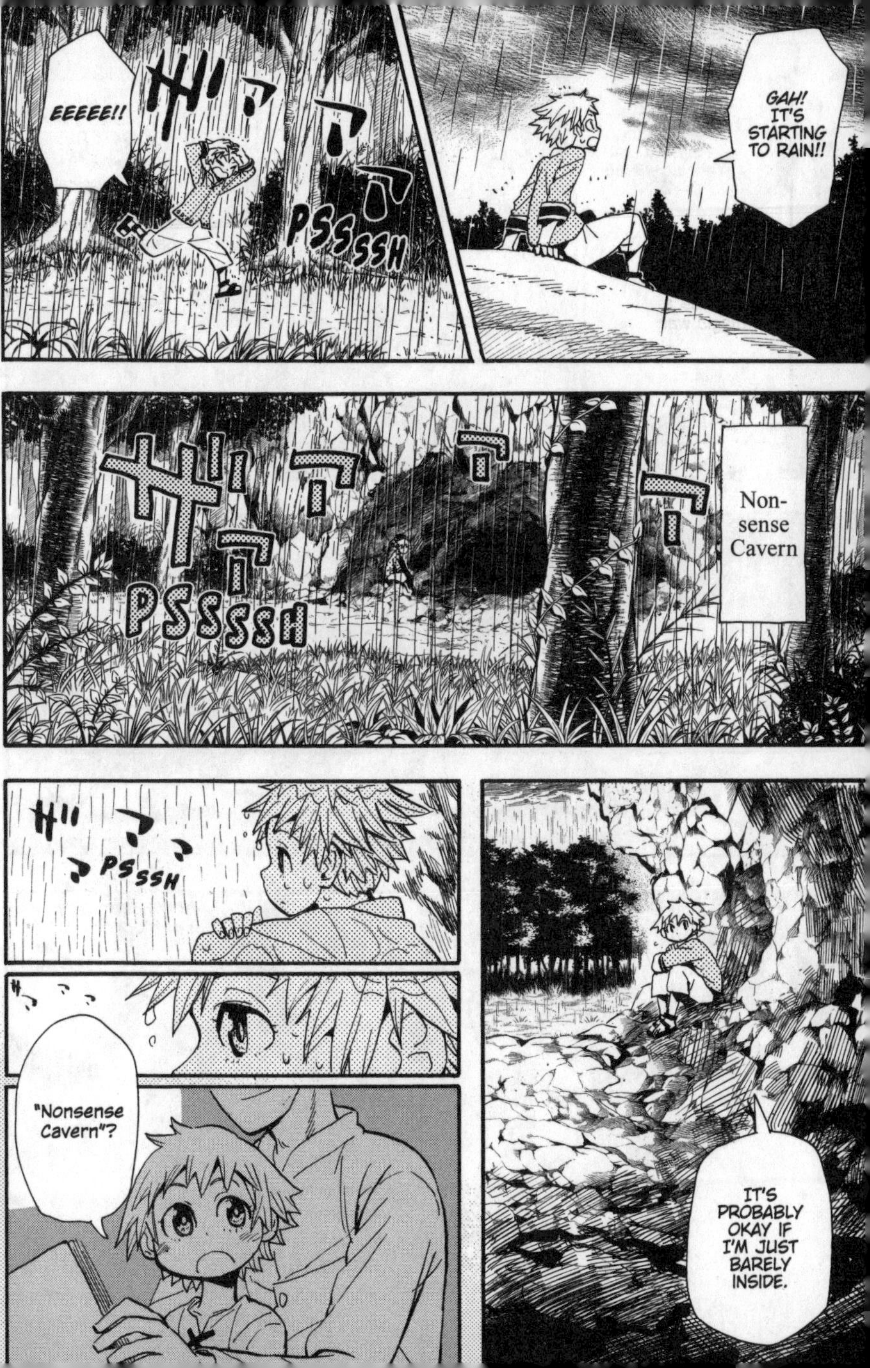
GAH! IT'S STARTING TO RAIN!!
EEEEE!!
PSSSSH
Non-sense Cavern
PSSSSH
IT'S PROBABLY OKAY IF I'M JUST BARELY INSIDE.
PSSSH
"Nonsense Cavern"?

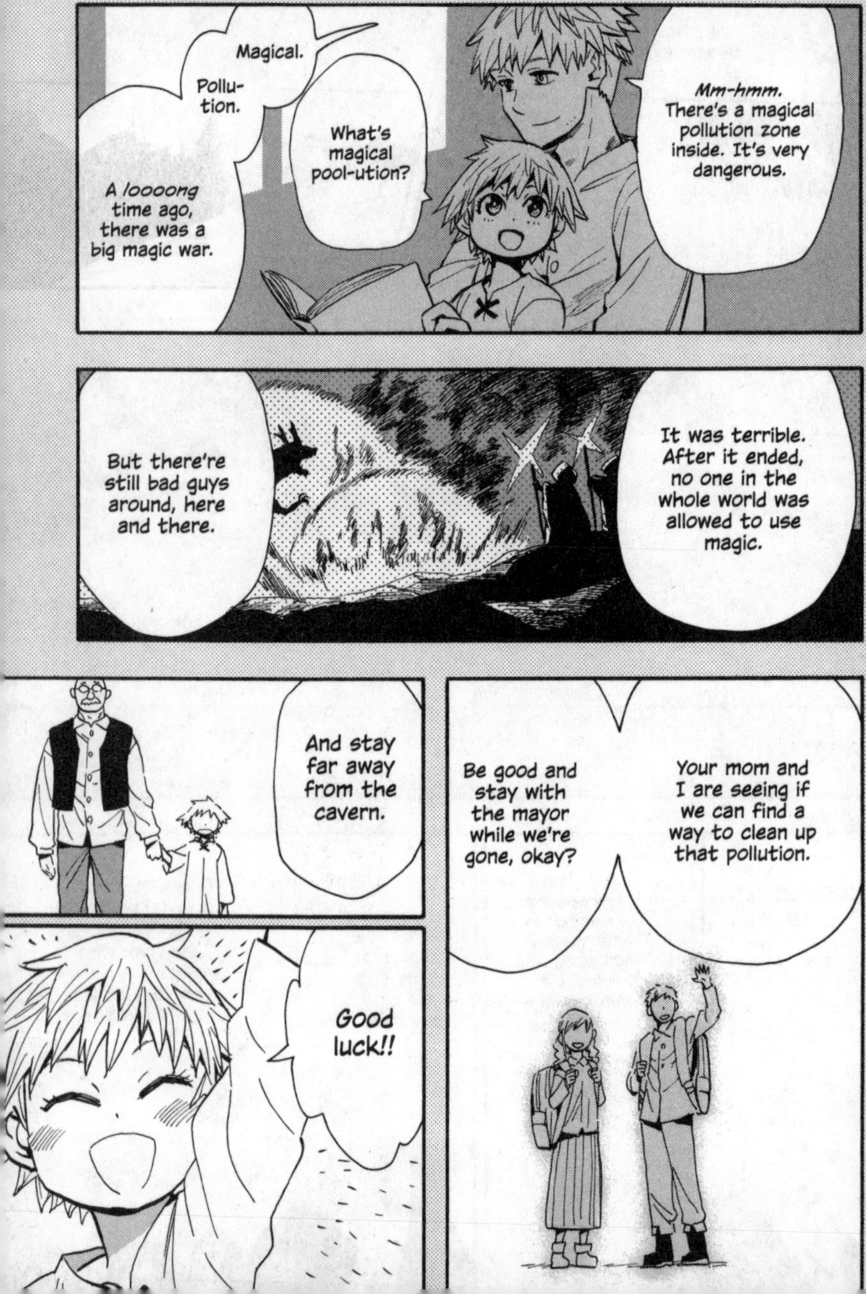
Mm-hmm. There's a magical pollution zone inside. It's very dangerous.
What's magical pool-ution?
Magical.
Pollu-tion.
A loooong time ago, there was a big magic war.
It was terrible. After it ended, no one in the whole world was allowed to use magic.
But there're still bad guys around, here and there.
Your mom and I are seeing if we can find a way to clean up that pollution.
Be good and stay with the mayor while we're gone, okay?
And stay far away from the cavern.
Good luck!!

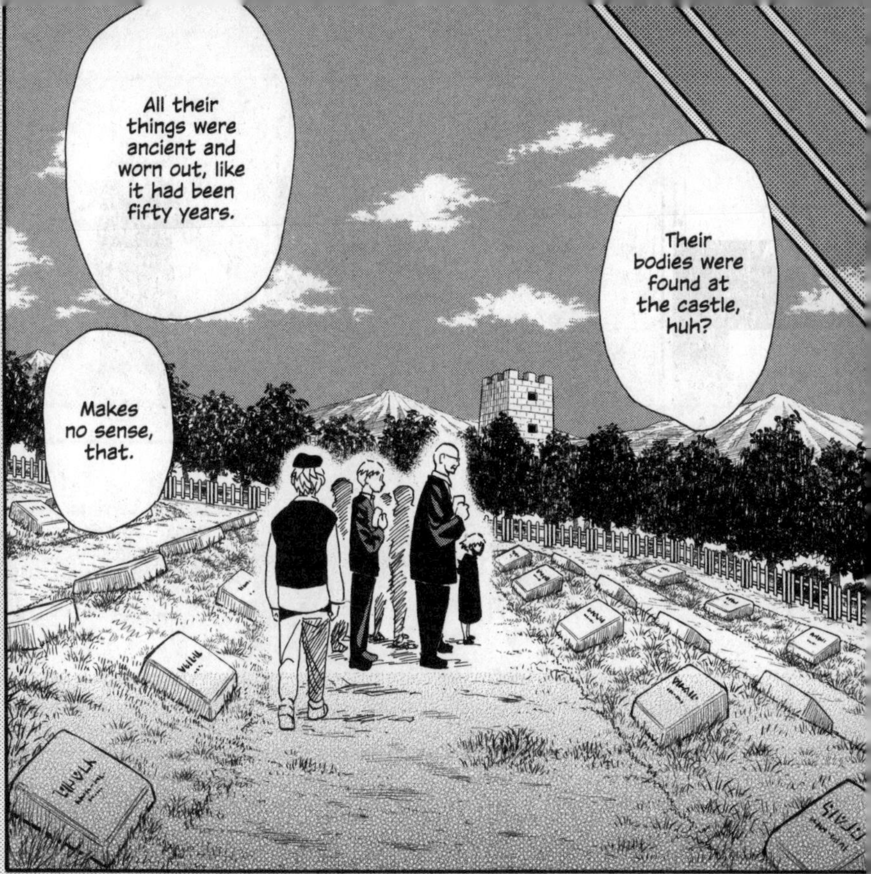
Their bodies were found at the castle, huh?
All their things were ancient and worn out, like it had been fifty years.
Makes no sense, that.

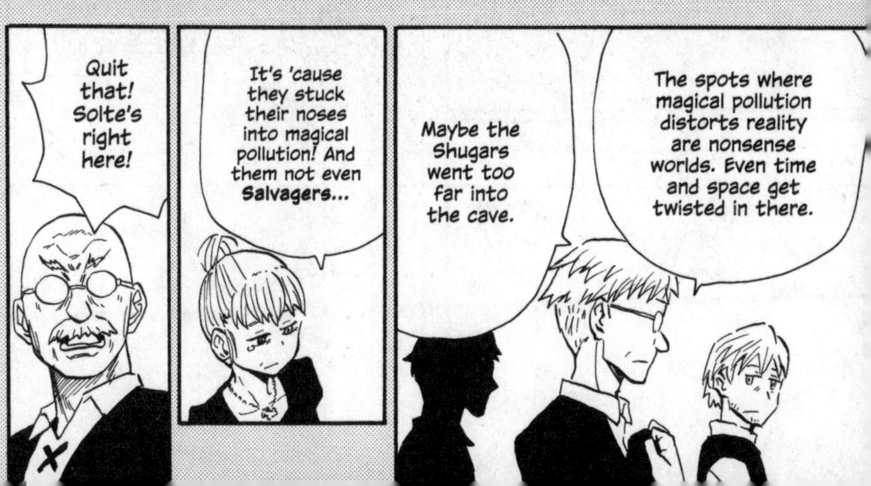
The spots where magical pollution distorts reality are nonsense worlds. Even time and space get twisted in there.
Maybe the Shugars went too far into the cave.
It's 'cause they stuck their noses into magical pollution! And them not even **Salvagers**...
Quit that! Solte's right here!

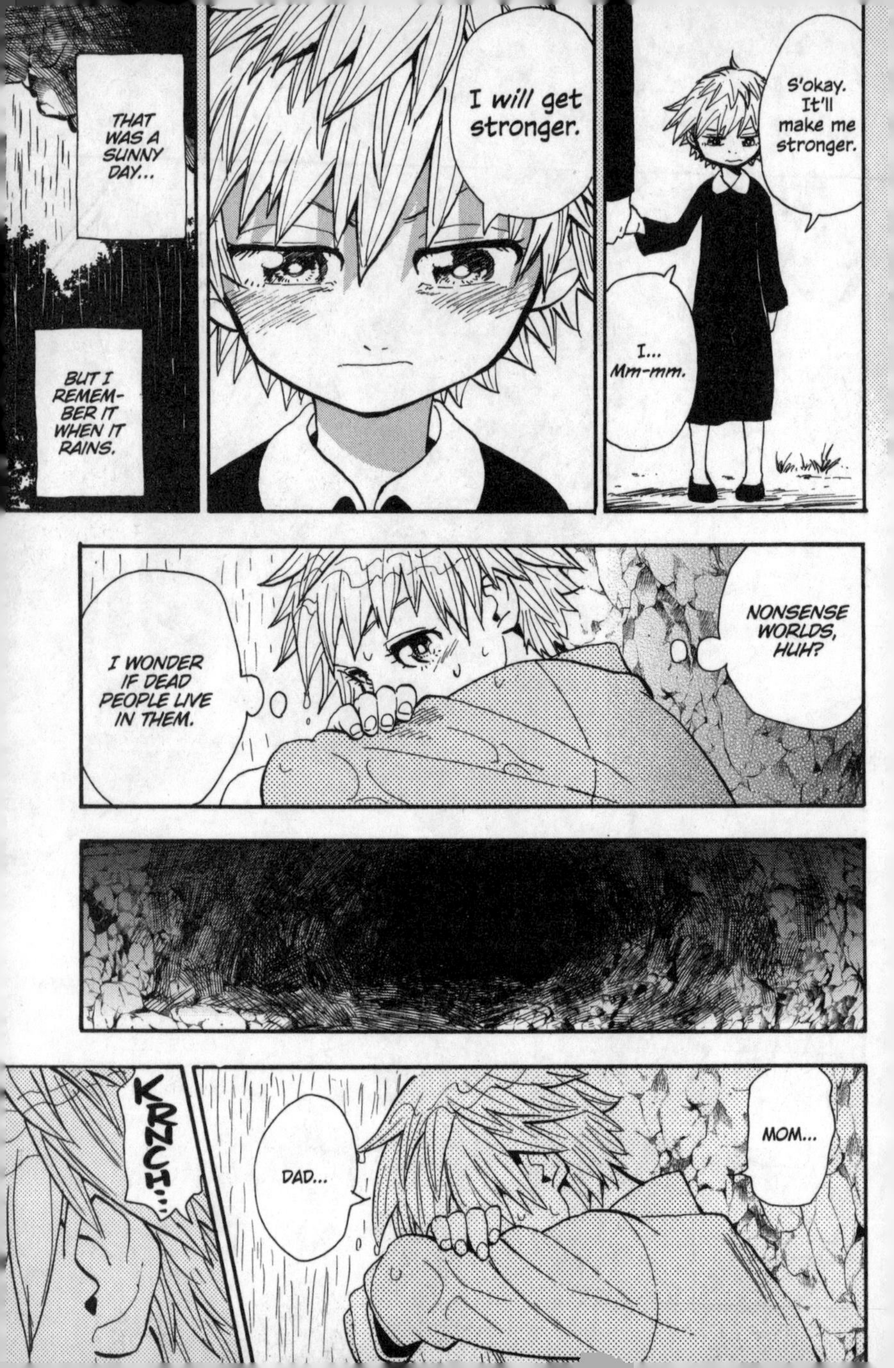
S'okay. It'll make me stronger.
I... Mm-mm.
I will get stronger.
THAT WAS A SUNNY DAY...
BUT I REMEMBER IT WHEN IT RAINS.
NONSENSE WORLDS, HUH?
I WONDER IF DEAD PEOPLE LIVE IN THEM.
MOM...
DAD...
KRNCH...

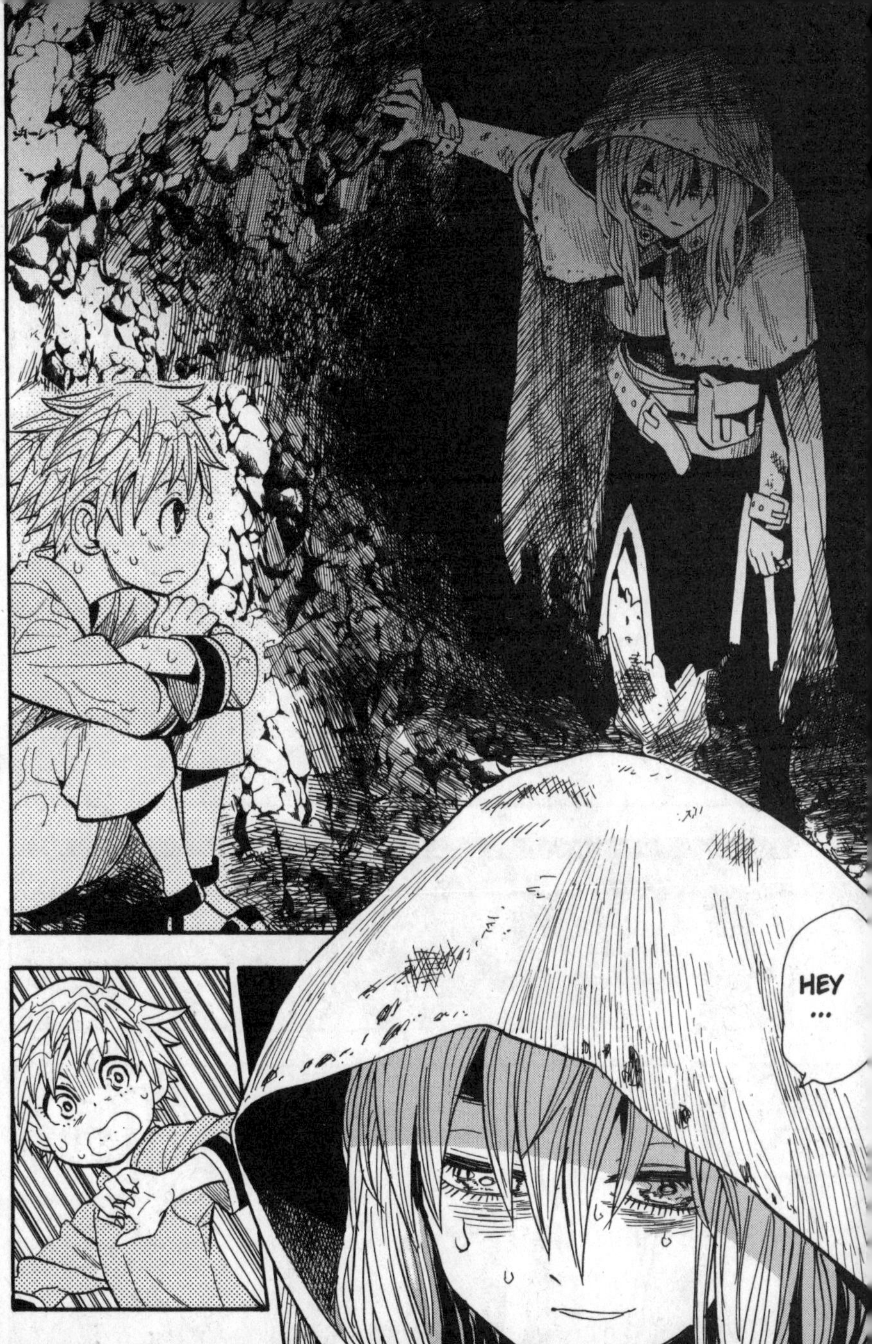
HEY ...

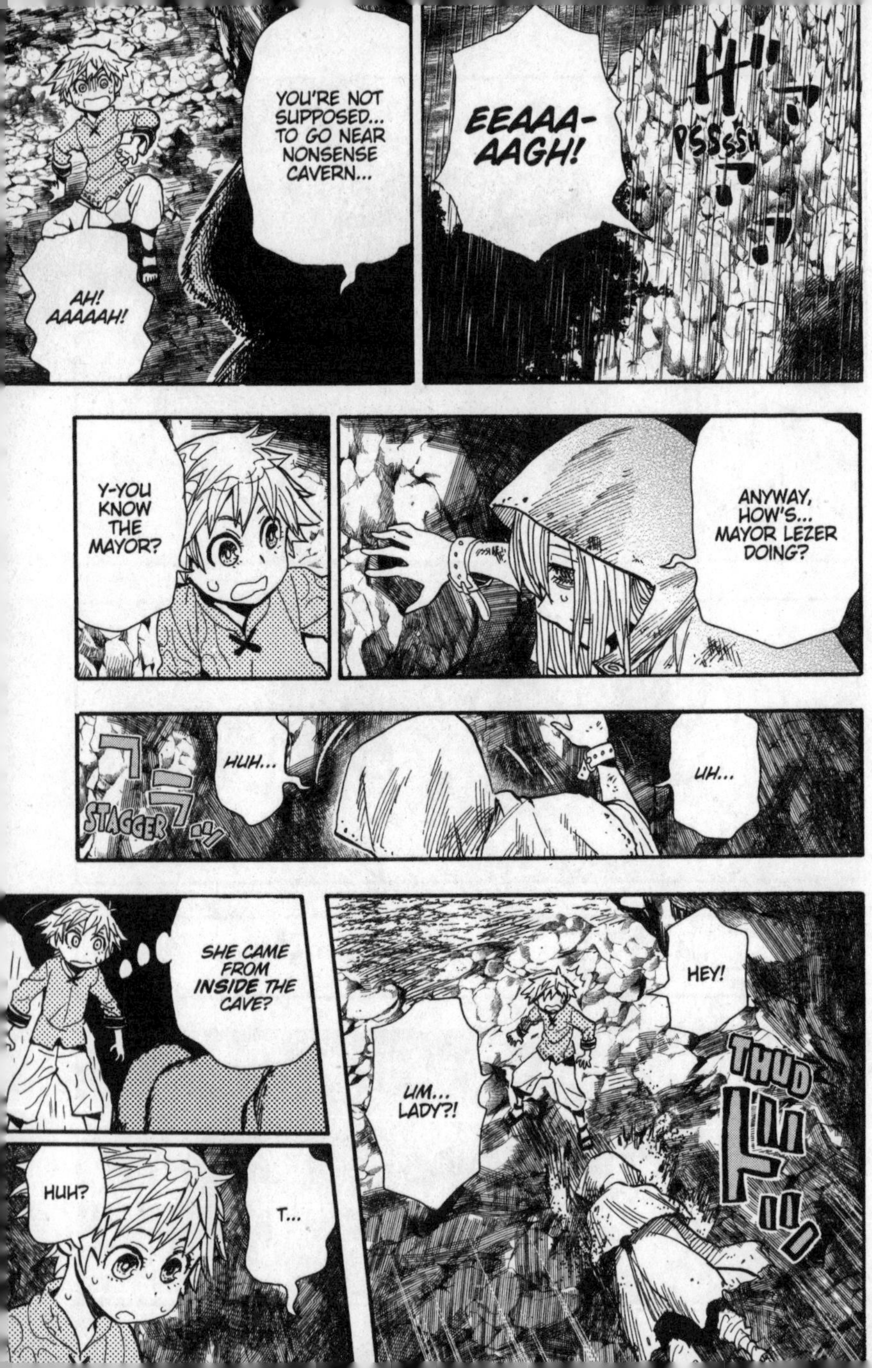
EEAAA-AAGH!
PSSSSH
YOU'RE NOT SUPPOSED... TO GO NEAR NONSENSE CAVERN...
AH! AAAAAH!
ANYWAY, HOW'S... MAYOR LEZER DOING?
Y-YOU KNOW THE MAYOR?
UH...
HUH...
STAGGER
HEY!
THUD
UM... LADY?!
SHE CAME FROM INSIDE THE CAVE?
T...
HUH?

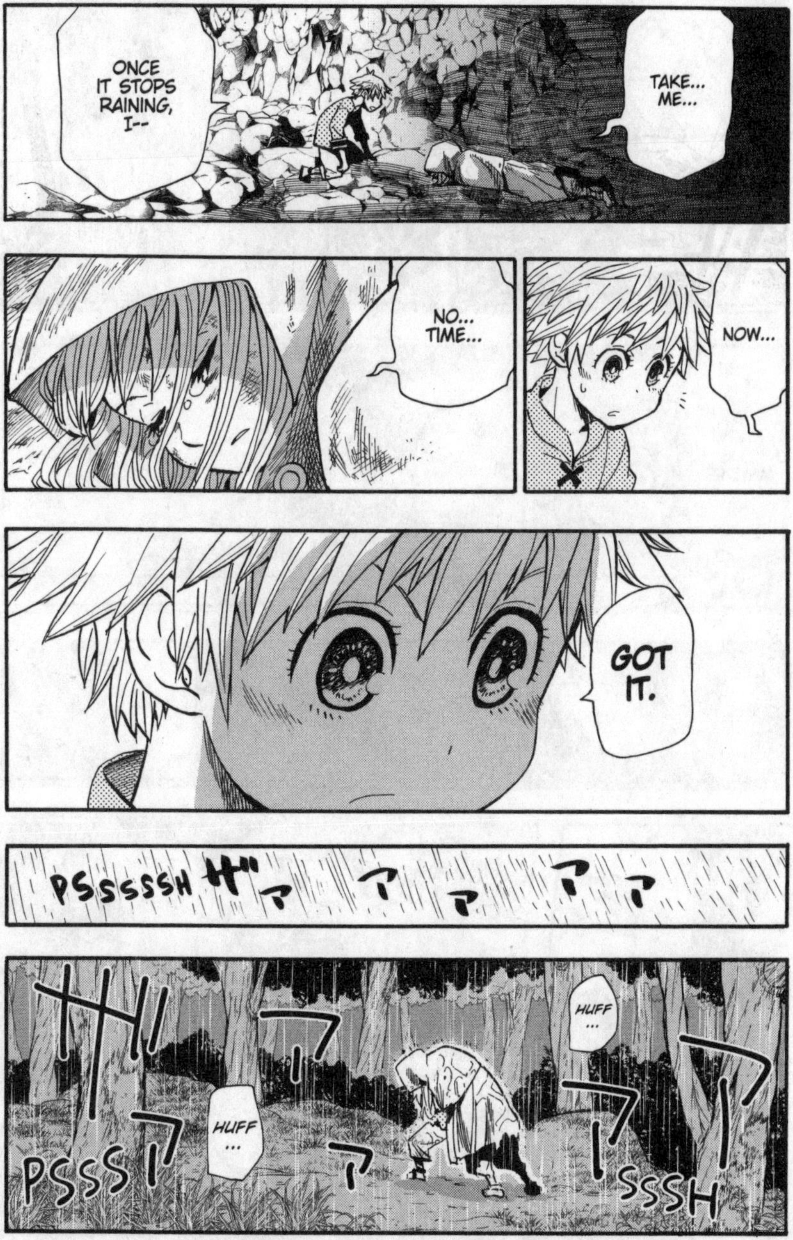
TAKE... ME...
ONCE IT STOPS RAINING, I--
NOW...
NO... TIME...
GOT IT.
PSSSSSH ザァアアア
HUFF ...
HUFF ...
PSSS SSSH

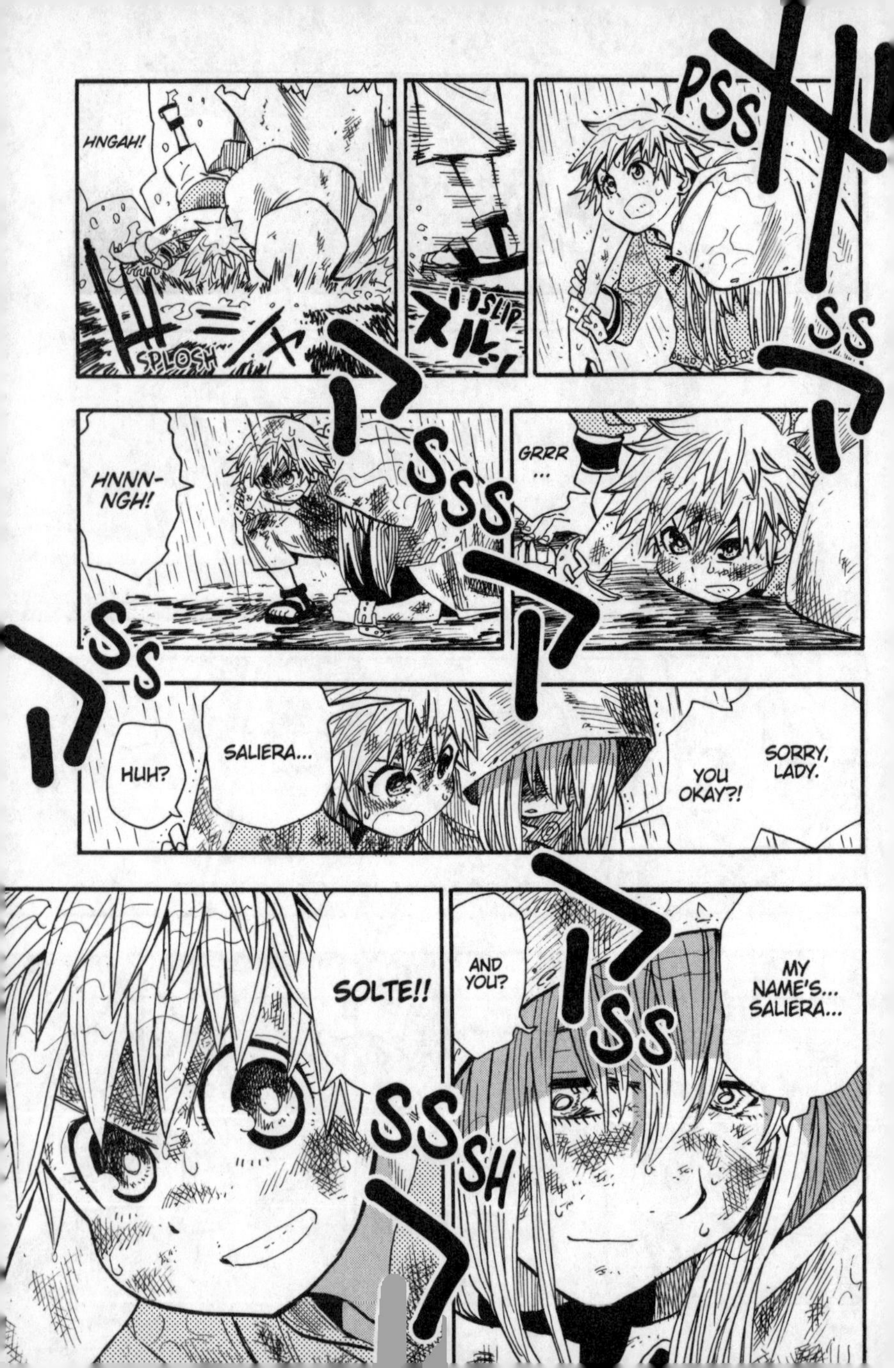
PSS
SS
SLIP
HNGAH!
SPLOSH
SS
GRRR ...
SSS
HNNN-NGH!
SS
SORRY, LADY.
YOU OKAY?!
SALIERA...
HUH?
MY NAME'S... SALIERA...
SS
AND YOU?
SOLTE!!
SSSH

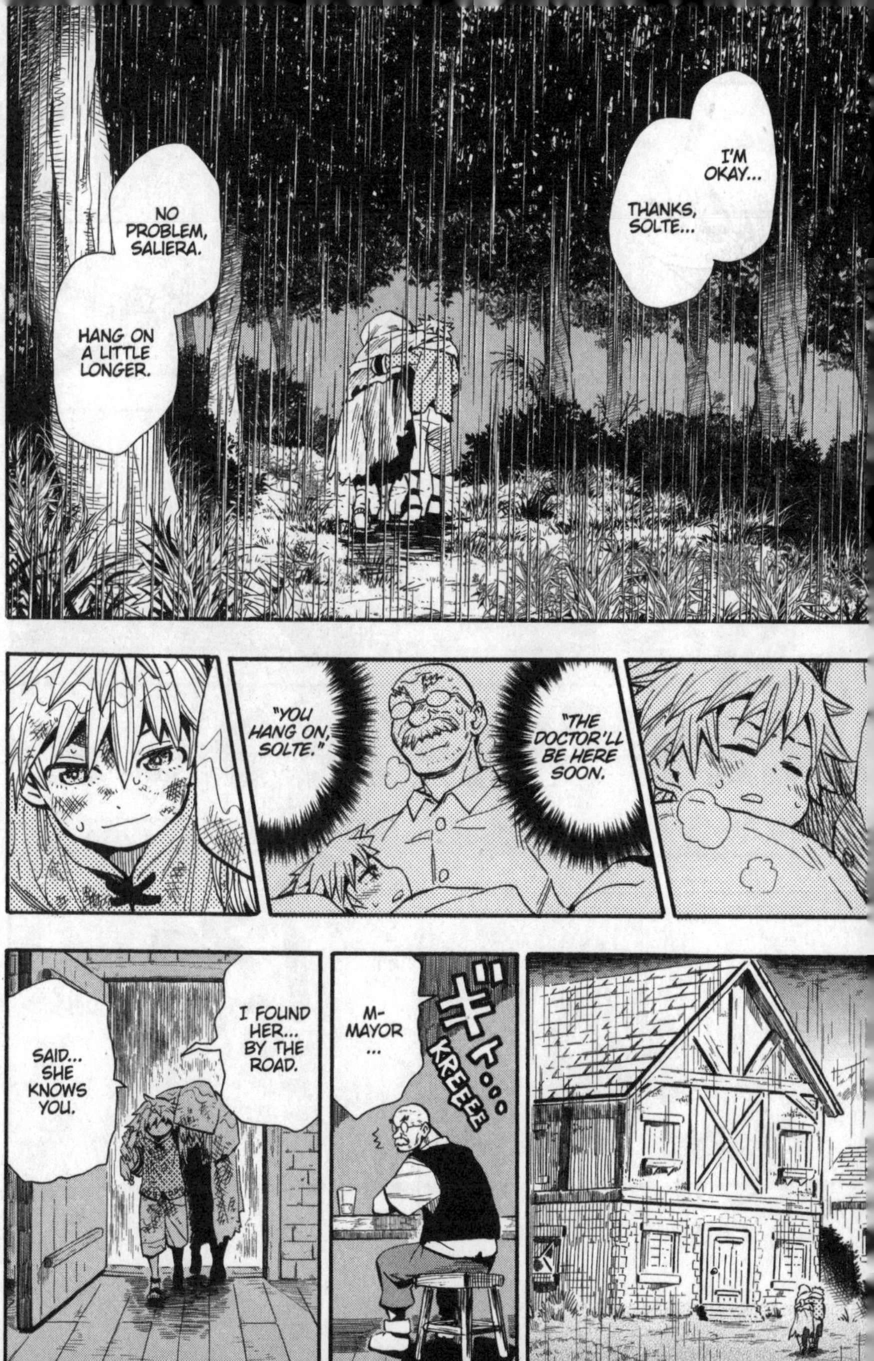
I'M OKAY...
THANKS, SOLTE...
NO PROBLEM, SALIERA.
HANG ON A LITTLE LONGER.
"THE DOCTOR'LL BE HERE SOON.
"YOU HANG ON, SOLTE."
ギイ
KREEEE
M-MAYOR ...
I FOUND HER... BY THE ROAD.
SAID... SHE KNOWS YOU.

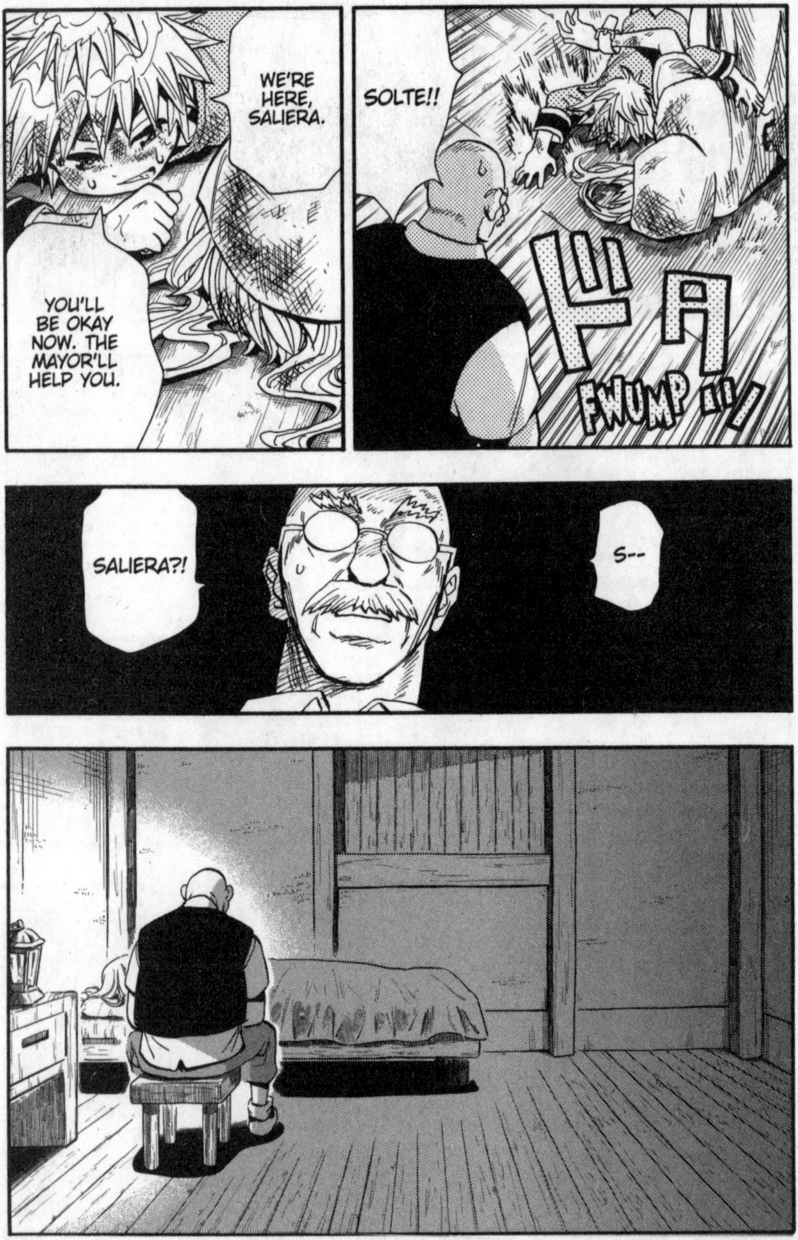

SOLTE!!
FWUMP!!!
WE'RE HERE, SALIERA.
YOU'LL BE OKAY NOW. THE MAYOR'LL HELP YOU.
S--
SALIERA?!

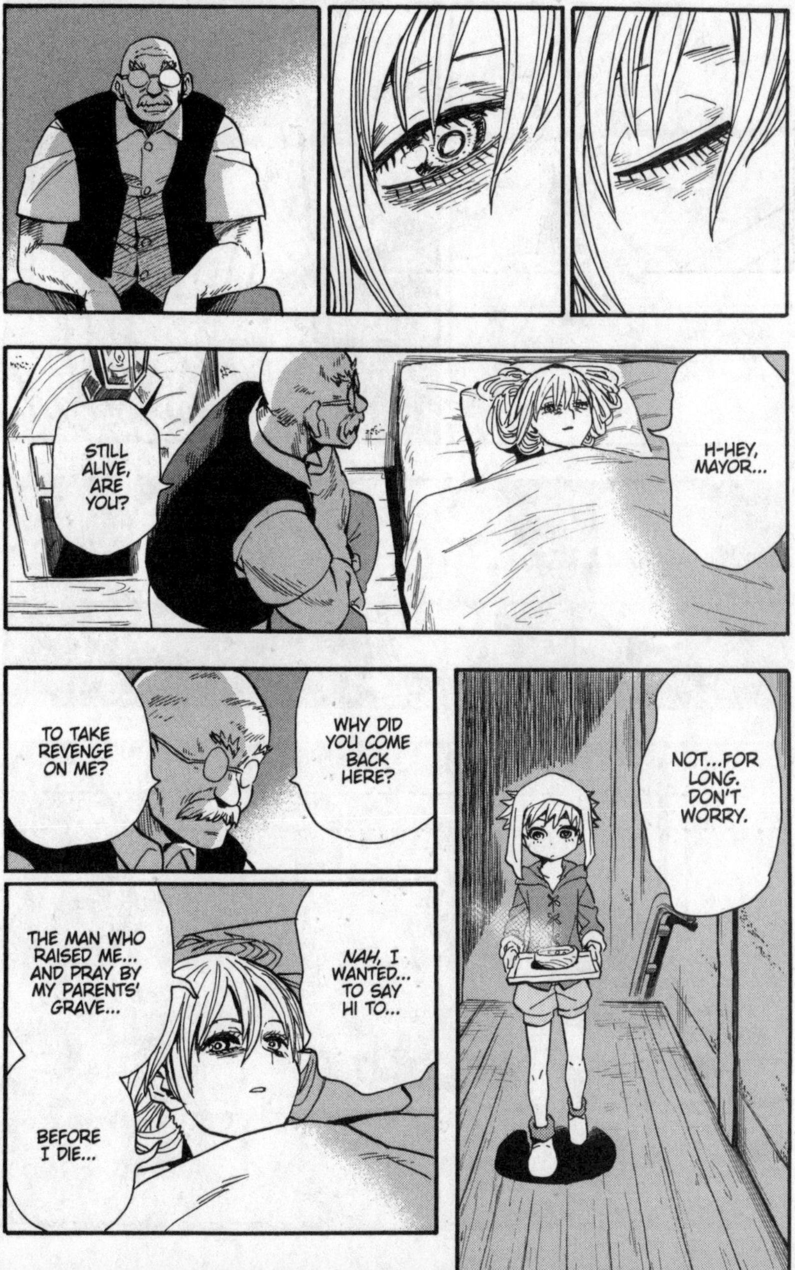
H-HEY, MAYOR...
STILL ALIVE, ARE YOU?
NOT...FOR LONG. DON'T WORRY.
WHY DID YOU COME BACK HERE?
TO TAKE REVENGE ON ME?
NAH, I WANTED... TO SAY HI TO...
THE MAN WHO RAISED ME... AND PRAY BY MY PARENTS' GRAVE...
BEFORE I DIE...

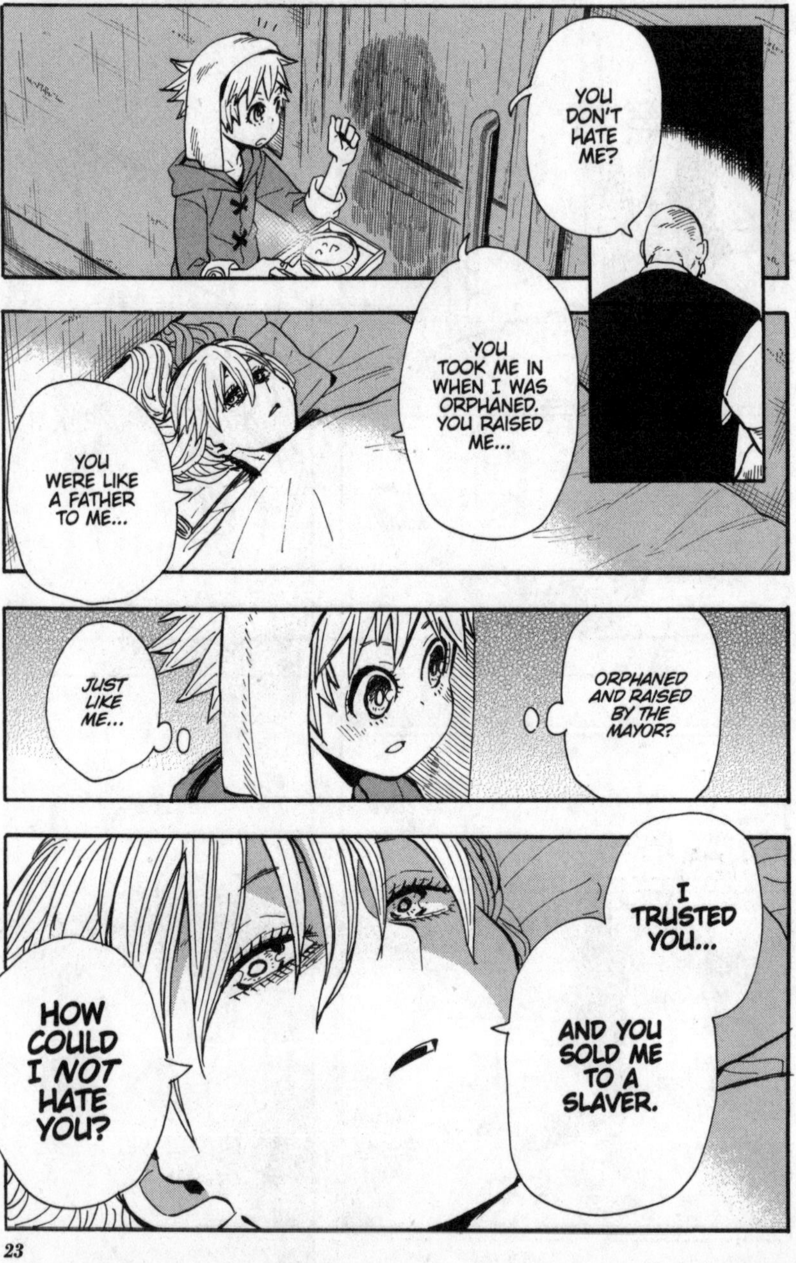
YOU DON'T HATE ME?
YOU TOOK ME IN WHEN I WAS ORPHANED. YOU RAISED ME...
YOU WERE LIKE A FATHER TO ME...
ORPHANED AND RAISED BY THE MAYOR?
JUST LIKE ME...
I TRUSTED YOU...
AND YOU SOLD ME TO A SLAVER.
HOW COULD I *NOT* HATE YOU?

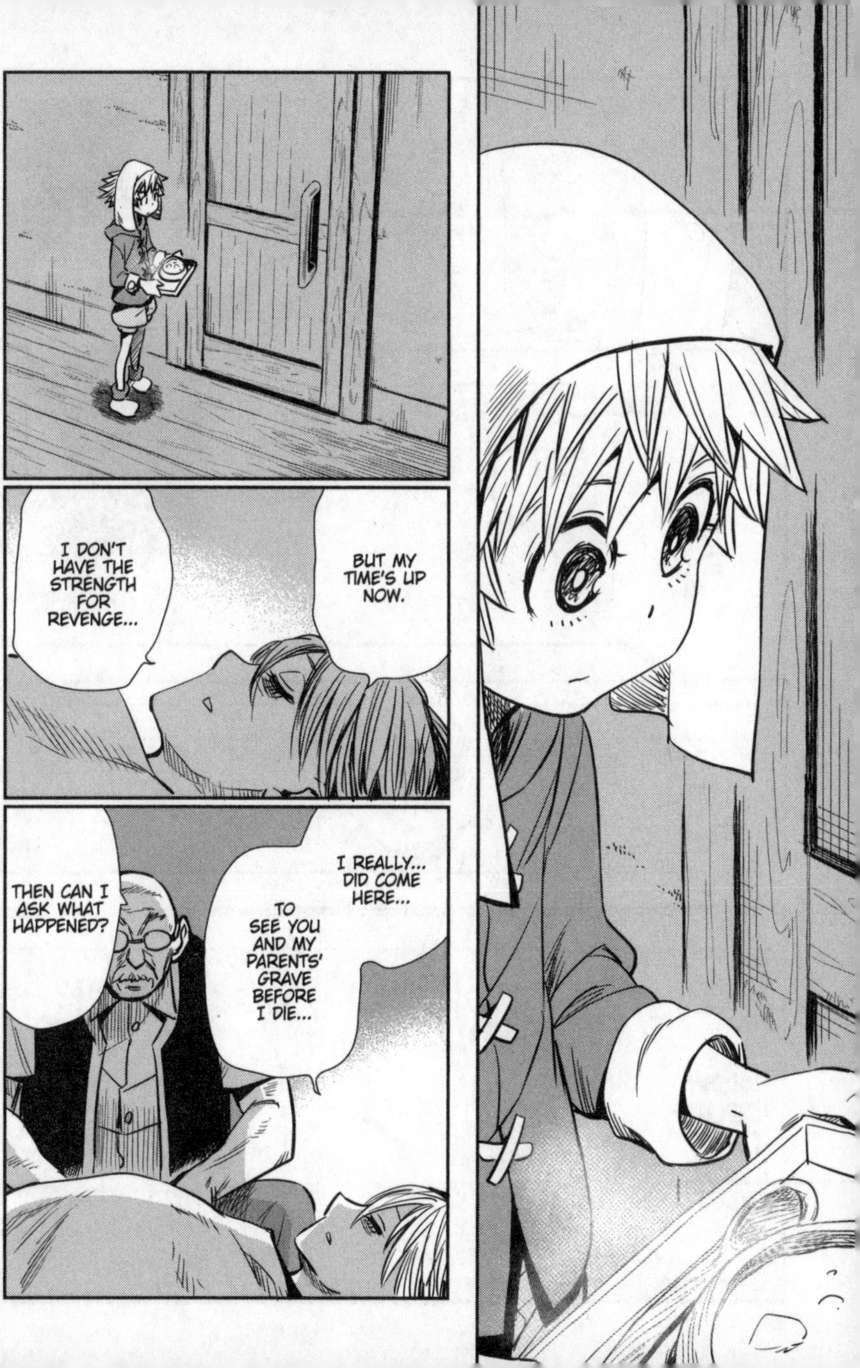
BUT MY TIME'S UP NOW.
I DON'T HAVE THE STRENGTH FOR REVENGE...
I REALLY... DID COME HERE...
TO SEE YOU AND MY PARENTS' GRAVE BEFORE I DIE...
THEN CAN I ASK WHAT HAPPENED?

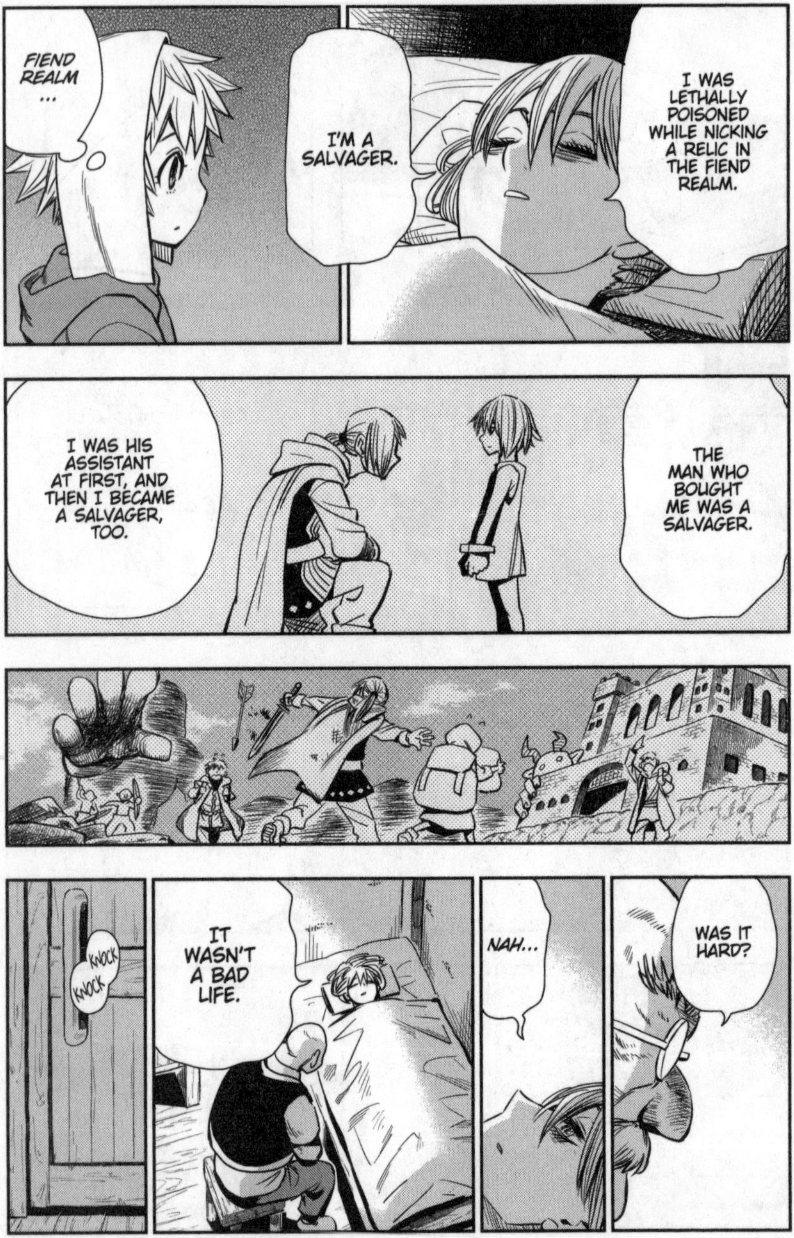
I WAS LETHALLY POISONED WHILE NICKING A RELIC IN THE FIEND REALM.
I'M A SALVAGER.
FIEND REALM ...
THE MAN WHO BOUGHT ME WAS A SALVAGER.
I WAS HIS ASSISTANT AT FIRST, AND THEN I BECAME A SALVAGER, TOO.
WAS IT HARD?
NAH...
IT WASN'T A BAD LIFE.
KNOCK
KNOCK

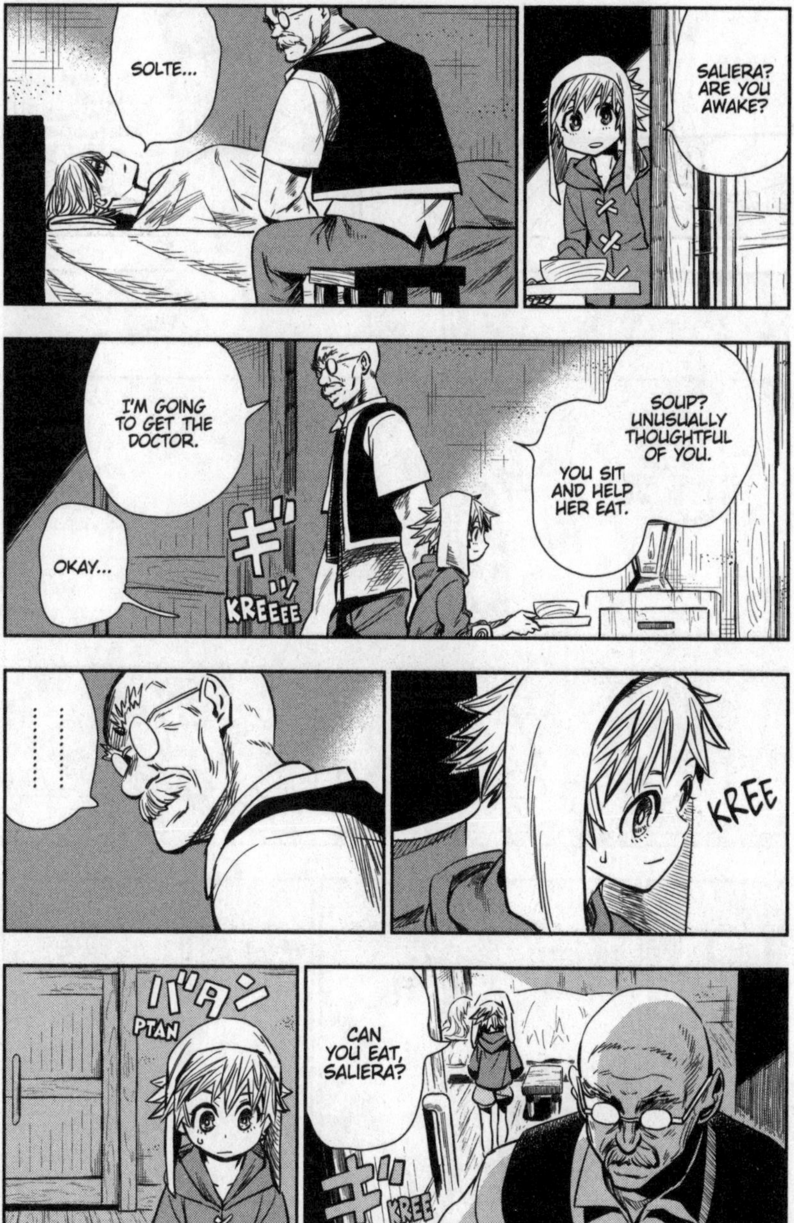
SALIERA? ARE YOU AWAKE?
SOLTE...
SOUP? UNUSUALLY THOUGHTFUL OF YOU.
YOU SIT AND HELP HER EAT.
I'M GOING TO GET THE DOCTOR.
ギッ
KREEEEE
OKAY...
KREE
......
CAN YOU EAT, SALIERA?
ギッ
KREE
バタン
PTAN

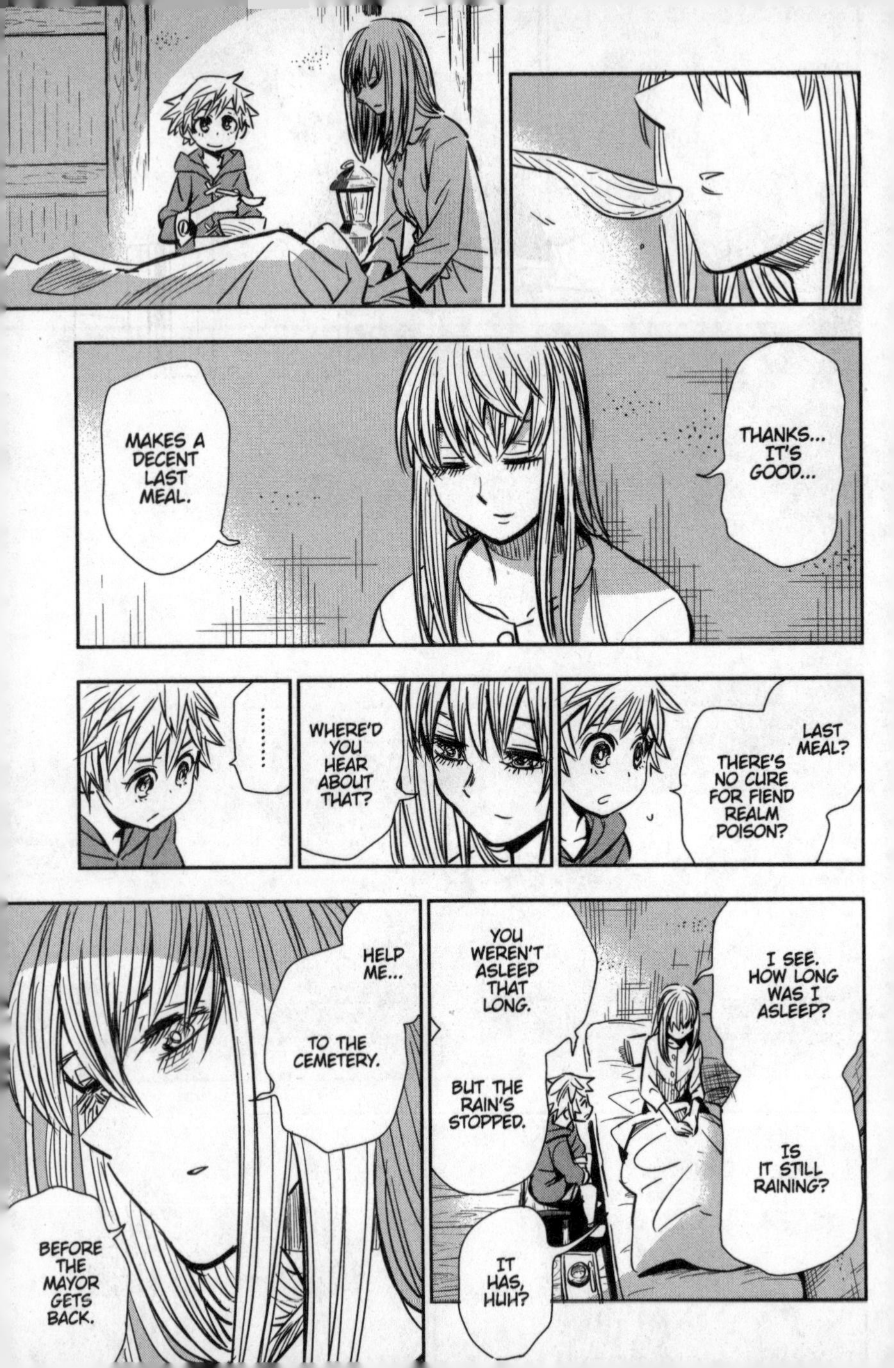
THANKS... IT'S GOOD...
MAKES A DECENT LAST MEAL.
LAST MEAL?
THERE'S NO CURE FOR FIEND REALM POISON?
WHERE'D YOU HEAR ABOUT THAT?
......
I SEE. HOW LONG WAS I ASLEEP?
YOU WEREN'T ASLEEP THAT LONG.
IS IT STILL RAINING?
BUT THE RAIN'S STOPPED.
IT HAS, HUH?
HELP ME...
TO THE CEMETERY.
BEFORE THE MAYOR GETS BACK.

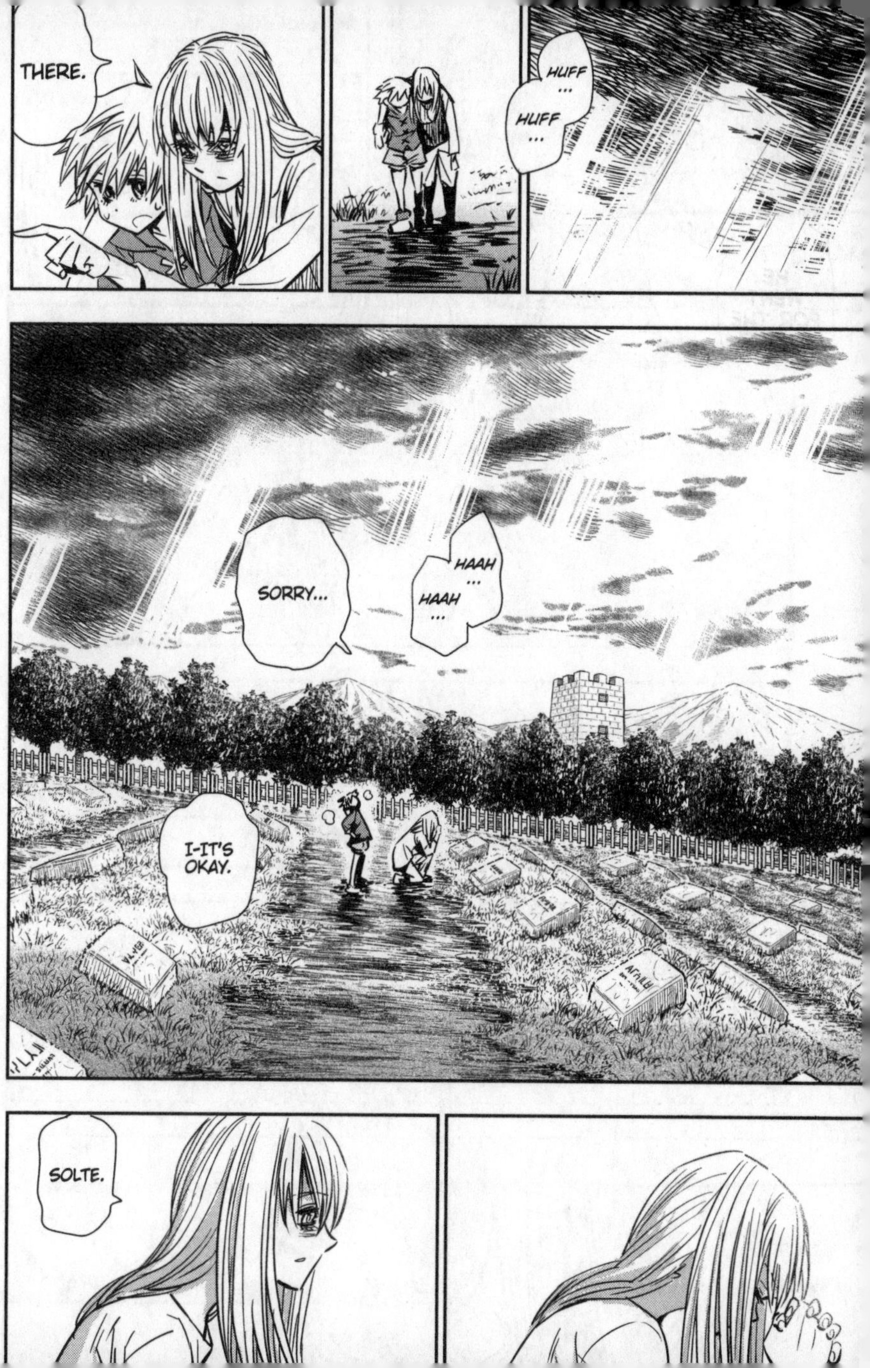
HUFF ...
HUFF ...
THERE.
HAAH ...
HAAH ...
SORRY...
I-IT'S OKAY.
SOLTE.

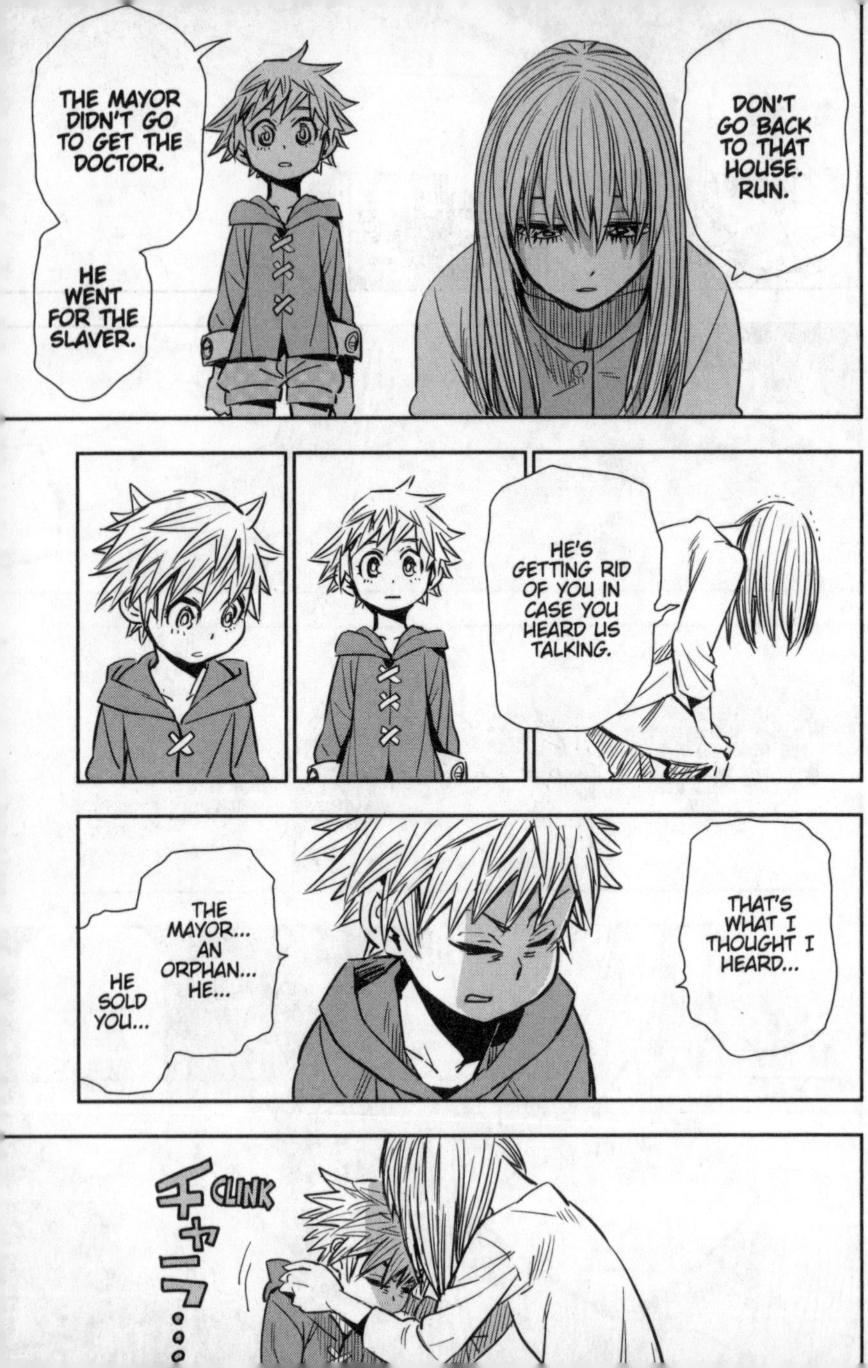
DON'T GO BACK TO THAT HOUSE. RUN.
THE MAYOR DIDN'T GO TO GET THE DOCTOR.
HE WENT FOR THE SLAVER.
HE'S GETTING RID OF YOU IN CASE YOU HEARD US TALKING.
THAT'S WHAT I THOUGHT I HEARD...
THE MAYOR... AN ORPHAN... HE...
HE SOLD YOU...
CLINK

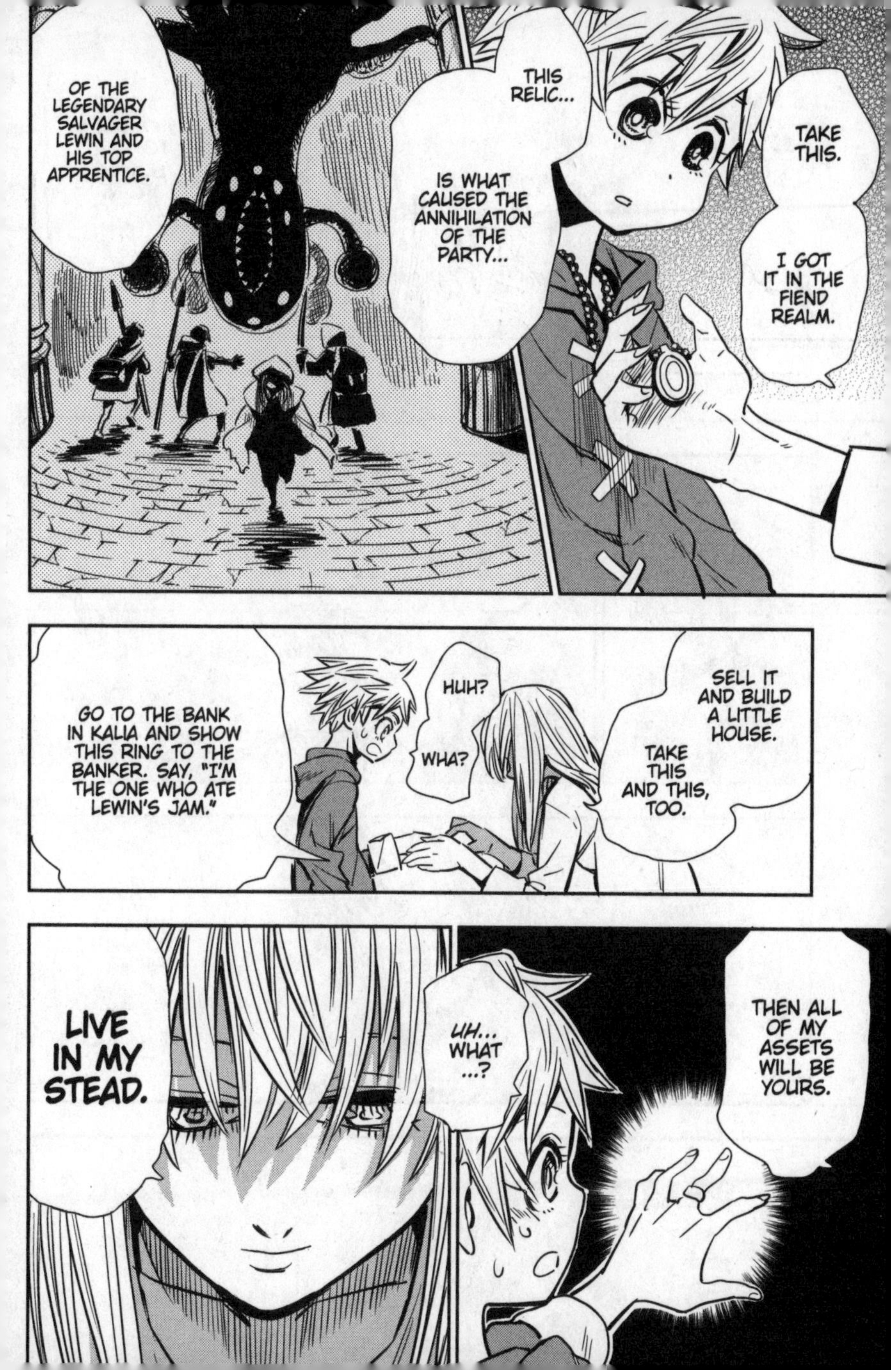
TAKE THIS.
I GOT IT IN THE FIEND REALM.
THIS RELIC...
IS WHAT CAUSED THE ANNIHILATION OF THE PARTY...
OF THE LEGENDARY SALVAGER LEWIN AND HIS TOP APPRENTICE.
SELL IT AND BUILD A LITTLE HOUSE.
TAKE THIS AND THIS, TOO.
HUH?
WHA?
GO TO THE BANK IN KALIA AND SHOW THIS RING TO THE BANKER. SAY, "I'M THE ONE WHO ATE LEWIN'S JAM."
THEN ALL OF MY ASSETS WILL BE YOURS.
UH... WHAT ...?
LIVE IN MY STEAD.

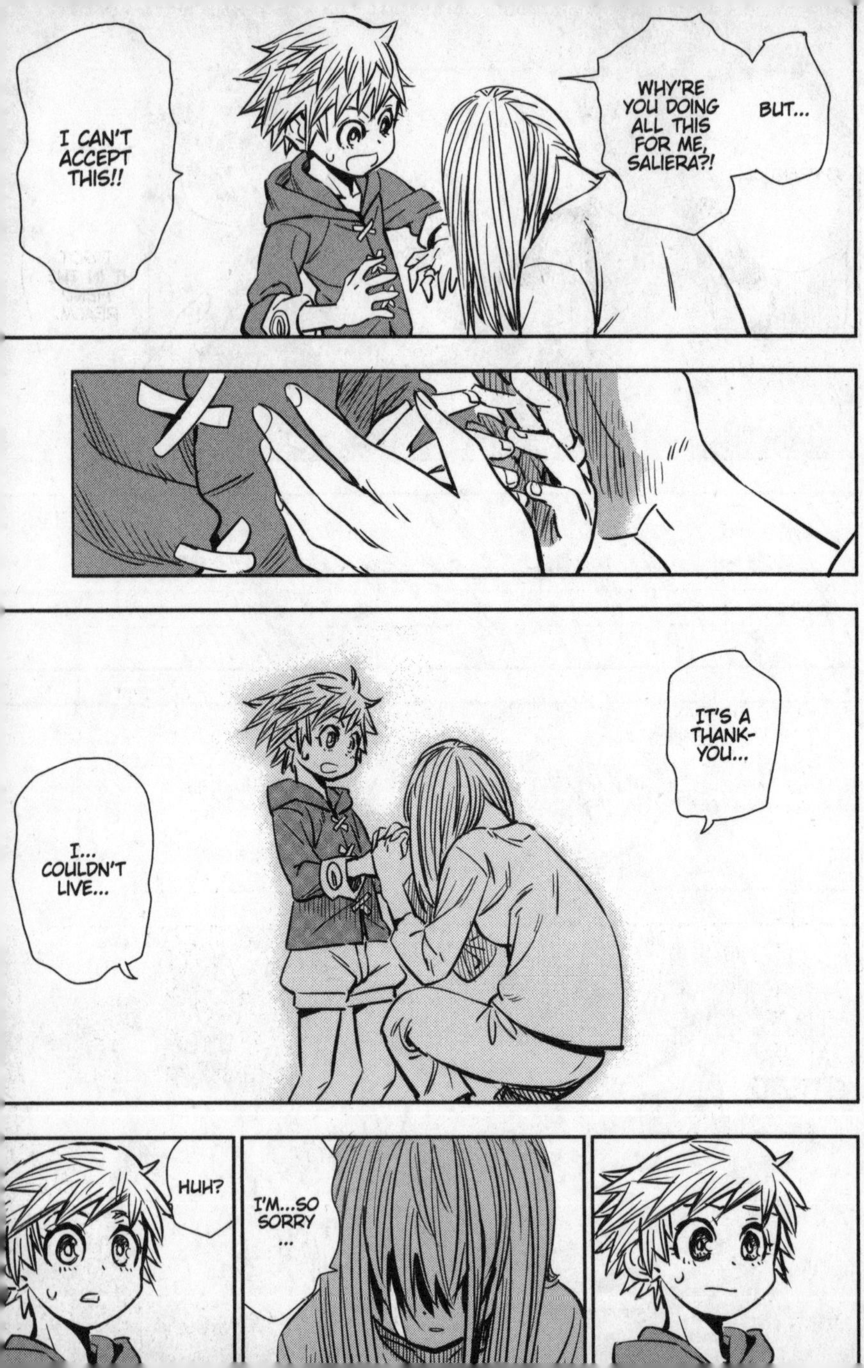
BUT...
WHY'RE YOU DOING ALL THIS FOR ME, SALIERA?!
I CAN'T ACCEPT THIS!!
IT'S A THANK-YOU...
I... COULDN'T LIVE...
I'M...SO SORRY ...
HUH?

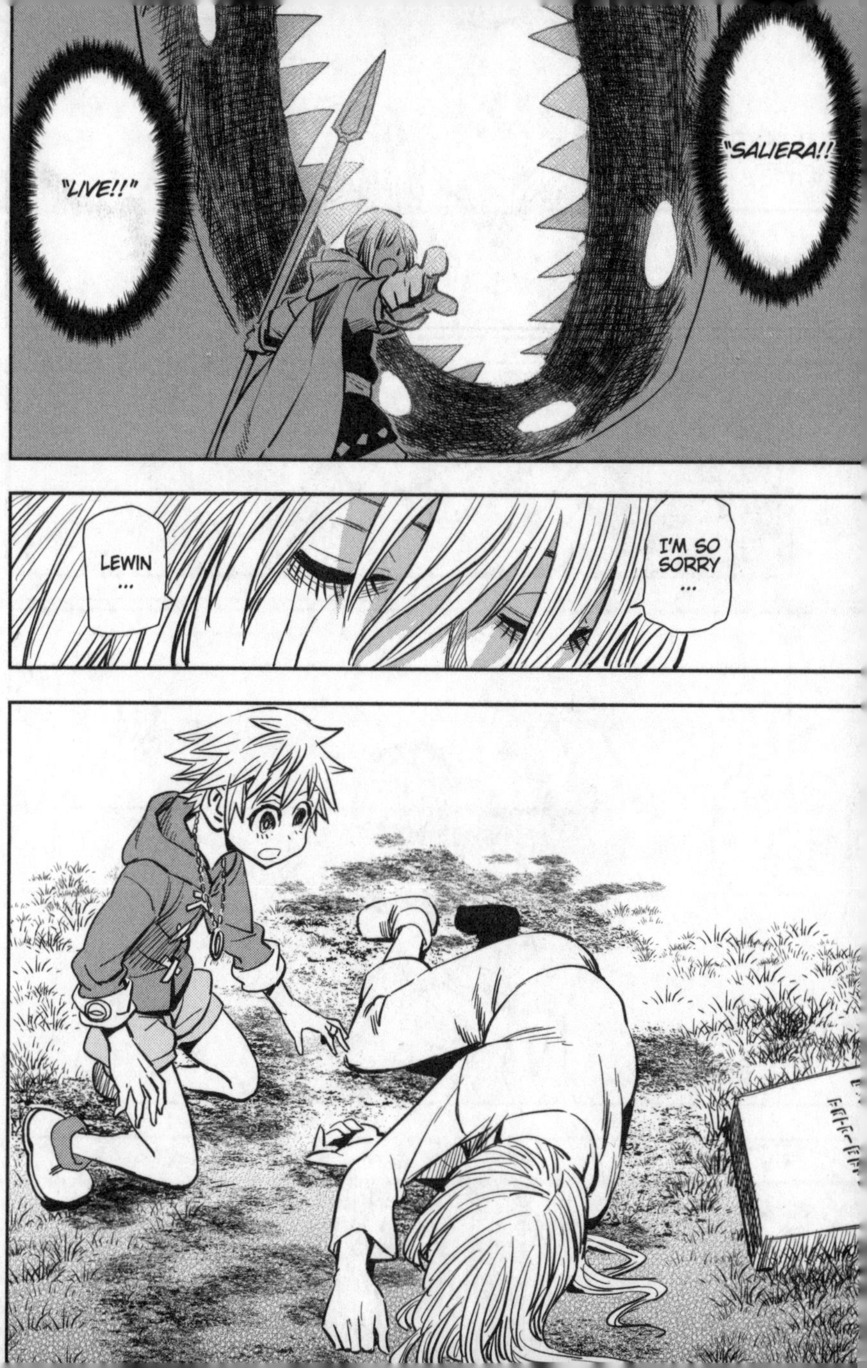
"SALIERA!!
"LIVE!!"
I'M SO SORRY ...
LEWIN ...

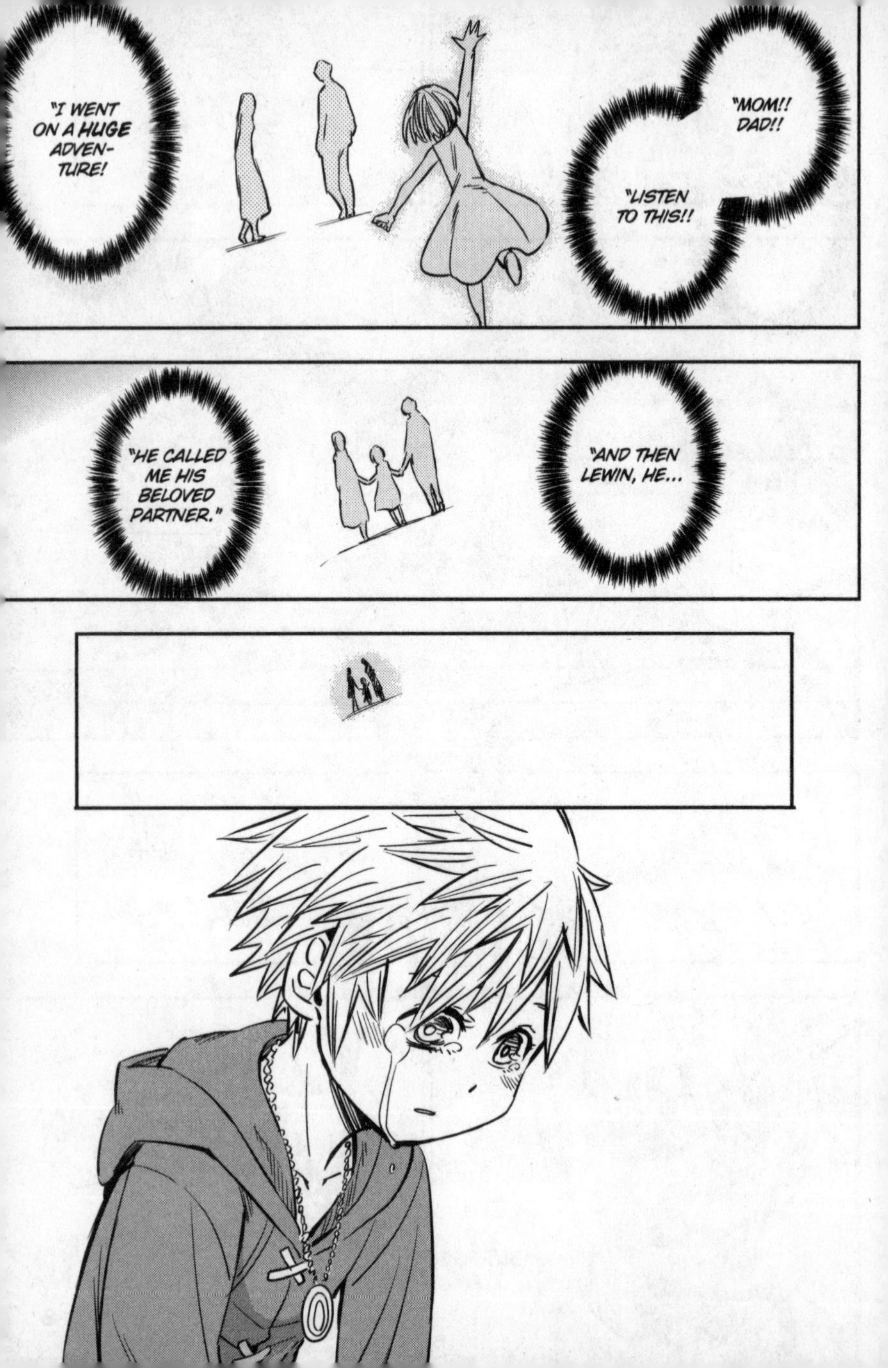
"MOM!! DAD!!
"LISTEN TO THIS!!
"I WENT ON A HUGE ADVEN-TURE!
"AND THEN LEWIN, HE...
"HE CALLED ME HIS BELOVED PARTNER."

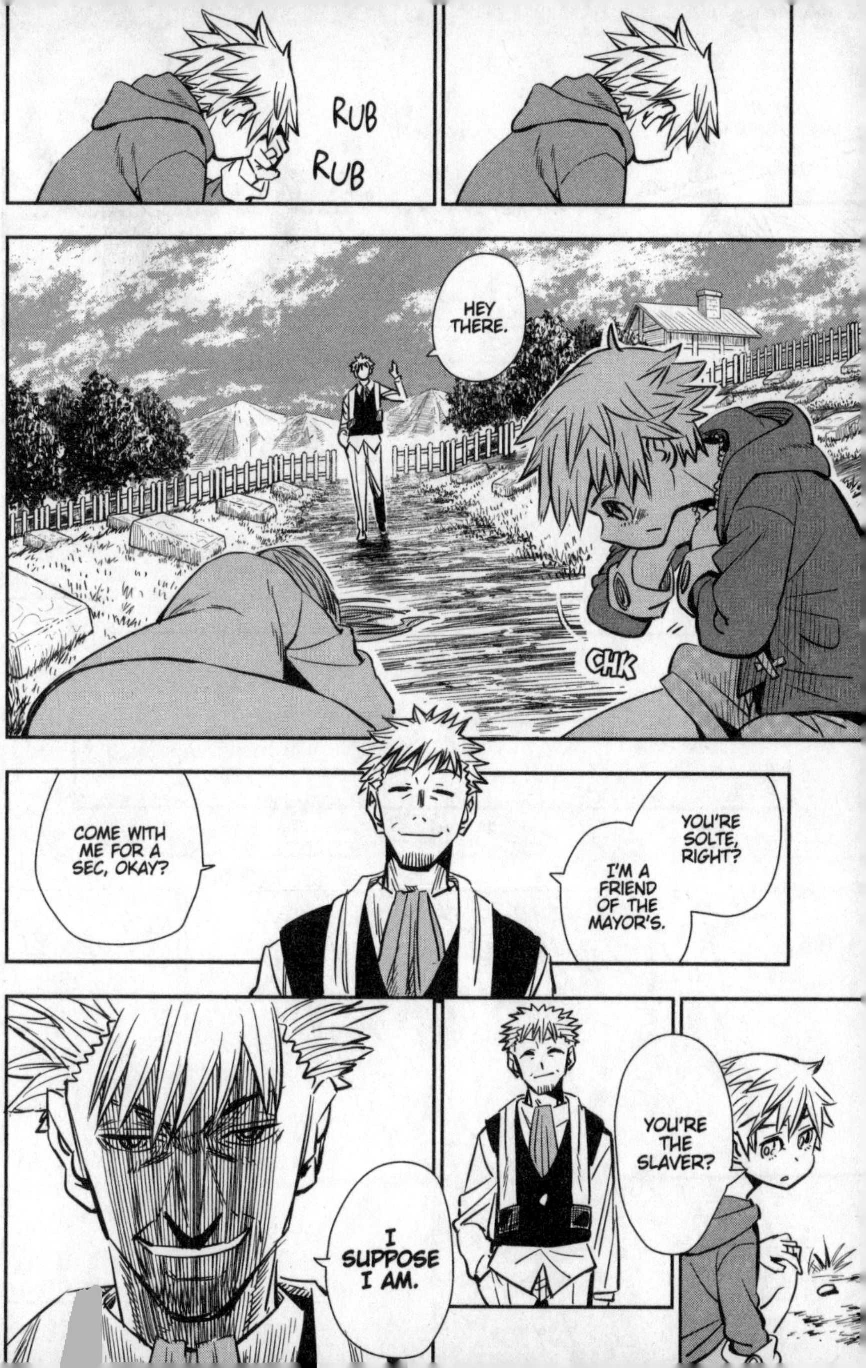
RUB
RUB
HEY THERE.
CHK
YOU'RE SOLTE, RIGHT?
I'M A FRIEND OF THE MAYOR'S.
COME WITH ME FOR A SEC, OKAY?
YOU'RE THE SLAVER?
I SUPPOSE I AM.

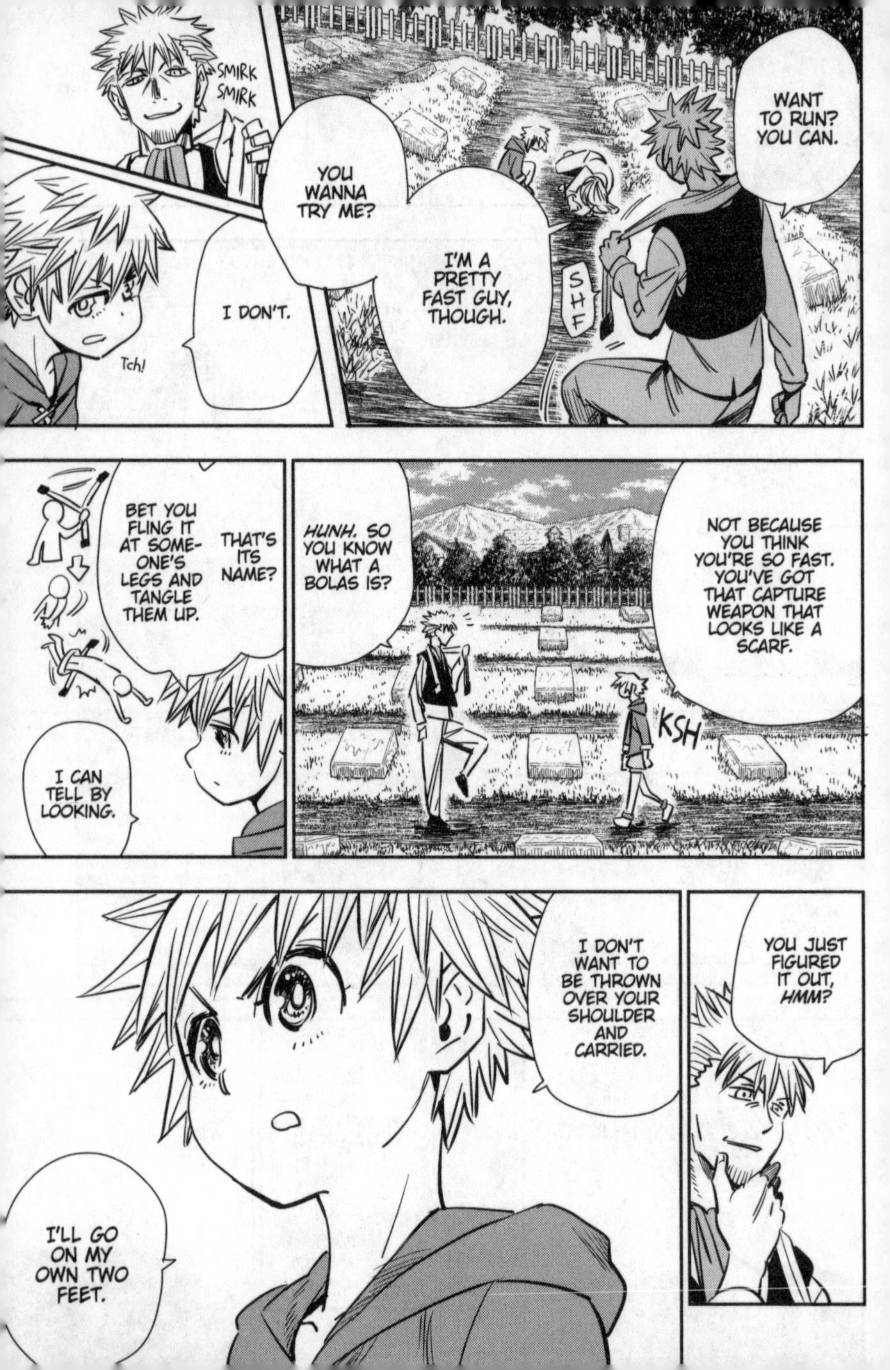
WANT TO RUN? YOU CAN.
SHF
I'M A PRETTY FAST GUY, THOUGH.
YOU WANNA TRY ME?
SMIRK SMIRK
I DON'T.
Tch!
NOT BECAUSE YOU THINK YOU'RE SO FAST. YOU'VE GOT THAT CAPTURE WEAPON THAT LOOKS LIKE A SCARF.
KSH
HUNH. SO YOU KNOW WHAT A BOLAS IS?
THAT'S ITS NAME?
BET YOU FLING IT AT SOME-ONE'S LEGS AND TANGLE THEM UP.
I CAN TELL BY LOOKING.
YOU JUST FIGURED IT OUT, *HMM?*
I DON'T WANT TO BE THROWN OVER YOUR SHOULDER AND CARRIED.
I'LL GO ON MY OWN TWO FEET.

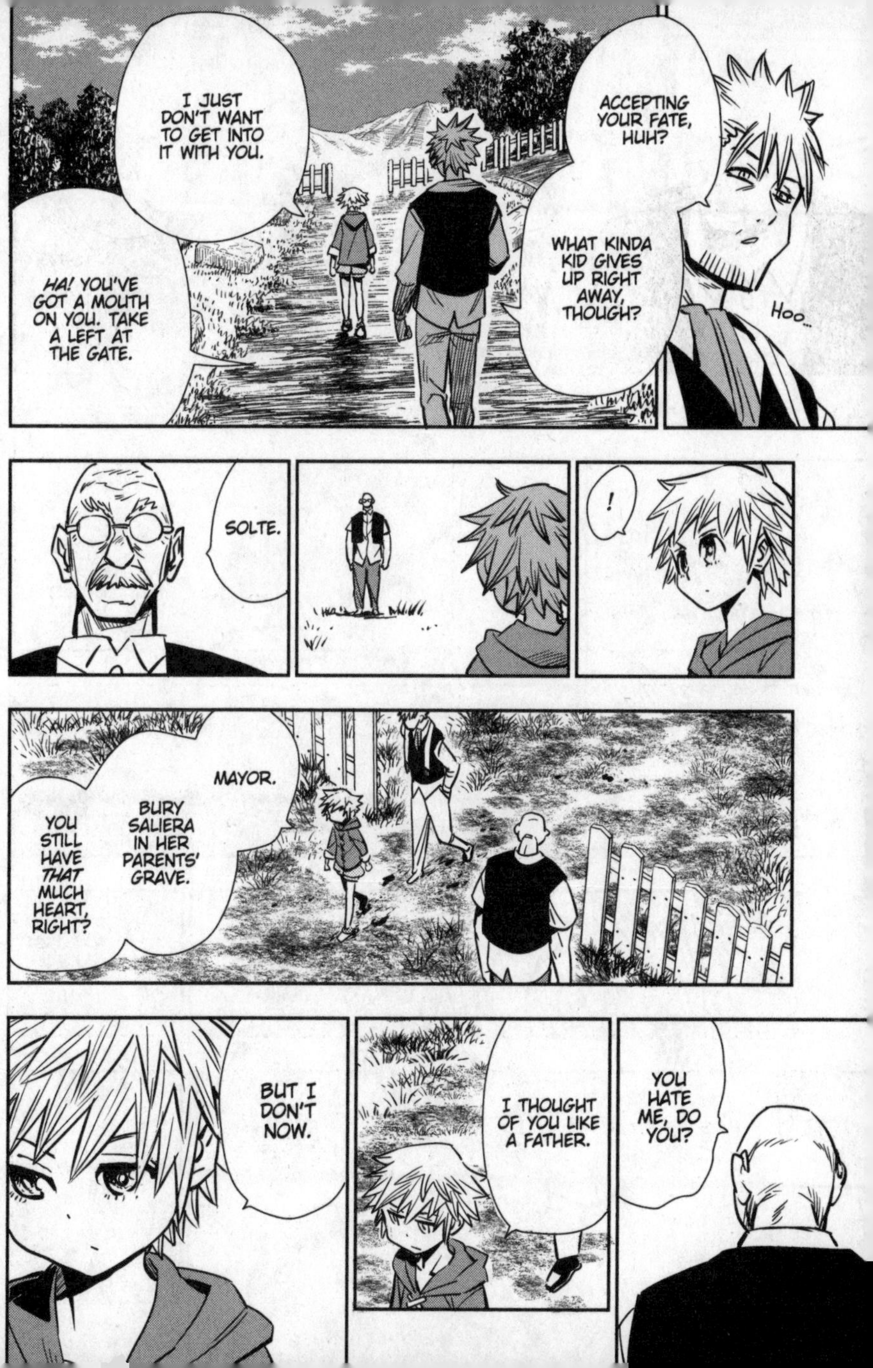
ACCEPTING YOUR FATE, HUH?
WHAT KINDA KID GIVES UP RIGHT AWAY, THOUGH?
Hoo...
I JUST DON'T WANT TO GET INTO IT WITH YOU.
HA! YOU'VE GOT A MOUTH ON YOU. TAKE A LEFT AT THE GATE.
!
SOLTE.
MAYOR.
BURY SALIERA IN HER PARENTS' GRAVE.
YOU STILL HAVE *THAT* MUCH HEART, RIGHT?
YOU HATE ME, DO YOU?
I THOUGHT OF YOU LIKE A FATHER.
BUT I DON'T NOW.

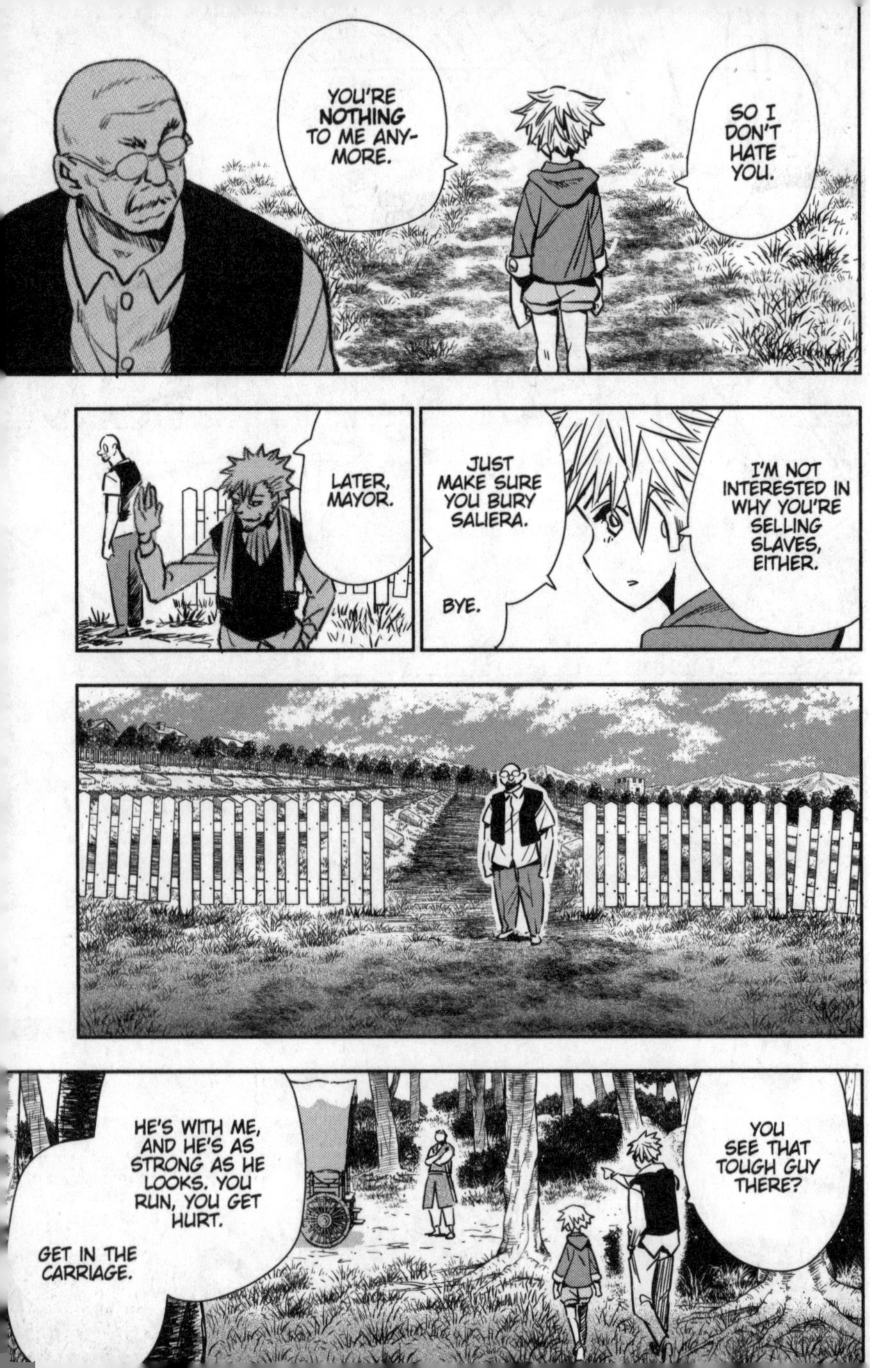
YOU'RE NOTHING TO ME ANY-MORE.
SO I DON'T HATE YOU.
I'M NOT INTERESTED IN WHY YOU'RE SELLING SLAVES, EITHER.
JUST MAKE SURE YOU BURY SALIERA.
BYE.
LATER, MAYOR.
YOU SEE THAT TOUGH GUY THERE?
HE'S WITH ME, AND HE'S AS STRONG AS HE LOOKS. YOU RUN, YOU GET HURT.
GET IN THE CARRIAGE.

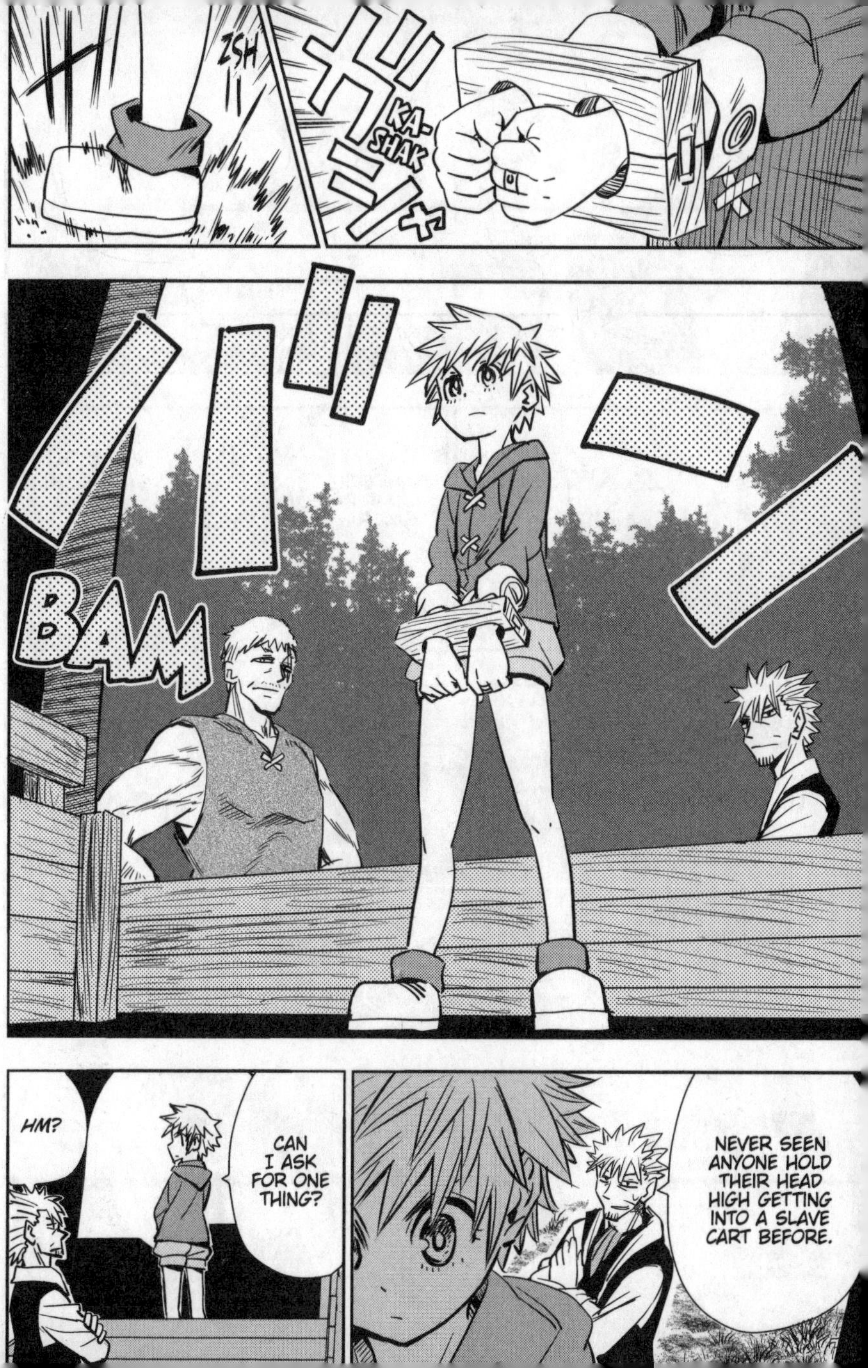
KA-SHAK
ZSH
BAM
NEVER SEEN ANYONE HOLD THEIR HEAD HIGH GETTING INTO A SLAVE CART BEFORE.
CAN I ASK FOR ONE THING?
HM?

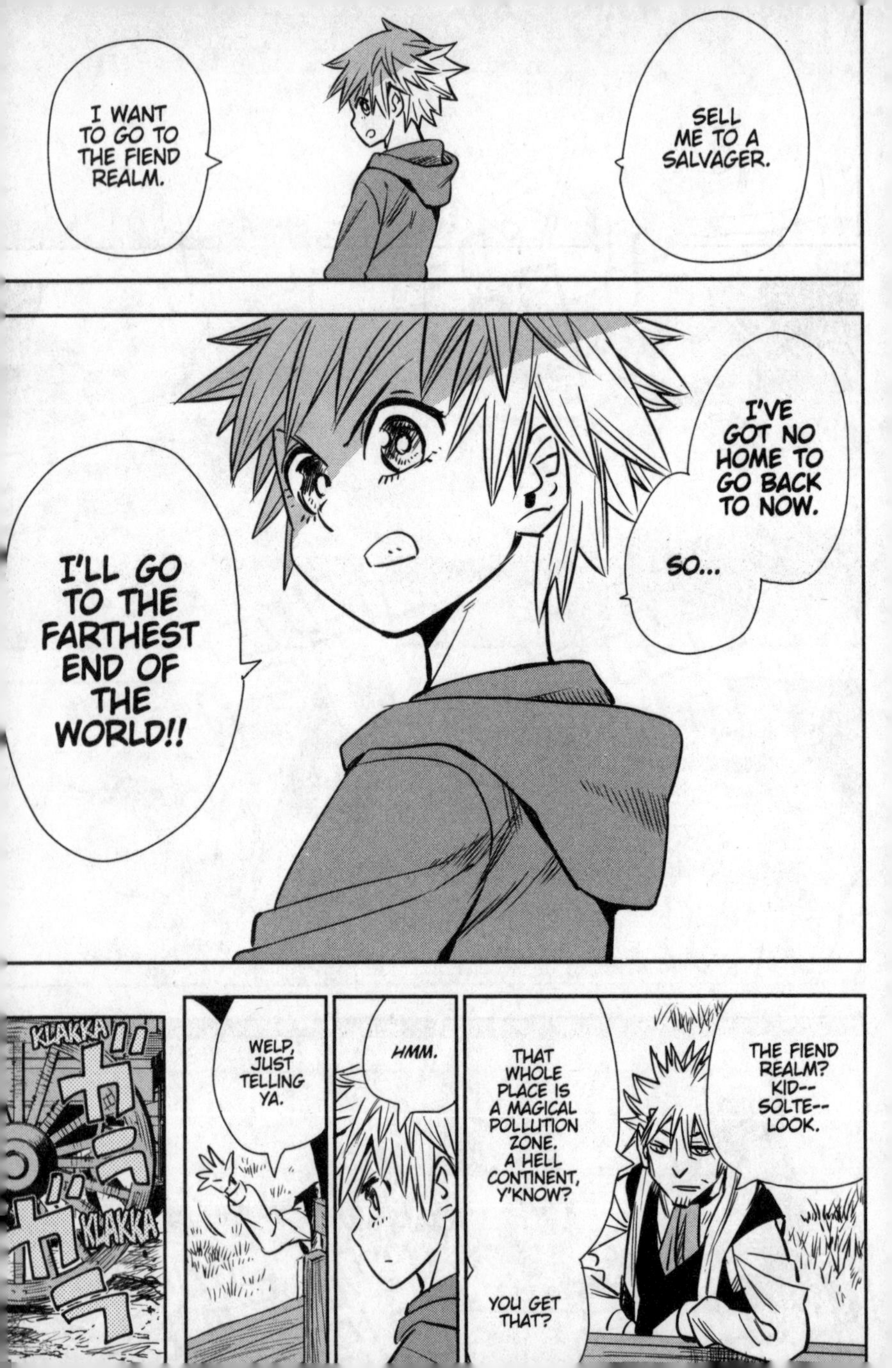
SELL ME TO A SALVAGER.
I WANT TO GO TO THE FIEND REALM.
I'VE GOT NO HOME TO GO BACK TO NOW.
SO...
I'LL GO TO THE FARTHEST END OF THE WORLD!!
THE FIEND REALM? KID-- SOLTE-- LOOK.
THAT WHOLE PLACE IS A MAGICAL POLLUTION ZONE. A HELL CONTINENT, Y'KNOW?
YOU GET THAT?
HMM.
WELP, JUST TELLING YA.
KLAKKA!!
KLAKKA

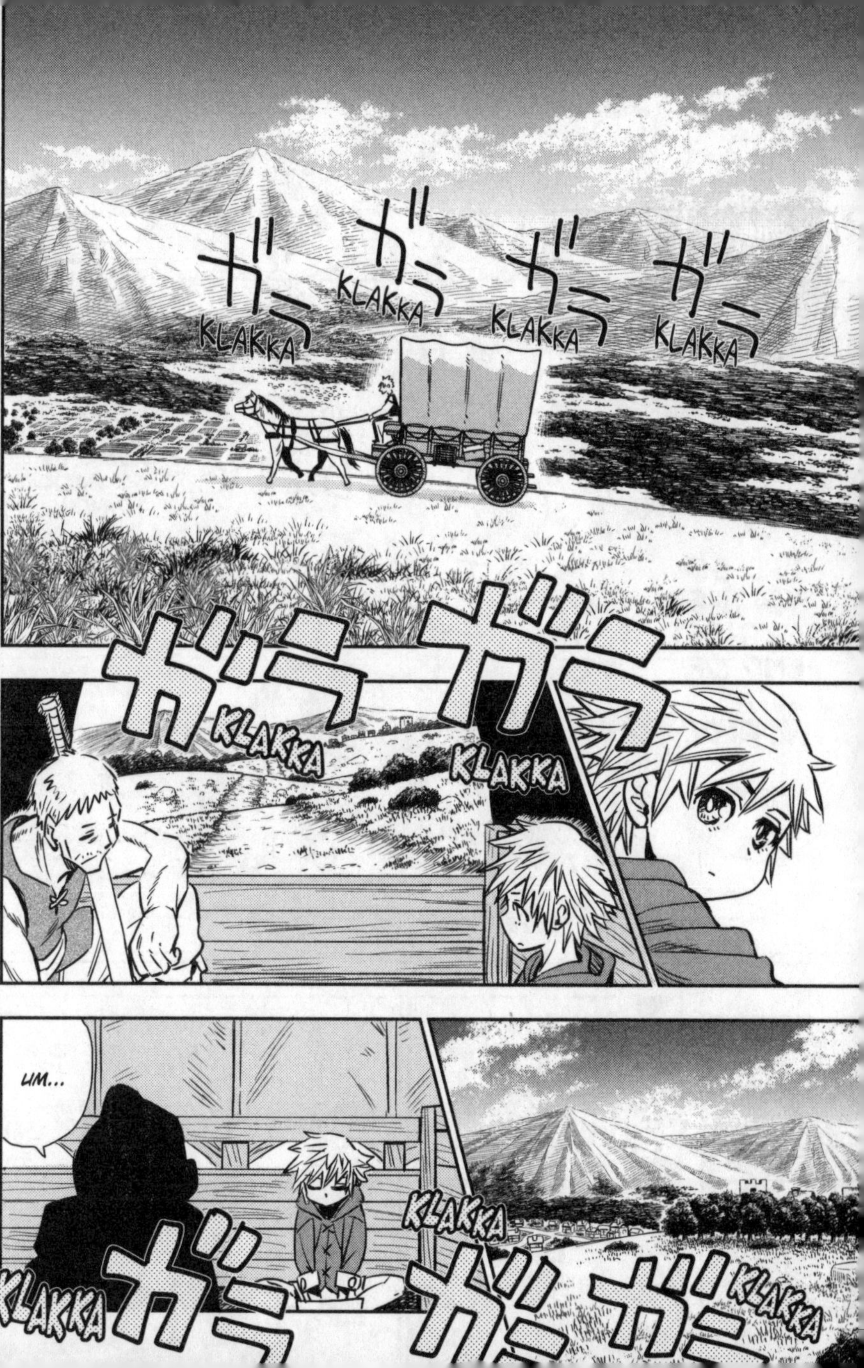
ガラ
KLAKKA
ガラ
KLAKKA
ガラ
KLAKKA
ガラ
KLAKKA
ガラ
KLAKKA
ガラ
KLAKKA
KLAKKA
ガラ
KLAKKA
ガラ
UM...
ガラ
KLAKKA

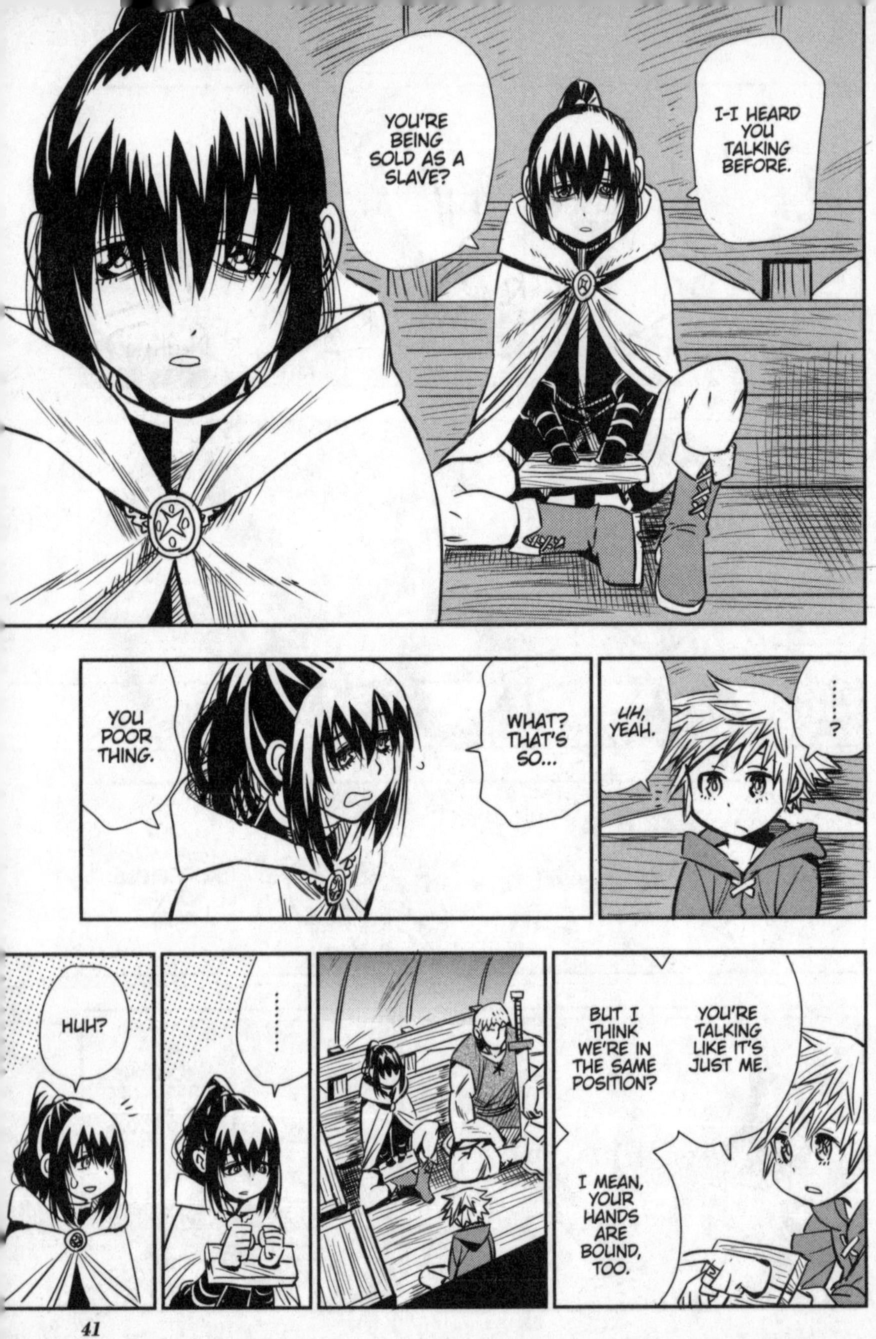
I-I HEARD YOU TALKING BEFORE.
YOU'RE BEING SOLD AS A SLAVE?
......?
UH, YEAH.
WHAT? THAT'S SO...
YOU POOR THING.
YOU'RE TALKING LIKE IT'S JUST ME.
BUT I THINK WE'RE IN THE SAME POSITION?
I MEAN, YOUR HANDS ARE BOUND, TOO.
......
HUH?

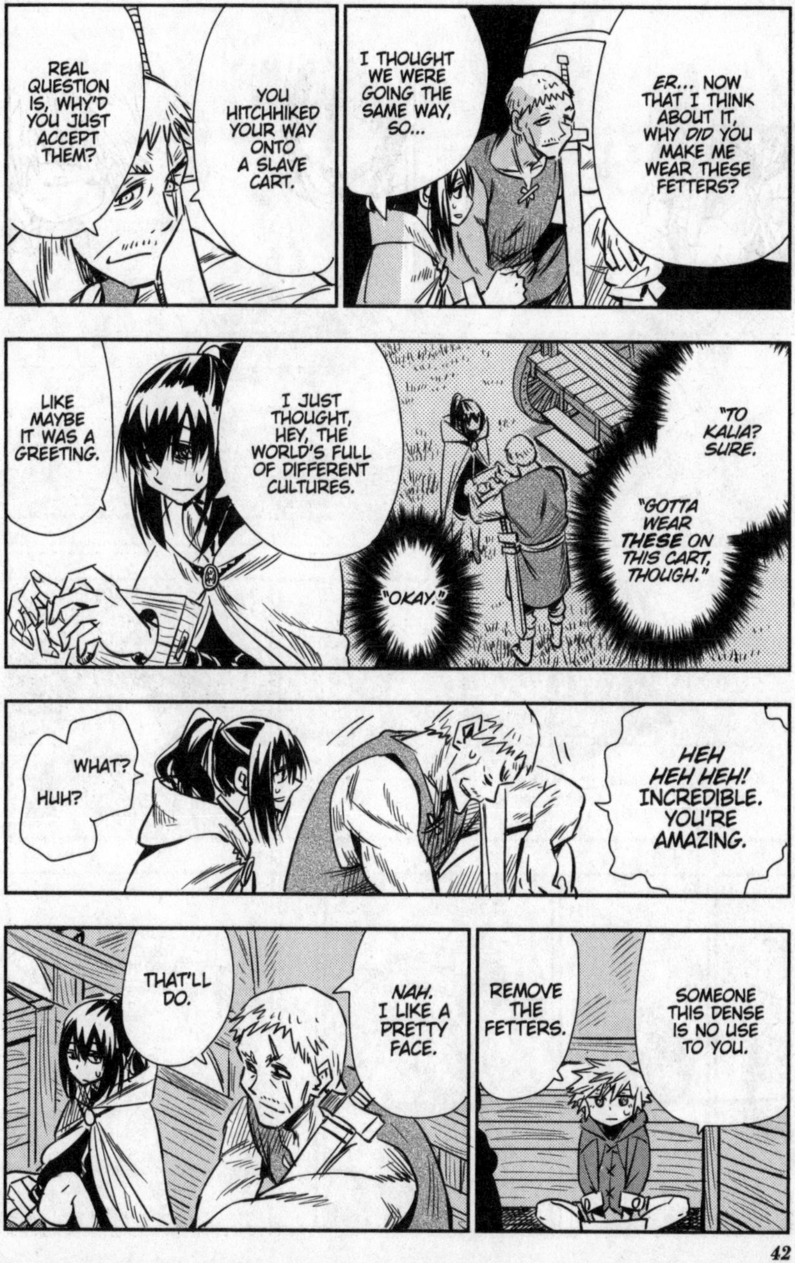
ER... NOW THAT I THINK ABOUT IT, WHY *DID* YOU MAKE ME WEAR THESE FETTERS?
I THOUGHT WE WERE GOING THE SAME WAY, SO...
YOU HITCHHIKED YOUR WAY ONTO A SLAVE CART.
REAL QUESTION IS, WHY'D YOU JUST ACCEPT THEM?
"TO KALIA? SURE.
"GOTTA WEAR **THESE** ON THIS CART, THOUGH."
"OKAY."
I JUST THOUGHT, HEY, THE WORLD'S FULL OF DIFFERENT CULTURES.
LIKE MAYBE IT WAS A GREETING.
HEH HEH HEH! INCREDIBLE. YOU'RE AMAZING.
WHAT?
HUH?
SOMEONE THIS DENSE IS NO USE TO YOU.
REMOVE THE FETTERS.
NAH. I LIKE A PRETTY FACE.
THAT'LL DO.

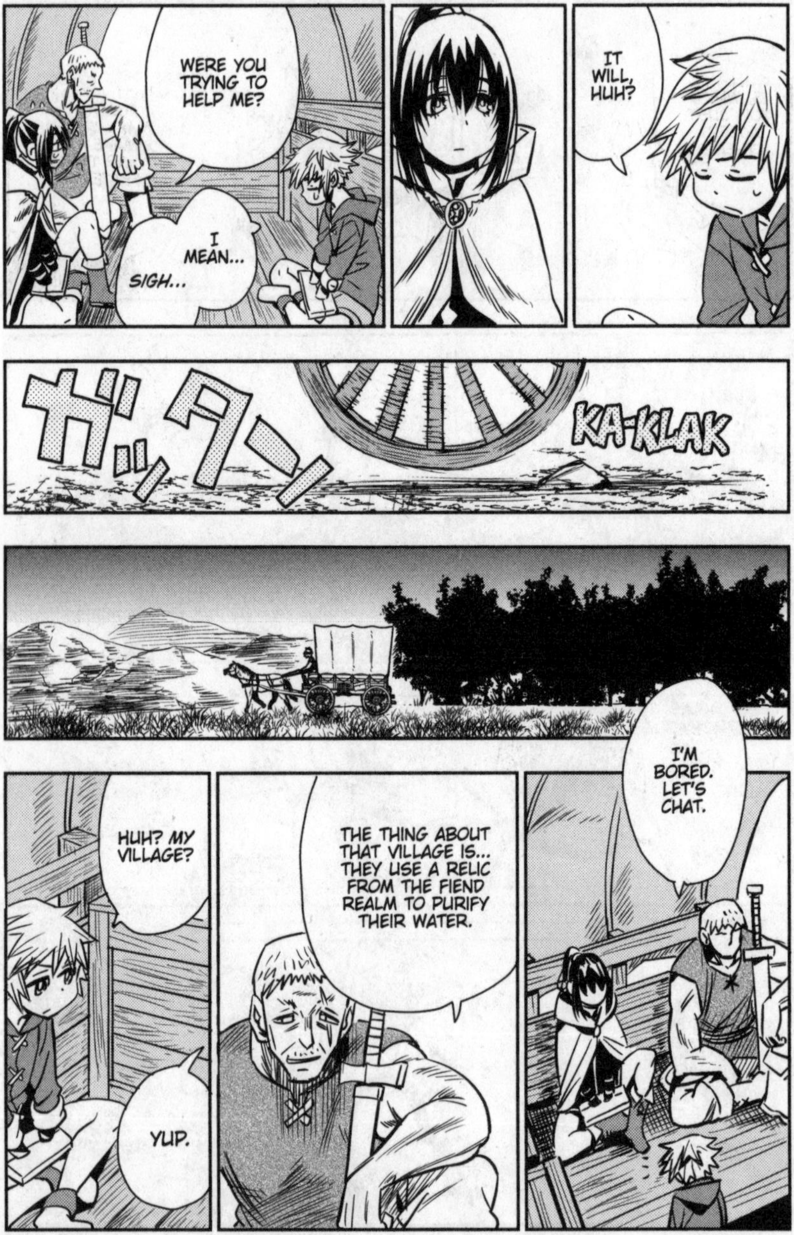
IT WILL, HUH?
WERE YOU TRYING TO HELP ME?
I MEAN...
SIGH...
KA-KLAK
ガッタン
I'M BORED. LET'S CHAT.
THE THING ABOUT THAT VILLAGE IS... THEY USE A RELIC FROM THE FIEND REALM TO PURIFY THEIR WATER.
HUH? MY VILLAGE?
YUP.

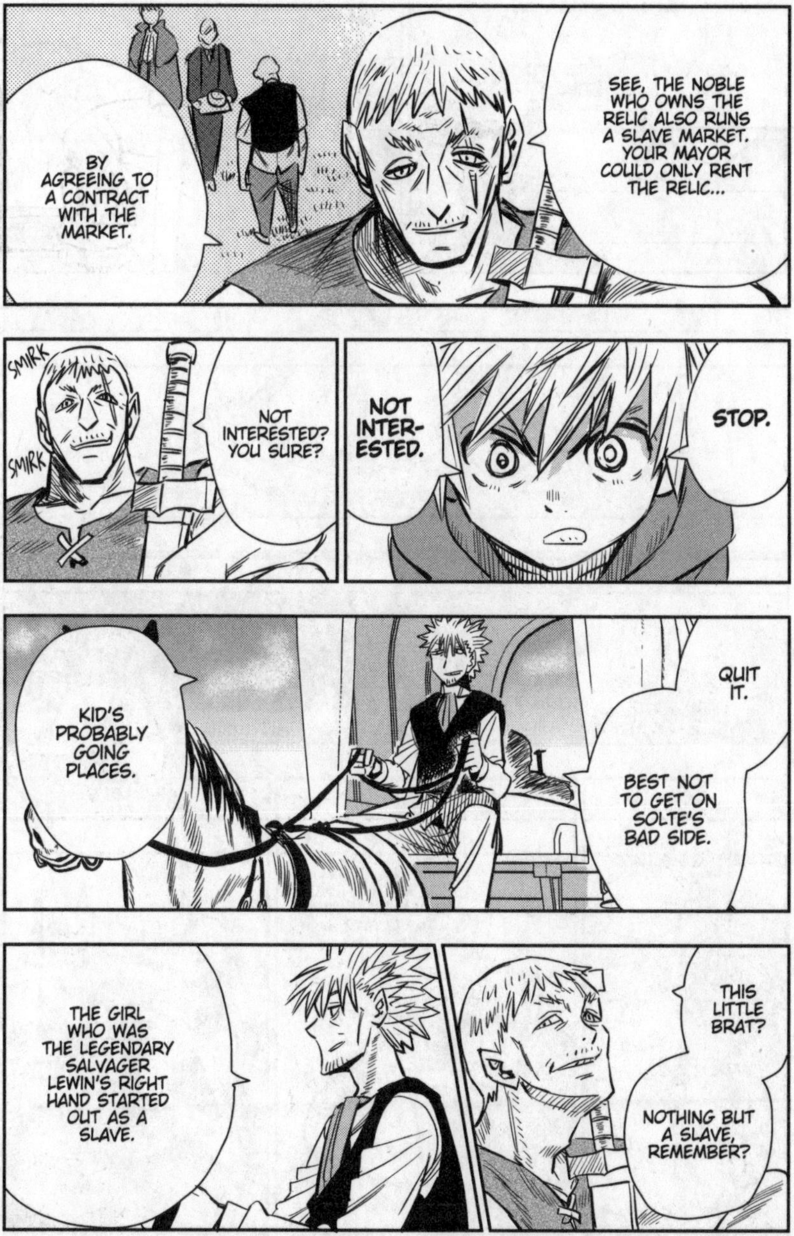
SEE, THE NOBLE WHO OWNS THE RELIC ALSO RUNS A SLAVE MARKET. YOUR MAYOR COULD ONLY RENT THE RELIC...
BY AGREEING TO A CONTRACT WITH THE MARKET.
STOP.
NOT INTER-ESTED.
NOT INTERESTED? YOU SURE?
SMIRK
SMIRK
KID'S PROBABLY GOING PLACES.
QUIT IT.
BEST NOT TO GET ON SOLTE'S BAD SIDE.
THIS LITTLE BRAT?
NOTHING BUT A SLAVE, REMEMBER?
THE GIRL WHO WAS THE LEGENDARY SALVAGER LEWIN'S RIGHT HAND STARTED OUT AS A SLAVE.

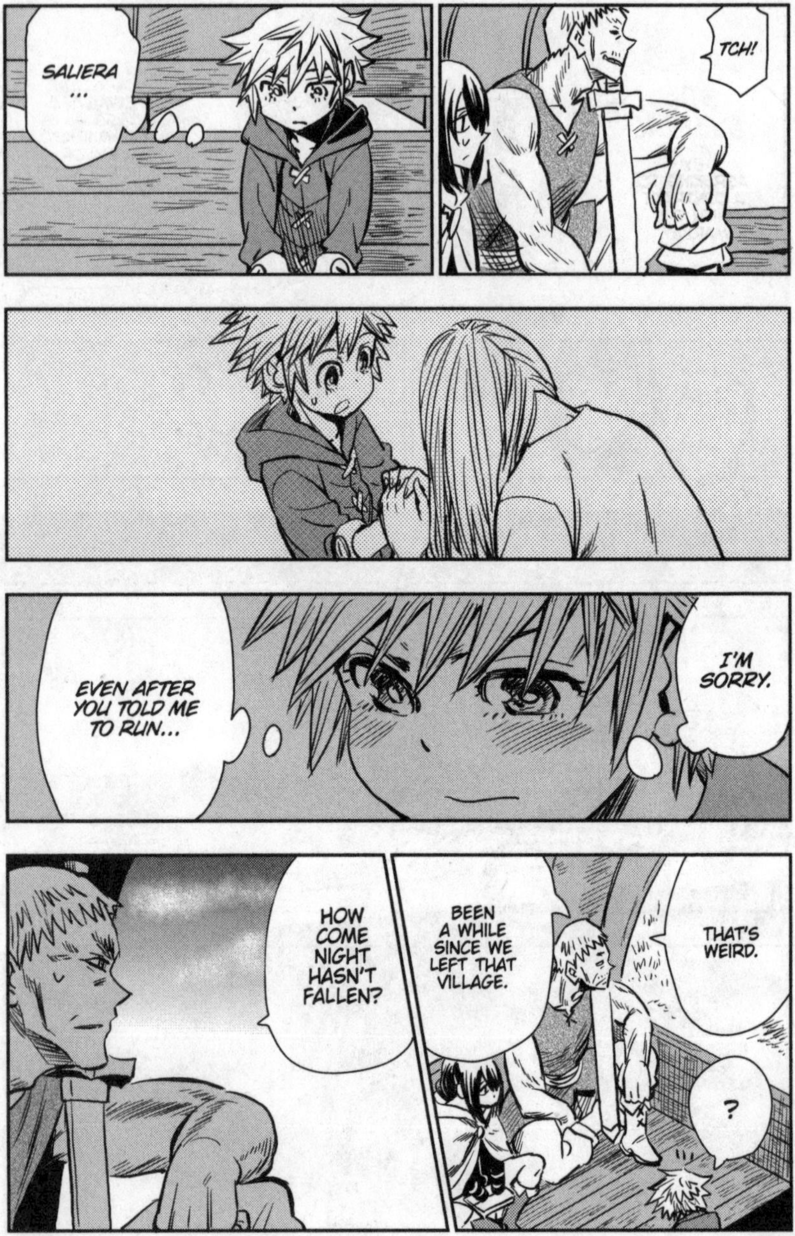
TCH!
SALIERA ...
I'M SORRY.
EVEN AFTER YOU TOLD ME TO RUN...
THAT'S WEIRD.
BEEN A WHILE SINCE WE LEFT THAT VILLAGE.
?
HOW COME NIGHT HASN'T FALLEN?

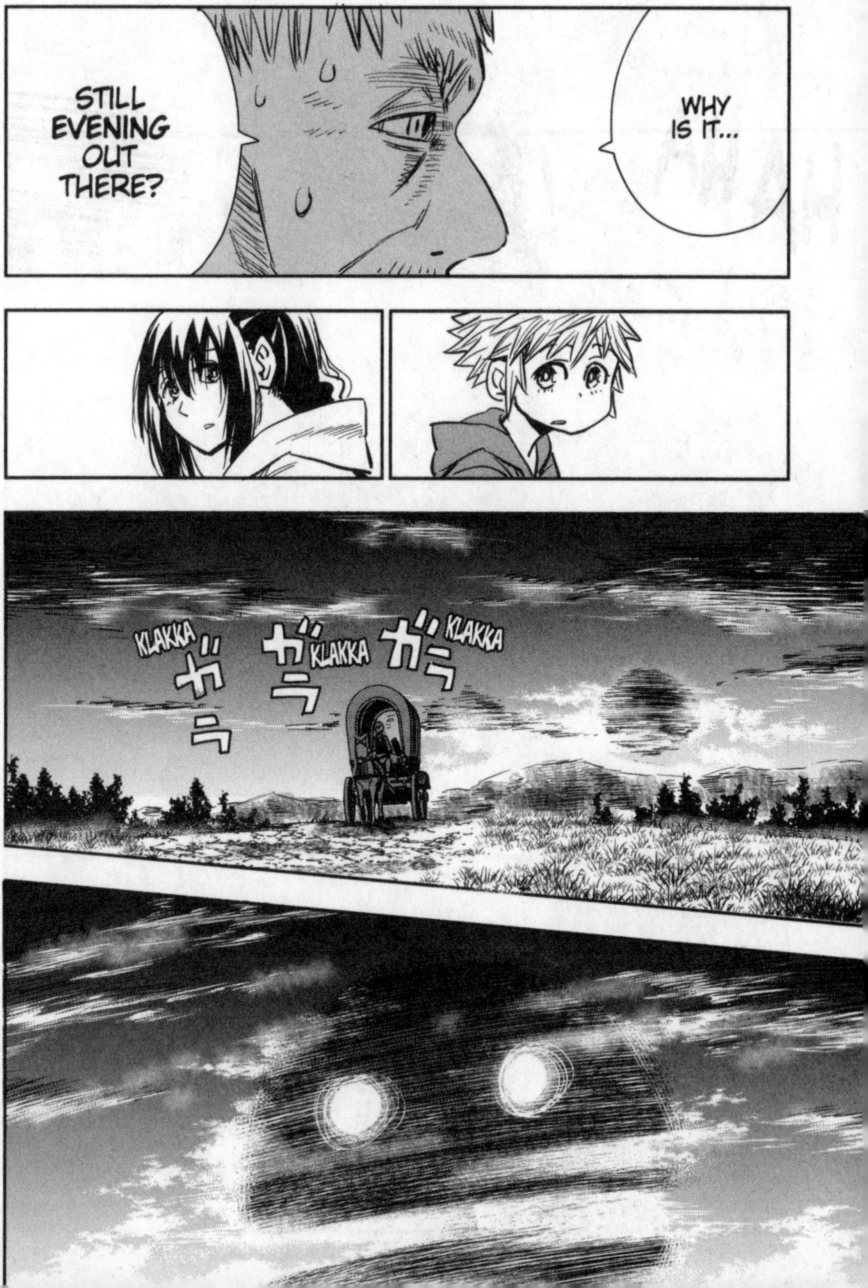
WHY IS IT...
STILL EVENING OUT THERE?
KLAKKA
ガラ
KLAKKA
ガラ
KLAKKA
ガラ

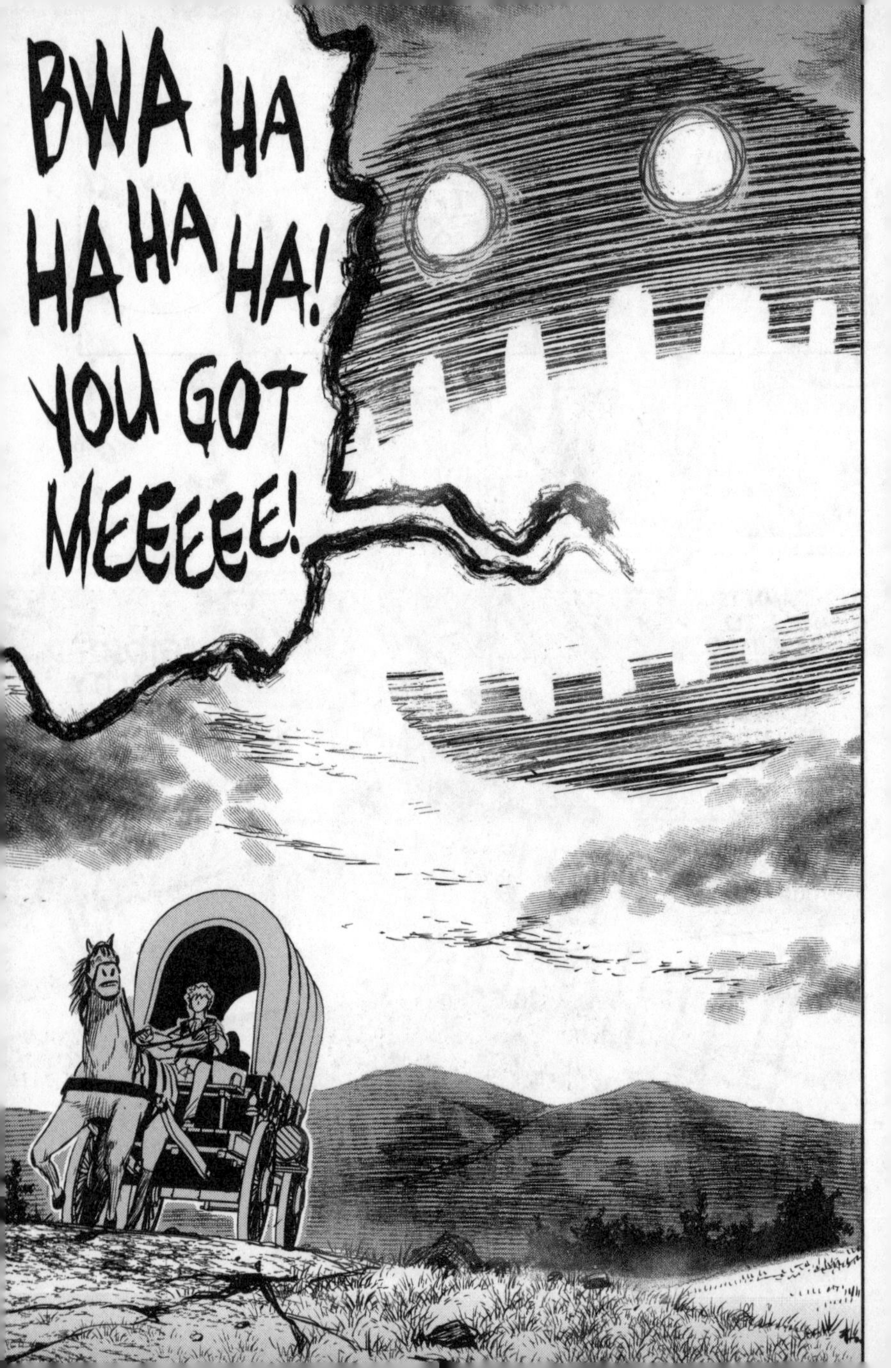
BWA HA HA HA HA HA! YOU GOT MEEEEE!

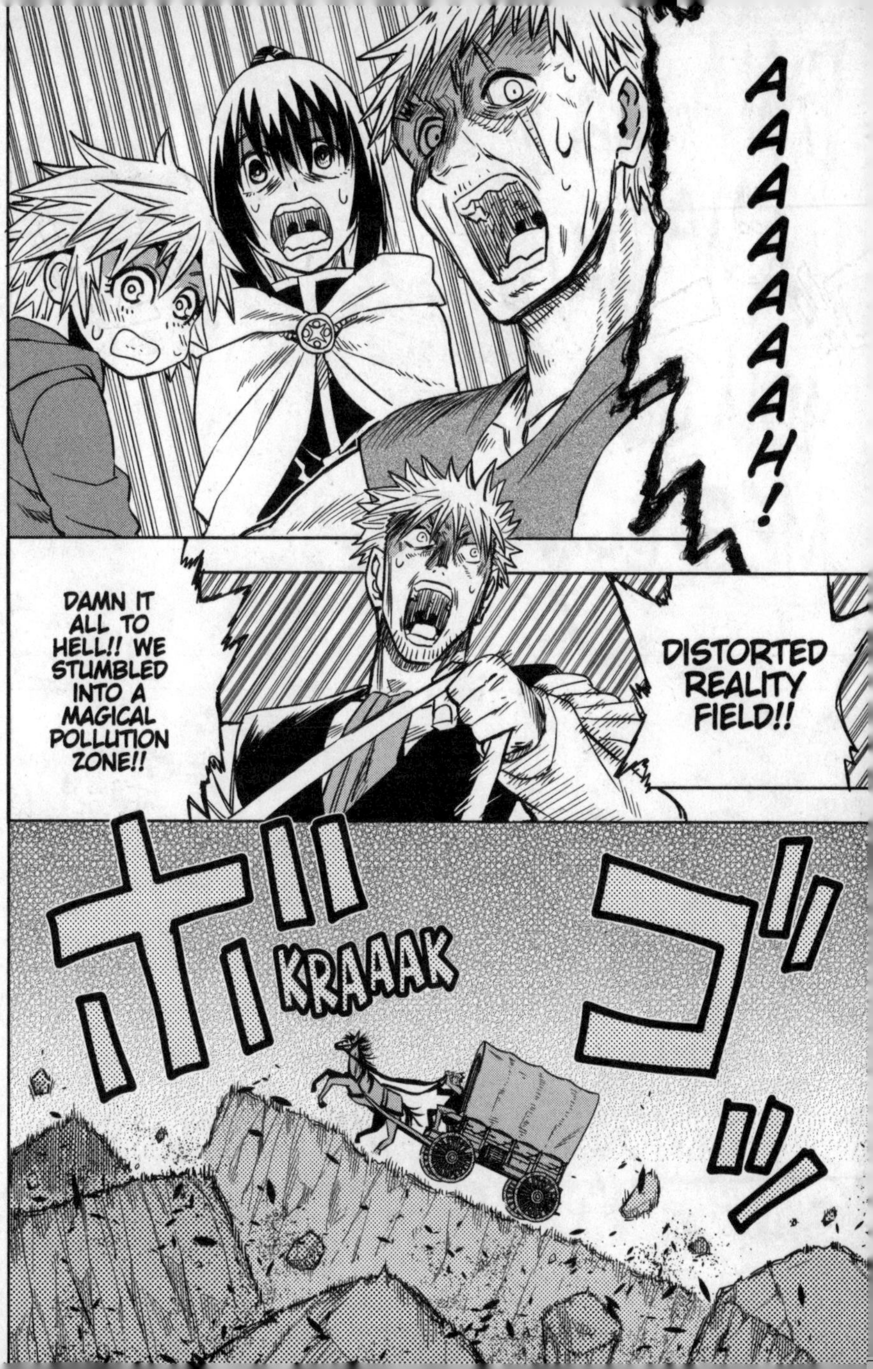
AAAAAAAH!
DISTORTED REALITY FIELD!!
DAMN IT ALL TO HELL!! WE STUMBLED INTO A MAGICAL POLLUTION ZONE!!
KRAAAK

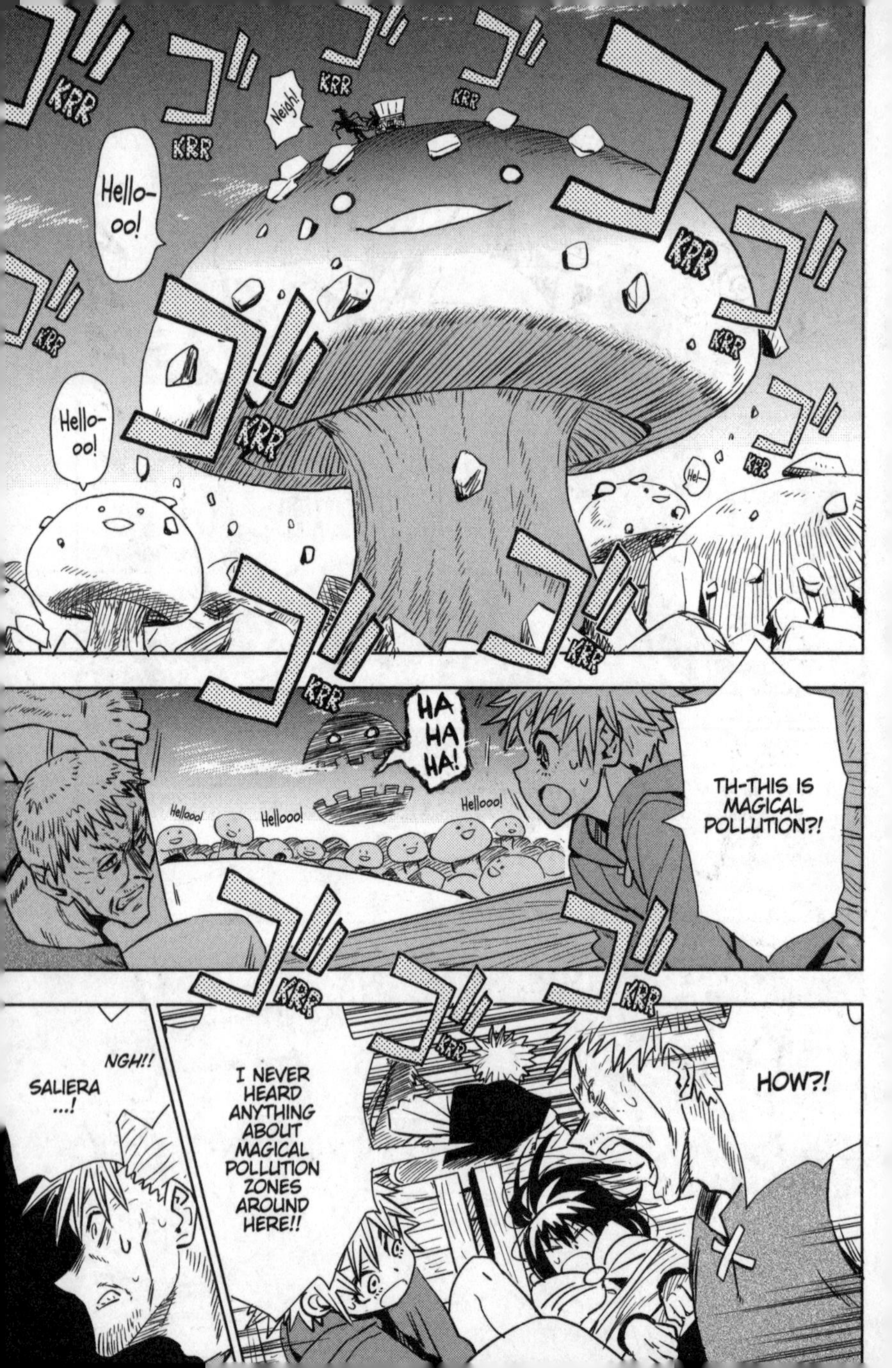
KRR
KRR
KRR
KRR
Neigh!
KRR
Hello-
oo!
KRR
KRR
KRR
Hel-
KRR
Hello-
oo!
KRR
TH-THIS IS MAGICAL POLLUTION?!
HA HA HA!
Hellooo!
Hellooo!
Hellooo!
KRR
KRR
KRR
HOW?!
I NEVER HEARD ANYTHING ABOUT MAGICAL POLLUTION ZONES AROUND HERE!!
NGH!!
SALIERA ...!

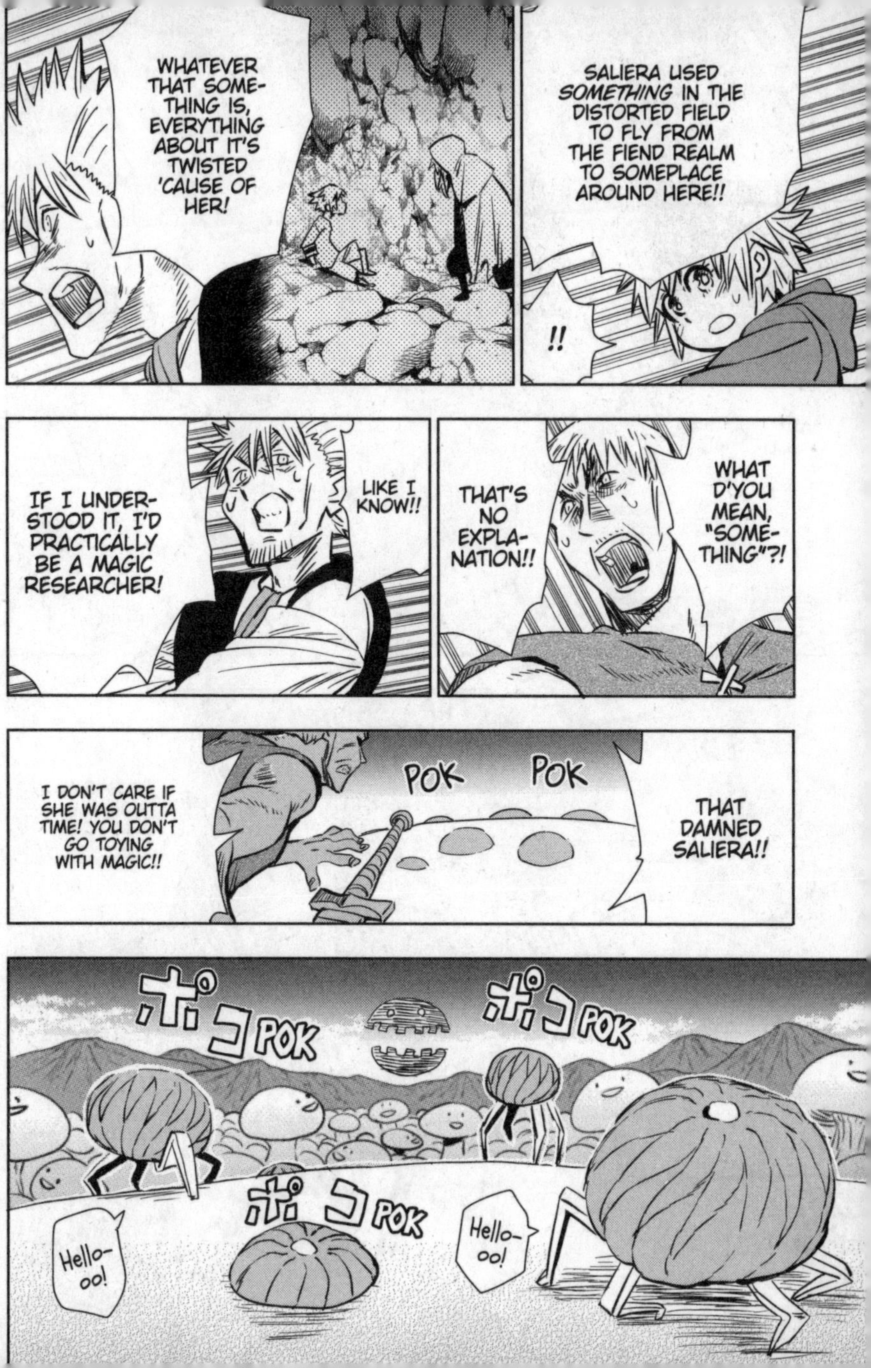
SALIERA USED *SOMETHING* IN THE DISTORTED FIELD TO FLY FROM THE FIEND REALM TO SOMEPLACE AROUND HERE!!
!!
WHATEVER THAT SOMETHING IS, EVERYTHING ABOUT IT'S TWISTED 'CAUSE OF HER!
WHAT D'YOU MEAN, "SOMETHING"?!
THAT'S NO EXPLANATION!!
LIKE I KNOW!!
IF I UNDERSTOOD IT, I'D PRACTICALLY BE A MAGIC RESEARCHER!
THAT DAMNED SALIERA!!
POK POK
I DON'T CARE IF SHE WAS OUTTA TIME! YOU DON'T GO TOYING WITH MAGIC!!
ポコ POK
ポコ POK
Hello-oo!
ポコ POK
Hello-oo!

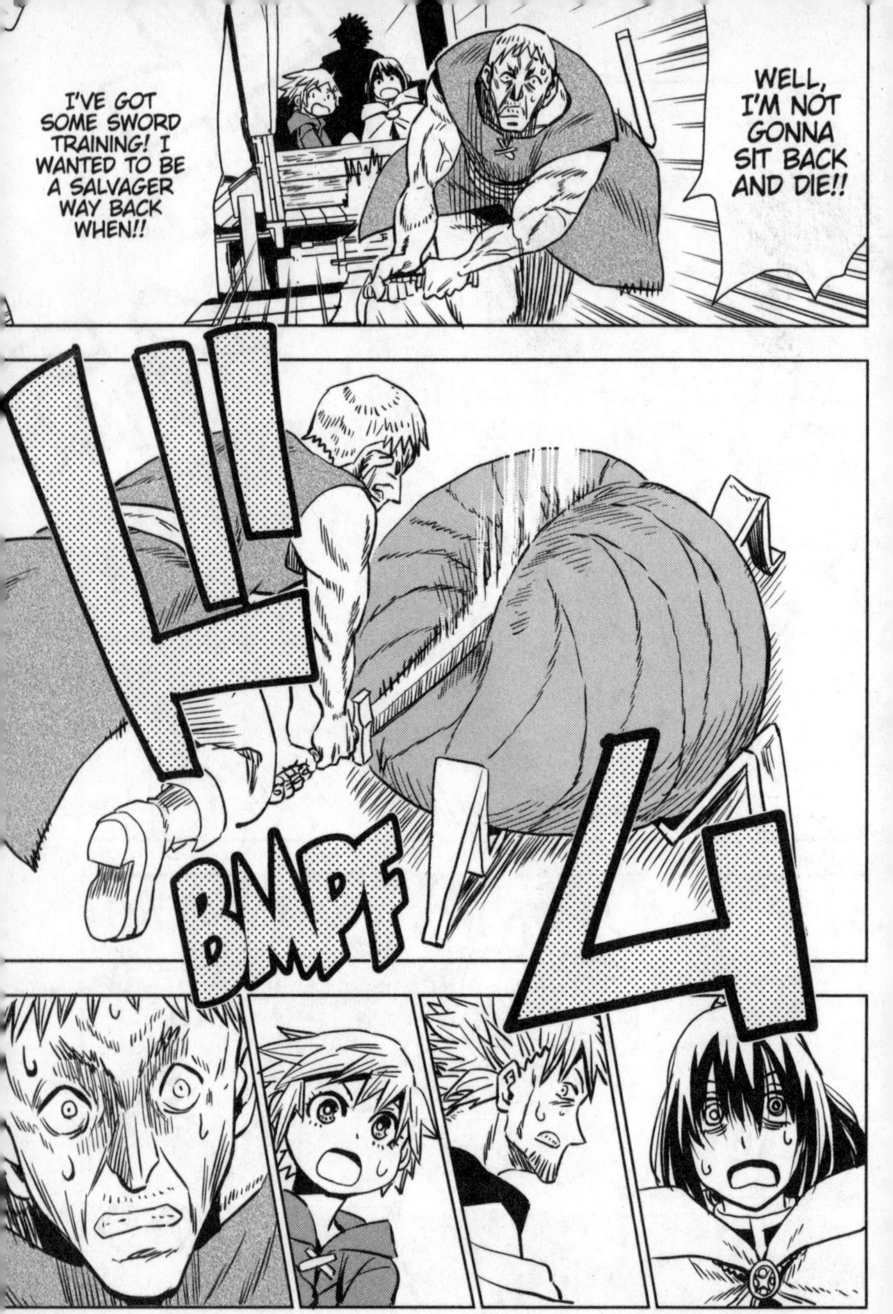
WELL, I'M NOT GONNA SIT BACK AND DIE!!
I'VE GOT SOME SWORD TRAINING! I WANTED TO BE A SALVAGER WAY BACK WHEN!!
BMPF

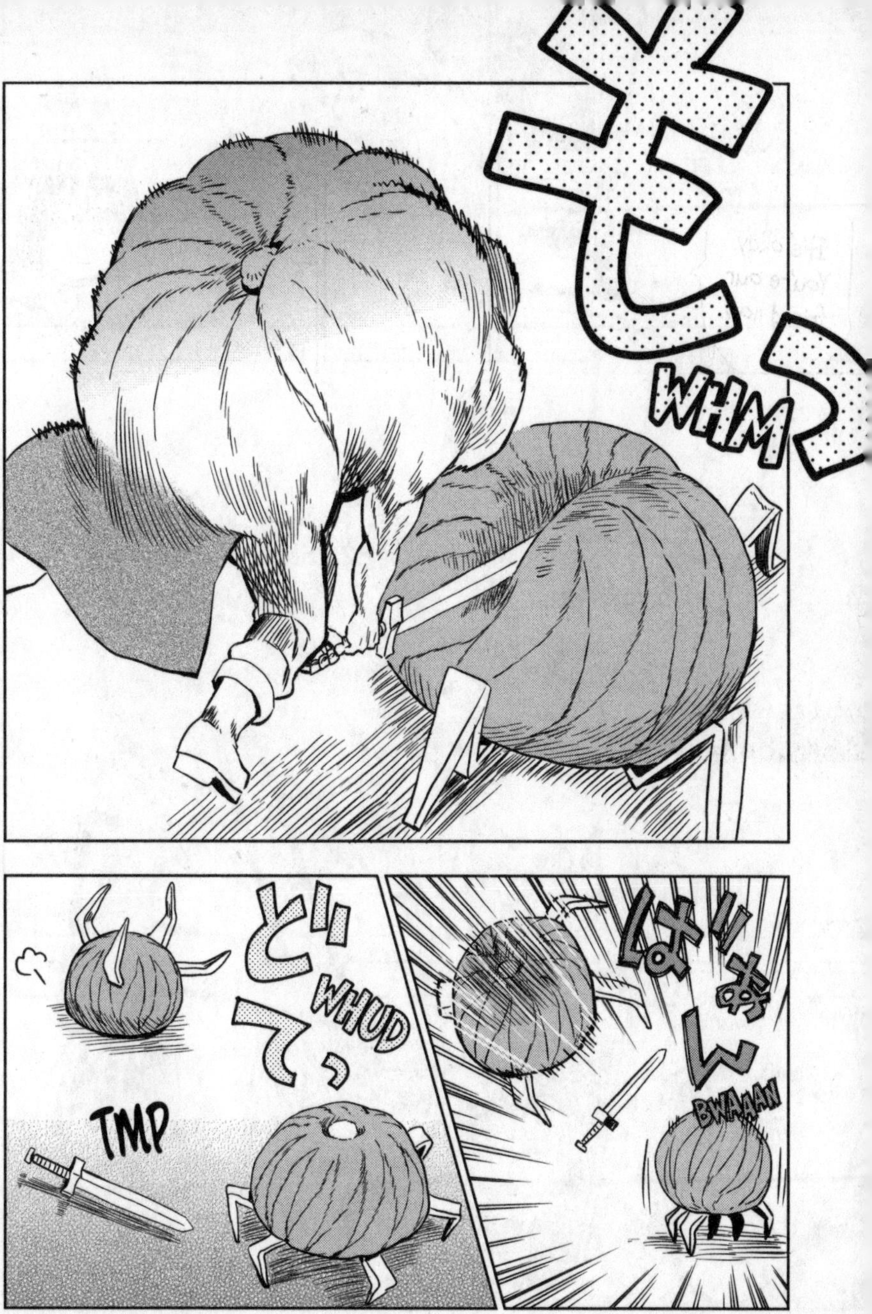
ずしっ
WHM
ぱぁん
BWAAAN
どてっ
WHUD
TMP

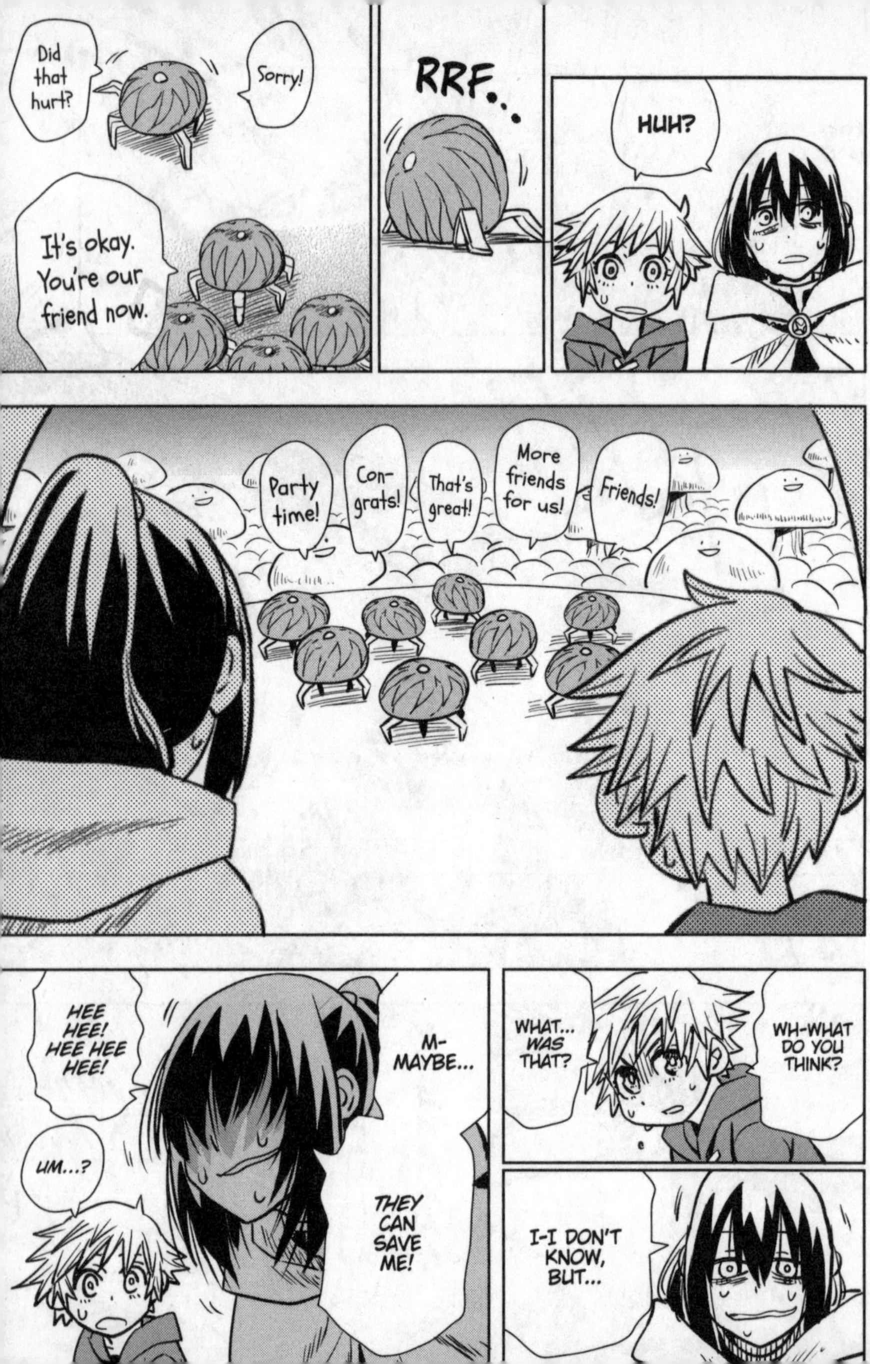
HUH?
RRF...
Sorry!
Did that hurt?
It's okay. You're our friend now.
Friends!
More friends for us!
That's great!
Con-grats!
Party time!
WH-WHAT DO YOU THINK?
WHAT... WAS THAT?
I-I DON'T KNOW, BUT...
M-MAYBE...
HEE HEE! HEE HEE HEE!
THEY CAN SAVE ME!
UM...?

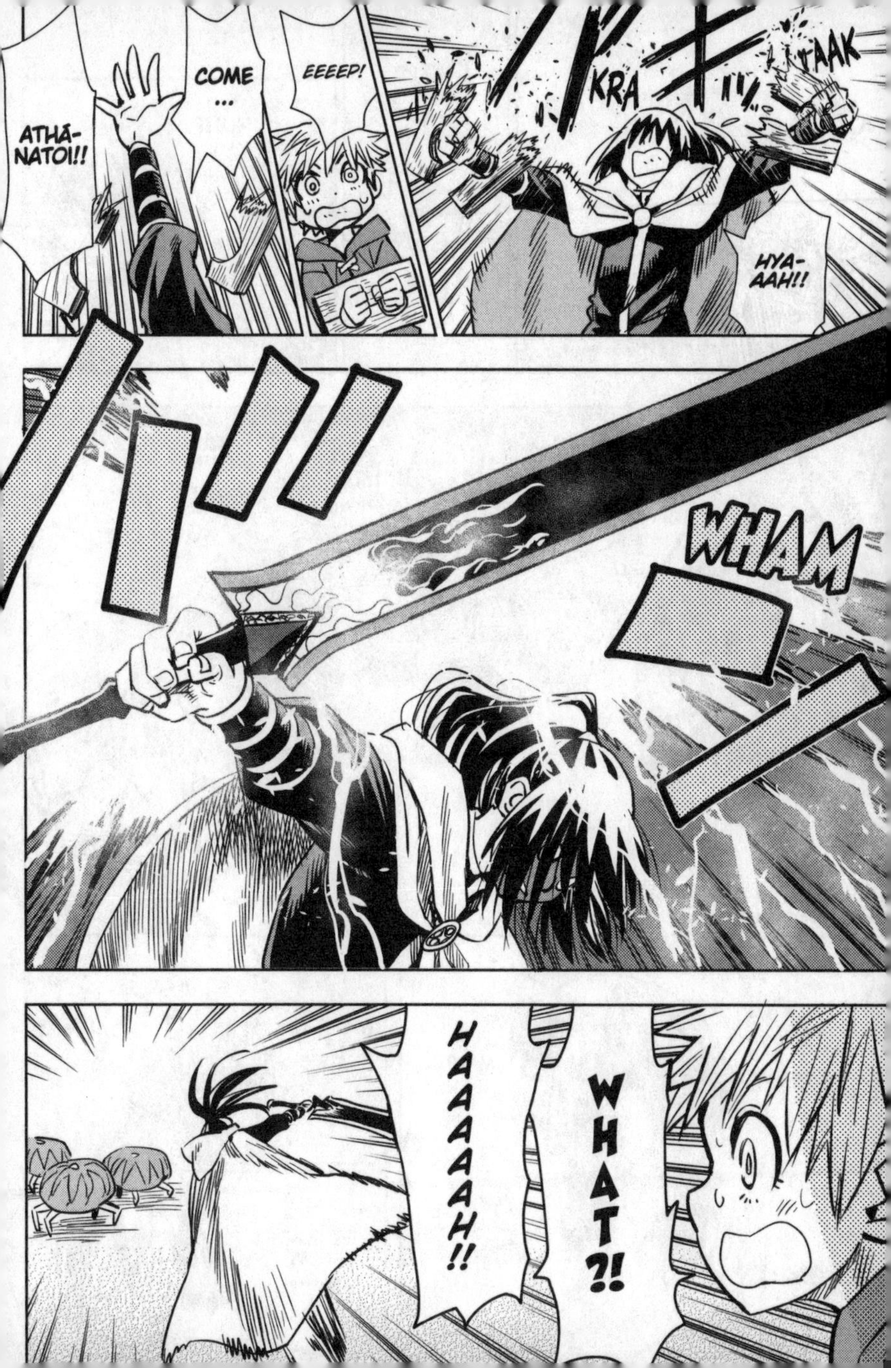
KRA TAAK
HYA-AAH!!
EEEEP!
COME ...
ATHÁ-NATOI!!
WHAM
WHAT?!
HAAAAAAH!!

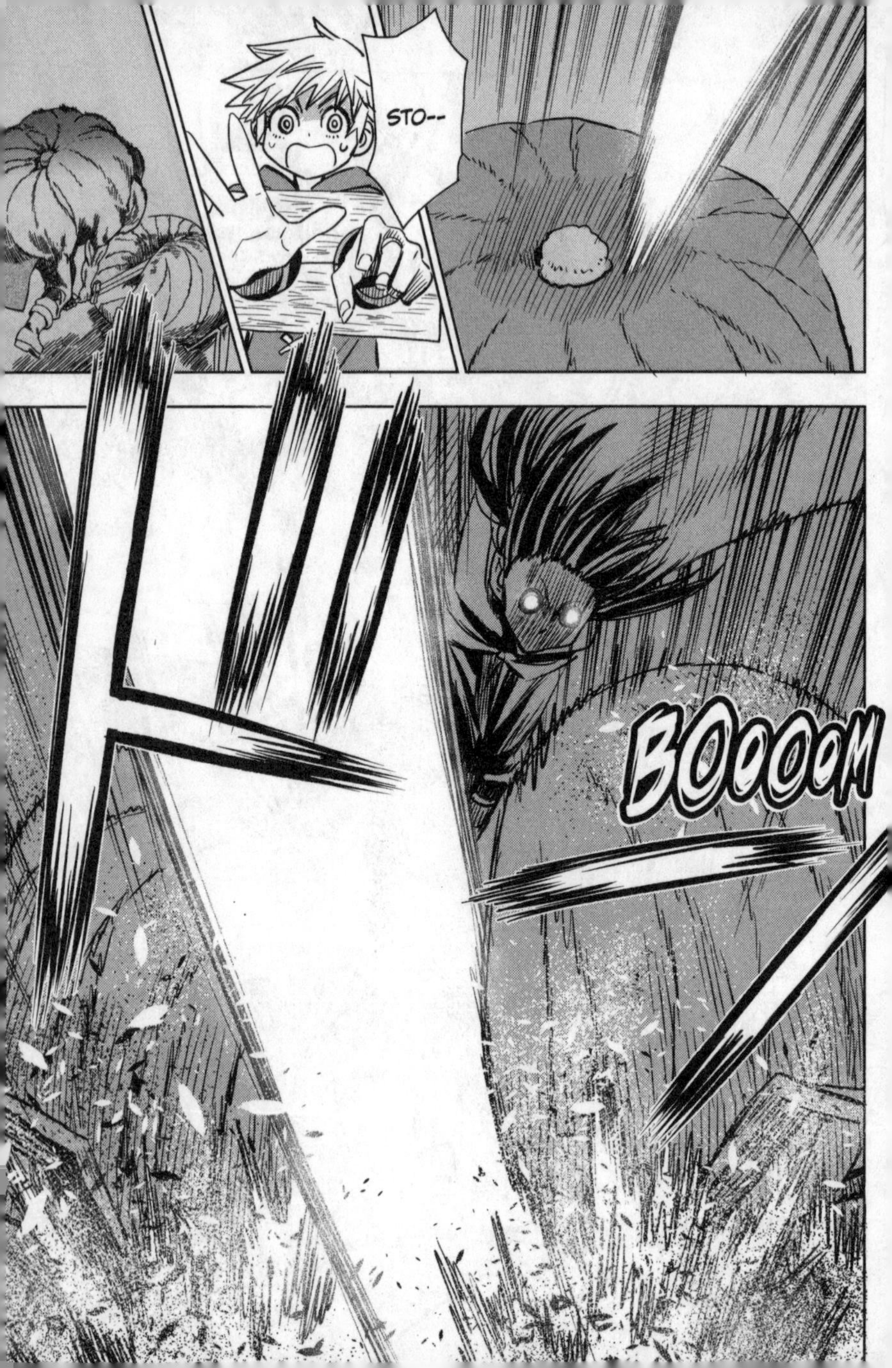
STO--
BOOOOM

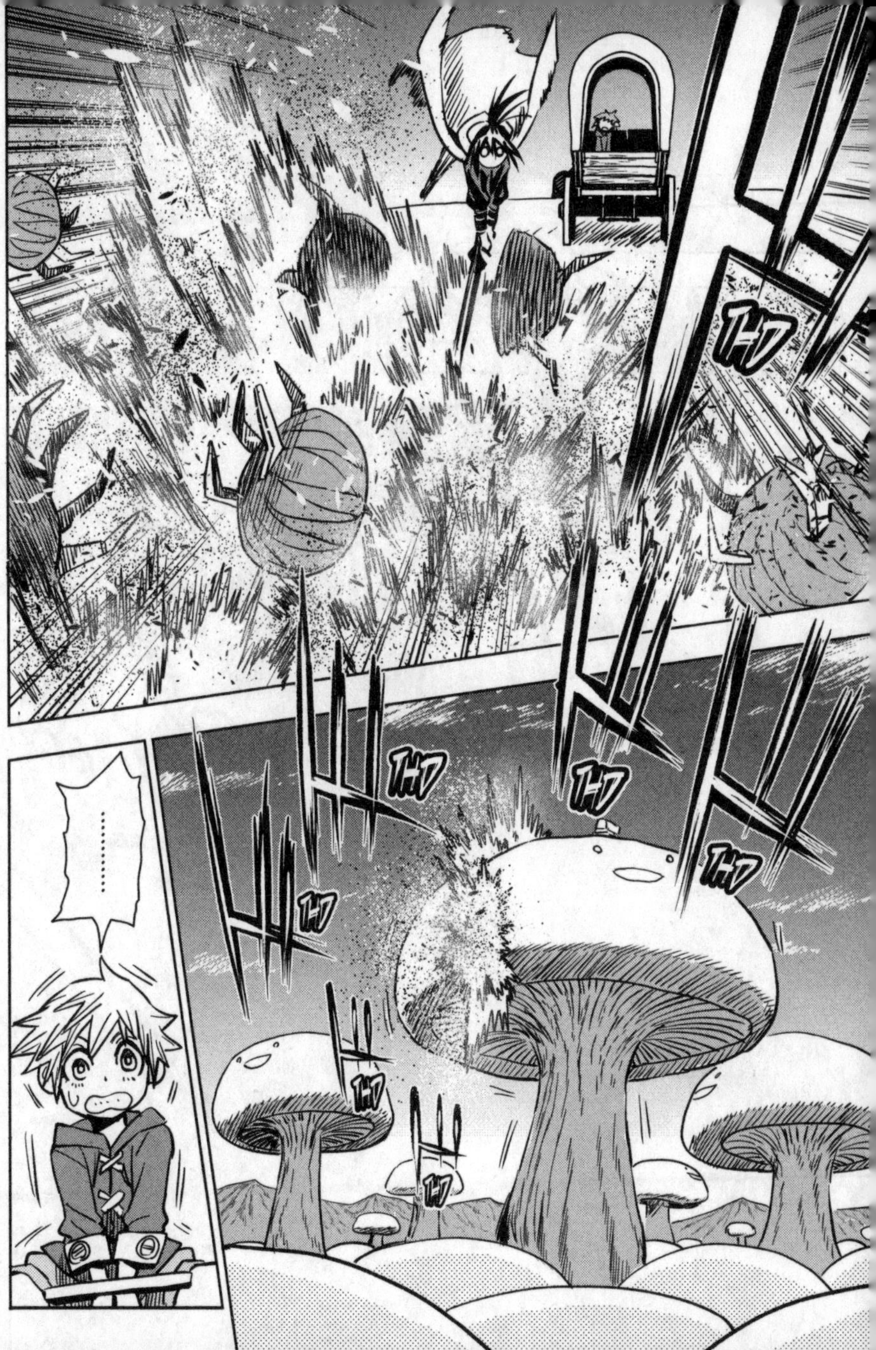
THD
THD
THD
THD
THD
THD
THD
......

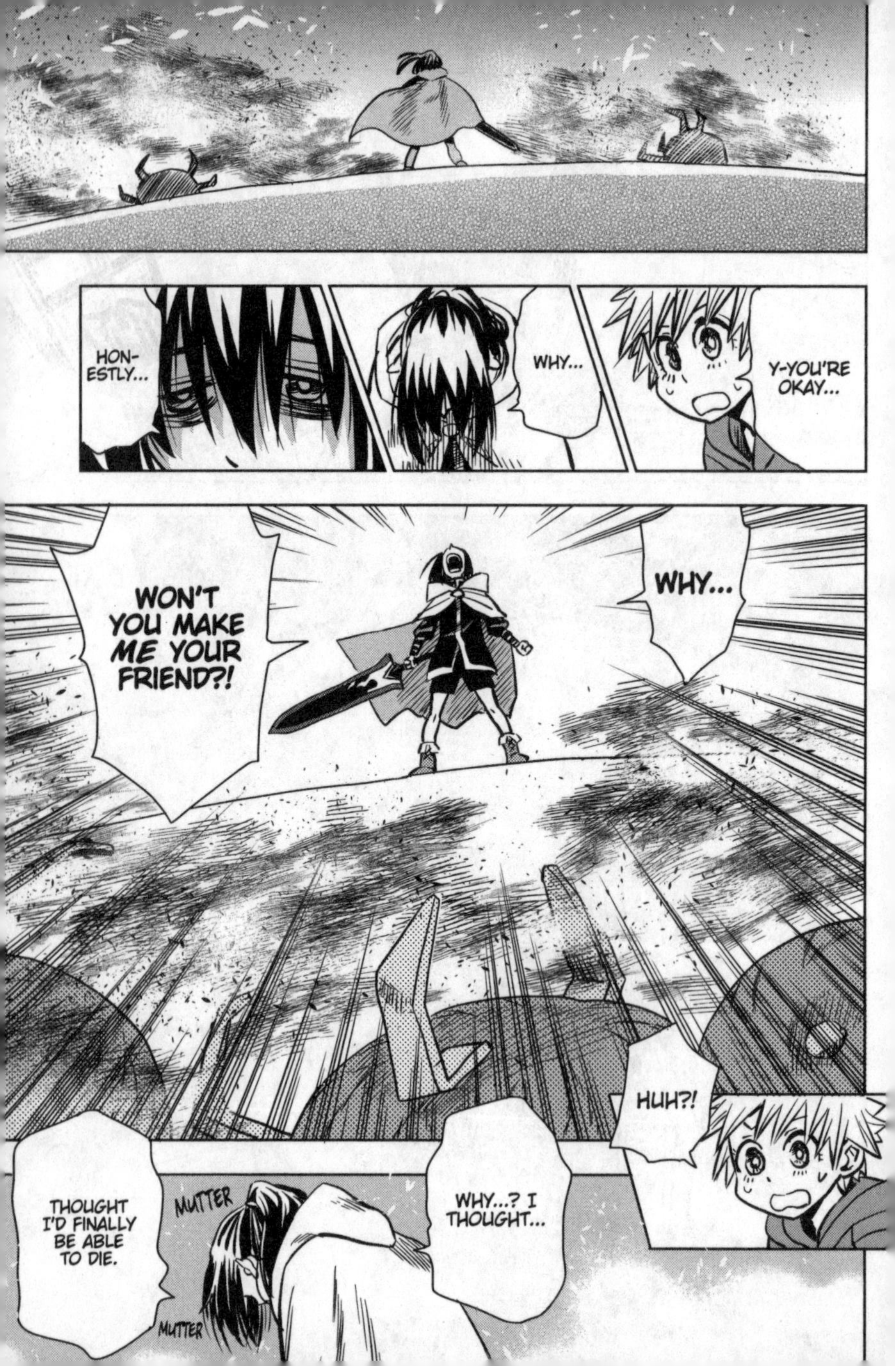
Y-YOU'RE OKAY...
WHY...
HON-ESTLY...
WHY...
WON'T YOU MAKE *ME* YOUR FRIEND?!
HUH?!
WHY...? I THOUGHT...
MUTTER
THOUGHT I'D FINALLY BE ABLE TO DIE.
MUTTER

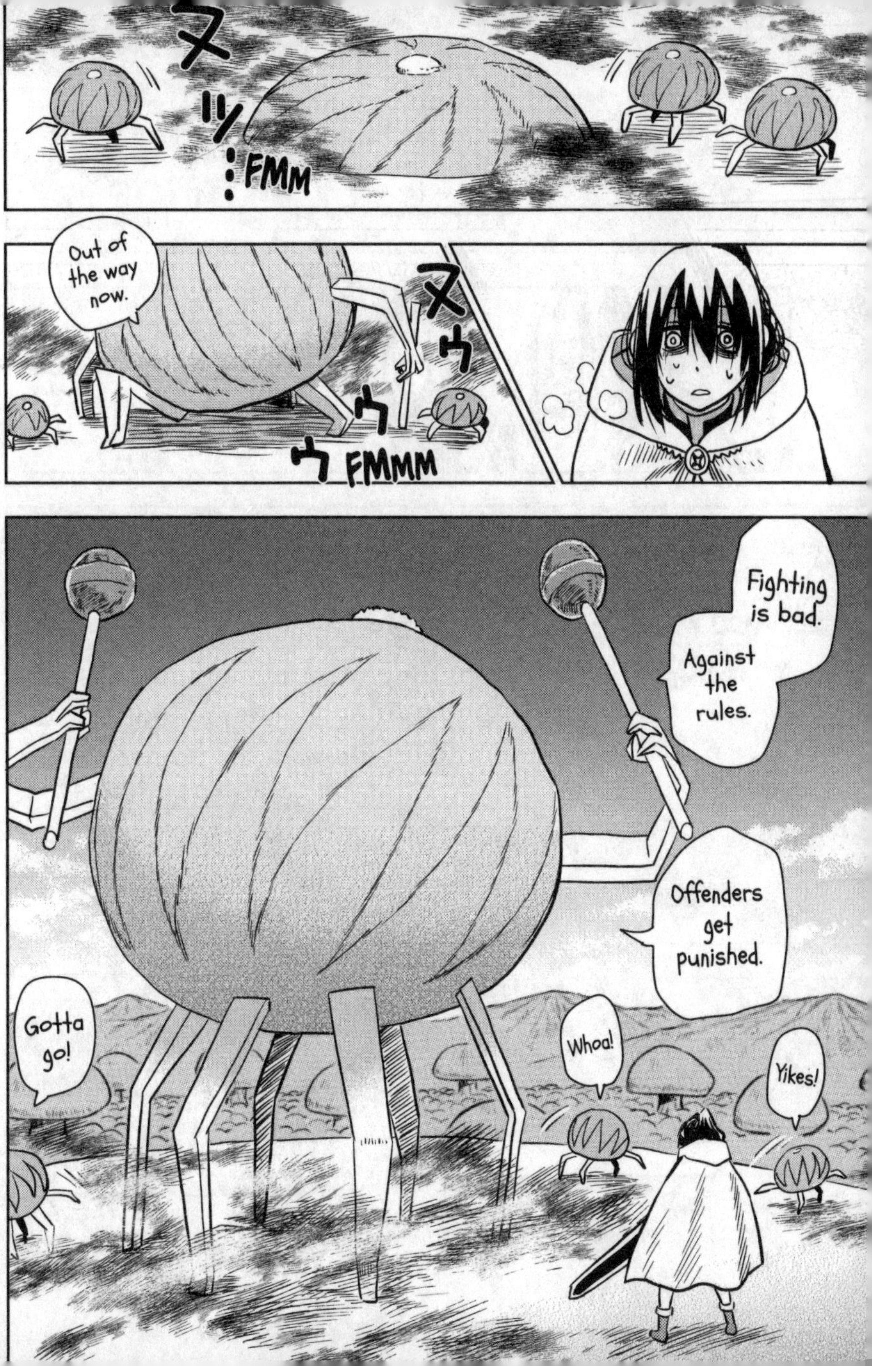
ヌッ
FMM
Out of the way now.
ヌゥゥゥ
FMMM
Fighting is bad.
Against the rules.
Offenders get punished.
Yikes!
Whoa!
Gotta go!

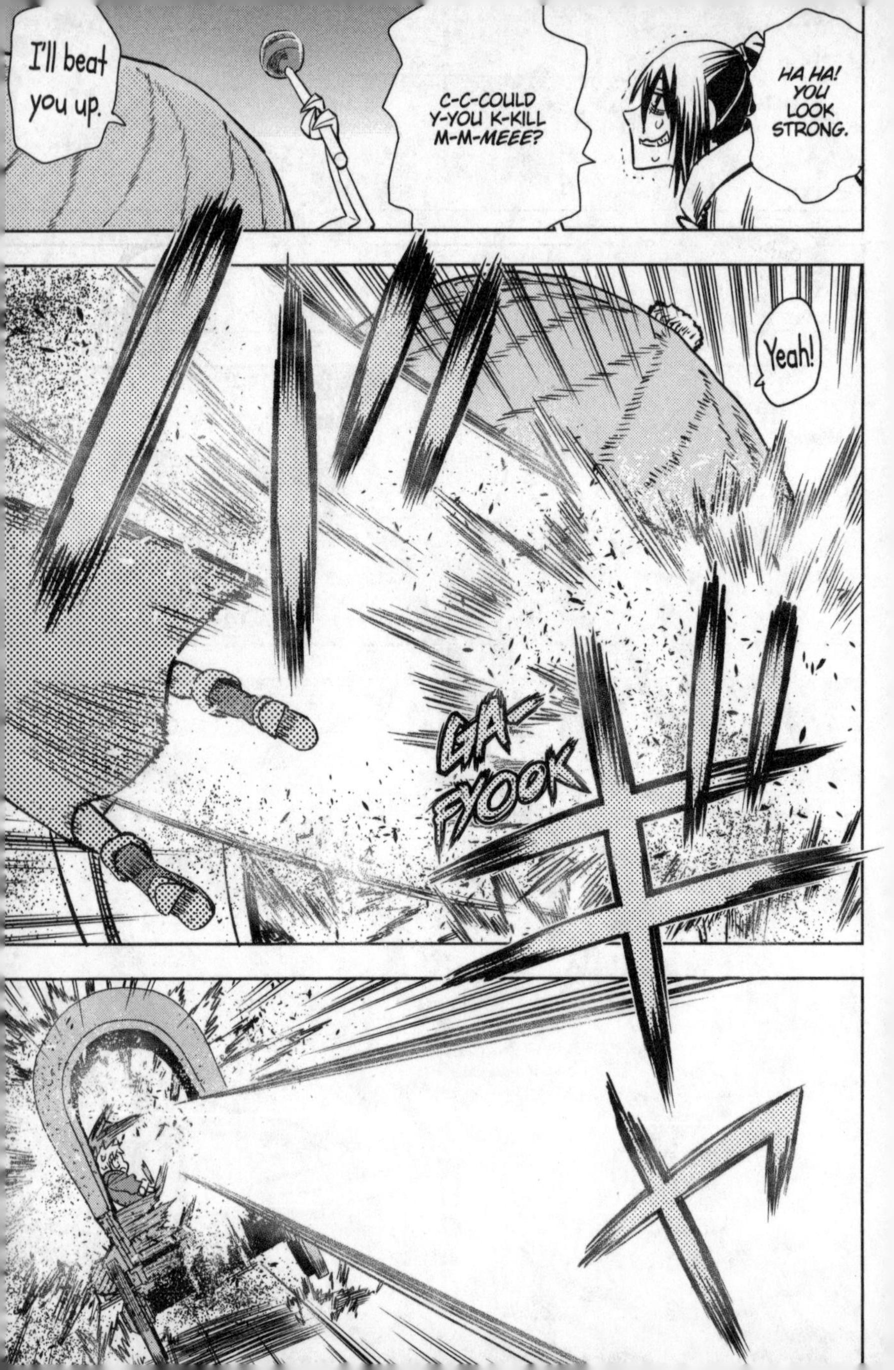
HA HA! YOU LOOK STRONG.
C-C-COULD Y-YOU K-KILL M-M-MEEE?
I'll beat you up.
Yeah!
GA-FYOOK

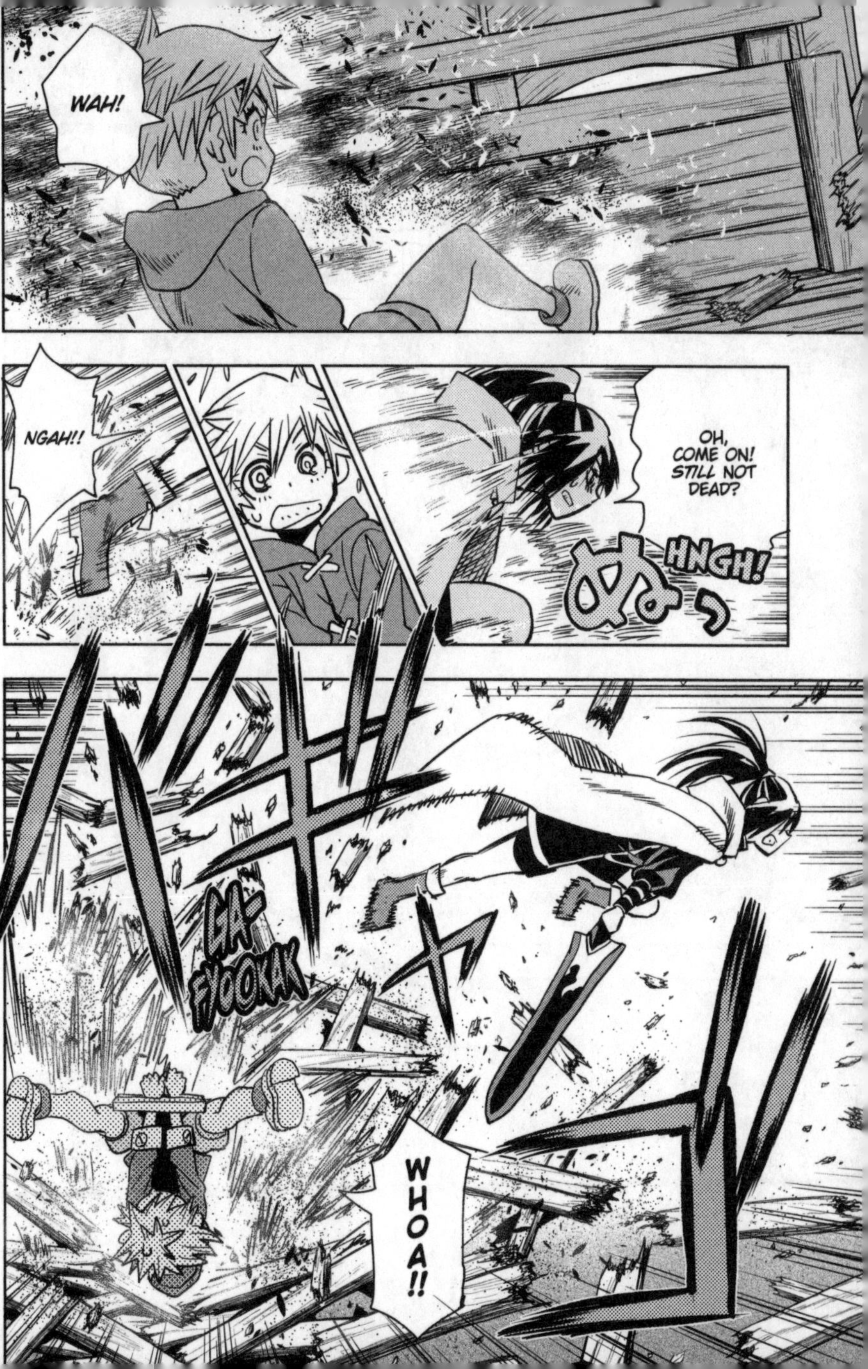
WAH!
OH, COME ON! STILL NOT DEAD?
ぬっ
HNGH!
NGAH!!
GA-FYOOKAK
WHOA!!

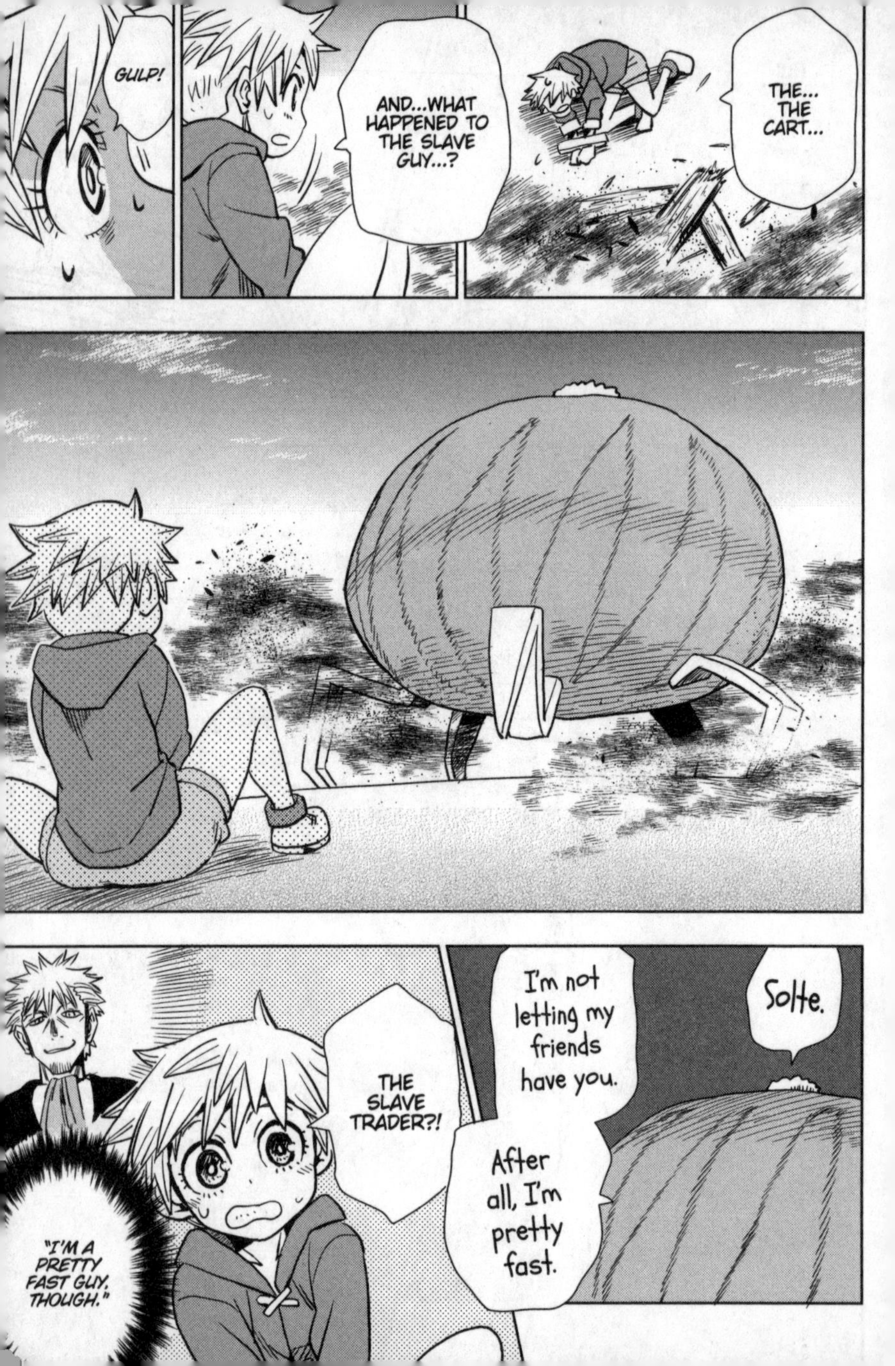
THE... THE CART...
AND...WHAT HAPPENED TO THE SLAVE GUY...?
GULP!
Solte.
I'm not letting my friends have you.
After all, I'm pretty fast.
THE SLAVE TRADER?!
"I'M A PRETTY FAST GUY, THOUGH."

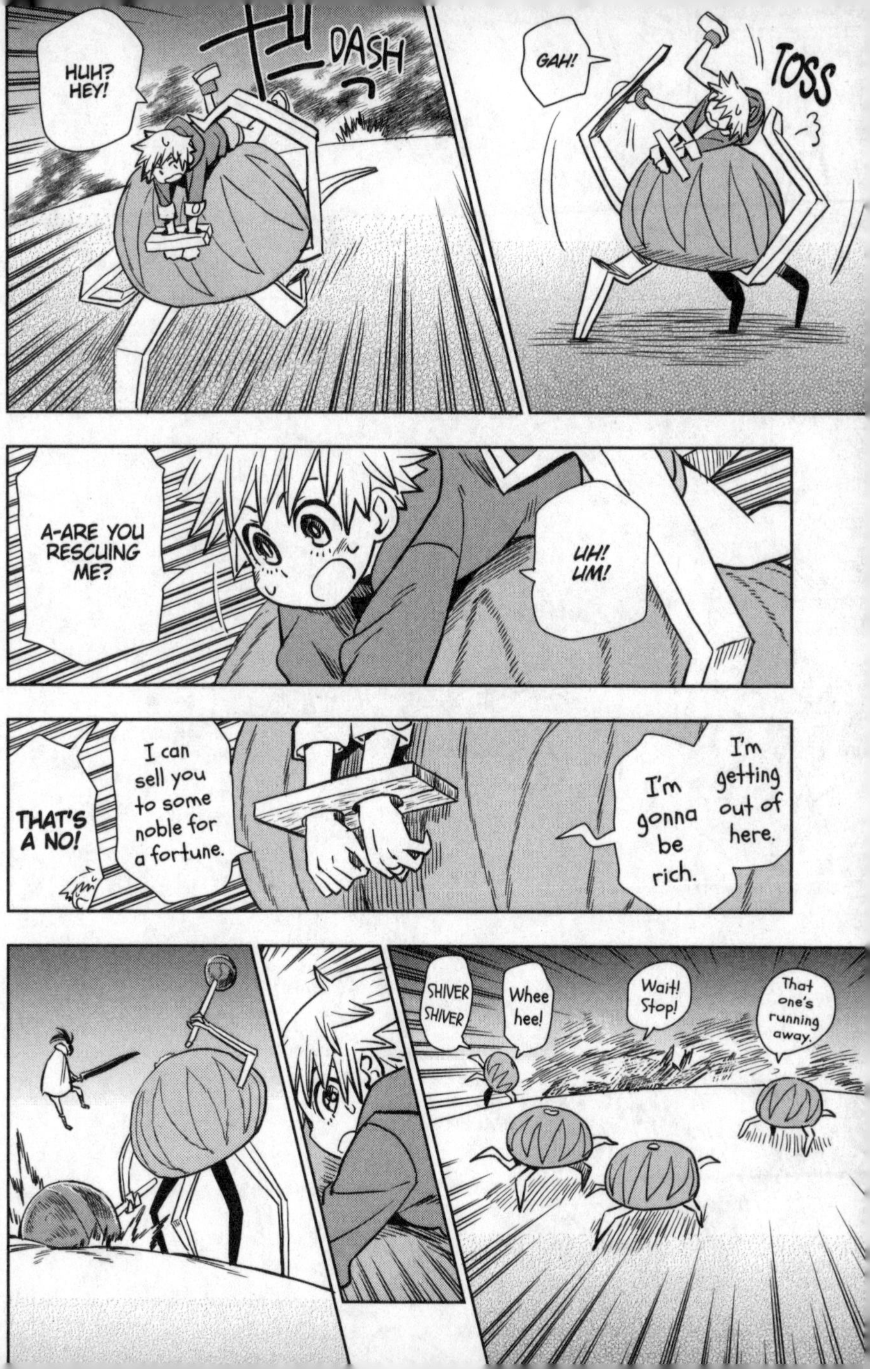
GAH!
TOSS
HUH? HEY!
DASH
UH! UM!
A-ARE YOU RESCUING ME?
I'm getting out of here.
I'm gonna be rich.
I can sell you to some noble for a fortune.
THAT'S A NO!
That one's running away.
Wait! Stop!
Whee hee!
SHIVER SHIVER

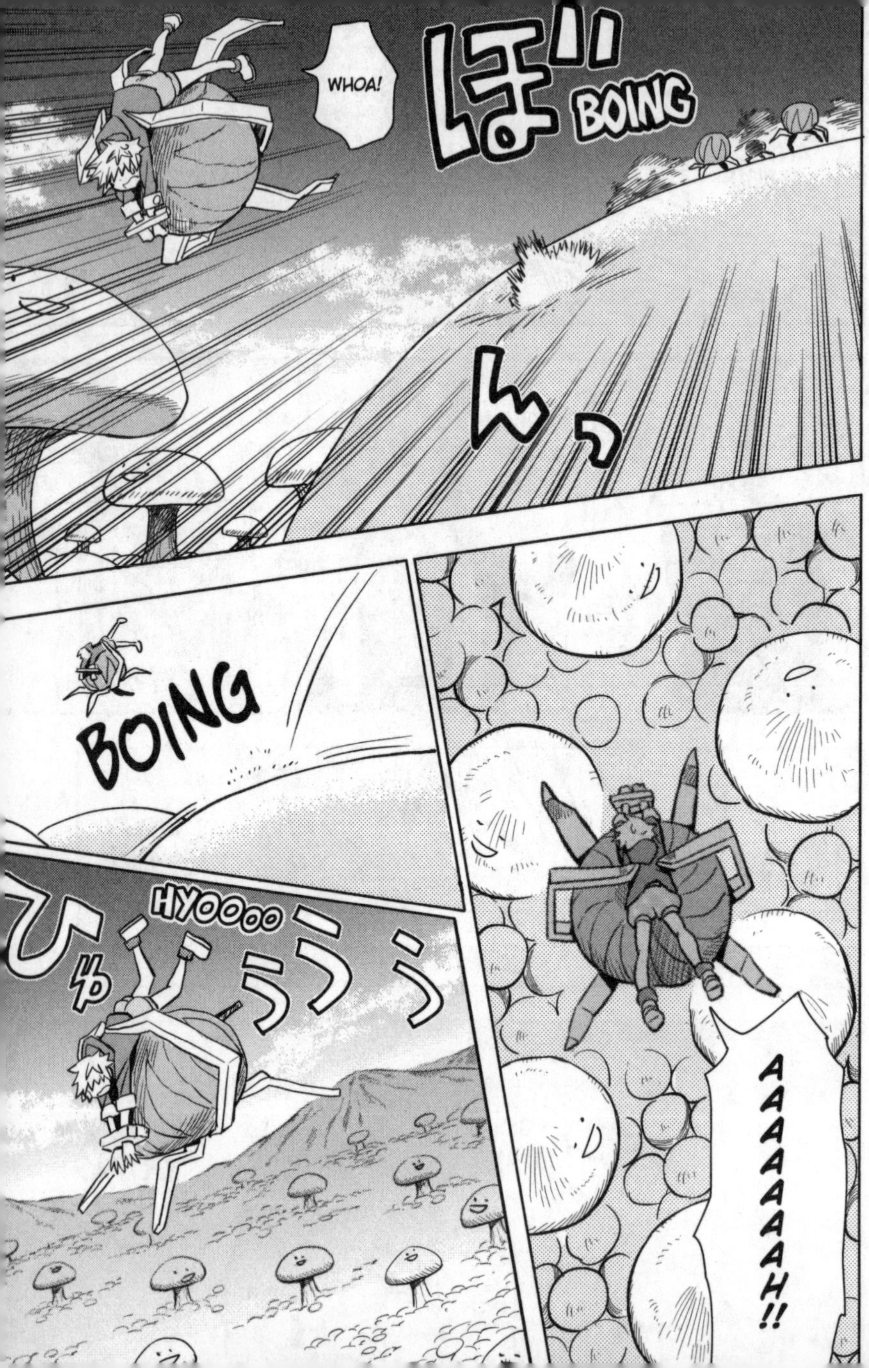
WHOA!
ぼぃ
BOING
んっ
AAAAAAAAH!!
BOING
ひゅううう
HYOOOOO

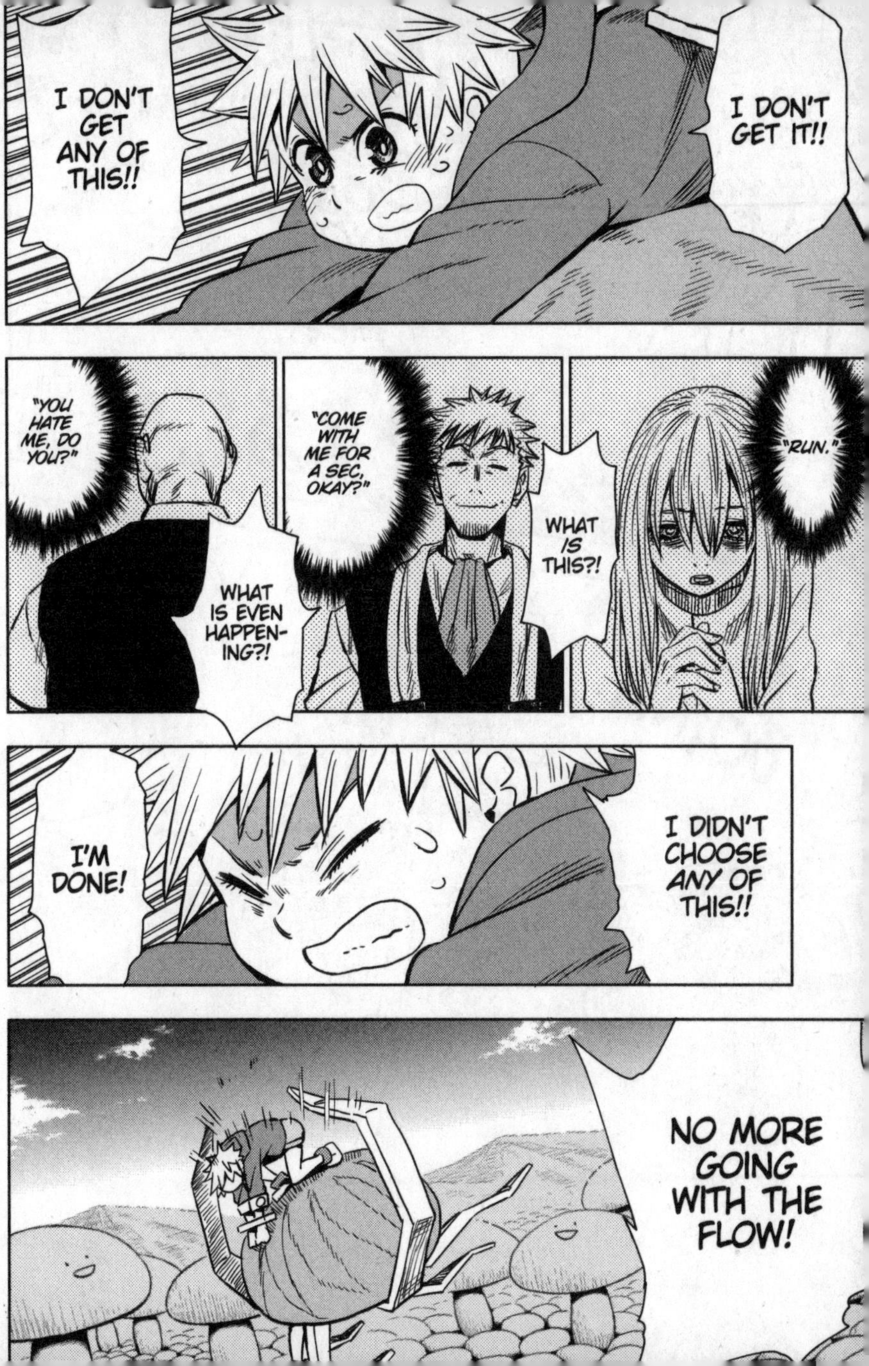
I DON'T GET IT!!
I DON'T GET ANY OF THIS!!
"RUN."
WHAT IS THIS?!
"COME WITH ME FOR A SEC, OKAY?"
"YOU HATE ME, DO YOU?"
WHAT IS EVEN HAPPENING?!
I DIDN'T CHOOSE ANY OF THIS!!
I'M DONE!
NO MORE GOING WITH THE FLOW!

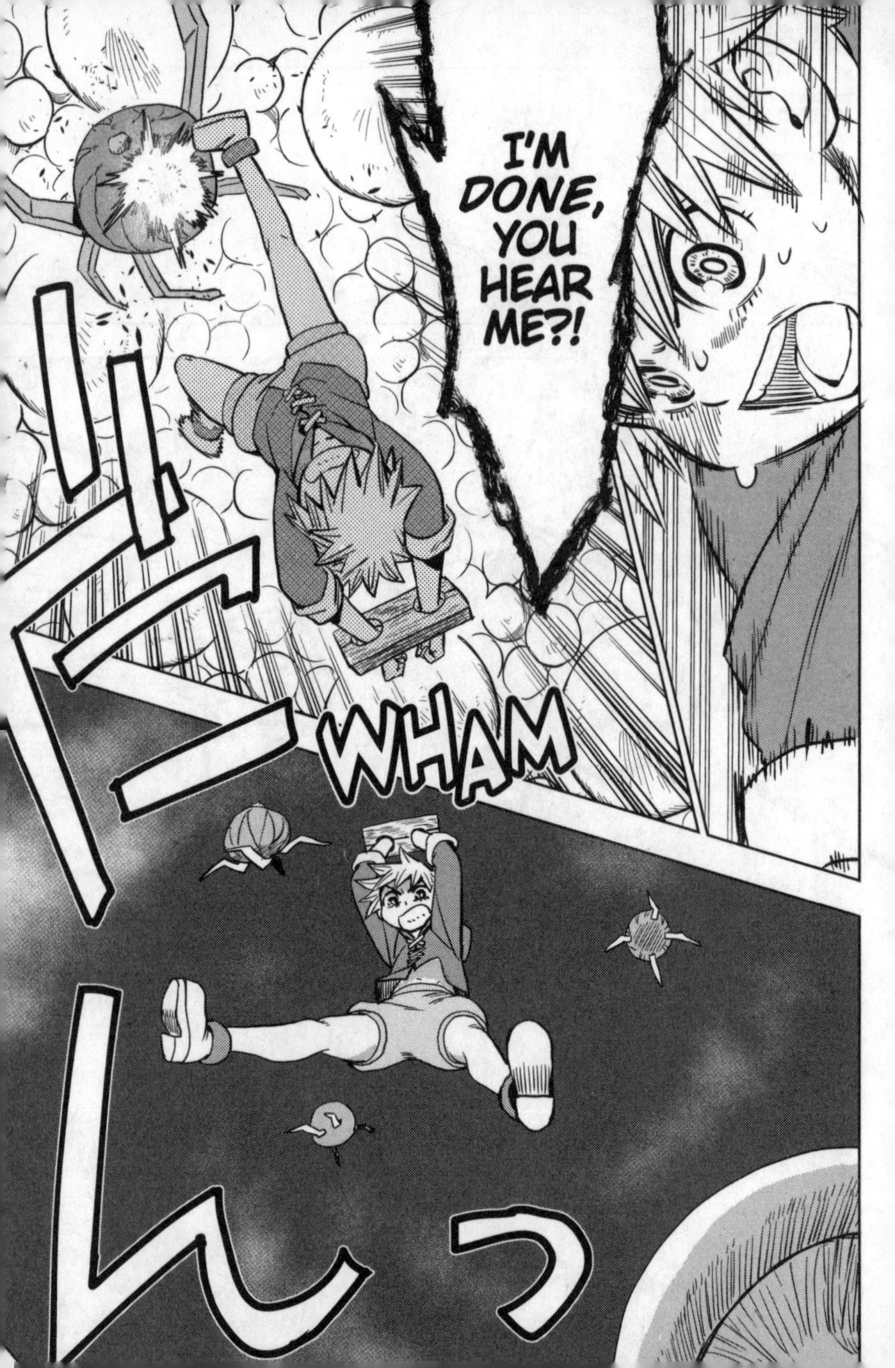
I'M DONE, YOU HEAR ME?!
WHAM

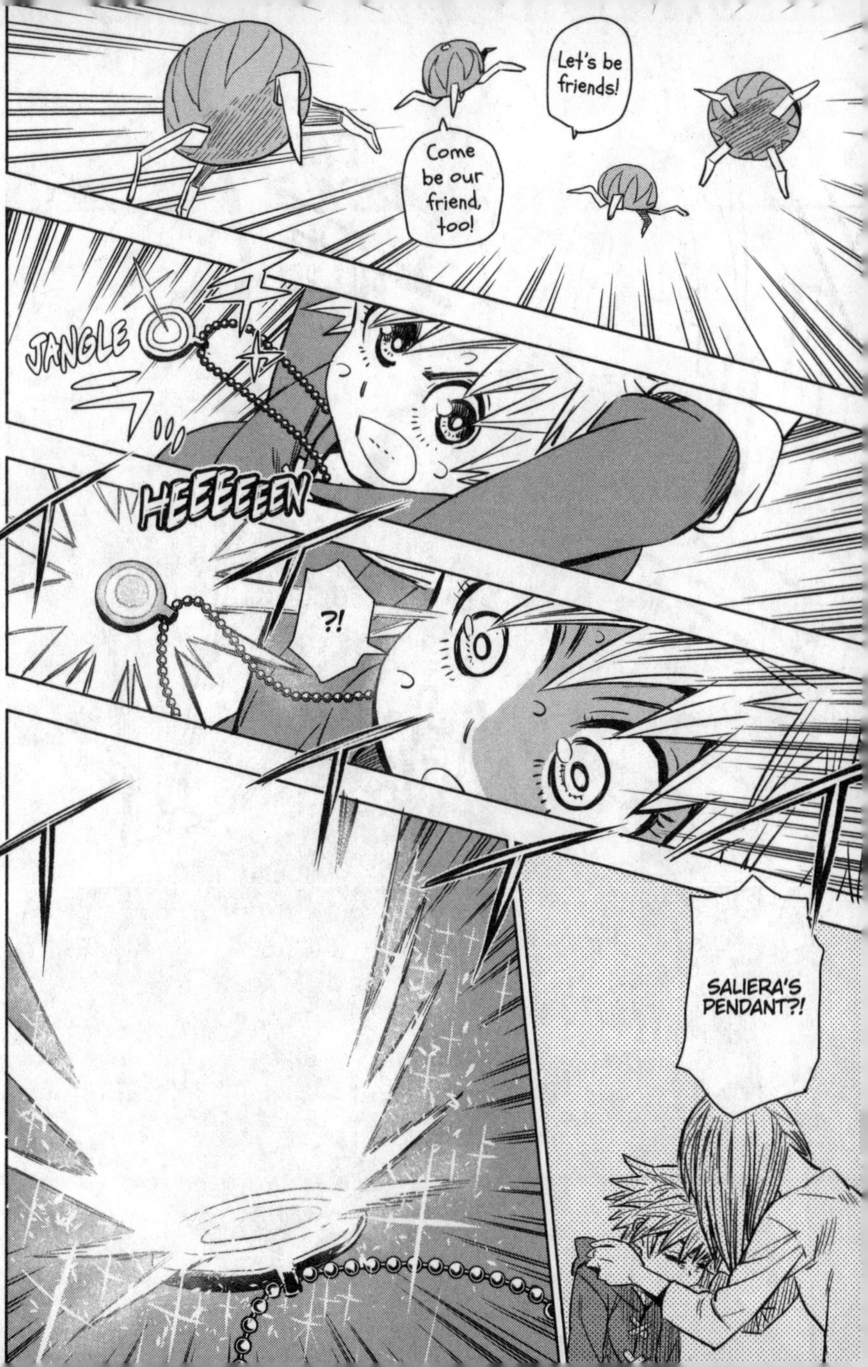
Let's be friends!
Come be our friend, too!
JANGLE
HEEEEEEEN
?!
SALIERA'S PENDANT?!

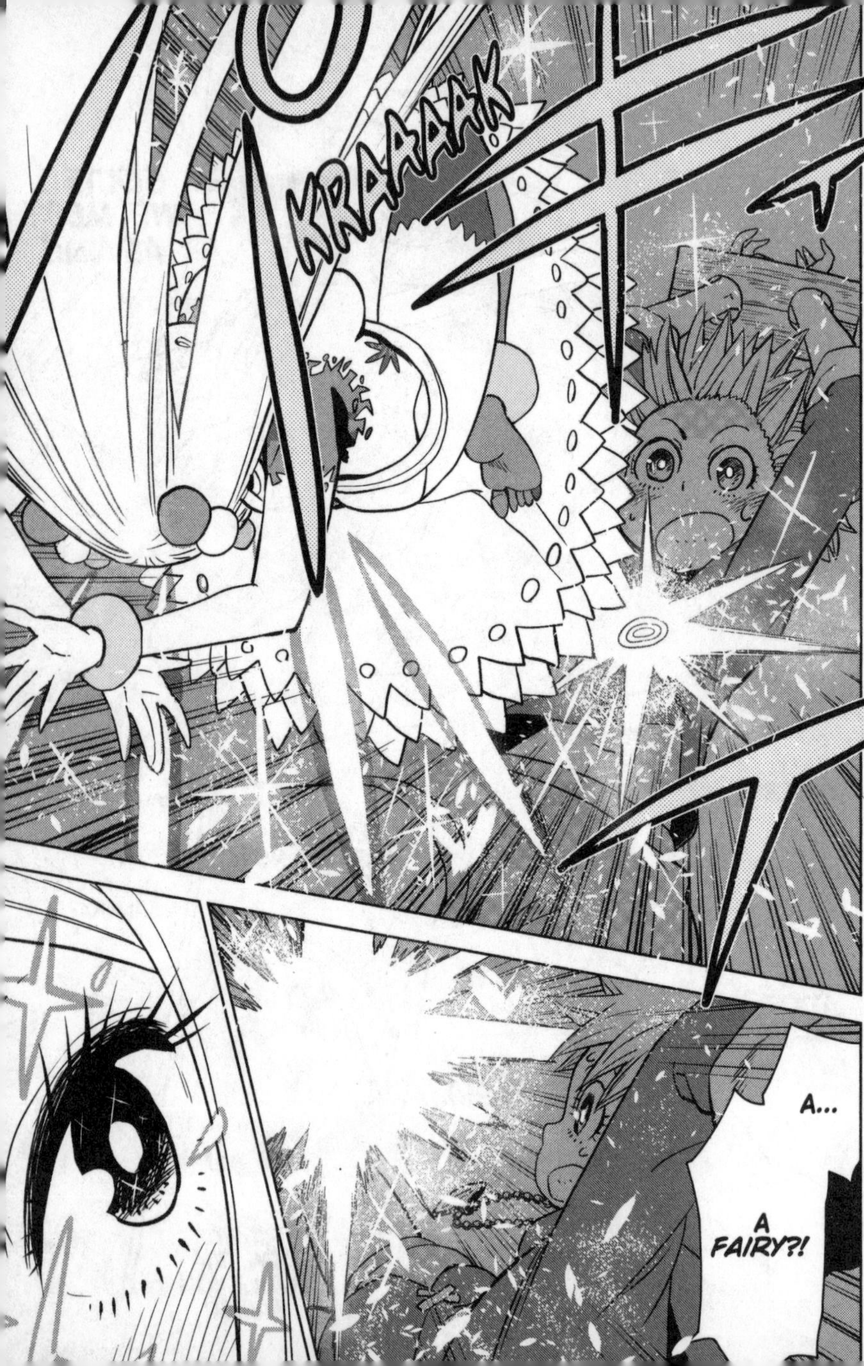
KRAAAAK
A...
A FAIRY?!

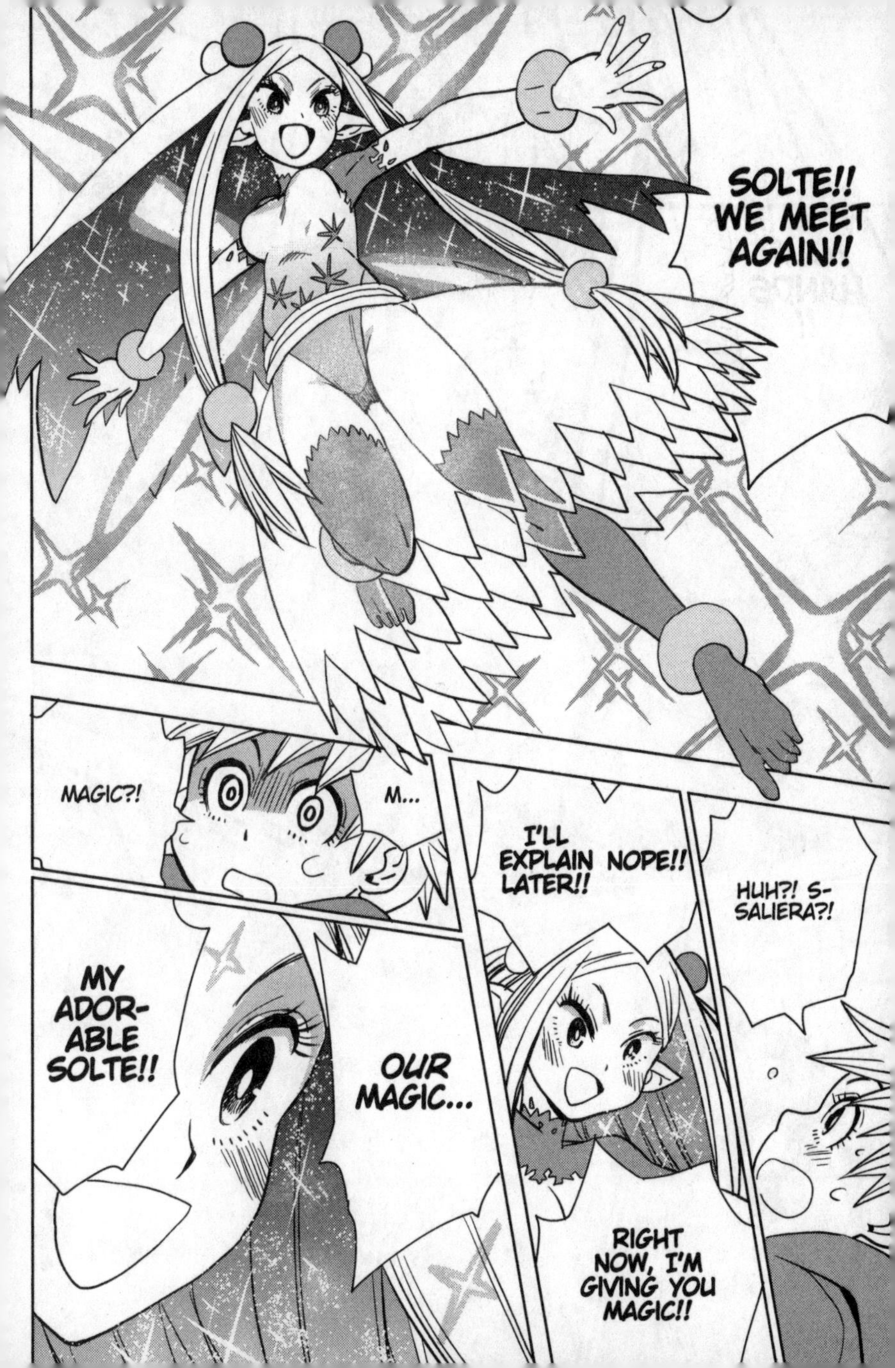
SOLTE!! WE MEET AGAIN!!
HUH?! S-SALIERA?!
NOPE!!
I'LL EXPLAIN LATER!!
RIGHT NOW, I'M GIVING YOU MAGIC!!
M...
MAGIC?!
OUR MAGIC...
MY ADORABLE SOLTE!!

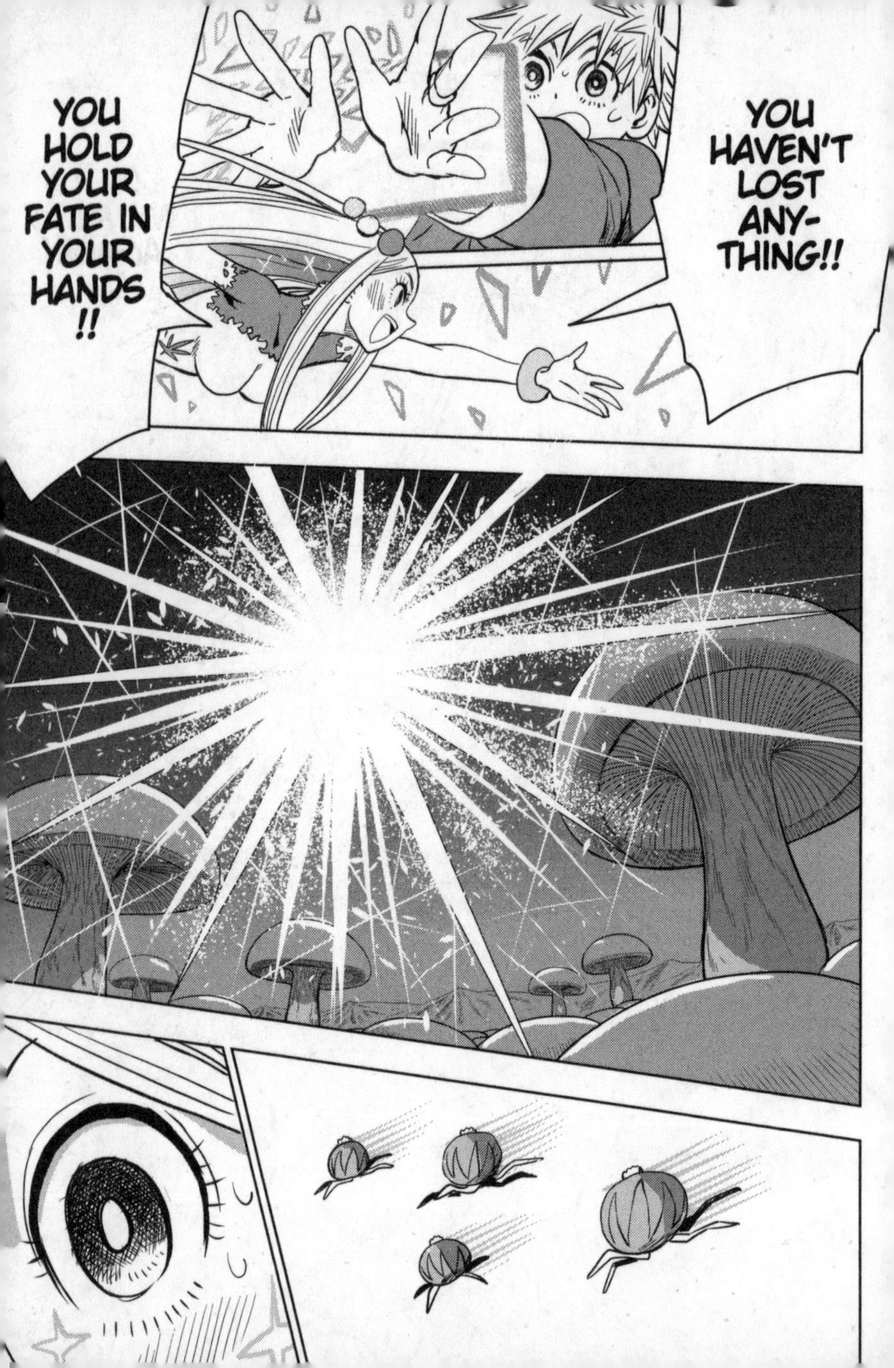
YOU HAVEN'T LOST ANYTHING!!
YOU HOLD YOUR FATE IN YOUR HANDS!!

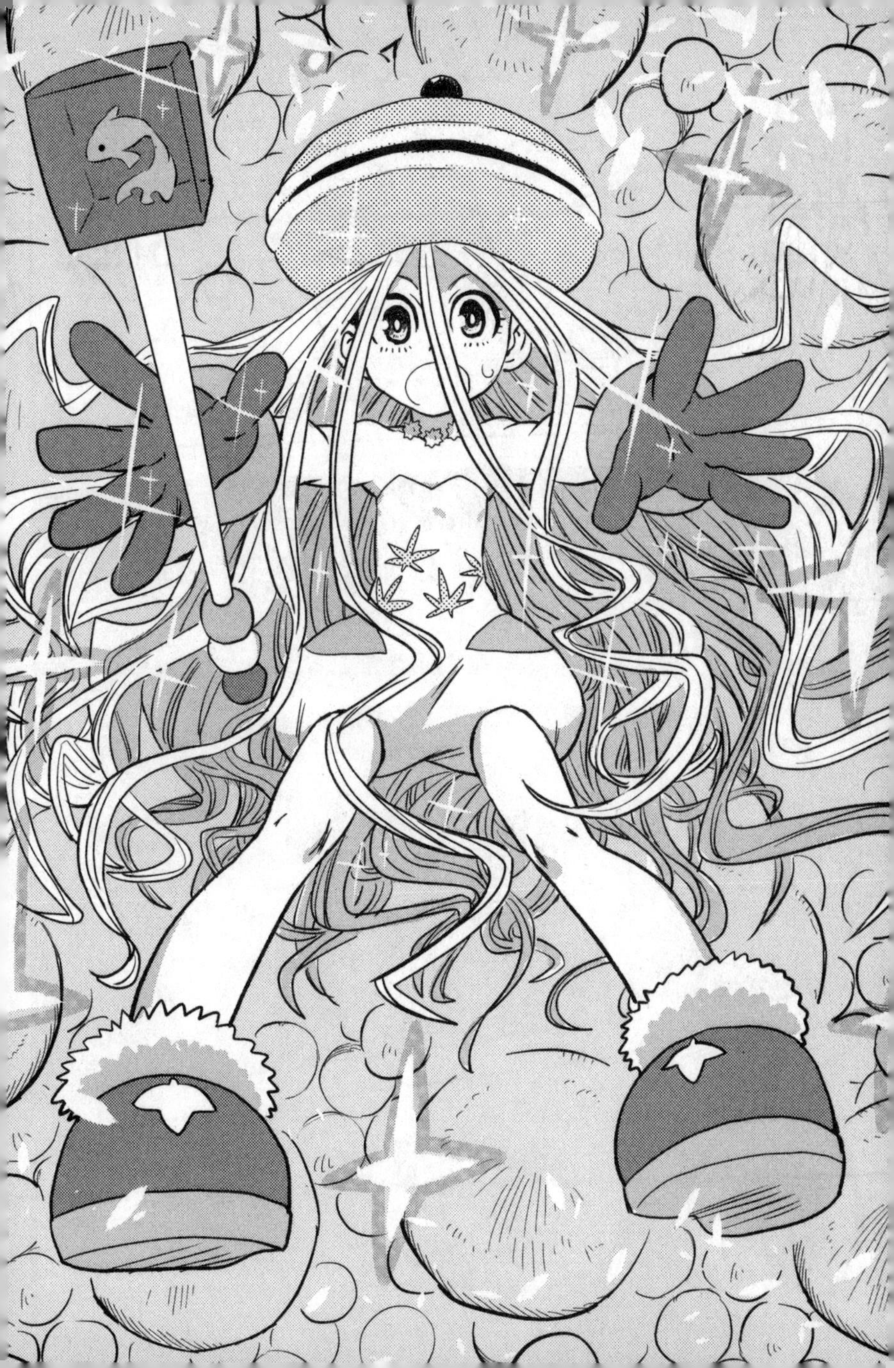

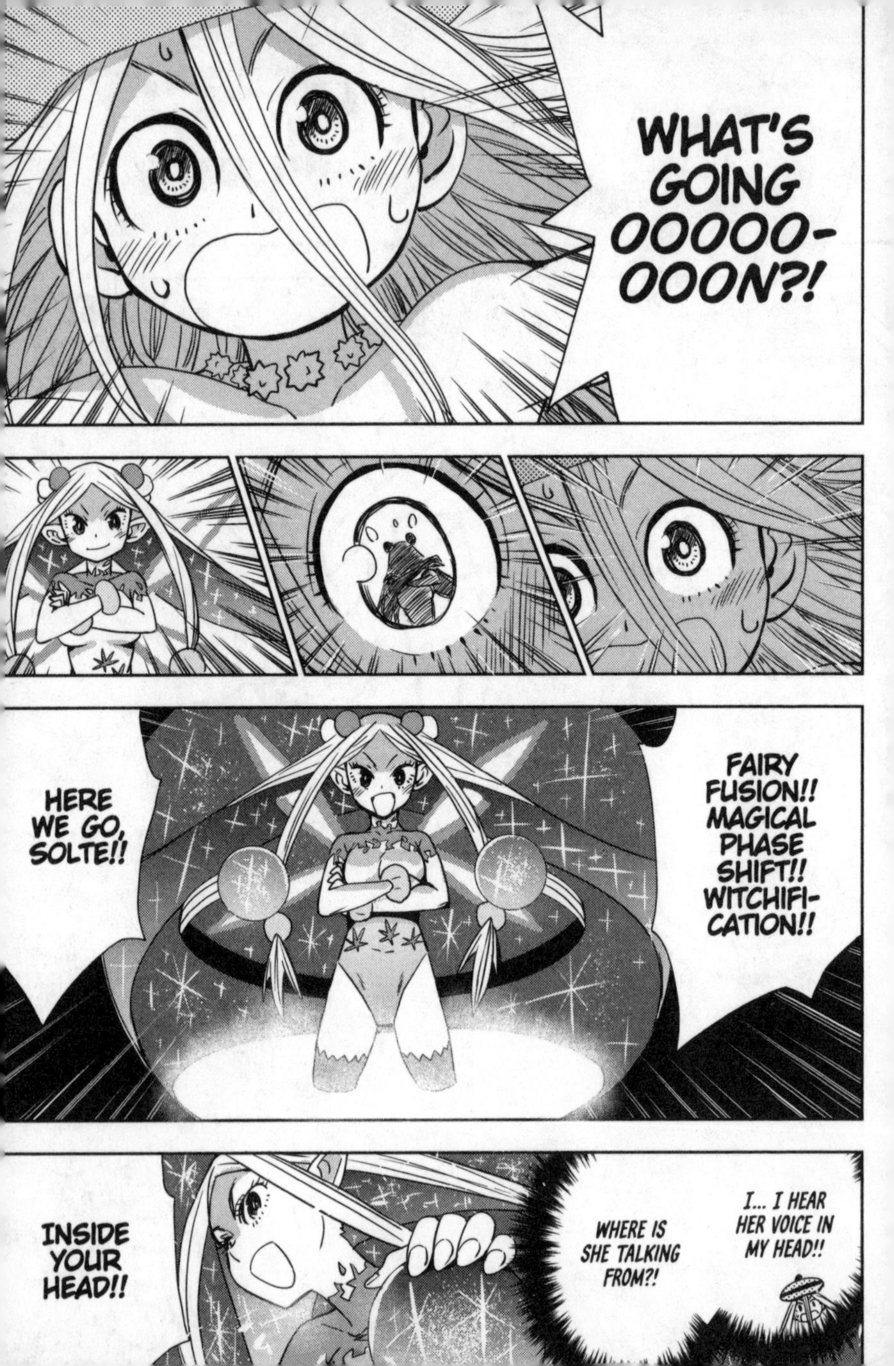

WHAT'S GOING OOOOO-OOON?!
FAIRY FUSION!! MAGICAL PHASE SHIFT!! WITCHIFI-CATION!!
HERE WE GO, SOLTE!!
I... I HEAR HER VOICE IN MY HEAD!!
WHERE IS SHE TALKING FROM?!
INSIDE YOUR HEAD!!

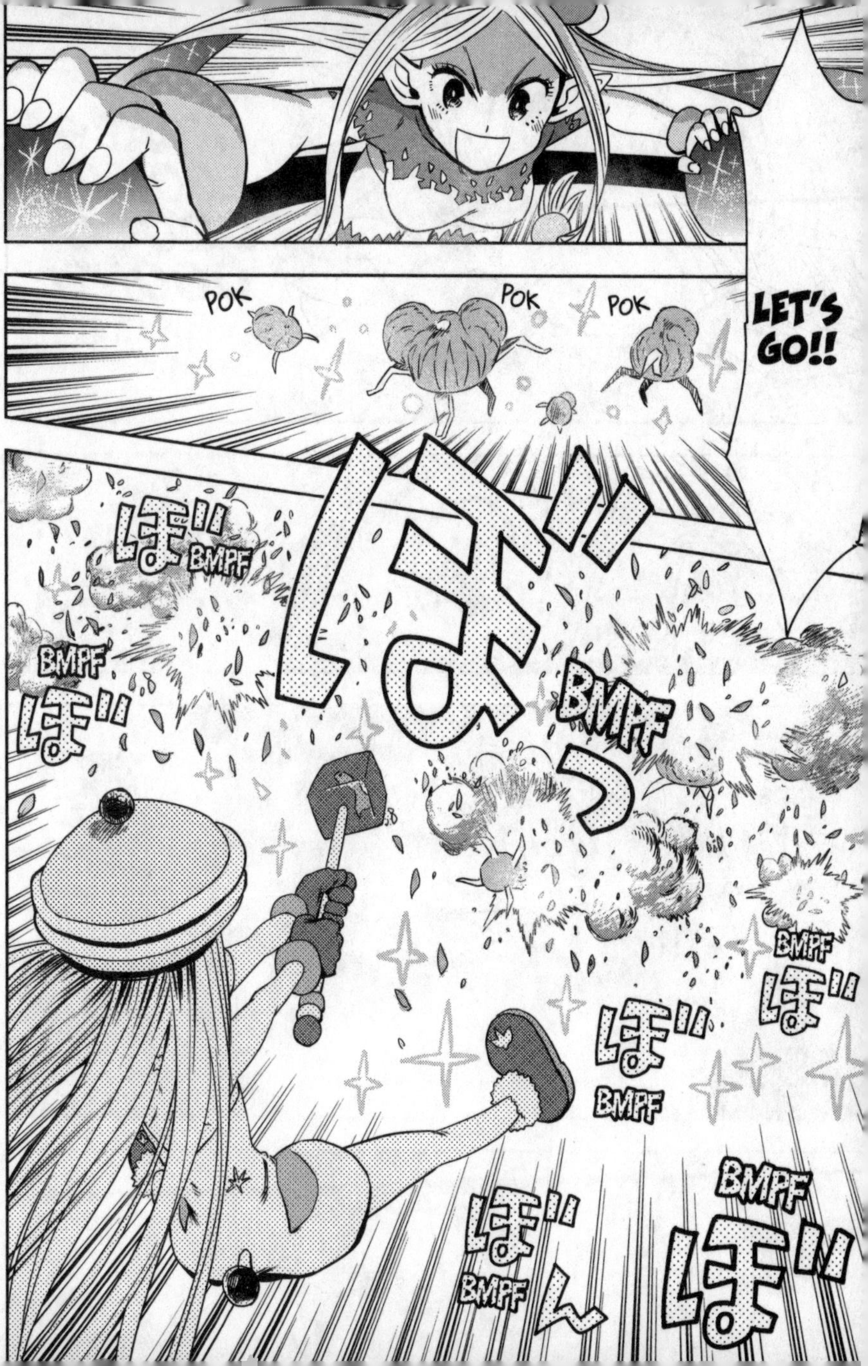

LET'S GO!!
POK
POK
POK
ぼっ
BMPF
BMPF
ぼ"
ぼ"
BMPF
ぼ"
BMPF
ぼ"
BMPF
BMPF
ぼ"
BMPF
ぼ!!
ぼ"ん
BMPF

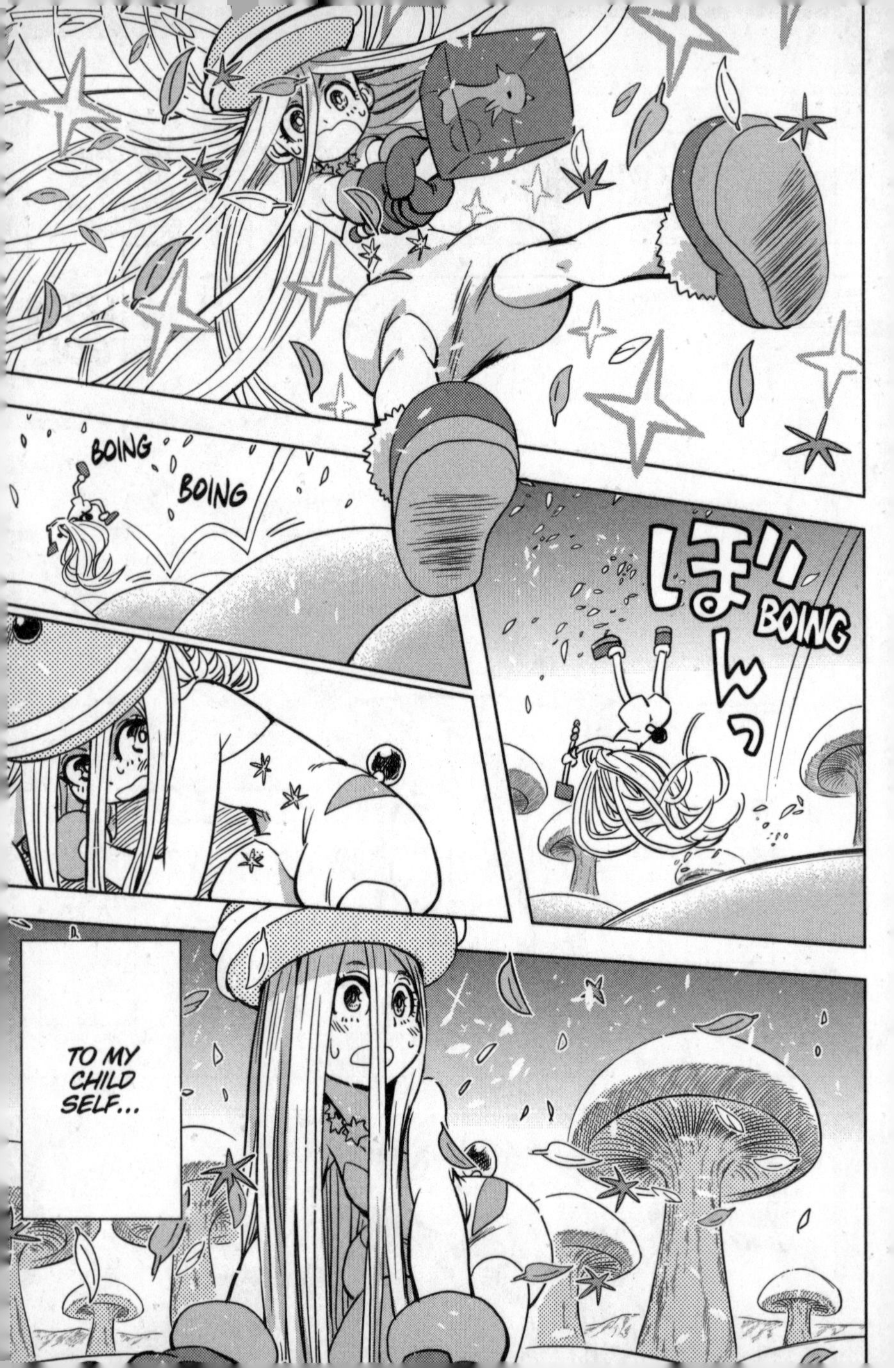

ぼんっ
BOING
BOING
BOING
TO MY CHILD SELF...

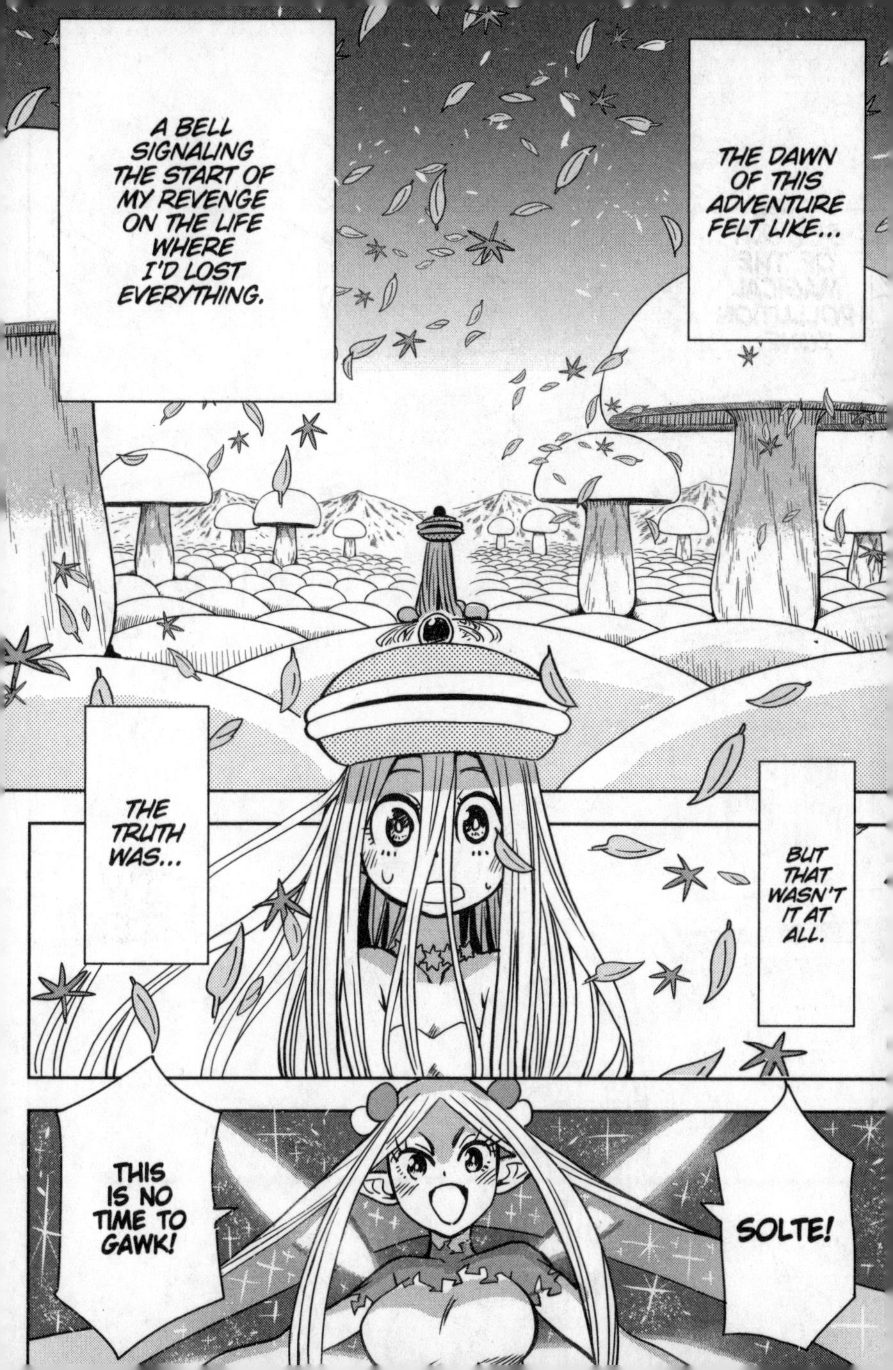
THE DAWN OF THIS ADVENTURE FELT LIKE...
A BELL SIGNALING THE START OF MY REVENGE ON THE LIFE WHERE I'D LOST EVERYTHING.
BUT THAT WASN'T IT AT ALL.
THE TRUTH WAS...
SOLTE!
THIS IS NO TIME TO GAWK!

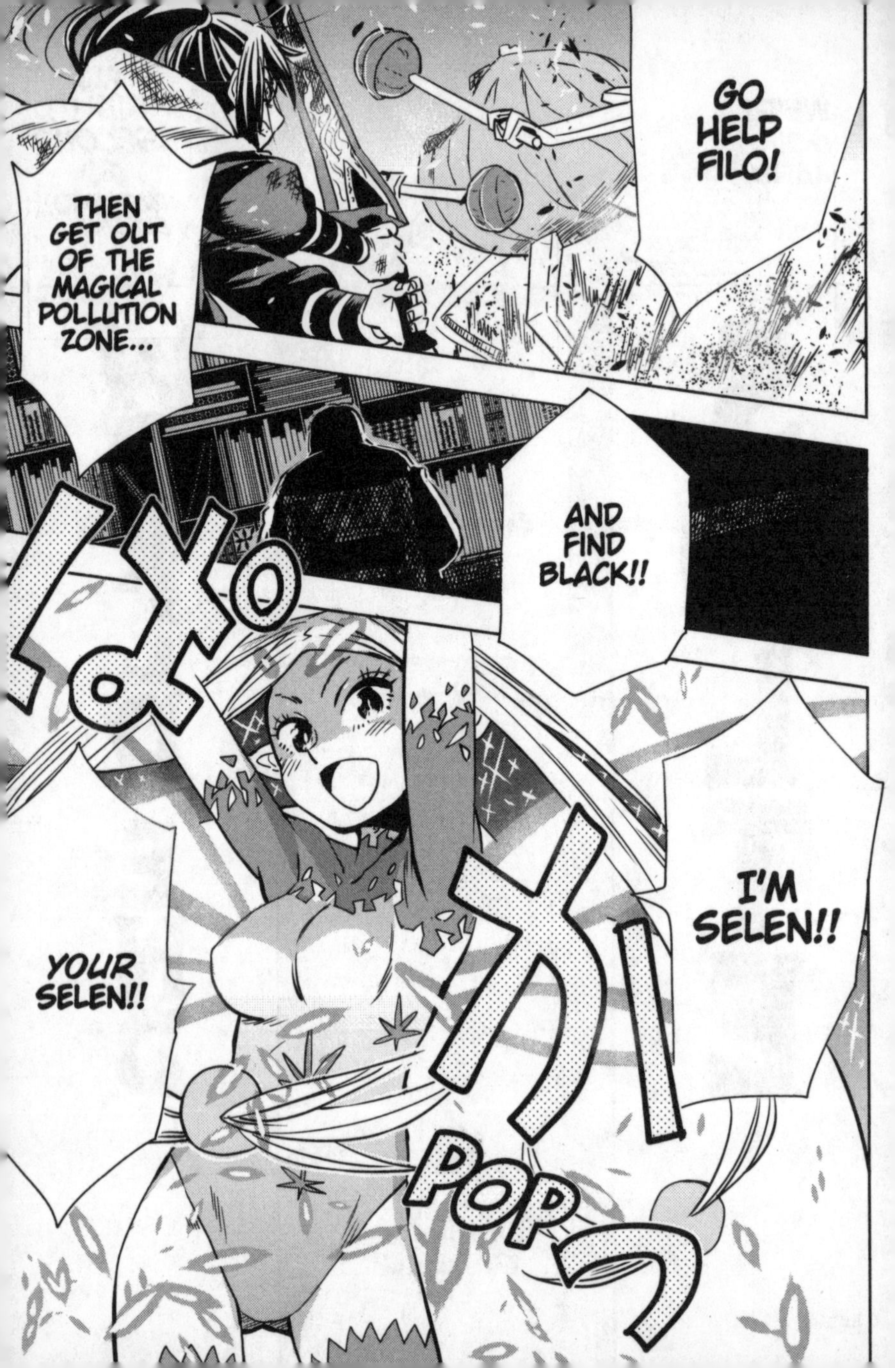
GO HELP FILO!
THEN GET OUT OF THE MAGICAL POLLUTION ZONE...
AND FIND BLACK!!
I'M SELEN!!
YOUR SELEN!!
POP

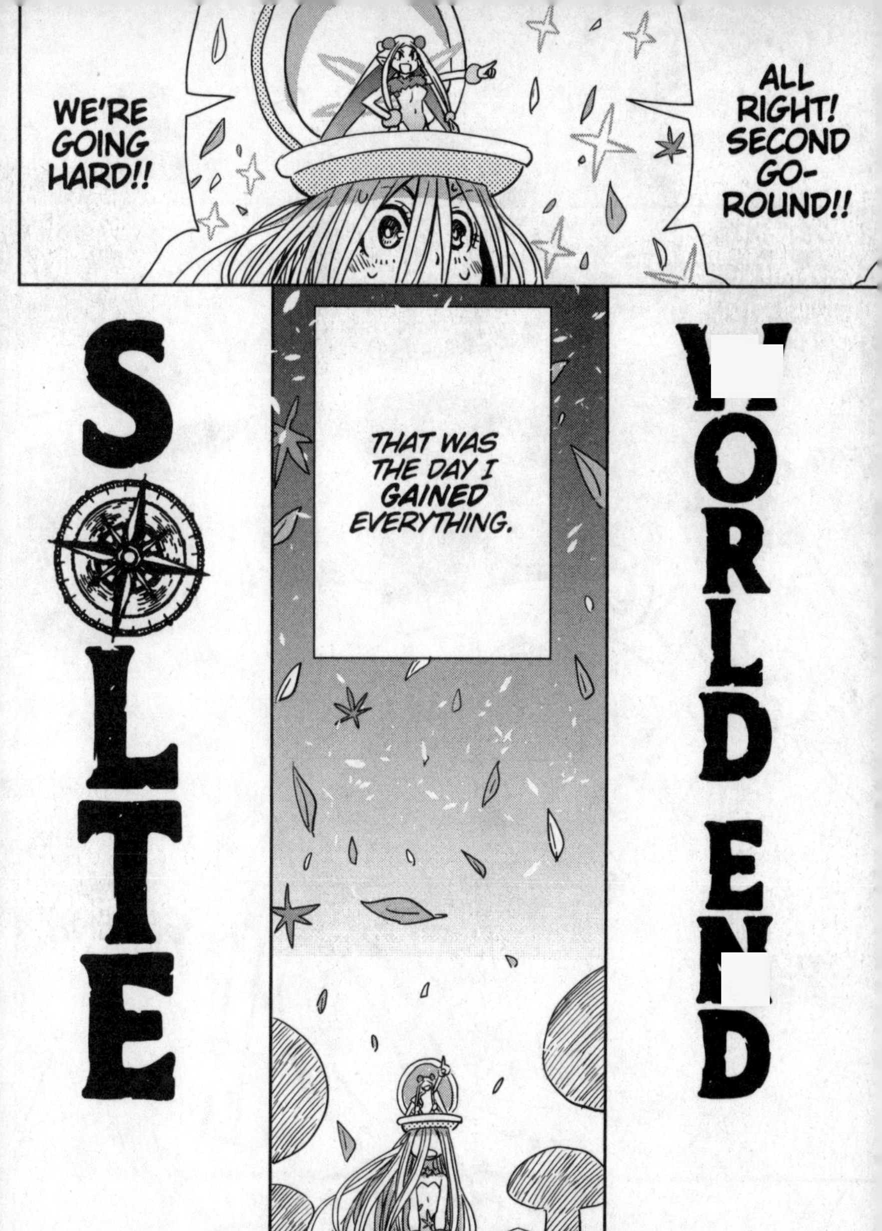
ALL RIGHT! SECOND GO-ROUND!!
WE'RE GOING HARD!!
SOLTE
WORLD END
THAT WAS THE DAY I GAINED EVERYTHING.

Chapter 1/END

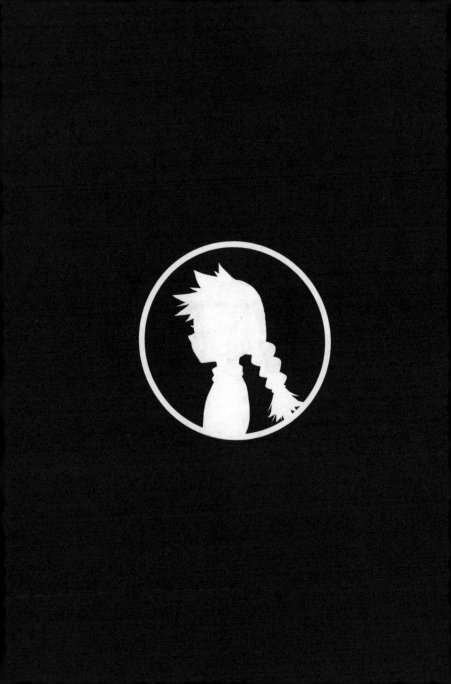

WORLD END SOLTE

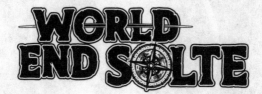

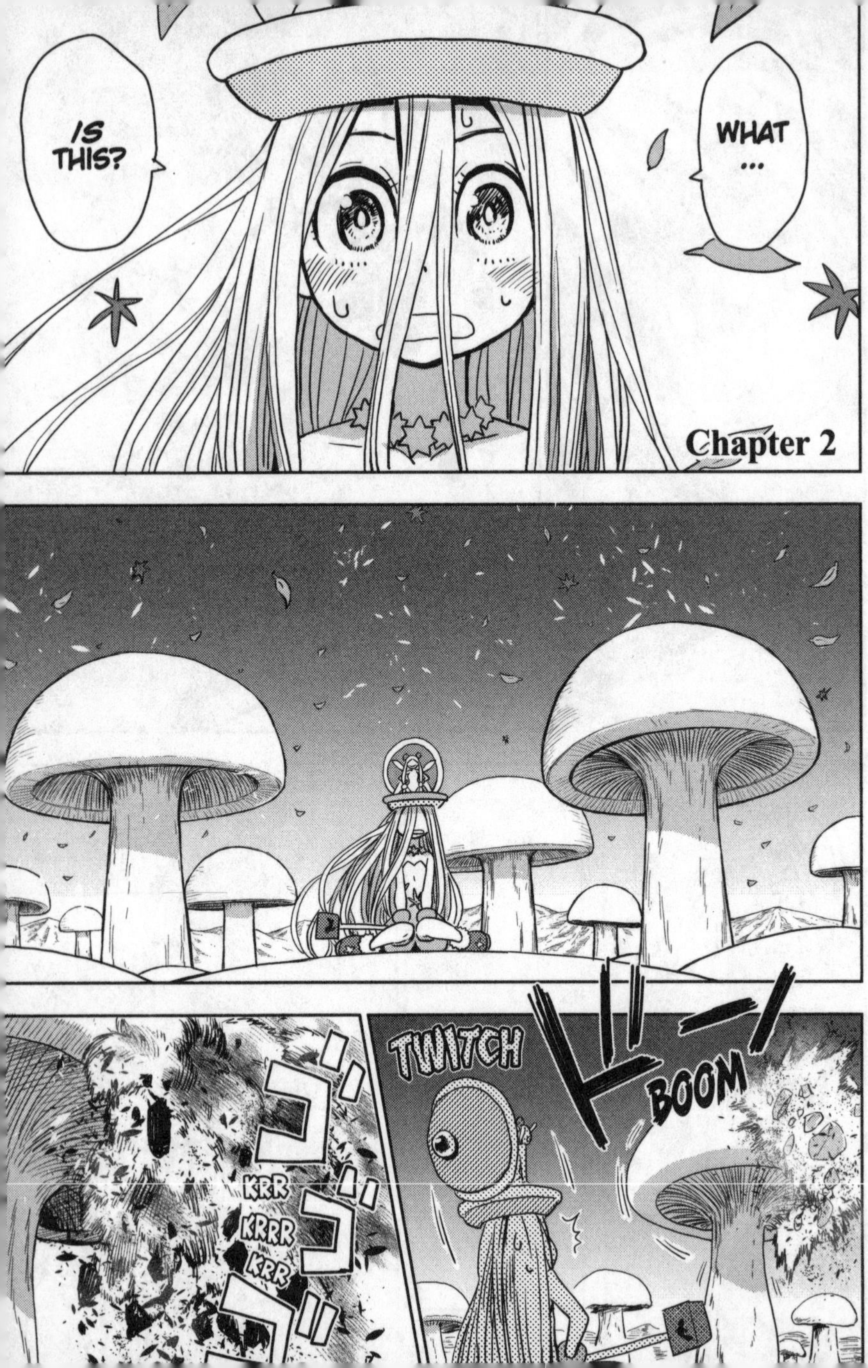
WHAT ...
IS THIS?
Chapter 2
BOOM
TWITCH
KRR
KRRR
KRR

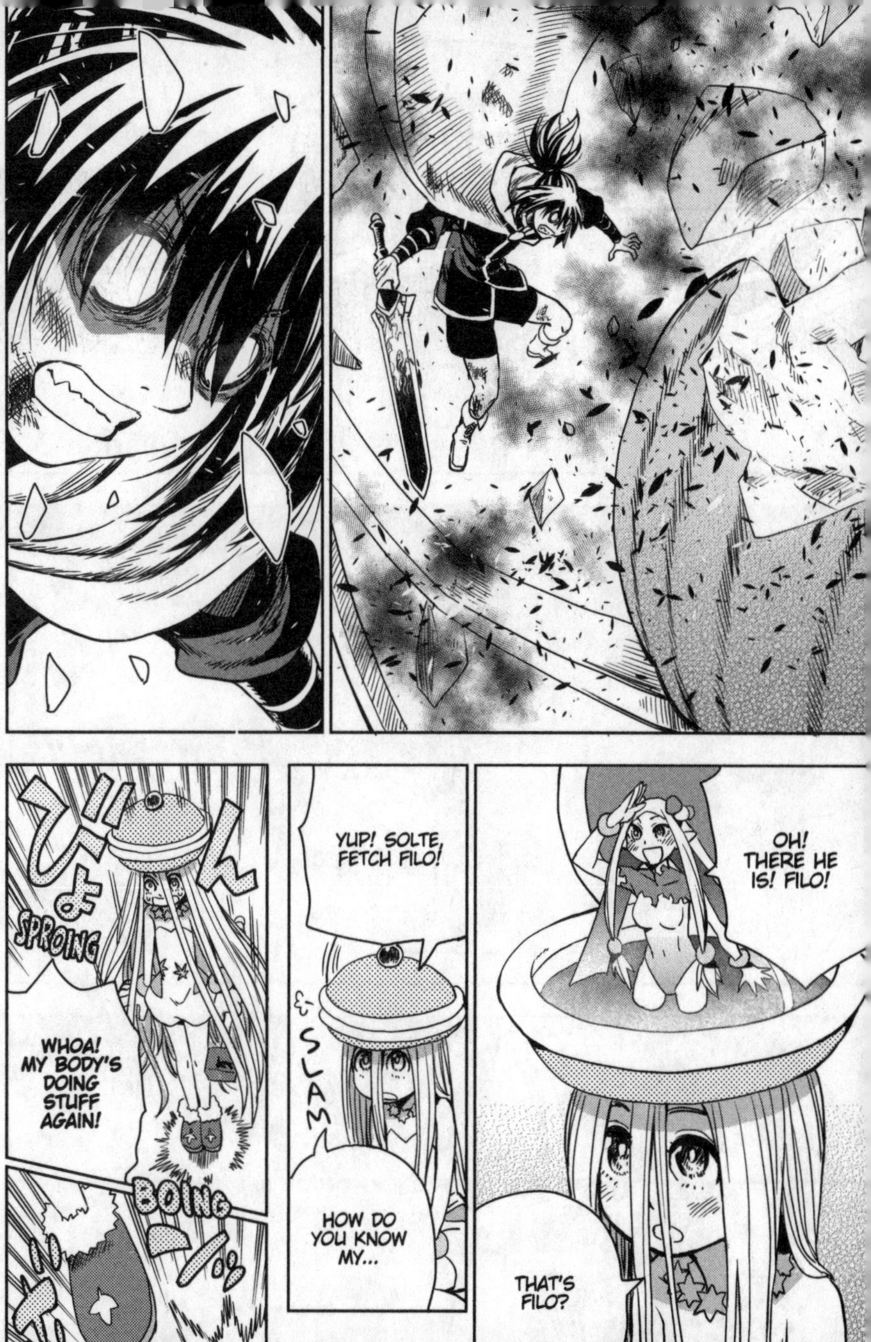

OH! THERE HE IS! FILO!
THAT'S FILO?
YUP! SOLTE, FETCH FILO!
SLAM
HOW DO YOU KNOW MY...
SPROING
WHOA! MY BODY'S DOING STUFF AGAIN!
BOING

Chapter 2: The Child, the Fairy, the Death Wish, and the Mole

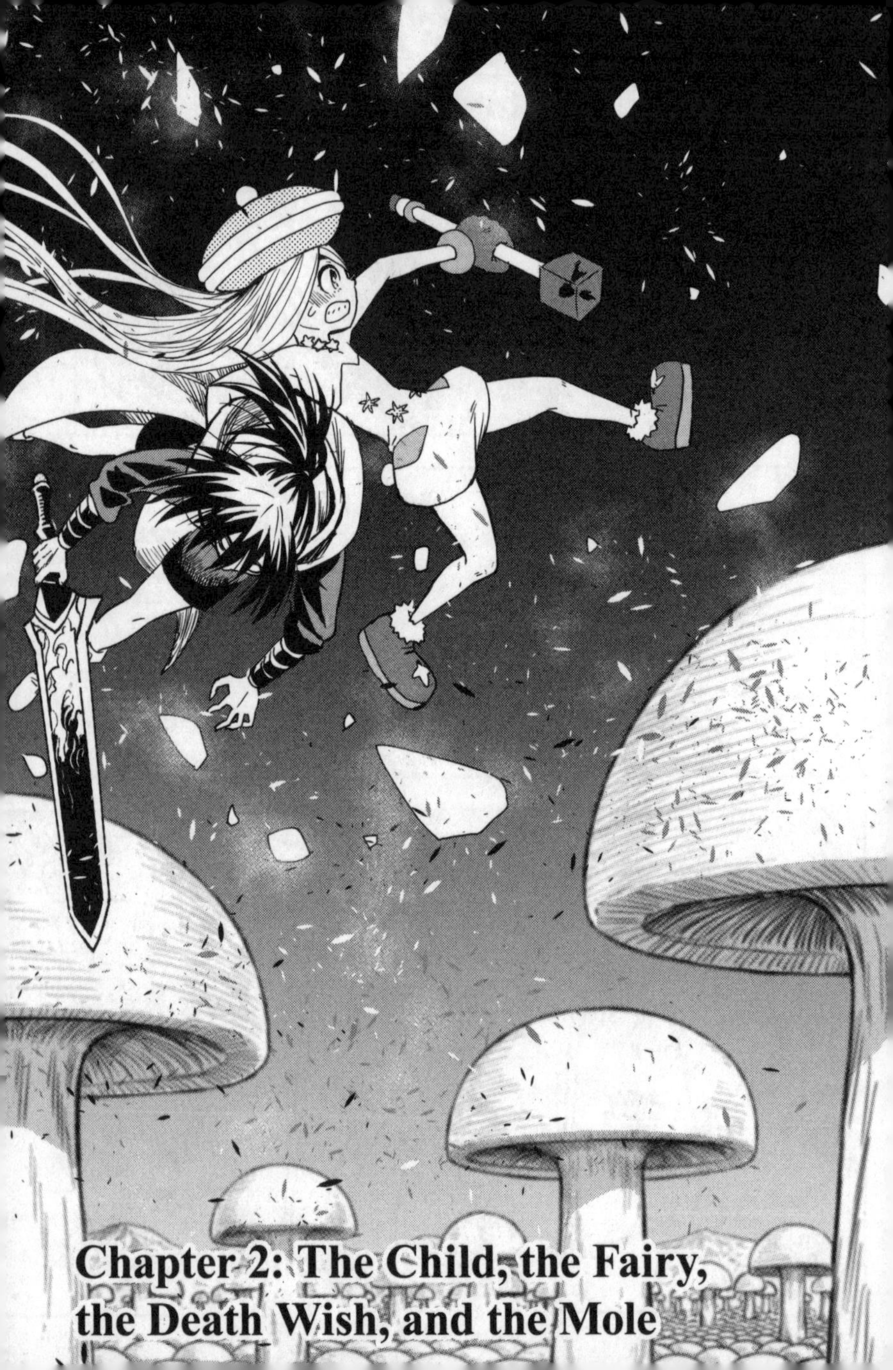

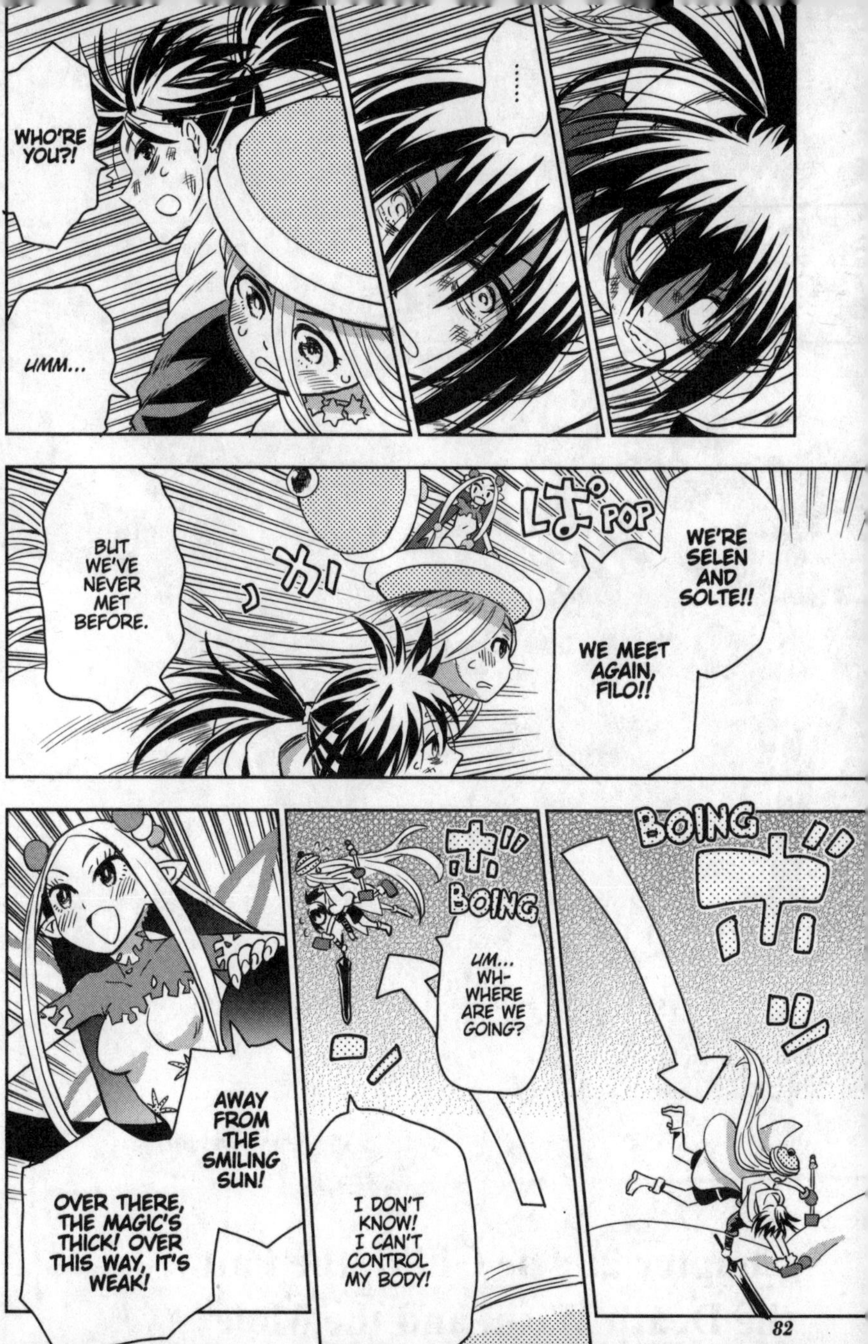
......
WHO'RE YOU?!
UMM...
POP
WE'RE SELEN AND SOLTE!!
WE MEET AGAIN, FILO!!
BUT WE'VE NEVER MET BEFORE.
BOING
BOING
UM... WH-WHERE ARE WE GOING?
I DON'T KNOW! I CAN'T CONTROL MY BODY!
AWAY FROM THE SMILING SUN!
OVER THERE, THE MAGIC'S THICK! OVER THIS WAY, IT'S WEAK!

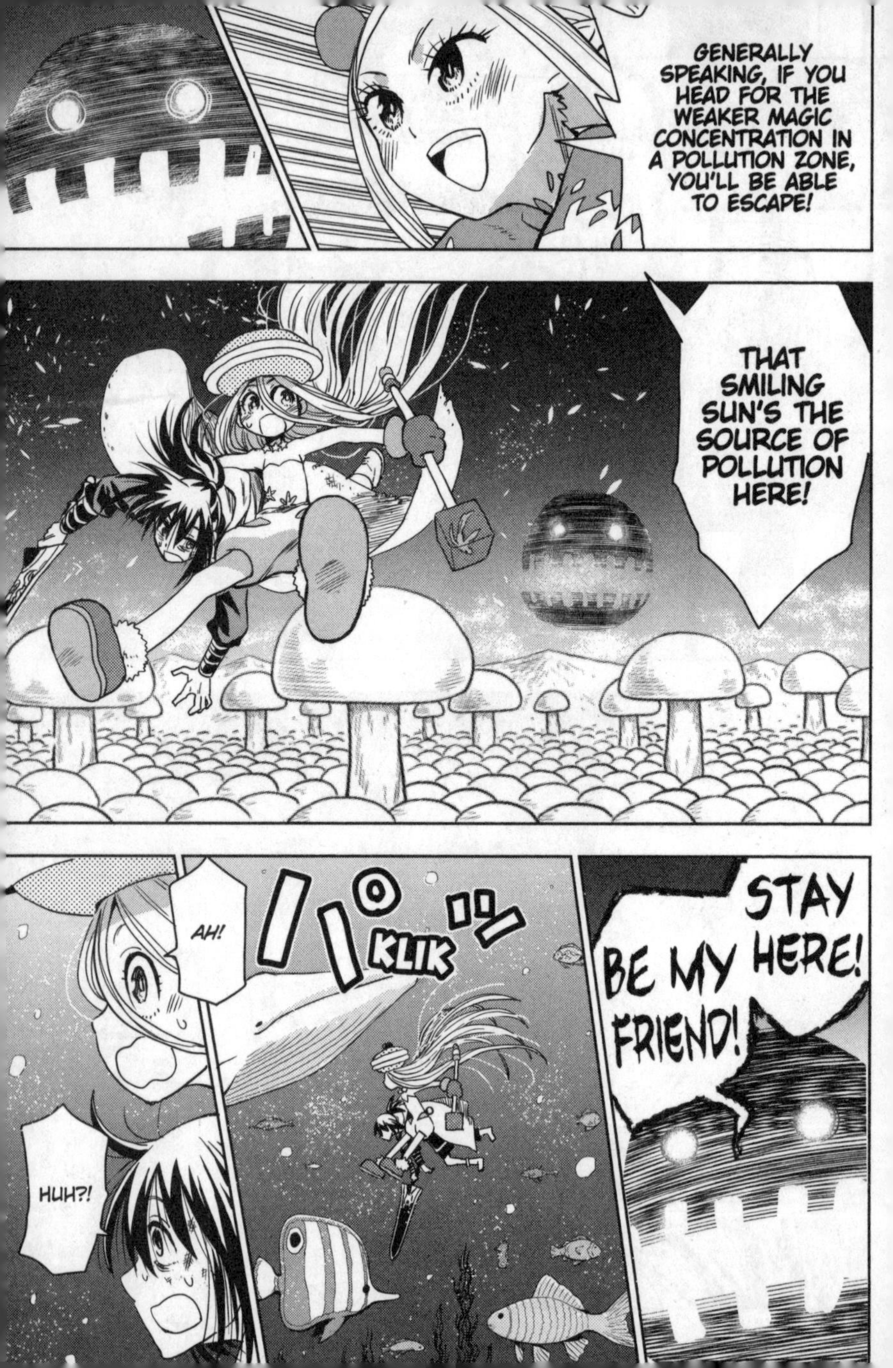
GENERALLY SPEAKING, IF YOU HEAD FOR THE WEAKER MAGIC CONCENTRATION IN A POLLUTION ZONE, YOU'LL BE ABLE TO ESCAPE!
THAT SMILING SUN'S THE SOURCE OF POLLUTION HERE!
STAY HERE! BE MY FRIEND!
KLIK
AH!
HUH?!

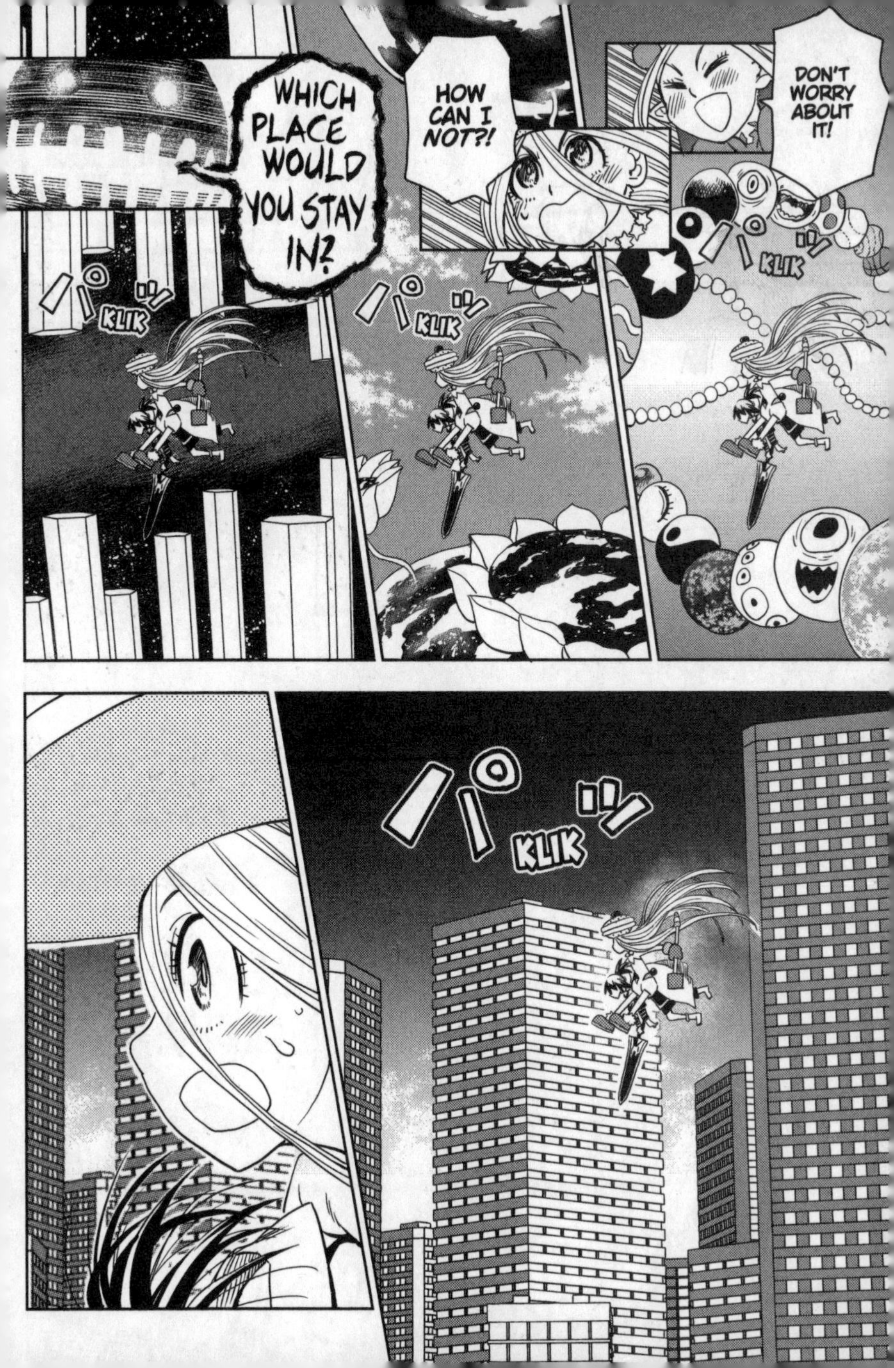
DON'T WORRY ABOUT IT!
KLIK
HOW CAN I NOT?!
KLIK
WHICH PLACE WOULD YOU STAY IN?
KLIK
KLIK

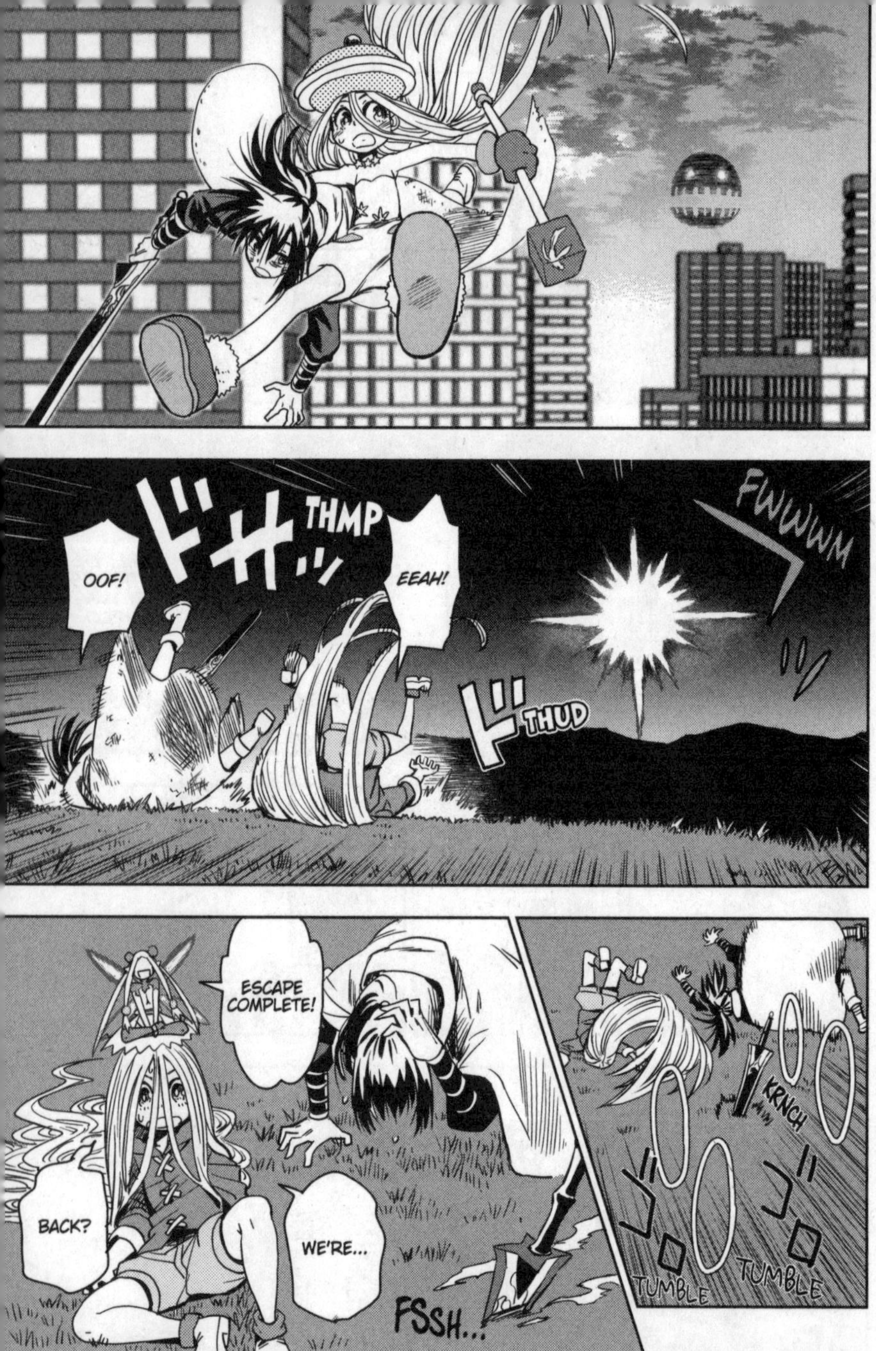
FWWWM
ド
THUD
EEAH!
ドサッ
THMP
OOF!
KRNCH
ゴロ
TUMBLE
ゴロ
TUMBLE
ESCAPE COMPLETE!
WE'RE...
BACK?
FSSH...

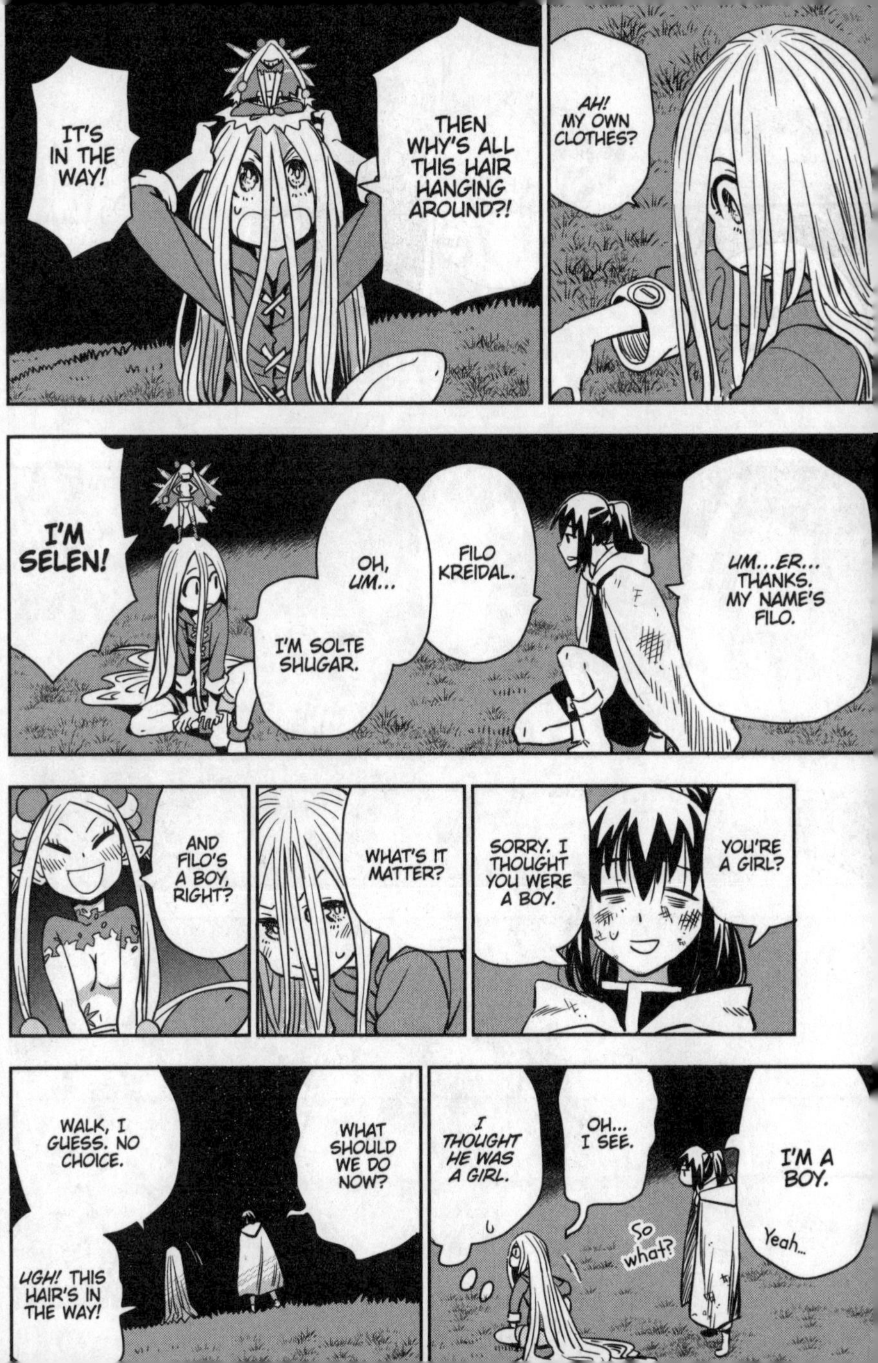
AH! MY OWN CLOTHES?
THEN WHY'S ALL THIS HAIR HANGING AROUND?!
IT'S IN THE WAY!
UM...ER... THANKS. MY NAME'S FILO.
FILO KREIDAL.
OH, UM...
I'M SOLTE SHUGAR.
I'M SELEN!
YOU'RE A GIRL?
SORRY. I THOUGHT YOU WERE A BOY.
WHAT'S IT MATTER?
AND FILO'S A BOY, RIGHT?
I'M A BOY.
Yeah...
OH... I SEE.
So what?
I THOUGHT HE WAS A GIRL.
WHAT SHOULD WE DO NOW?
WALK, I GUESS. NO CHOICE.
UGH! THIS HAIR'S IN THE WAY!

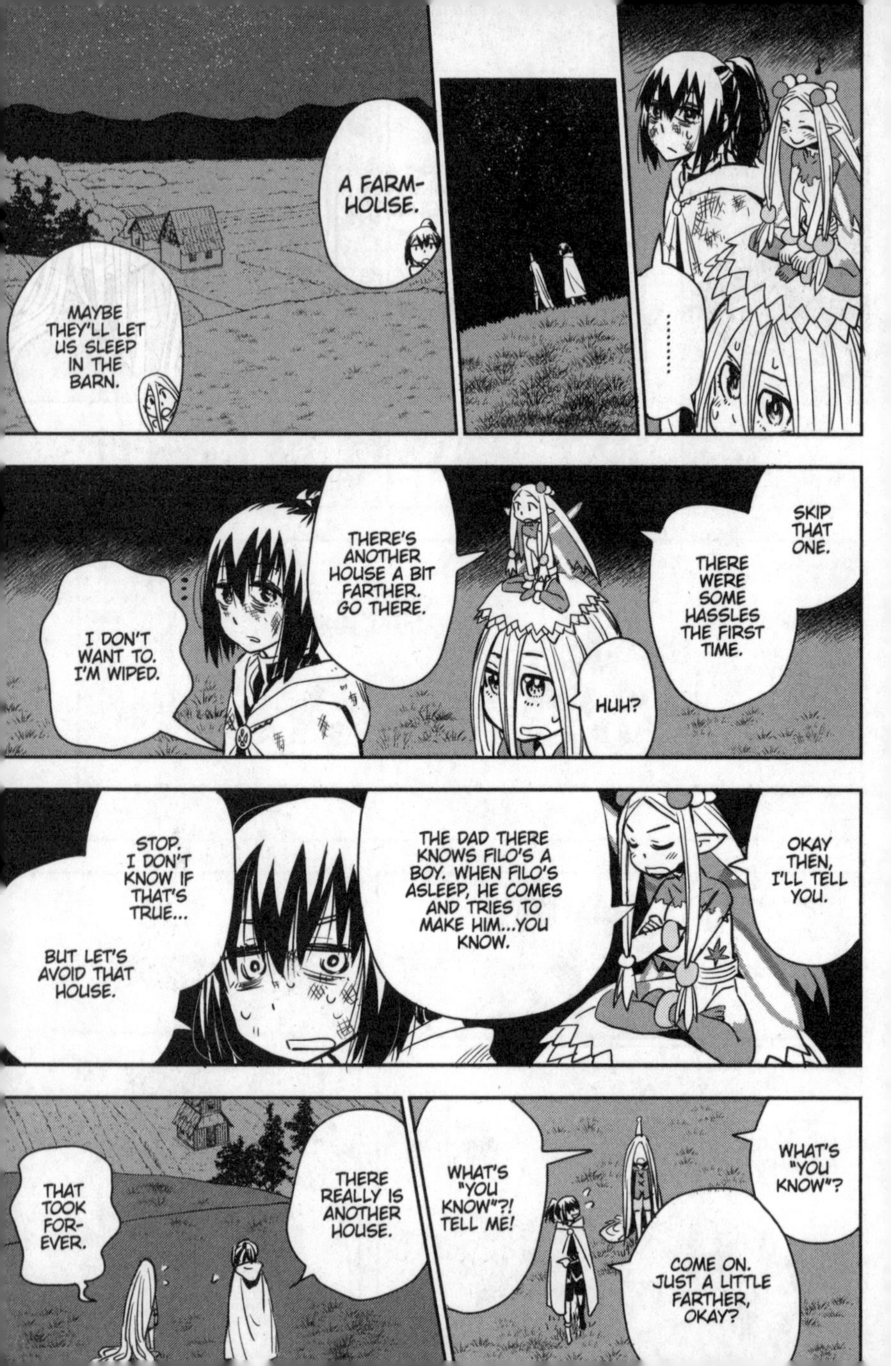
......
A FARM-HOUSE.
MAYBE THEY'LL LET US SLEEP IN THE BARN.
SKIP THAT ONE.
THERE WERE SOME HASSLES THE FIRST TIME.
HUH?
THERE'S ANOTHER HOUSE A BIT FARTHER. GO THERE.
...
I DON'T WANT TO. I'M WIPED.
OKAY THEN, I'LL TELL YOU.
THE DAD THERE KNOWS FILO'S A BOY. WHEN FILO'S ASLEEP, HE COMES AND TRIES TO MAKE HIM...YOU KNOW.
STOP. I DON'T KNOW IF THAT'S TRUE...
BUT LET'S AVOID THAT HOUSE.
WHAT'S "YOU KNOW"?
COME ON. JUST A LITTLE FARTHER, OKAY?
WHAT'S "YOU KNOW"?! TELL ME!
THERE REALLY IS ANOTHER HOUSE.
THAT TOOK FOR-EVER.

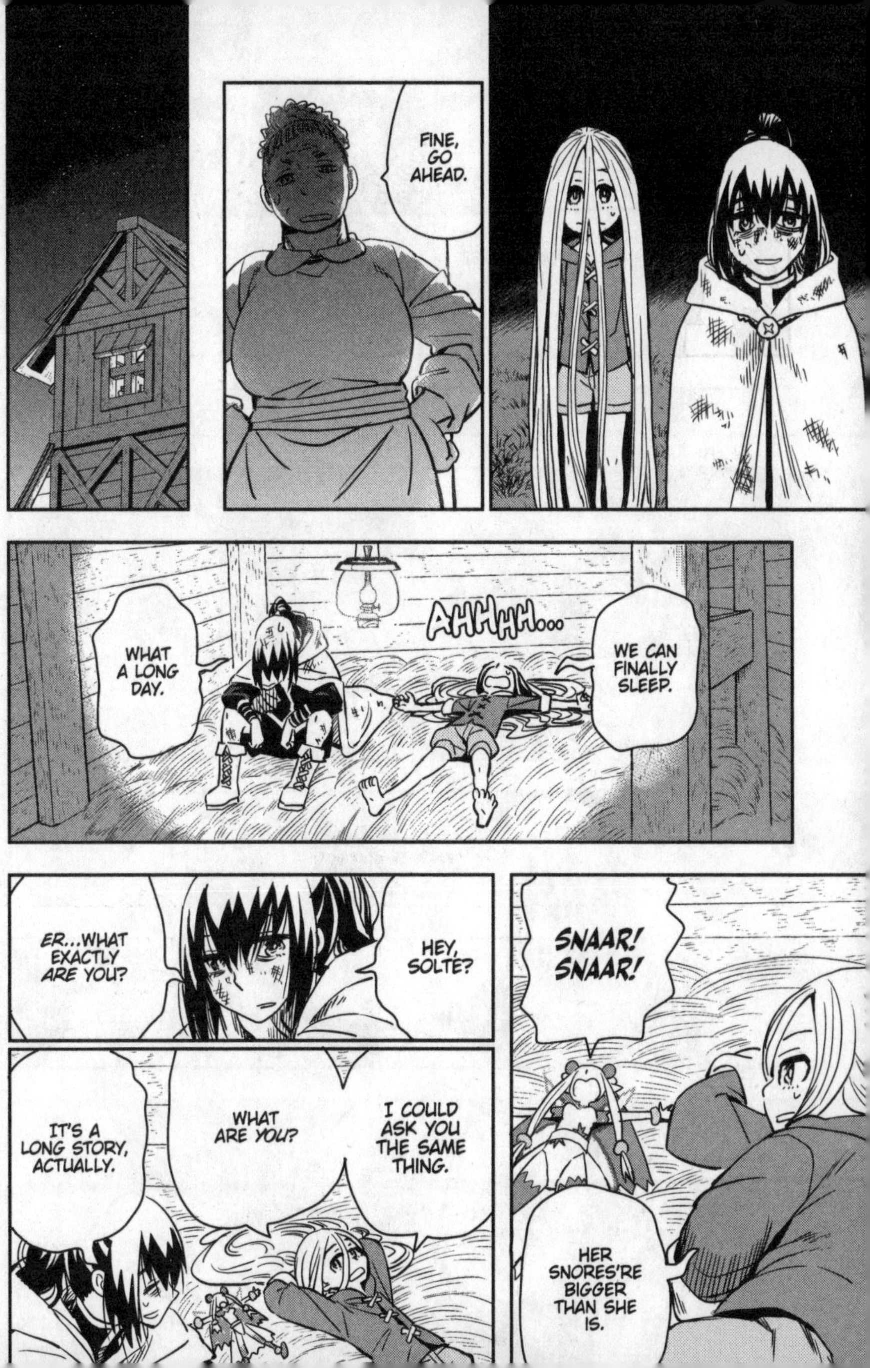
FINE, GO AHEAD.
WE CAN FINALLY SLEEP.
AHHHH...
WHAT A LONG DAY.
SNAAR! SNAAR!
HER SNORES'RE BIGGER THAN SHE IS.
HEY, SOLTE?
ER...WHAT EXACTLY ARE YOU?
I COULD ASK YOU THE SAME THING.
WHAT ARE YOU?
IT'S A LONG STORY, ACTUALLY.

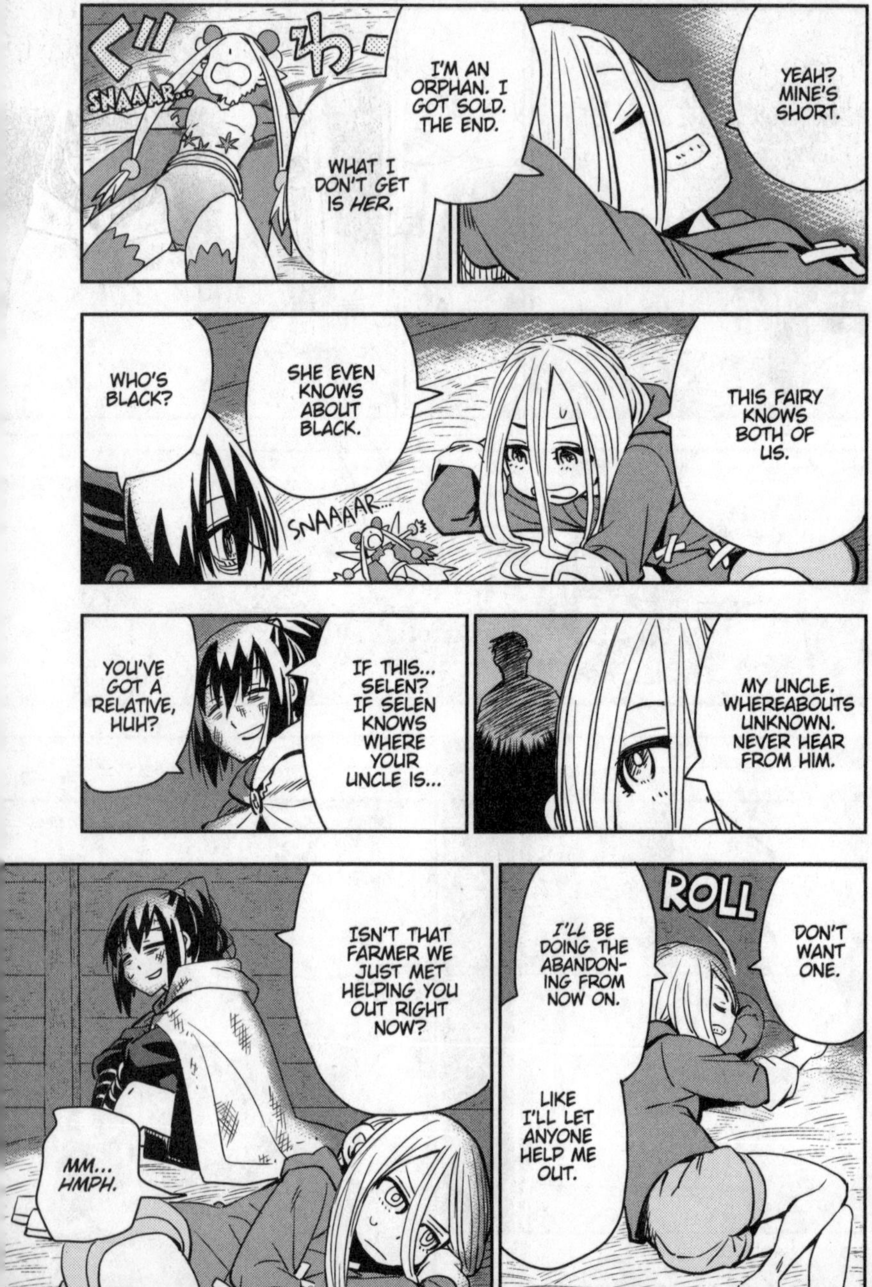
YEAH? MINE'S SHORT.
I'M AN ORPHAN. I GOT SOLD. THE END.
WHAT I DON'T GET IS *HER*.
SNAAAR...
THIS FAIRY KNOWS BOTH OF US.
SHE EVEN KNOWS ABOUT BLACK.
WHO'S BLACK?
SNAAAAR...
MY UNCLE. WHEREABOUTS UNKNOWN. NEVER HEAR FROM HIM.
IF THIS... SELEN? IF SELEN KNOWS WHERE YOUR UNCLE IS...
YOU'VE GOT A RELATIVE, HUH?
ROLL
DON'T WANT ONE.
I'LL BE DOING THE ABANDONING FROM NOW ON.
LIKE I'LL LET ANYONE HELP ME OUT.
ISN'T THAT FARMER WE JUST MET HELPING YOU OUT RIGHT NOW?
MM... HMPH.

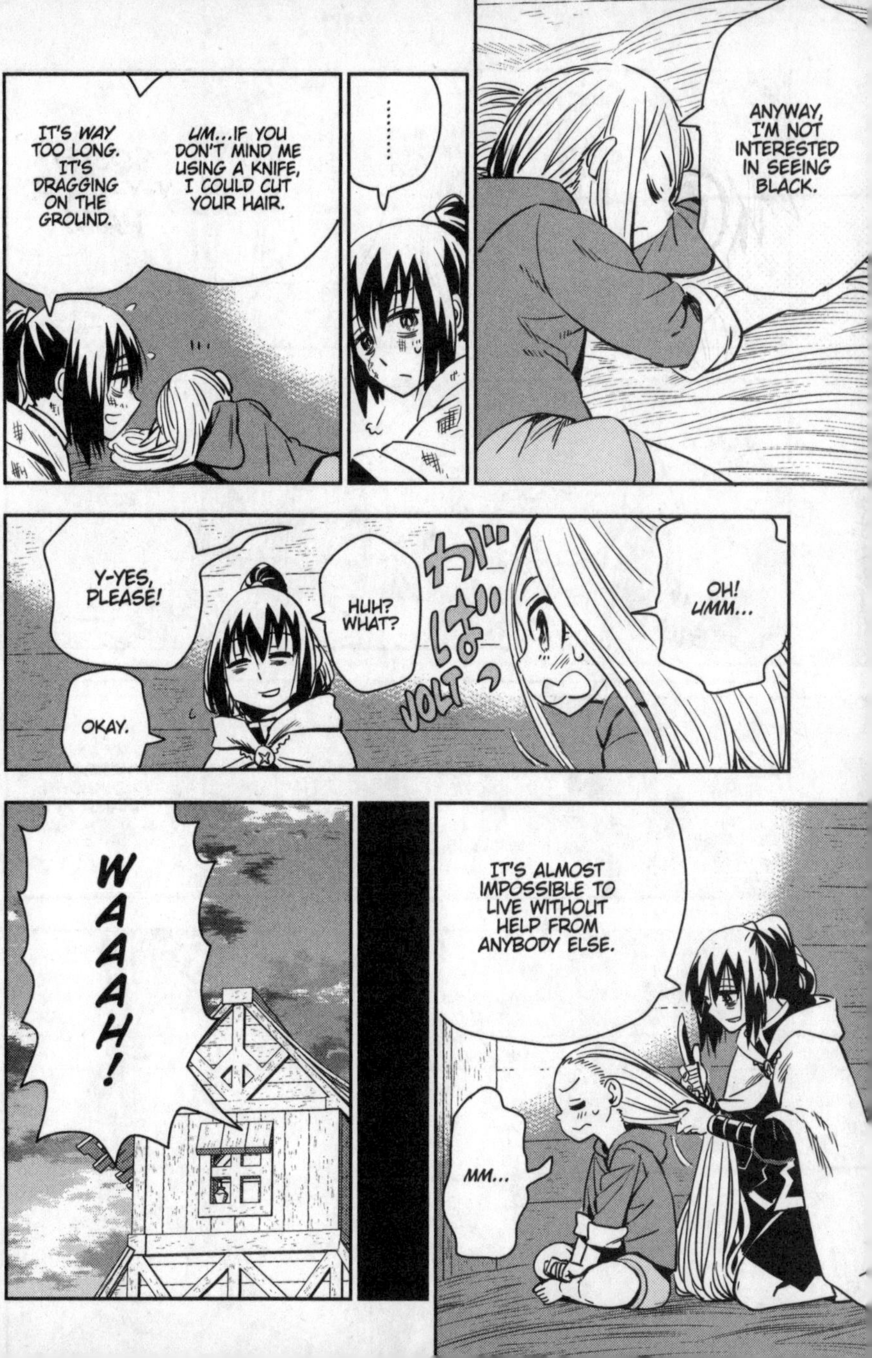
ANYWAY, I'M NOT INTERESTED IN SEEING BLACK.
......
UM...IF YOU DON'T MIND ME USING A KNIFE, I COULD CUT YOUR HAIR.
IT'S WAY TOO LONG. IT'S DRAGGING ON THE GROUND.
OH! UMM...
わ゙ばっ
JOLT
HUH? WHAT?
Y-YES, PLEASE!
OKAY.
IT'S ALMOST IMPOSSIBLE TO LIVE WITHOUT HELP FROM ANYBODY ELSE.
MM...
WAAAAH!

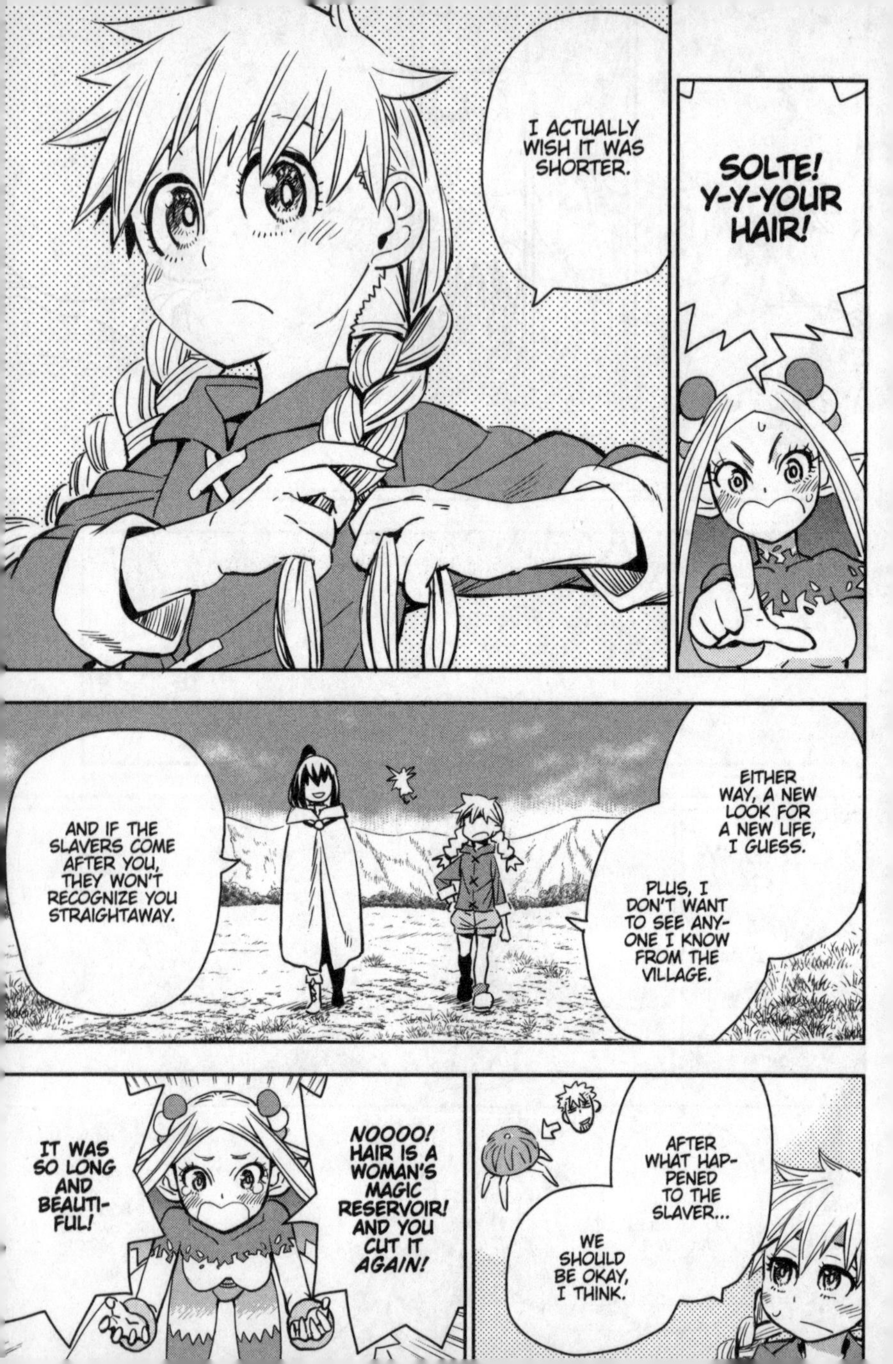
SOLTE! Y-Y-YOUR HAIR!
I ACTUALLY WISH IT WAS SHORTER.
EITHER WAY, A NEW LOOK FOR A NEW LIFE, I GUESS.
PLUS, I DON'T WANT TO SEE ANYONE I KNOW FROM THE VILLAGE.
AND IF THE SLAVERS COME AFTER YOU, THEY WON'T RECOGNIZE YOU STRAIGHTAWAY.
AFTER WHAT HAPPENED TO THE SLAVER...
WE SHOULD BE OKAY, I THINK.
NOOOO! HAIR IS A WOMAN'S MAGIC RESERVOIR! AND YOU CUT IT AGAIN!
IT WAS SO LONG AND BEAUTIFUL!

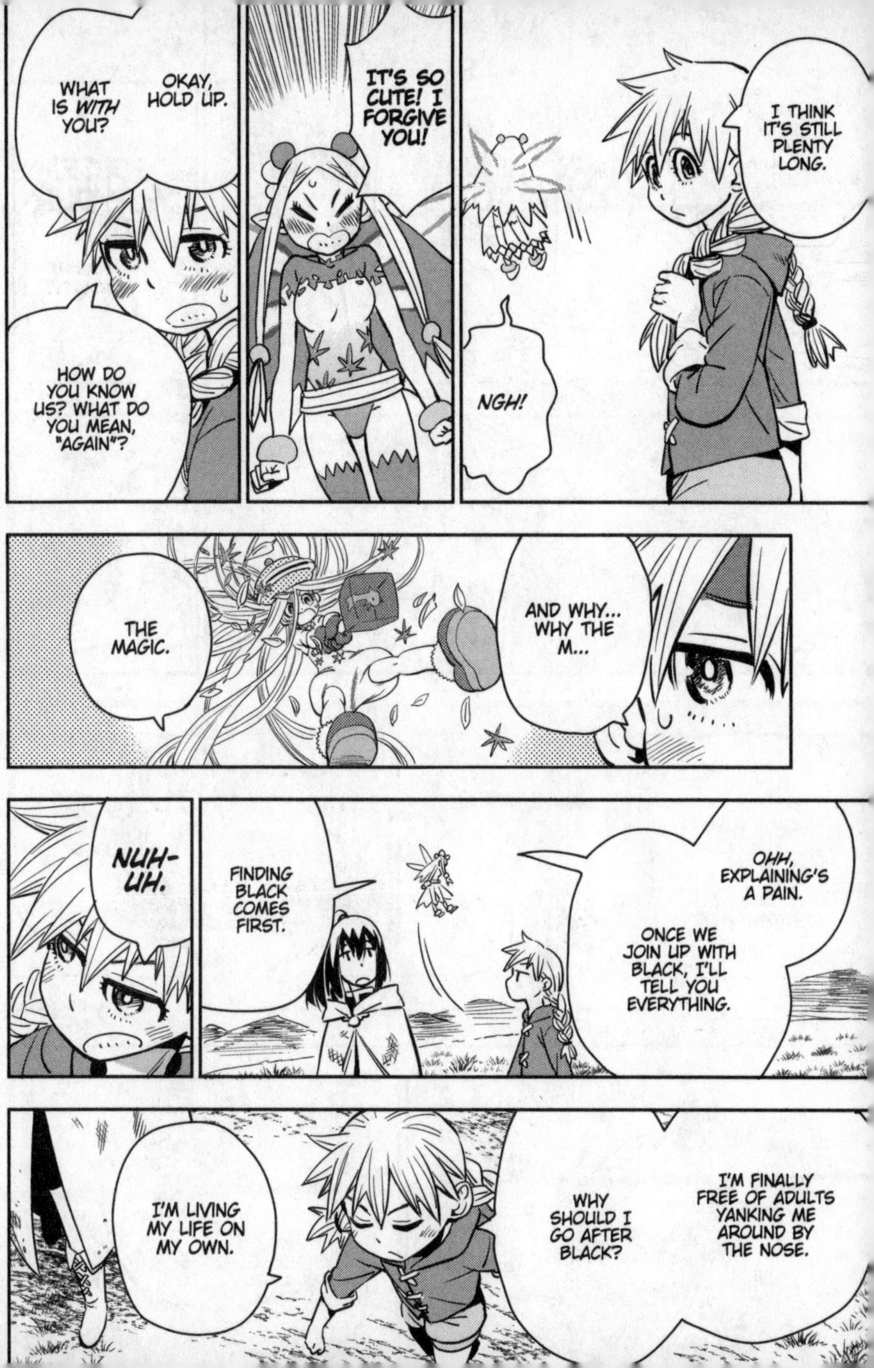
I THINK IT'S STILL PLENTY LONG.
NGH!
IT'S SO CUTE! I FORGIVE YOU!
OKAY, HOLD UP.
WHAT IS *WITH* YOU?
HOW DO YOU KNOW US? WHAT DO YOU MEAN, "AGAIN"?
AND WHY... WHY THE M...
THE MAGIC.
OHH, EXPLAINING'S A PAIN.
ONCE WE JOIN UP WITH BLACK, I'LL TELL YOU EVERYTHING.
FINDING BLACK COMES FIRST.
NUH-UH.
I'M FINALLY FREE OF ADULTS YANKING ME AROUND BY THE NOSE.
WHY SHOULD I GO AFTER BLACK?
I'M LIVING MY LIFE ON MY OWN.

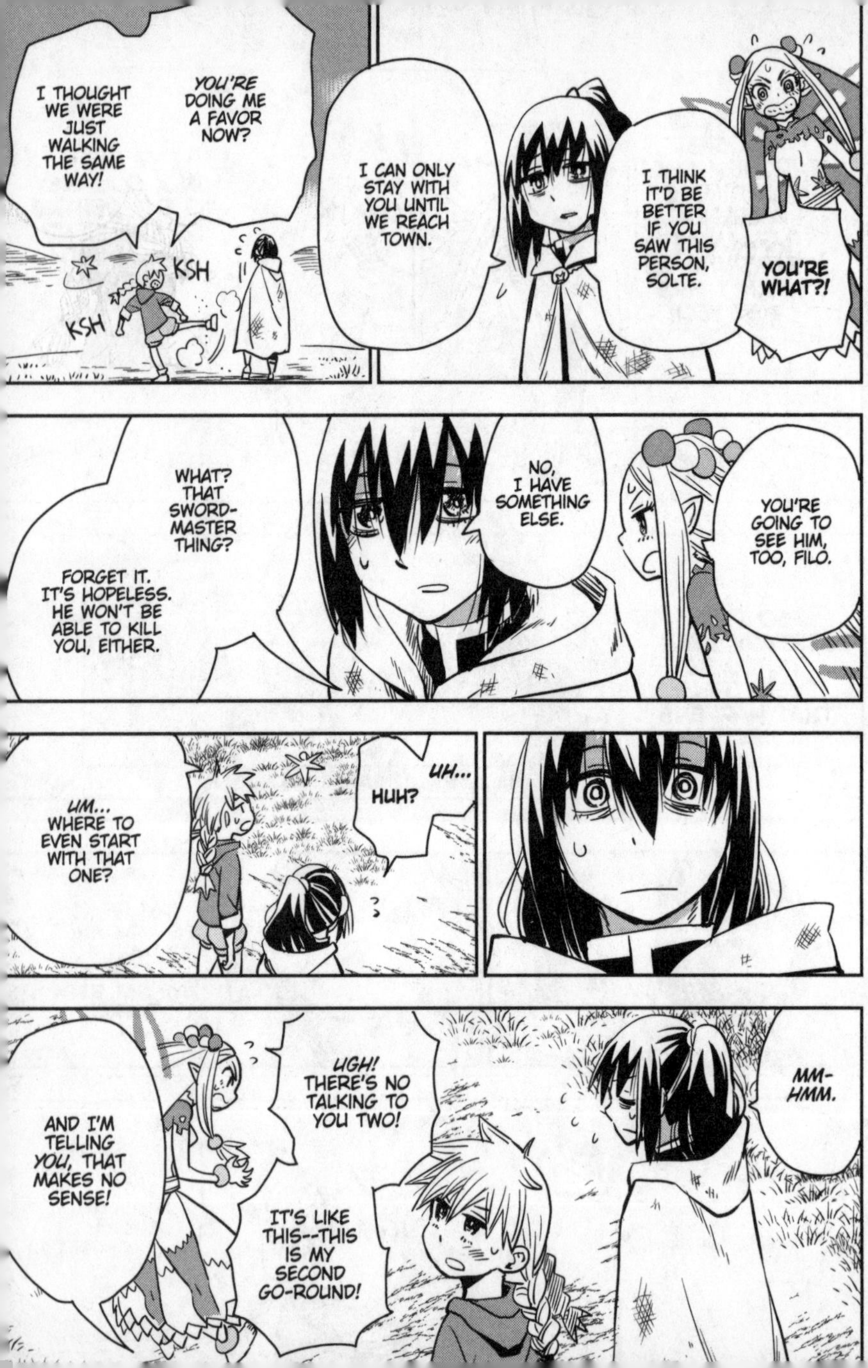
YOU'RE WHAT?!
I THINK IT'D BE BETTER IF YOU SAW THIS PERSON, SOLTE.
I CAN ONLY STAY WITH YOU UNTIL WE REACH TOWN.
YOU'RE DOING ME A FAVOR NOW?
I THOUGHT WE WERE JUST WALKING THE SAME WAY!
KSH
KSH
YOU'RE GOING TO SEE HIM, TOO, FILO.
NO, I HAVE SOMETHING ELSE.
WHAT? THAT SWORD-MASTER THING?
FORGET IT. IT'S HOPELESS. HE WON'T BE ABLE TO KILL YOU, EITHER.
UH...
HUH?
UM... WHERE TO EVEN START WITH THAT ONE?
MM-HMM.
UGH! THERE'S NO TALKING TO YOU TWO!
IT'S LIKE THIS--THIS IS MY SECOND GO-ROUND!
AND I'M TELLING *YOU*, THAT MAKES NO SENSE!

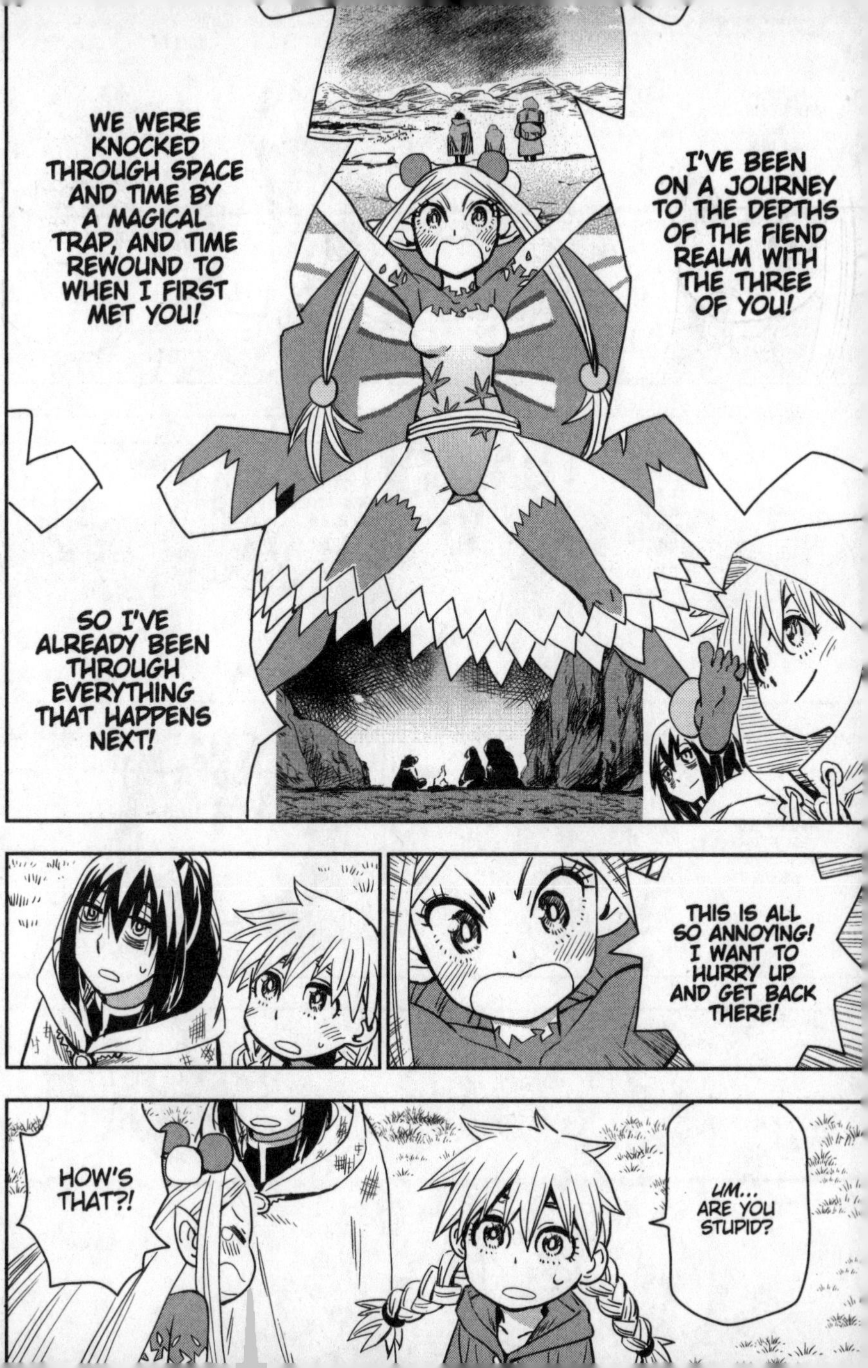
I'VE BEEN ON A JOURNEY TO THE DEPTHS OF THE FIEND REALM WITH THE THREE OF YOU!
WE WERE KNOCKED THROUGH SPACE AND TIME BY A MAGICAL TRAP, AND TIME REWOUND TO WHEN I FIRST MET YOU!
SO I'VE ALREADY BEEN THROUGH EVERYTHING THAT HAPPENS NEXT!
THIS IS ALL SO ANNOYING! I WANT TO HURRY UP AND GET BACK THERE!
UM... ARE YOU STUPID?
HOW'S THAT?!

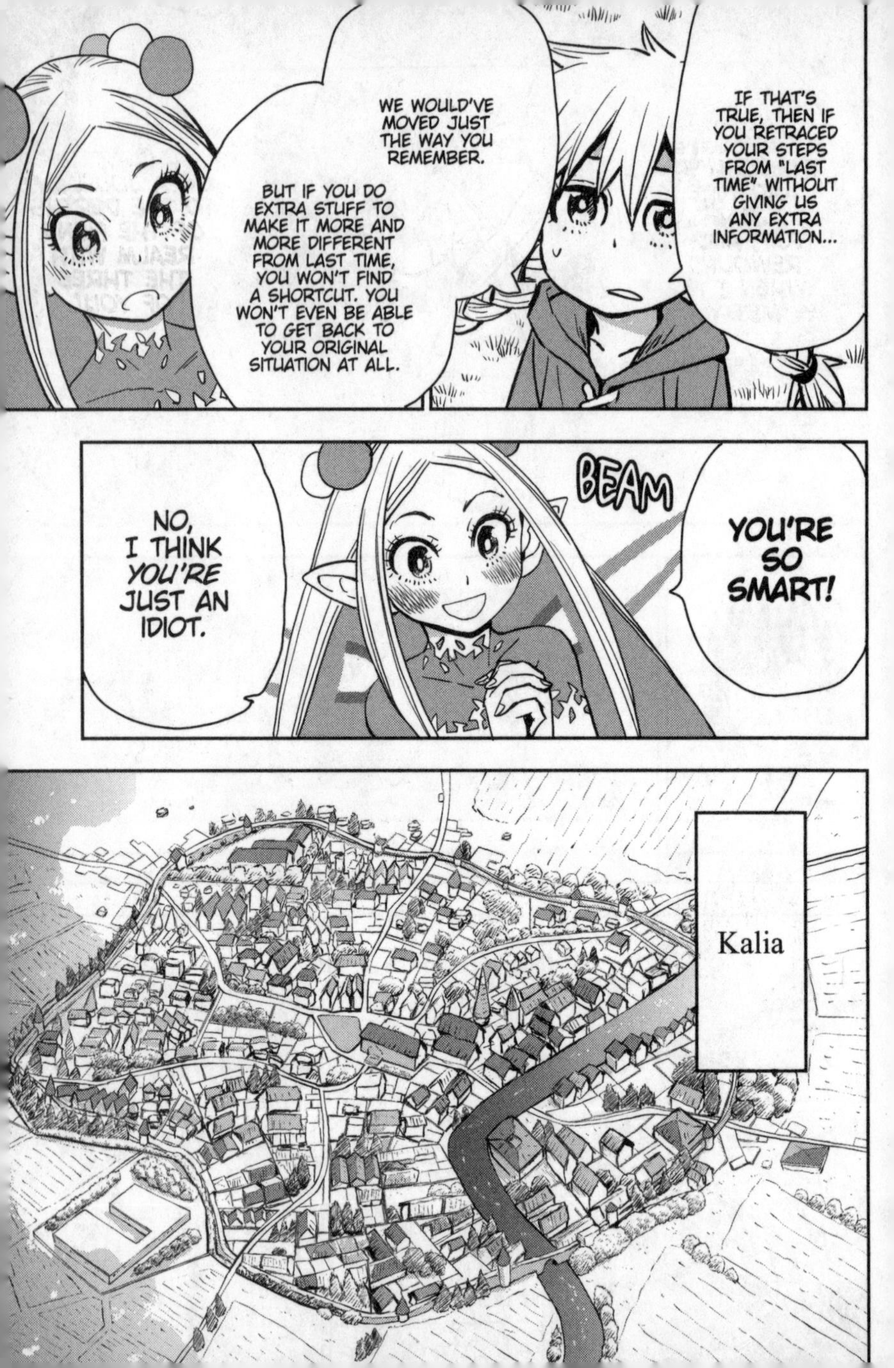
IF THAT'S TRUE, THEN IF YOU RETRACED YOUR STEPS FROM "LAST TIME" WITHOUT GIVING US ANY EXTRA INFORMATION...
WE WOULD'VE MOVED JUST THE WAY YOU REMEMBER.
BUT IF YOU DO EXTRA STUFF TO MAKE IT MORE AND MORE DIFFERENT FROM LAST TIME, YOU WON'T FIND A SHORTCUT. YOU WON'T EVEN BE ABLE TO GET BACK TO YOUR ORIGINAL SITUATION AT ALL.
YOU'RE SO SMART!
BEAM
NO, I THINK *YOU'RE* JUST AN IDIOT.
Kalia

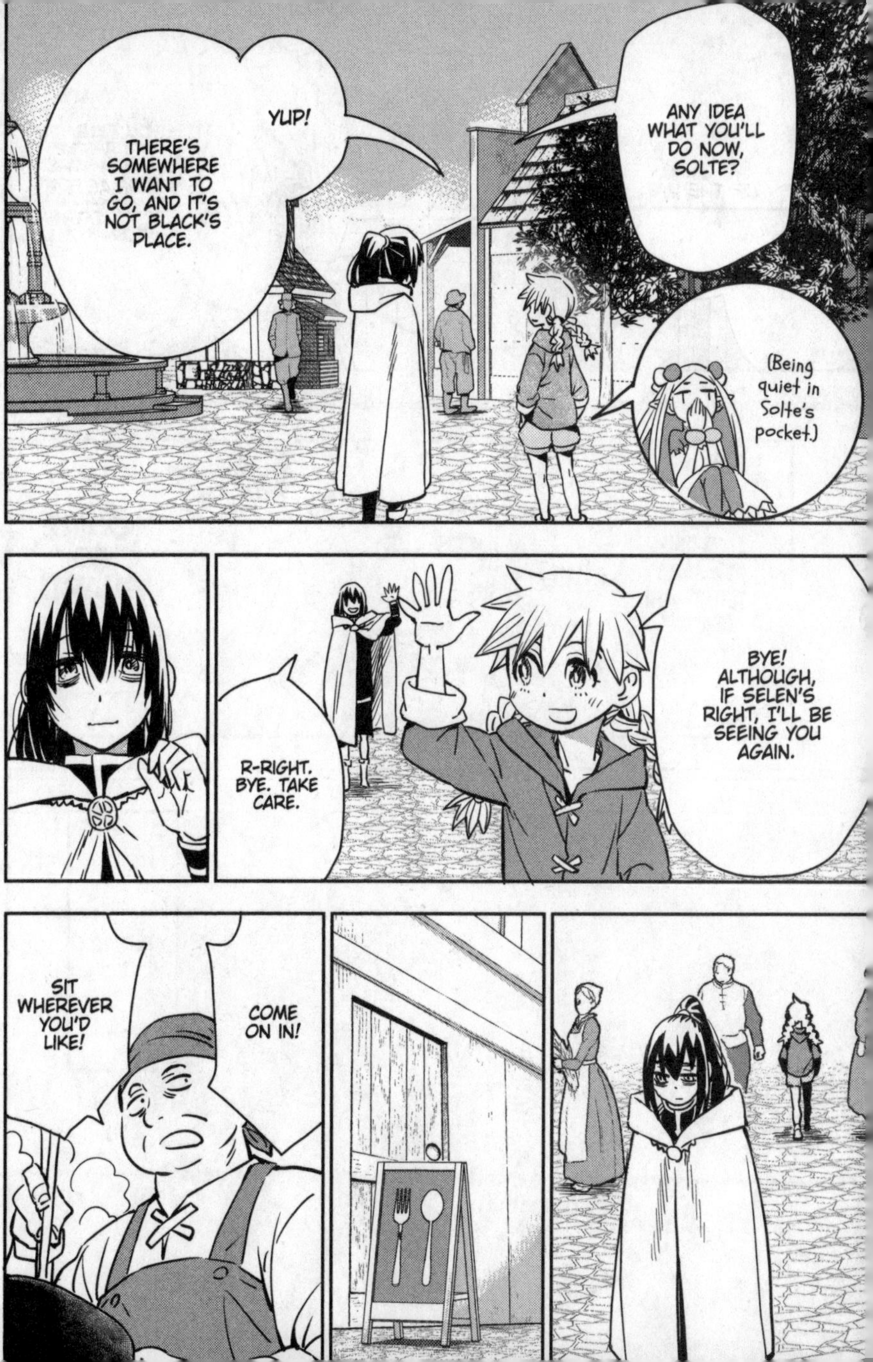
ANY IDEA WHAT YOU'LL DO NOW, SOLTE?
YUP!
THERE'S SOMEWHERE I WANT TO GO, AND IT'S NOT BLACK'S PLACE.
(Being quiet in Solte's pocket.)
BYE! ALTHOUGH, IF SELEN'S RIGHT, I'LL BE SEEING YOU AGAIN.
R-RIGHT. BYE. TAKE CARE.
COME ON IN!
SIT WHEREVER YOU'D LIKE!

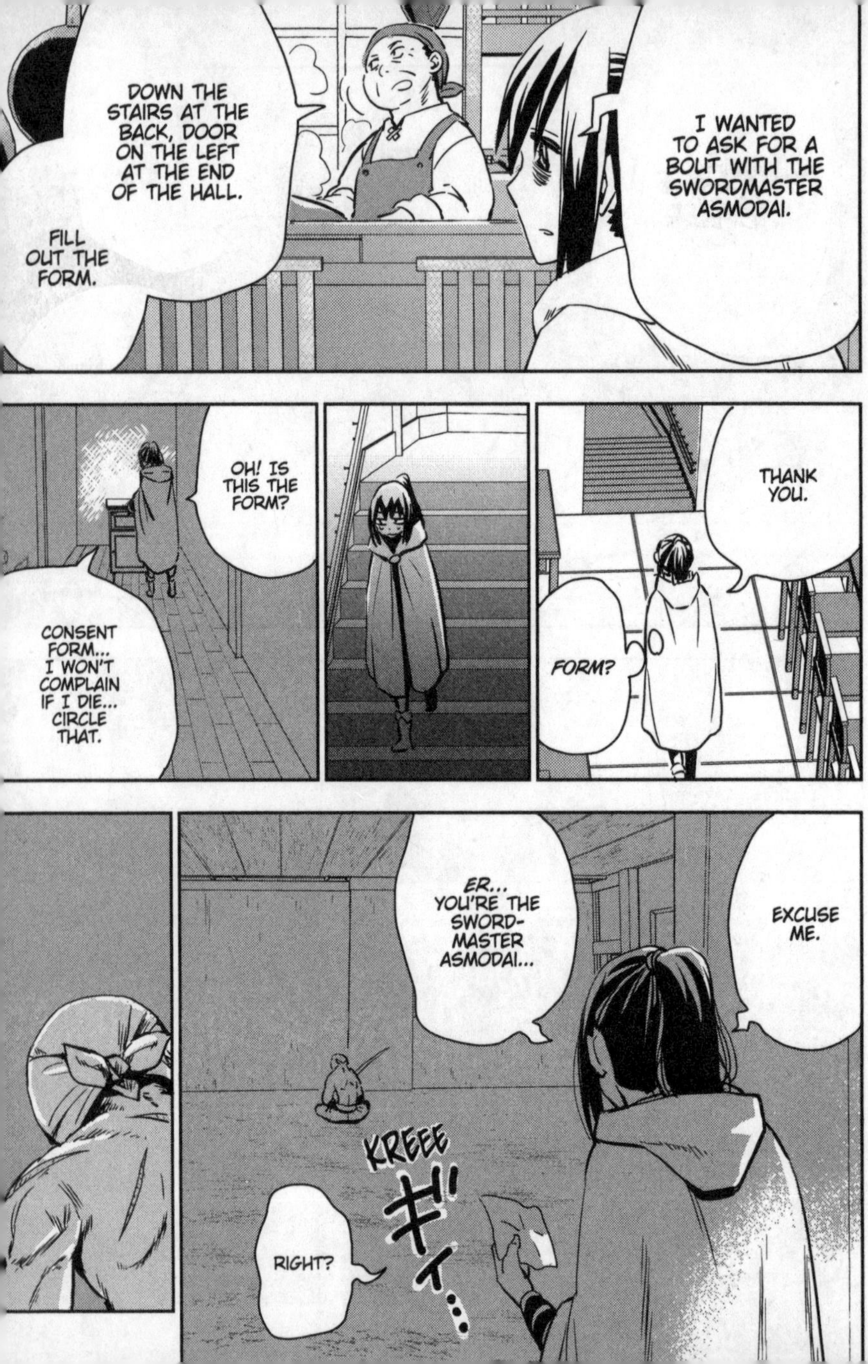
I WANTED TO ASK FOR A BOUT WITH THE SWORDMASTER ASMODAI.
DOWN THE STAIRS AT THE BACK, DOOR ON THE LEFT AT THE END OF THE HALL.
FILL OUT THE FORM.
THANK YOU.
FORM?
OH! IS THIS THE FORM?
CONSENT FORM... I WON'T COMPLAIN IF I DIE... CIRCLE THAT.
EXCUSE ME.
ER... YOU'RE THE SWORD-MASTER ASMODAI...
KREEE
ギィ…
RIGHT?

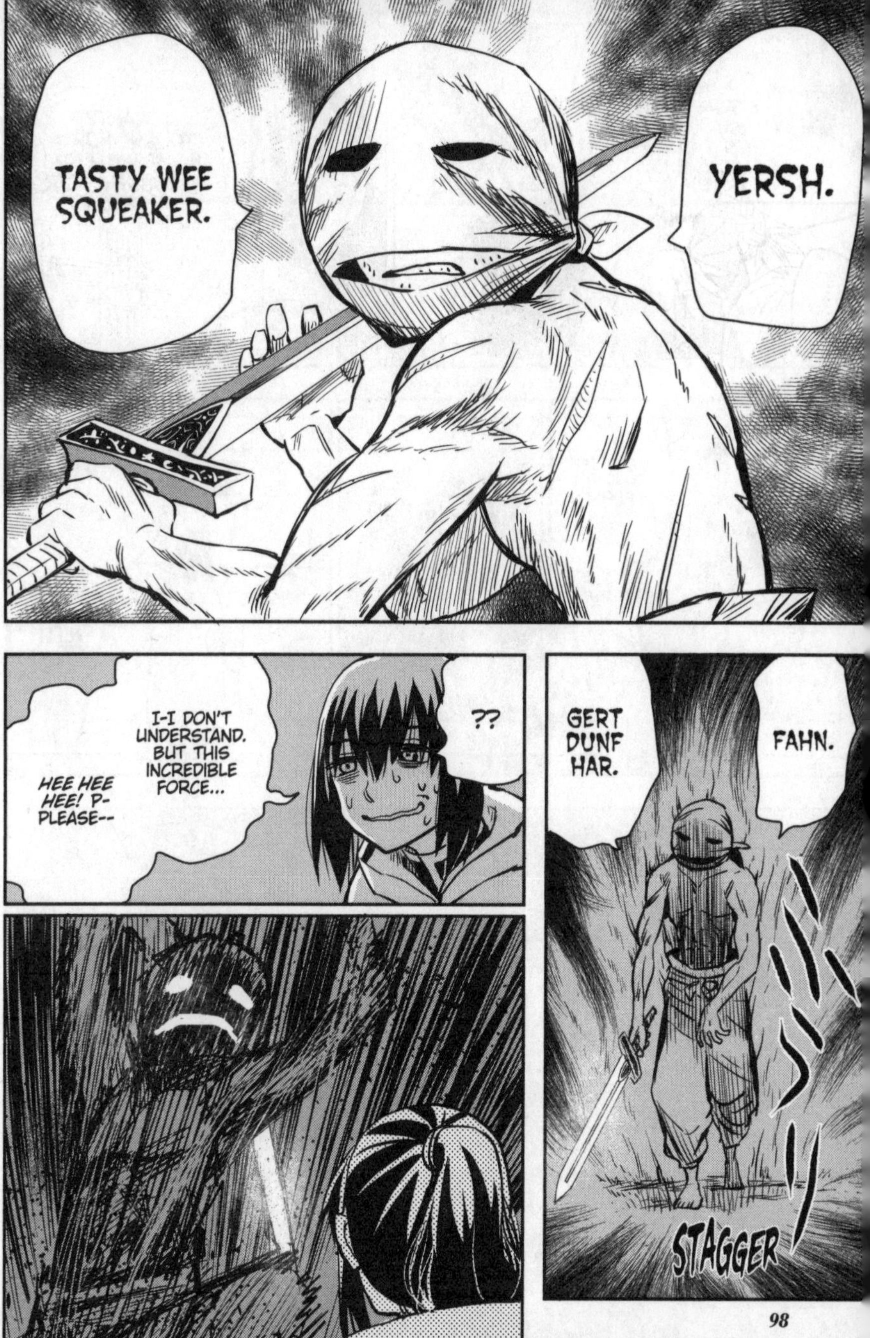
YERSH.
TASTY WEE SQUEAKER.
FAHN.
GERT DUNF HAR.
STAGGER
??
I-I DON'T UNDERSTAND. BUT THIS INCREDIBLE FORCE...
HEE HEE HEE! P-PLEASE--

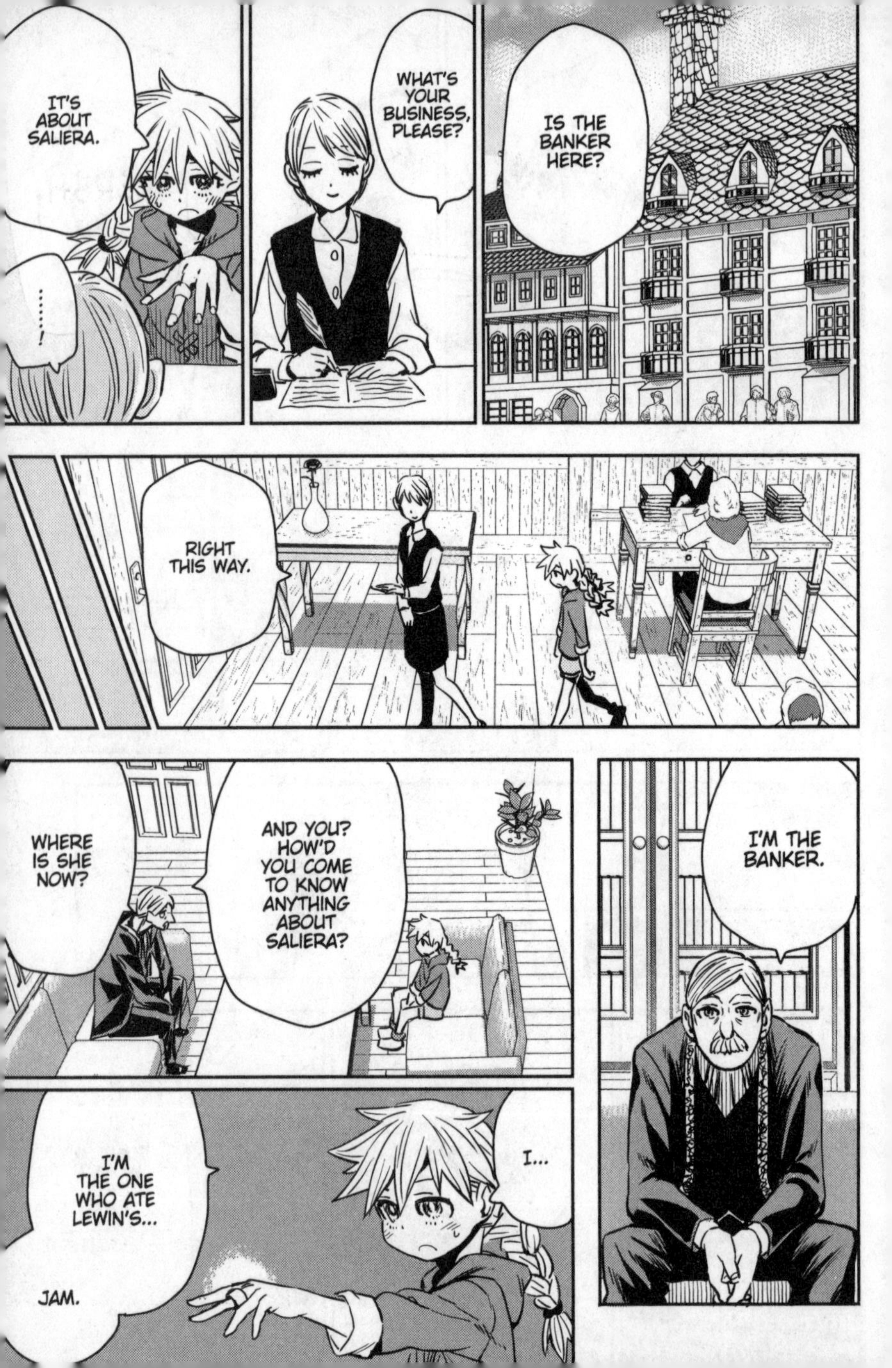
IS THE BANKER HERE?
WHAT'S YOUR BUSINESS, PLEASE?
IT'S ABOUT SALIERA.
......!
RIGHT THIS WAY.
I'M THE BANKER.
AND YOU? HOW'D YOU COME TO KNOW ANYTHING ABOUT SALIERA?
WHERE IS SHE NOW?
I...
I'M THE ONE WHO ATE LEWIN'S...
JAM.

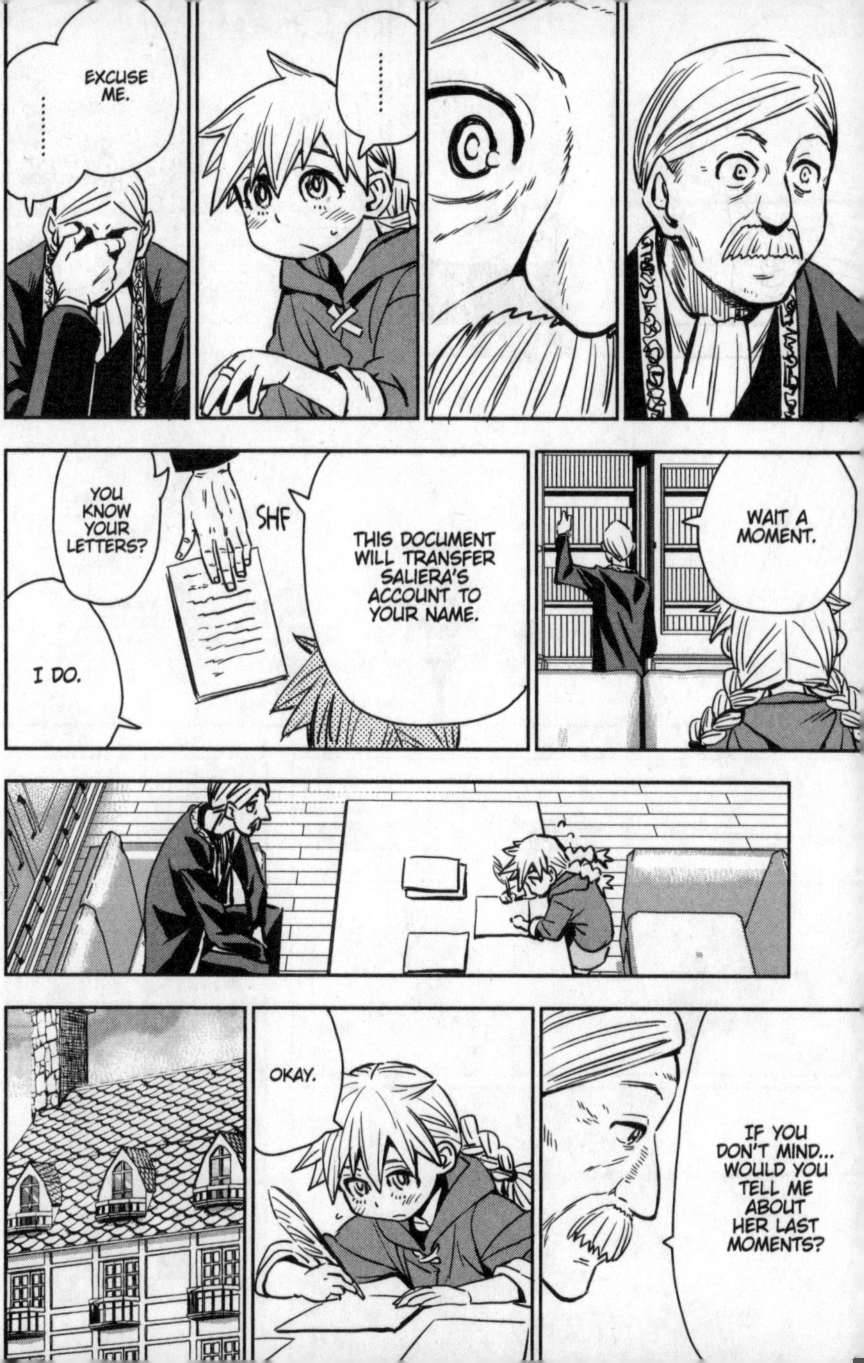
......
EXCUSE ME.
......
WAIT A MOMENT.
THIS DOCUMENT WILL TRANSFER SALIERA'S ACCOUNT TO YOUR NAME.
SHF
YOU KNOW YOUR LETTERS?
I DO.
IF YOU DON'T MIND... WOULD YOU TELL ME ABOUT HER LAST MOMENTS?
OKAY.

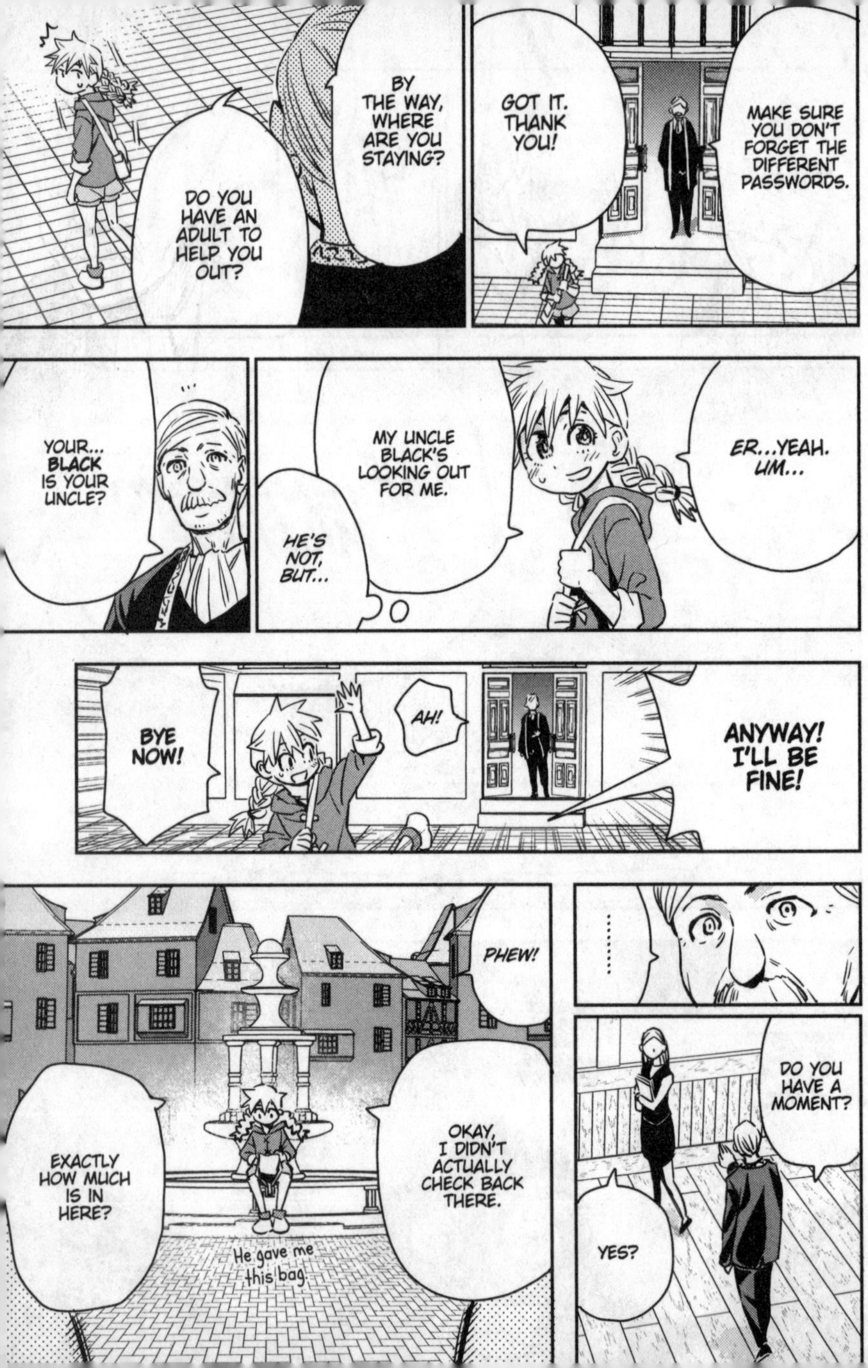
MAKE SURE YOU DON'T FORGET THE DIFFERENT PASSWORDS.
GOT IT. THANK YOU!
BY THE WAY, WHERE ARE YOU STAYING?
DO YOU HAVE AN ADULT TO HELP YOU OUT?
ER...YEAH. UM...
MY UNCLE BLACK'S LOOKING OUT FOR ME.
HE'S NOT, BUT...
...
YOUR... BLACK IS YOUR UNCLE?
ANYWAY! I'LL BE FINE!
AH!
BYE NOW!
......
DO YOU HAVE A MOMENT?
YES?
PHEW!
OKAY, I DIDN'T ACTUALLY CHECK BACK THERE.
He gave me this bag.
EXACTLY HOW MUCH IS IN HERE?

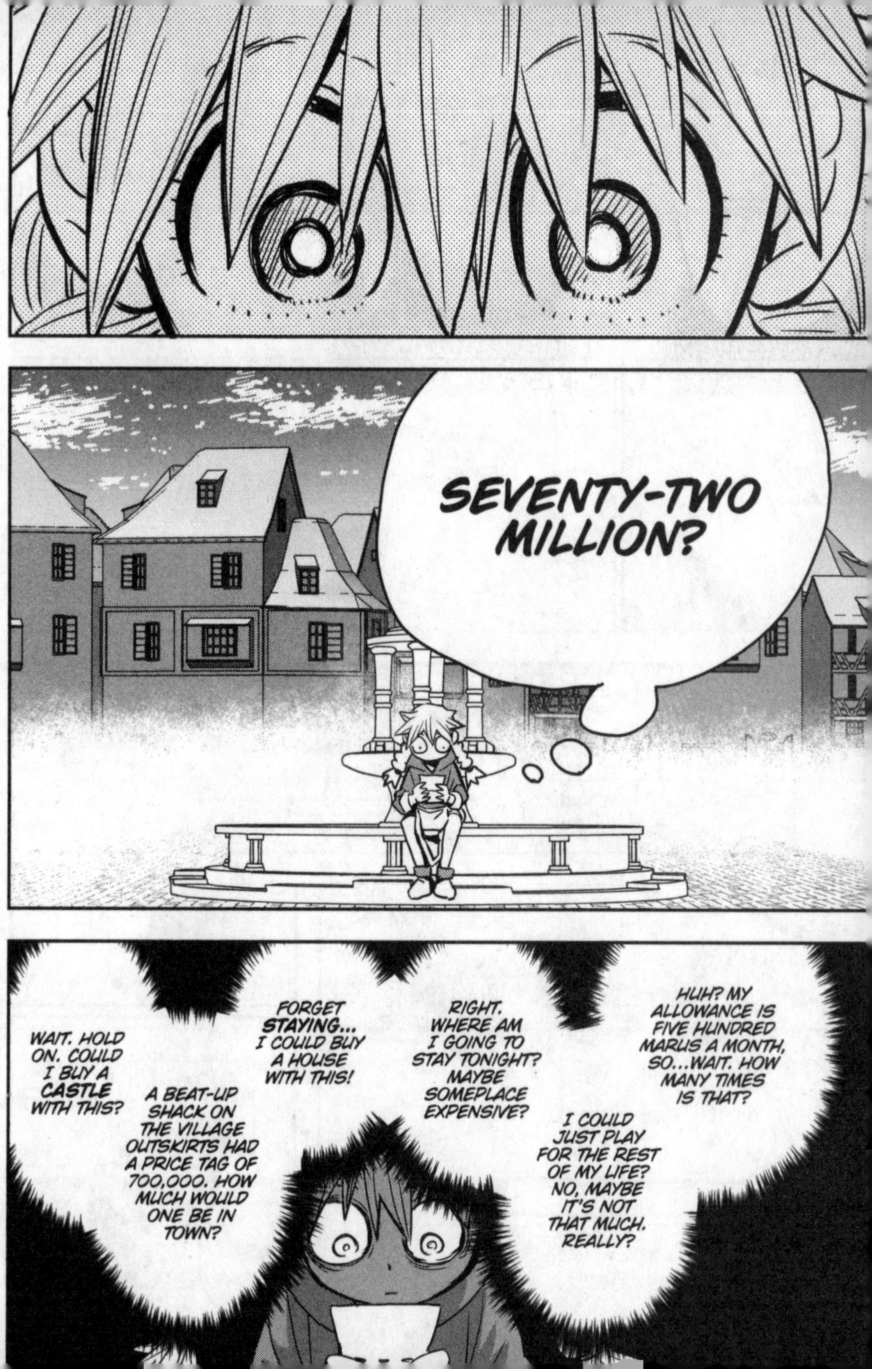
SEVENTY-TWO MILLION?
HUH? MY ALLOWANCE IS FIVE HUNDRED MARUS A MONTH, SO...WAIT. HOW MANY TIMES IS THAT?
I COULD JUST PLAY FOR THE REST OF MY LIFE? NO, MAYBE IT'S NOT THAT MUCH. REALLY?
RIGHT. WHERE AM I GOING TO STAY TONIGHT? MAYBE SOMEPLACE EXPENSIVE?
FORGET STAYING... I COULD BUY A HOUSE WITH THIS!
A BEAT-UP SHACK ON THE VILLAGE OUTSKIRTS HAD A PRICE TAG OF 700,000. HOW MUCH WOULD ONE BE IN TOWN?
WAIT. HOLD ON. COULD I BUY A CASTLE WITH THIS?

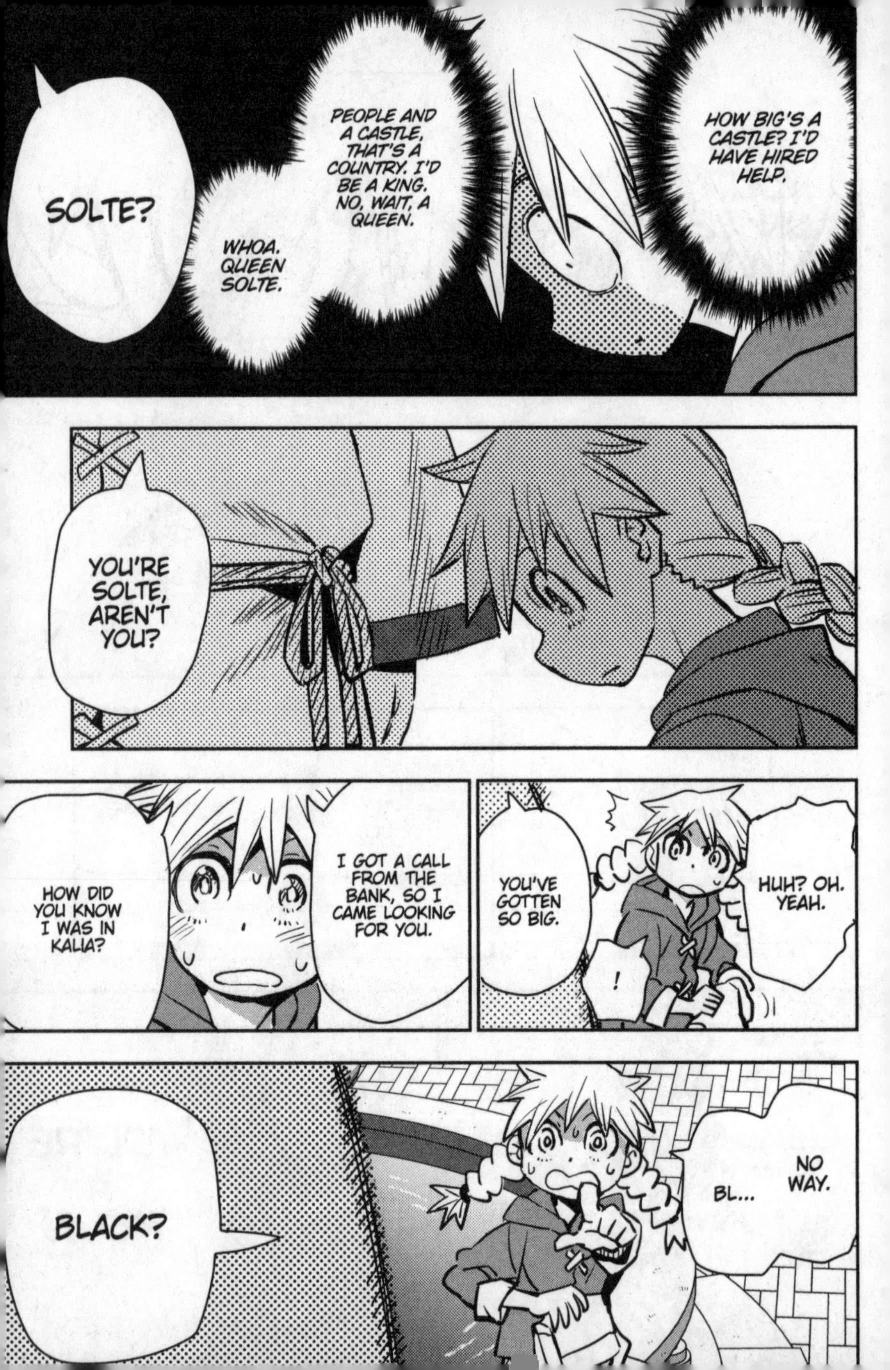
HOW BIG'S A CASTLE? I'D HAVE HIRED HELP.
PEOPLE AND A CASTLE, THAT'S A COUNTRY. I'D BE A KING. NO, WAIT, A QUEEN.
WHOA. QUEEN SOLTE.
SOLTE?
YOU'RE SOLTE, AREN'T YOU?
HUH? OH. YEAH.
!
YOU'VE GOTTEN SO BIG.
I GOT A CALL FROM THE BANK, SO I CAME LOOKING FOR YOU.
HOW DID YOU KNOW I WAS IN KALIA?
NO WAY.
BL...
BLACK?

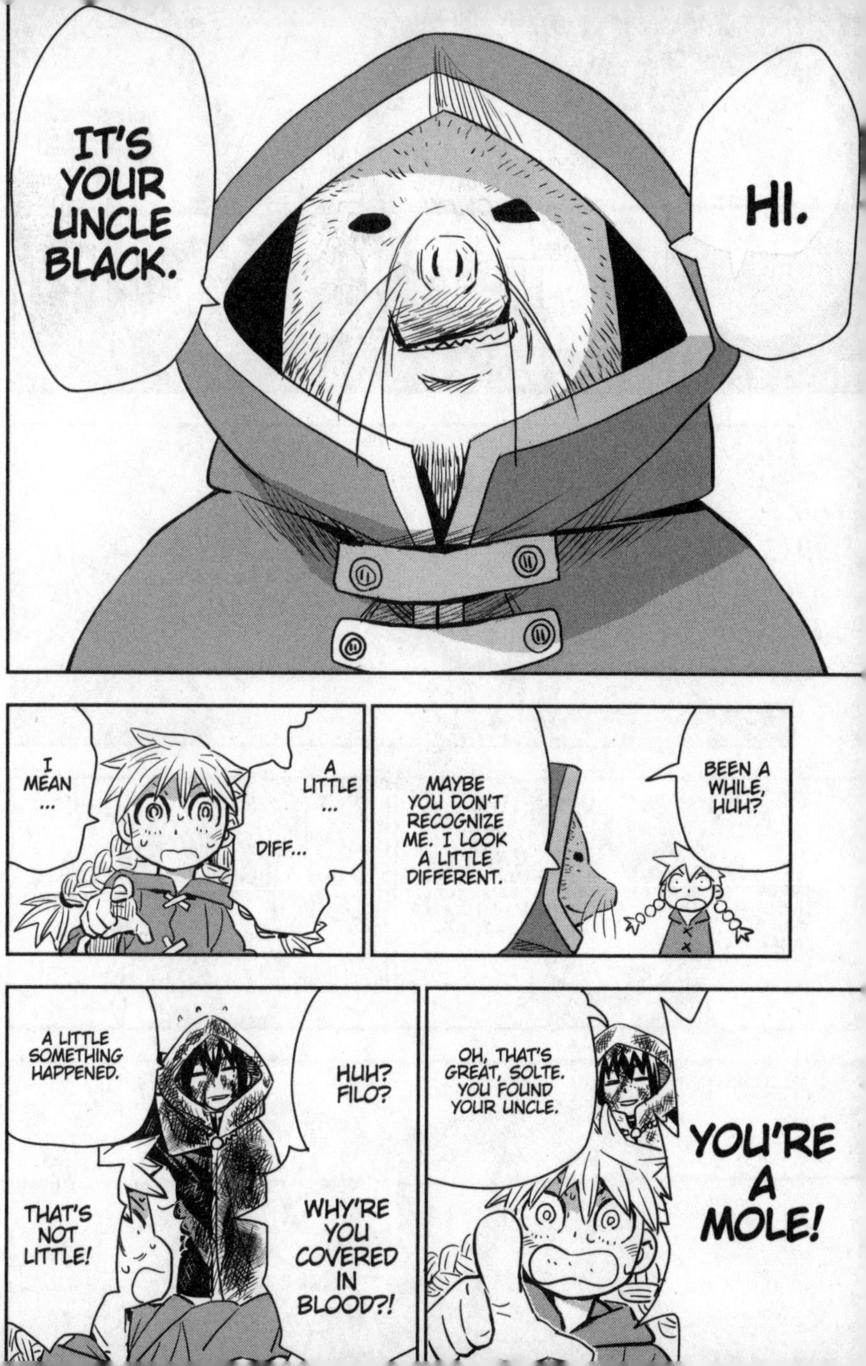
HI.
IT'S YOUR UNCLE BLACK.
BEEN A WHILE, HUH?
MAYBE YOU DON'T RECOGNIZE ME. I LOOK A LITTLE DIFFERENT.
A LITTLE ...
I MEAN ...
DIFF...
OH, THAT'S GREAT, SOLTE. YOU FOUND YOUR UNCLE.
YOU'RE A MOLE!
HUH? FILO?
WHY'RE YOU COVERED IN BLOOD?!
A LITTLE SOMETHING HAPPENED.
THAT'S NOT LITTLE!

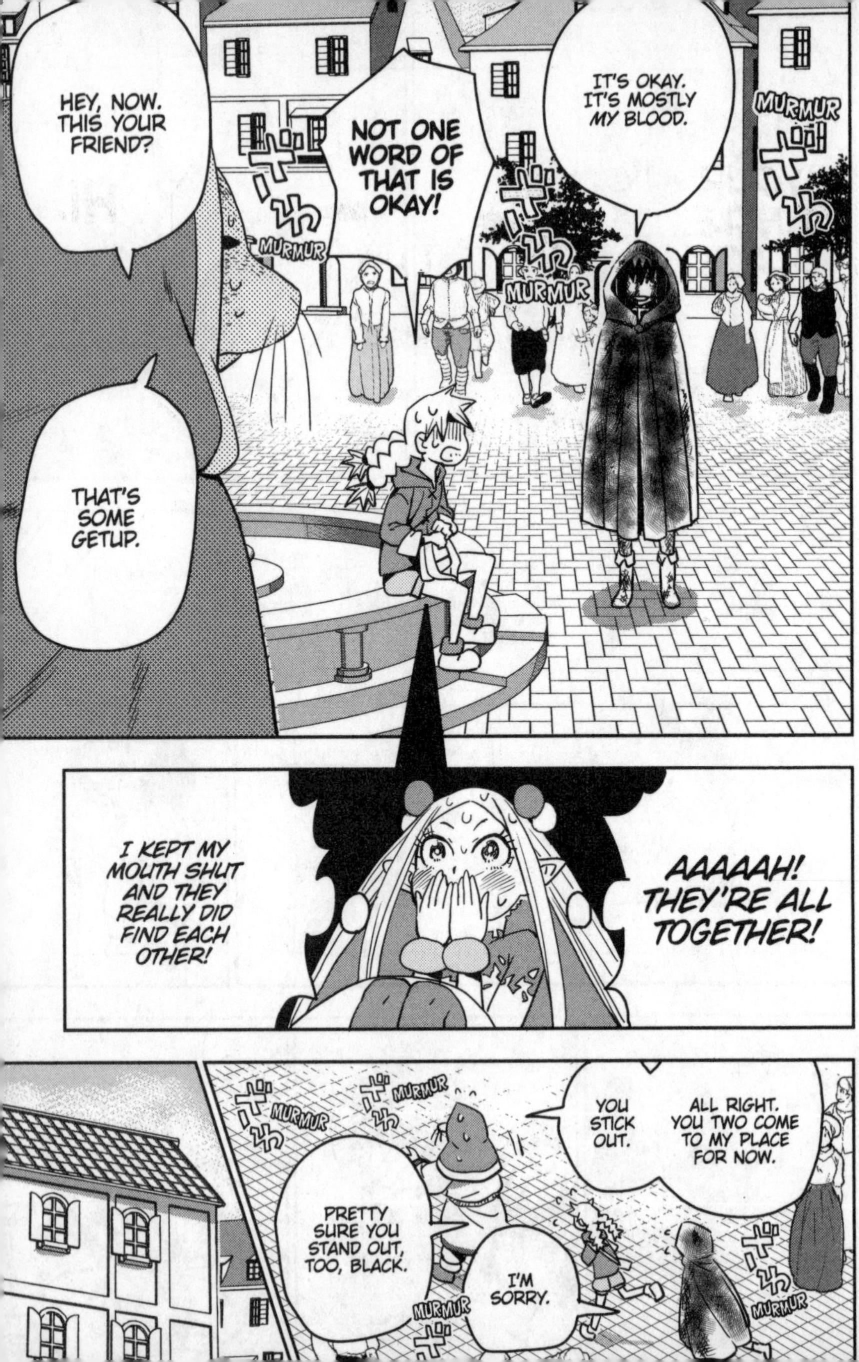
MURMUR
IT'S OKAY. IT'S MOSTLY MY BLOOD.
MURMUR
NOT ONE WORD OF THAT IS OKAY!
MURMUR
HEY, NOW. THIS YOUR FRIEND?
THAT'S SOME GETUP.
AAAAAH! THEY'RE ALL TOGETHER!
I KEPT MY MOUTH SHUT AND THEY REALLY DID FIND EACH OTHER!
ALL RIGHT. YOU TWO COME TO MY PLACE FOR NOW.
YOU STICK OUT.
MURMUR
MURMUR
MURMUR
PRETTY SURE YOU STAND OUT, TOO, BLACK.
I'M SORRY.
MURMUR

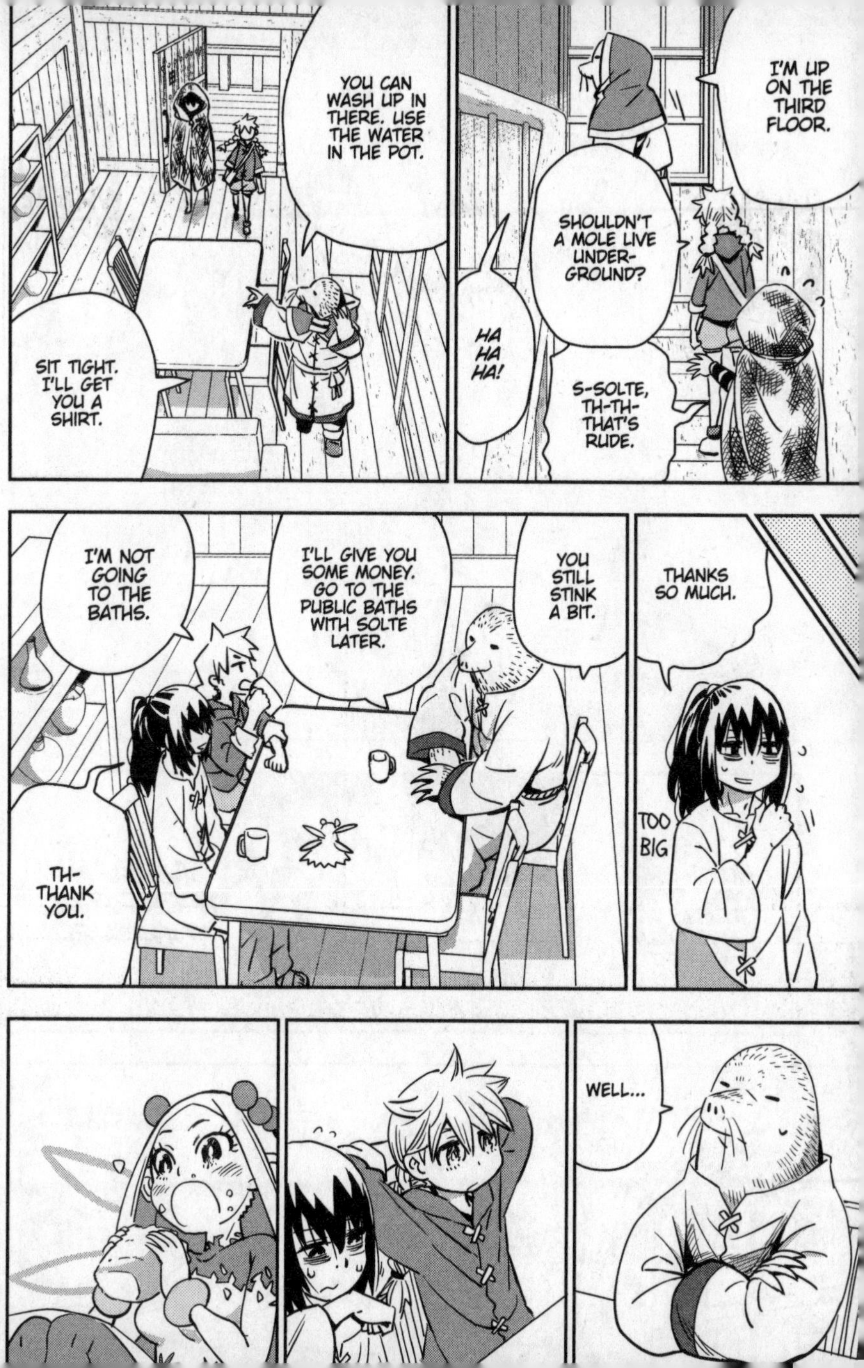
I'M UP ON THE THIRD FLOOR.
SHOULDN'T A MOLE LIVE UNDER-GROUND?
HA HA HA!
S-SOLTE, TH-TH-THAT'S RUDE.
YOU CAN WASH UP IN THERE. USE THE WATER IN THE POT.
SIT TIGHT. I'LL GET YOU A SHIRT.
THANKS SO MUCH.
TOO BIG
YOU STILL STINK A BIT.
I'LL GIVE YOU SOME MONEY. GO TO THE PUBLIC BATHS WITH SOLTE LATER.
I'M NOT GOING TO THE BATHS.
TH-THANK YOU.
WELL...

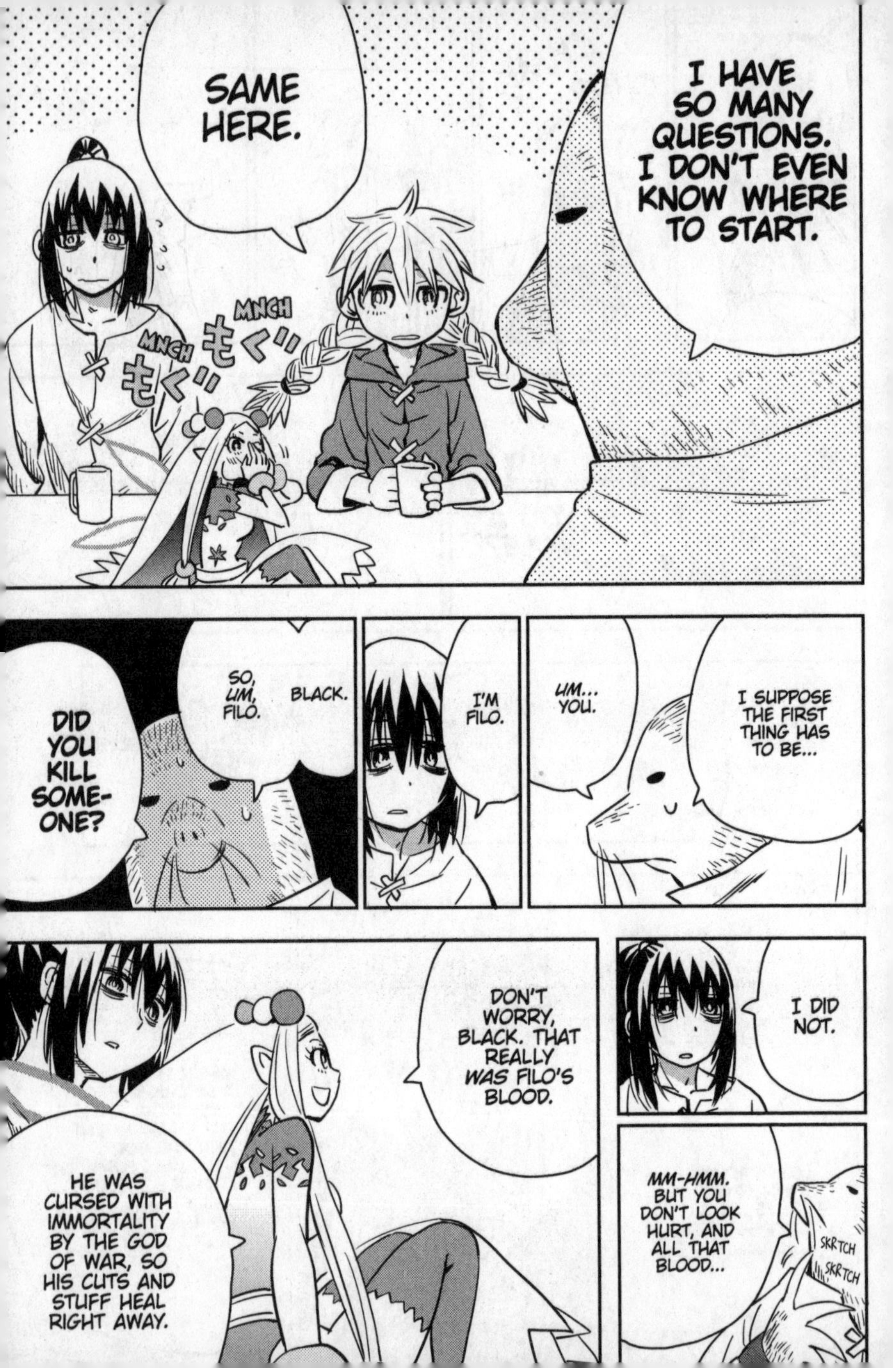
I HAVE SO MANY QUESTIONS. I DON'T EVEN KNOW WHERE TO START.
SAME HERE.
MNCH
もぐッ
MNCH
もぐッ
I SUPPOSE THE FIRST THING HAS TO BE...
UM... YOU.
I'M FILO.
BLACK.
SO, UM, FILO.
DID YOU KILL SOME-ONE?
I DID NOT.
MM-HMM. BUT YOU DON'T LOOK HURT, AND ALL THAT BLOOD...
SKRTCH
SKRTCH
DON'T WORRY, BLACK. THAT REALLY *WAS* FILO'S BLOOD.
HE WAS CURSED WITH IMMORTALITY BY THE GOD OF WAR, SO HIS CUTS AND STUFF HEAL RIGHT AWAY.

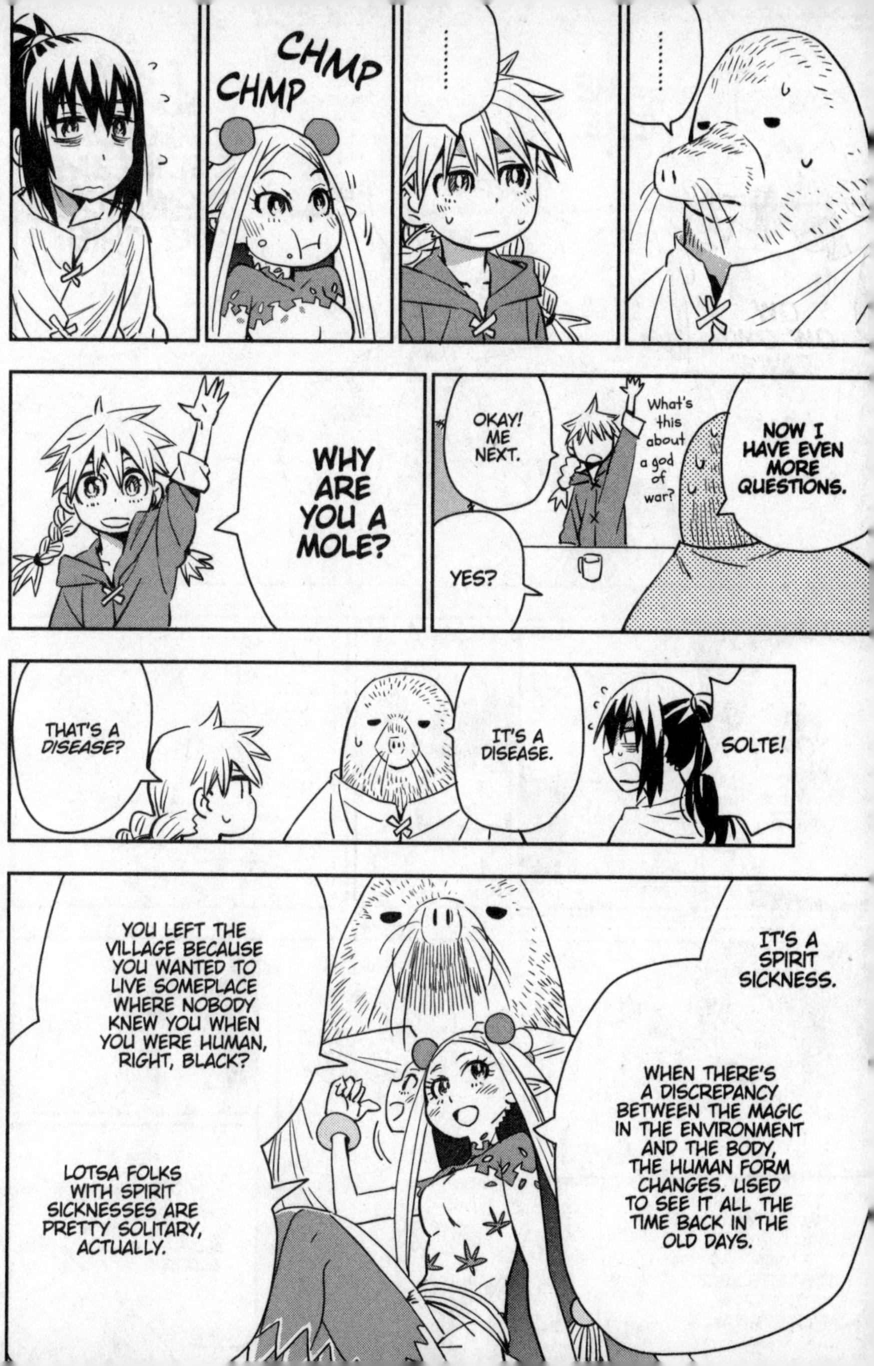

......
......
CHMP CHMP
NOW I HAVE EVEN MORE QUESTIONS.
What's this about a god of war?
OKAY! ME NEXT.
YES?
WHY ARE YOU A MOLE?
SOLTE!
IT'S A DISEASE.
THAT'S A *DISEASE?*
IT'S A SPIRIT SICKNESS.
WHEN THERE'S A DISCREPANCY BETWEEN THE MAGIC IN THE ENVIRONMENT AND THE BODY, THE HUMAN FORM CHANGES. USED TO SEE IT ALL THE TIME BACK IN THE OLD DAYS.
YOU LEFT THE VILLAGE BECAUSE YOU WANTED TO LIVE SOMEPLACE WHERE NOBODY KNEW YOU WHEN YOU WERE HUMAN, RIGHT, BLACK?
LOTSA FOLKS WITH SPIRIT SICKNESSES ARE PRETTY SOLITARY, ACTUALLY.

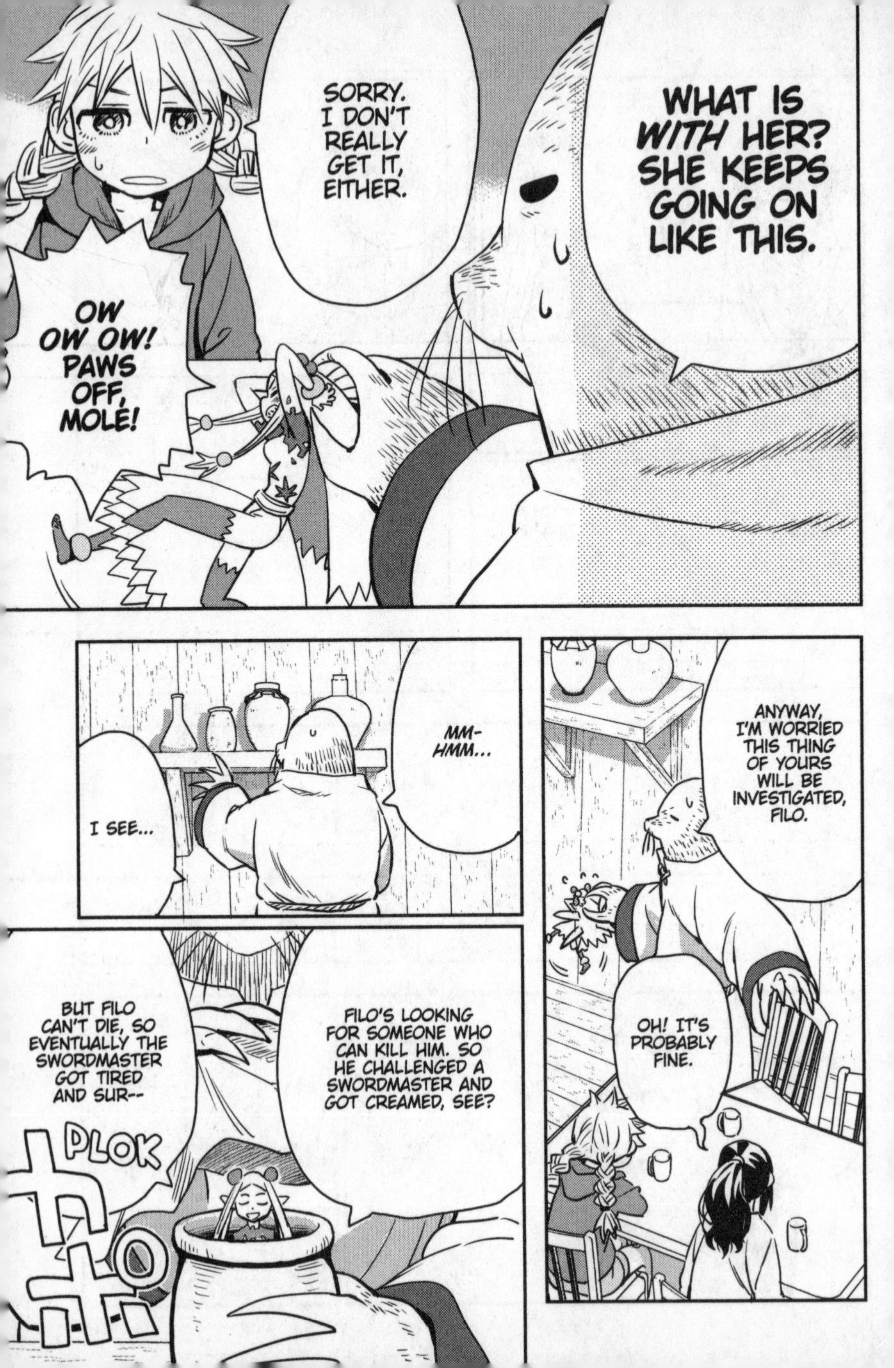
WHAT IS *WITH* HER? SHE KEEPS GOING ON LIKE THIS.
SORRY. I DON'T REALLY GET IT, EITHER.
OW OW OW! PAWS OFF, MOLE!
ANYWAY, I'M WORRIED THIS THING OF YOURS WILL BE INVESTIGATED, FILO.
OH! IT'S PROBABLY FINE.
MM-HMM...
I SEE...
FILO'S LOOKING FOR SOMEONE WHO CAN KILL HIM. SO HE CHALLENGED A SWORDMASTER AND GOT CREAMED, SEE?
BUT FILO CAN'T DIE, SO EVENTUALLY THE SWORDMASTER GOT TIRED AND SUR--
PLOK

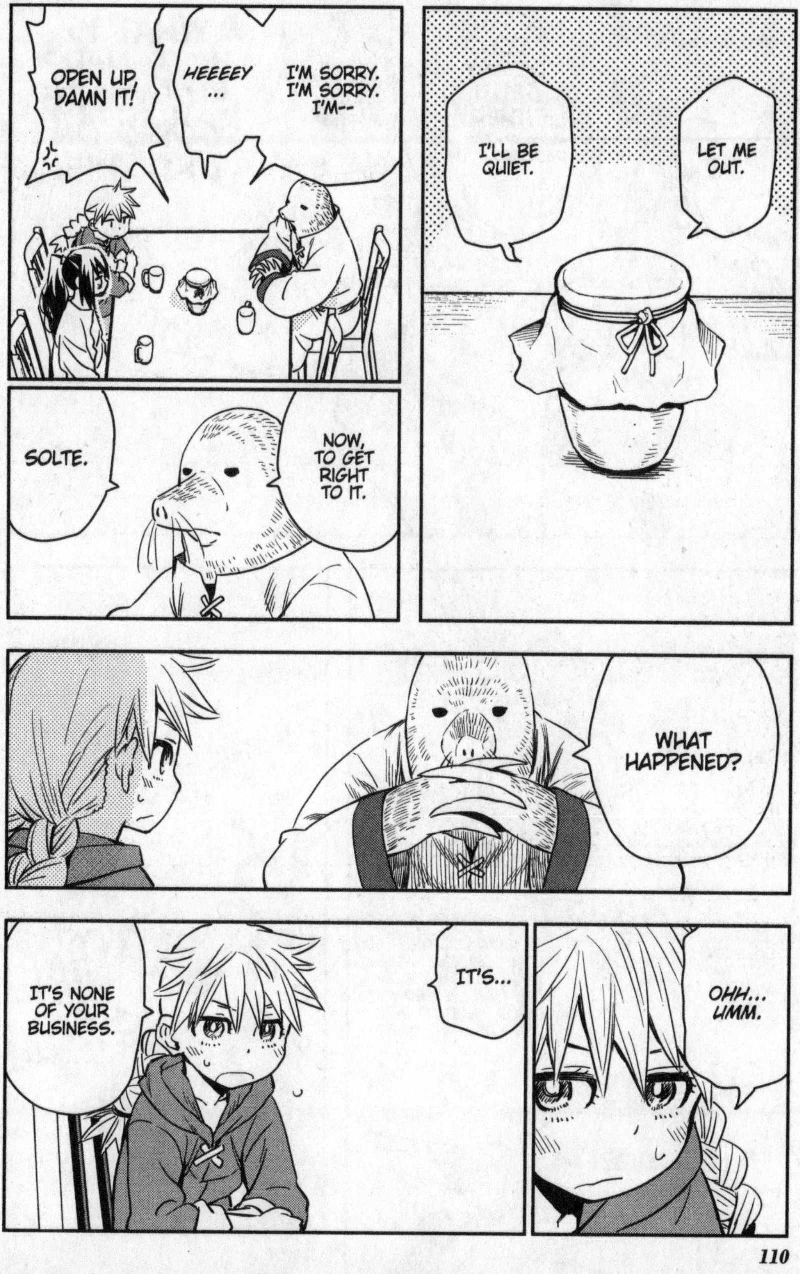
LET ME OUT.
I'LL BE QUIET.
I'M SORRY. I'M SORRY. I'M--
HEEEEY ...
OPEN UP, DAMN IT!
NOW, TO GET RIGHT TO IT.
SOLTE.
WHAT HAPPENED?
OHH... UMM.
IT'S...
IT'S NONE OF YOUR BUSINESS.

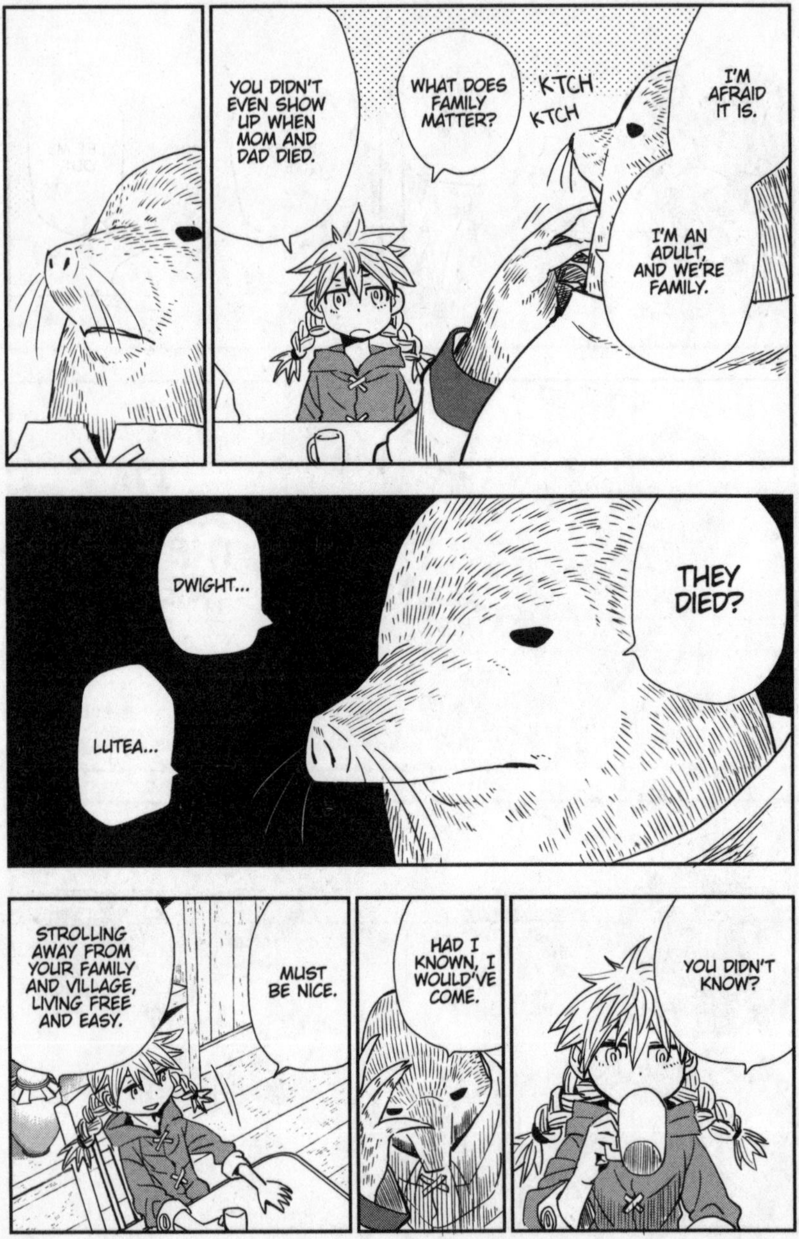

I'M AFRAID IT IS.
KTCH
KTCH
I'M AN ADULT, AND WE'RE FAMILY.
WHAT DOES FAMILY MATTER?
YOU DIDN'T EVEN SHOW UP WHEN MOM AND DAD DIED.
THEY DIED?
DWIGHT...
LUTEA...
YOU DIDN'T KNOW?
HAD I KNOWN, I WOULD'VE COME.
STROLLING AWAY FROM YOUR FAMILY AND VILLAGE, LIVING FREE AND EASY.
MUST BE NICE.

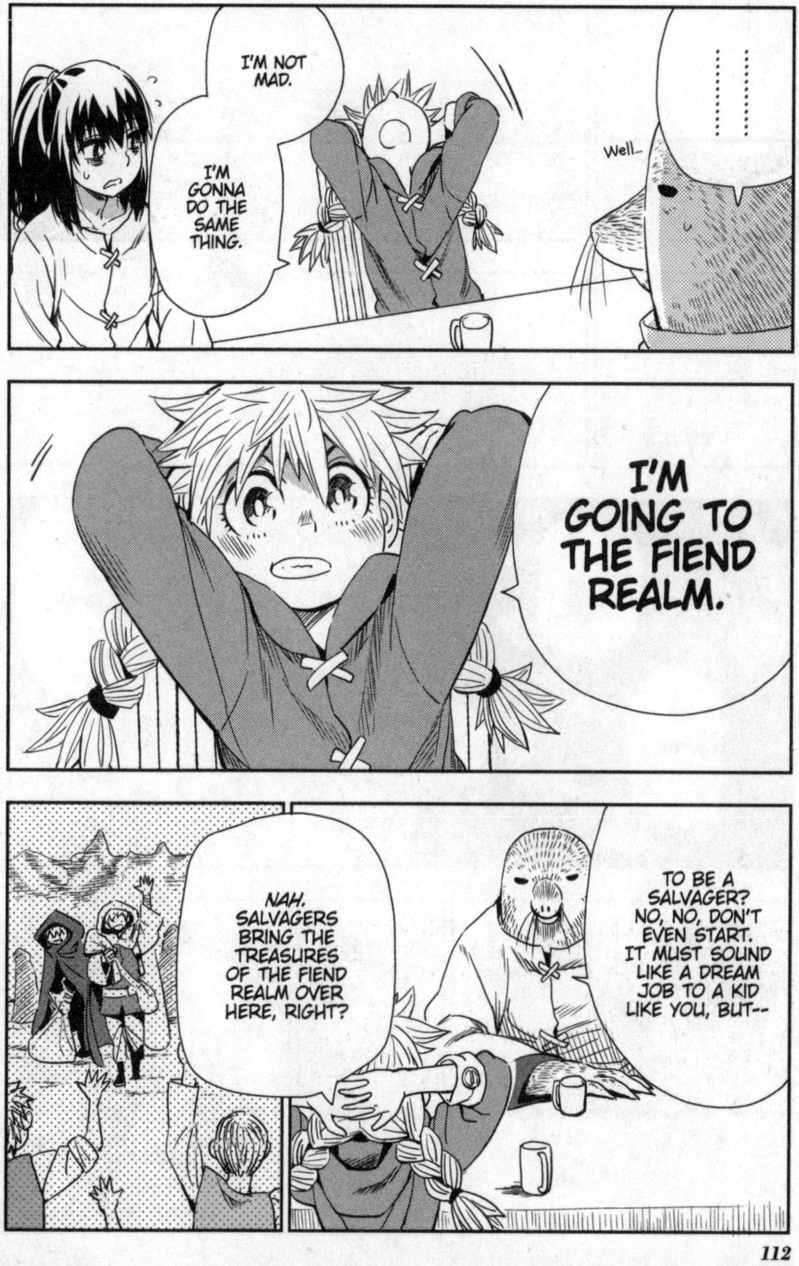
......
Well...
I'M NOT MAD.
I'M GONNA DO THE SAME THING.
I'M GOING TO THE FIEND REALM.
TO BE A SALVAGER? NO, NO, DON'T EVEN START. IT MUST SOUND LIKE A DREAM JOB TO A KID LIKE YOU, BUT--
NAH. SALVAGERS BRING THE TREASURES OF THE FIEND REALM OVER HERE, RIGHT?

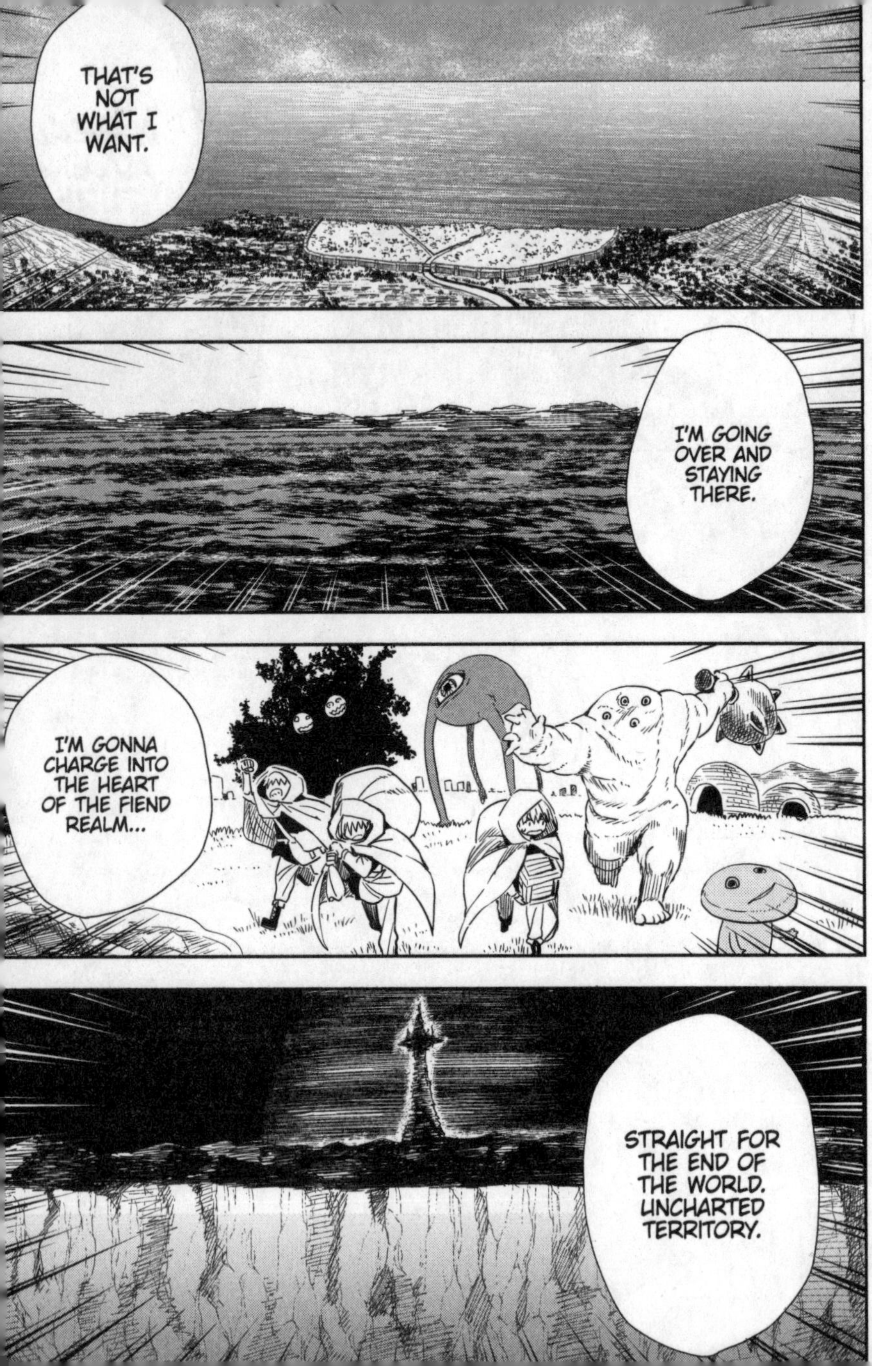
THAT'S NOT WHAT I WANT.
I'M GOING OVER AND STAYING THERE.
I'M GONNA CHARGE INTO THE HEART OF THE FIEND REALM...
STRAIGHT FOR THE END OF THE WORLD. UNCHARTED TERRITORY.

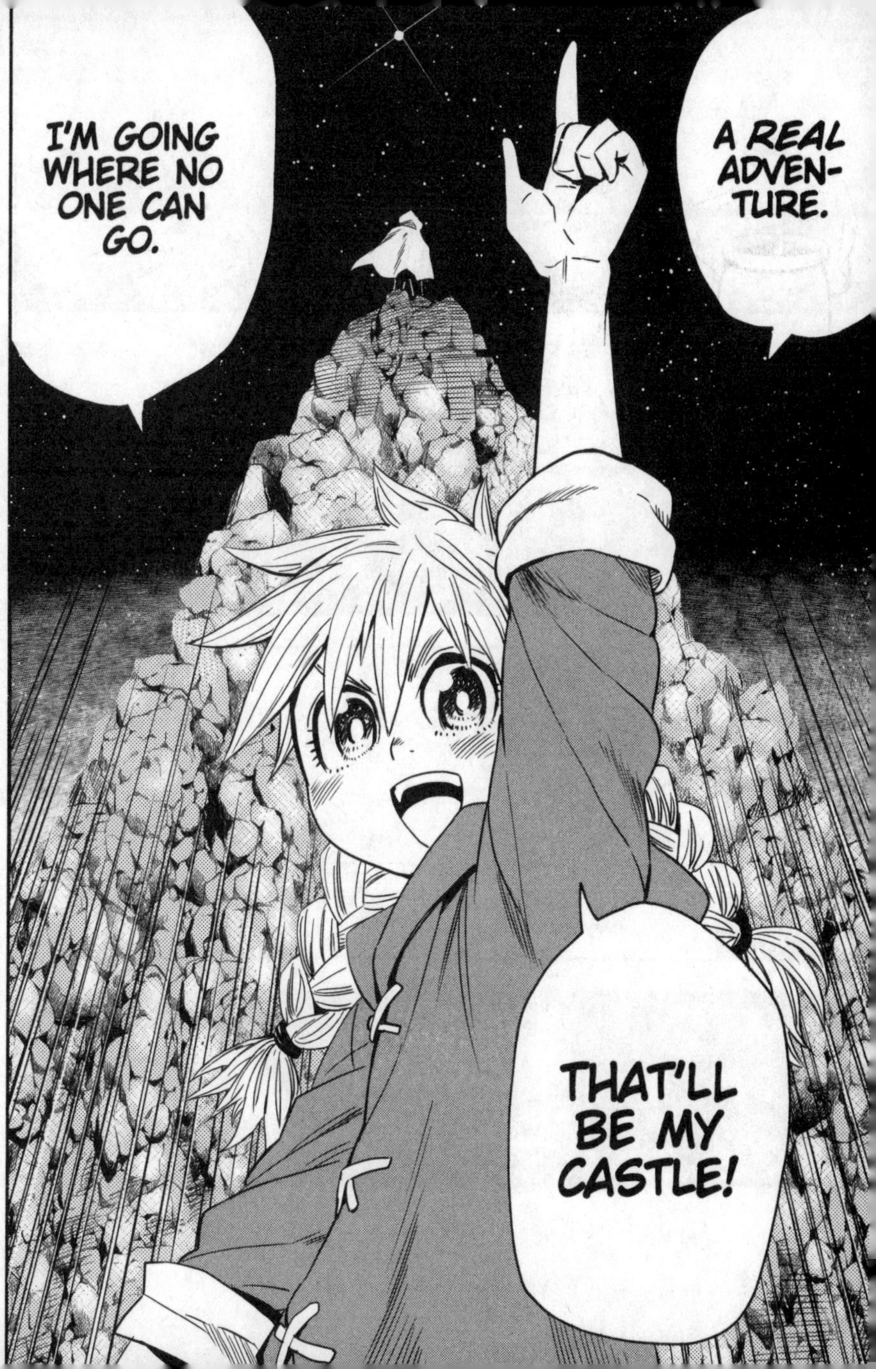
A *REAL* ADVEN-TURE.
I'M GOING WHERE NO ONE CAN GO.
THAT'LL BE MY CASTLE!

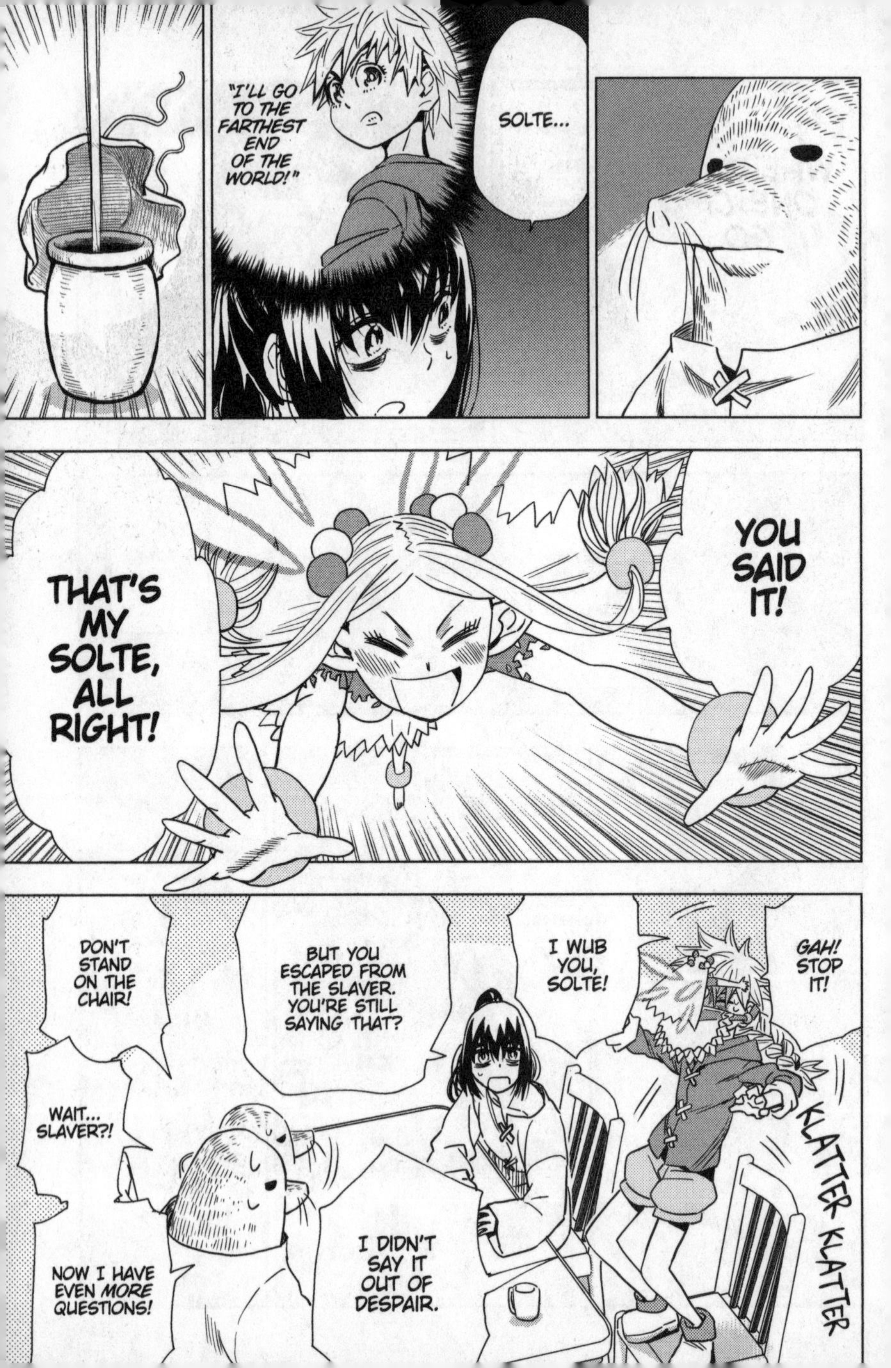
SOLTE...
"I'LL GO TO THE FARTHEST END OF THE WORLD!"
YOU SAID IT!
THAT'S MY SOLTE, ALL RIGHT!
GAH! STOP IT!
I WUB YOU, SOLTE!
KLATTER KLATTER
BUT YOU ESCAPED FROM THE SLAVER. YOU'RE STILL SAYING THAT?
DON'T STAND ON THE CHAIR!
WAIT... SLAVER?!
I DIDN'T SAY IT OUT OF DESPAIR.
NOW I HAVE EVEN *MORE* QUESTIONS!

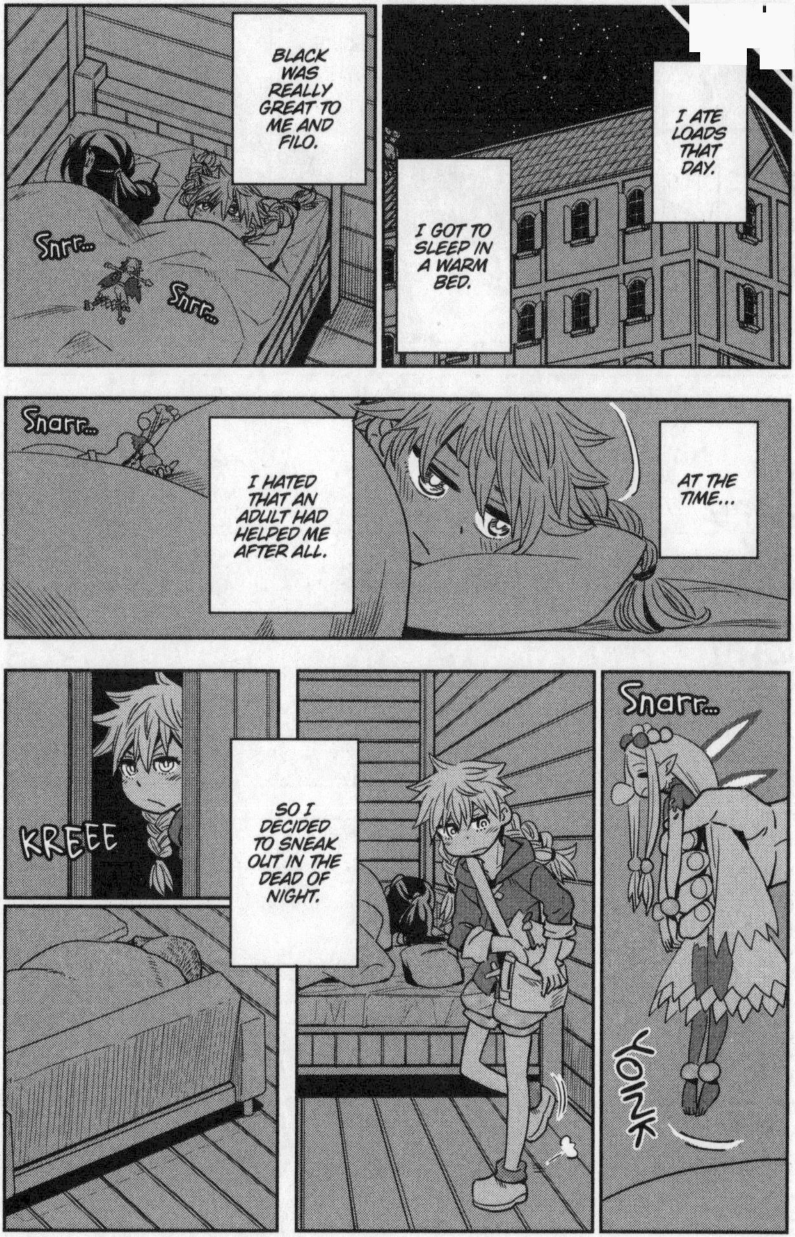
I ATE LOADS THAT DAY.
I GOT TO SLEEP IN A WARM BED.
BLACK WAS REALLY GREAT TO ME AND FILO.
Snrr...
Snrr...
AT THE TIME...
I HATED THAT AN ADULT HAD HELPED ME AFTER ALL.
Snarr...
Snarr...
YOINK
SO I DECIDED TO SNEAK OUT IN THE DEAD OF NIGHT.
KREEE

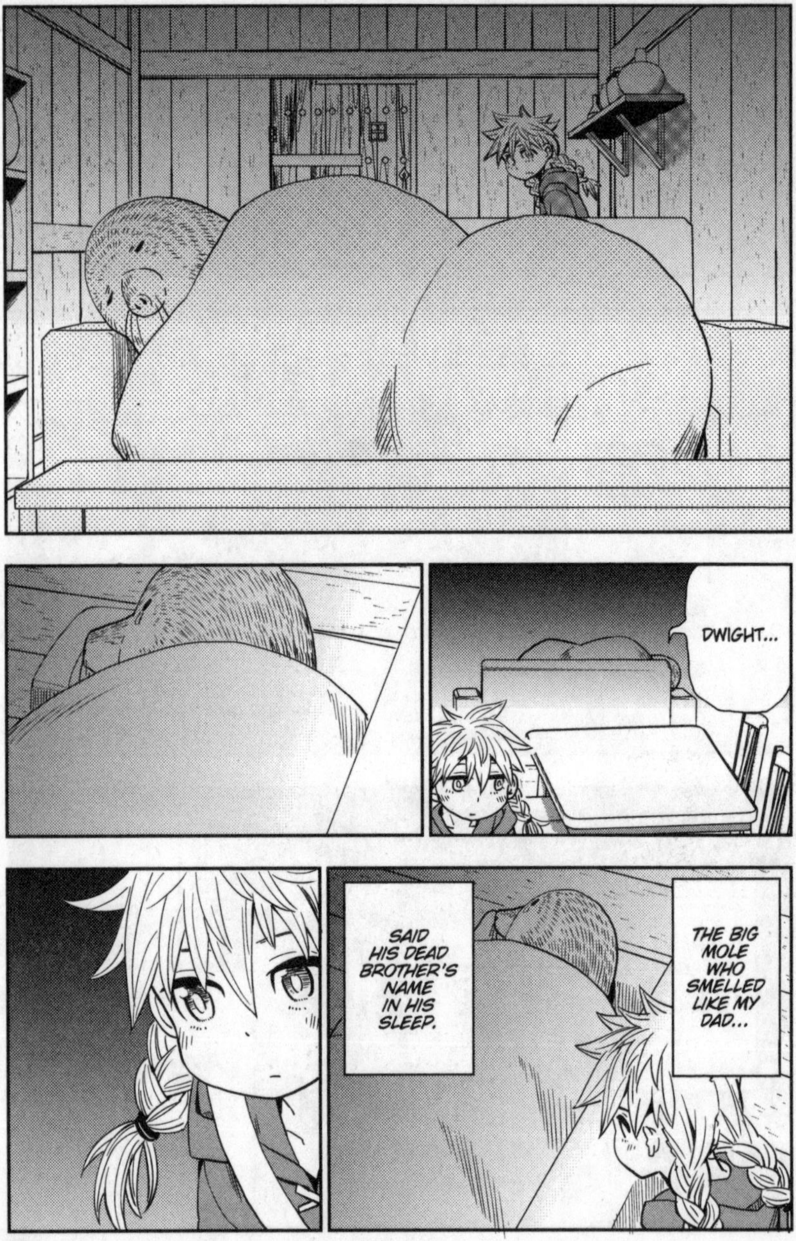
DWIGHT...
THE BIG MOLE WHO SMELLED LIKE MY DAD...
SAID HIS DEAD BROTHER'S NAME IN HIS SLEEP.

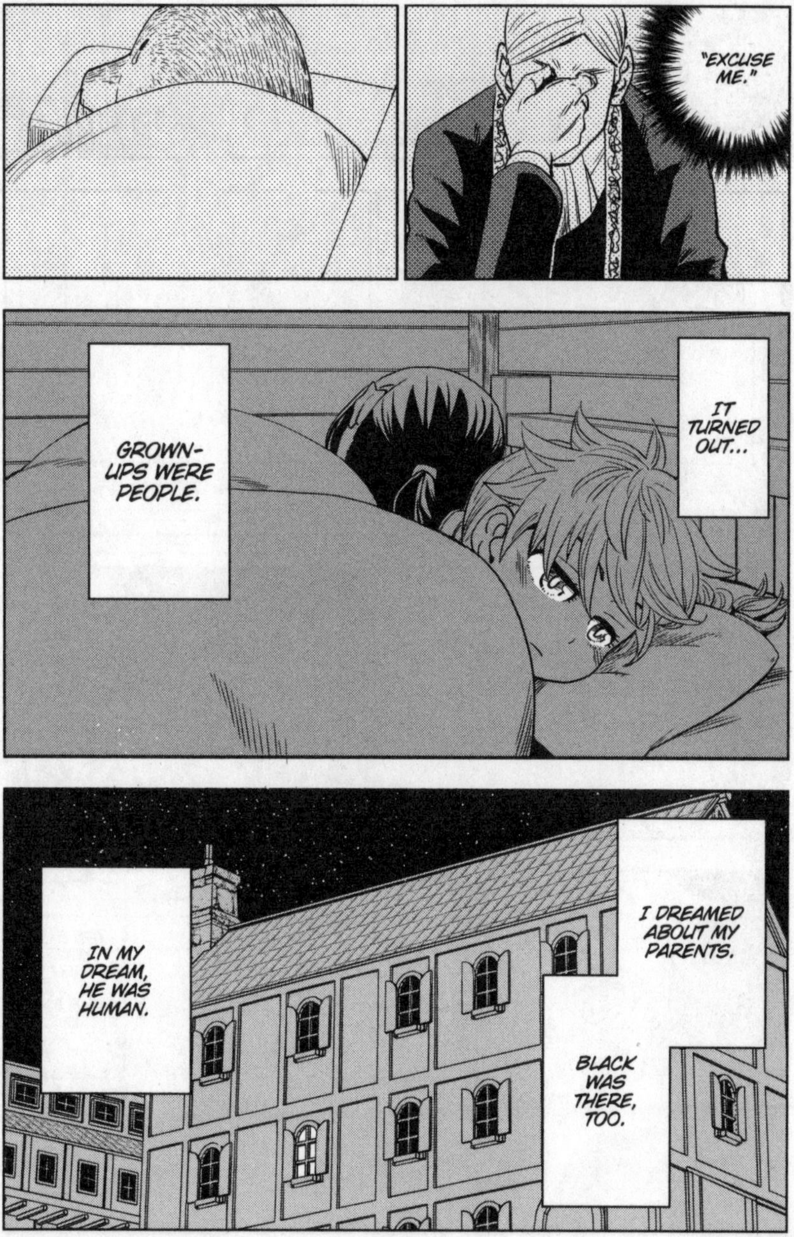
"EXCUSE ME."
IT TURNED OUT...
GROWN-UPS WERE PEOPLE.
I DREAMED ABOUT MY PARENTS.
BLACK WAS THERE, TOO.
IN MY DREAM, HE WAS HUMAN.

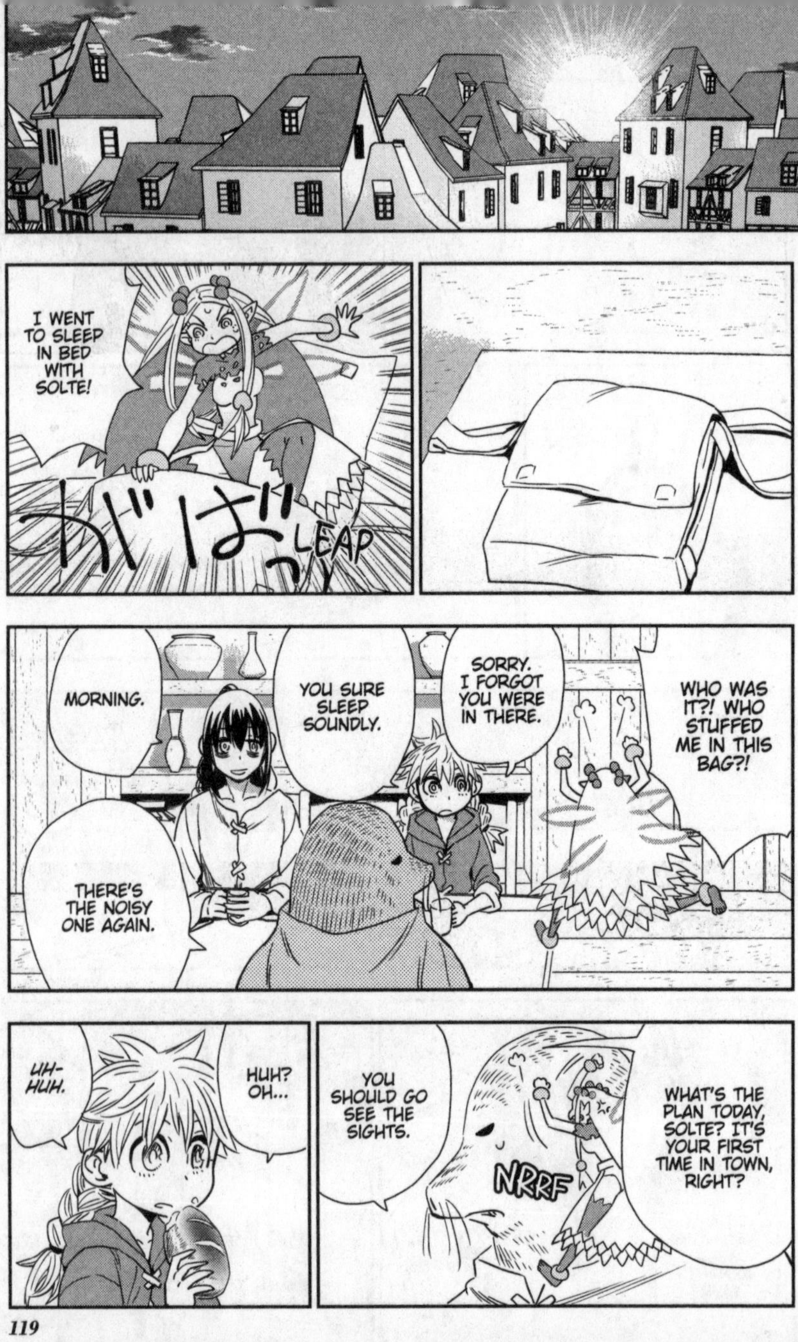
I WENT TO SLEEP IN BED WITH SOLTE!
LEAP
WHO WAS IT?! WHO STUFFED ME IN THIS BAG?!
SORRY. I FORGOT YOU WERE IN THERE.
YOU SURE SLEEP SOUNDLY.
MORNING.
THERE'S THE NOISY ONE AGAIN.
WHAT'S THE PLAN TODAY, SOLTE? IT'S YOUR FIRST TIME IN TOWN, RIGHT?
NRRF
YOU SHOULD GO SEE THE SIGHTS.
HUH? OH...
UH-HUH.

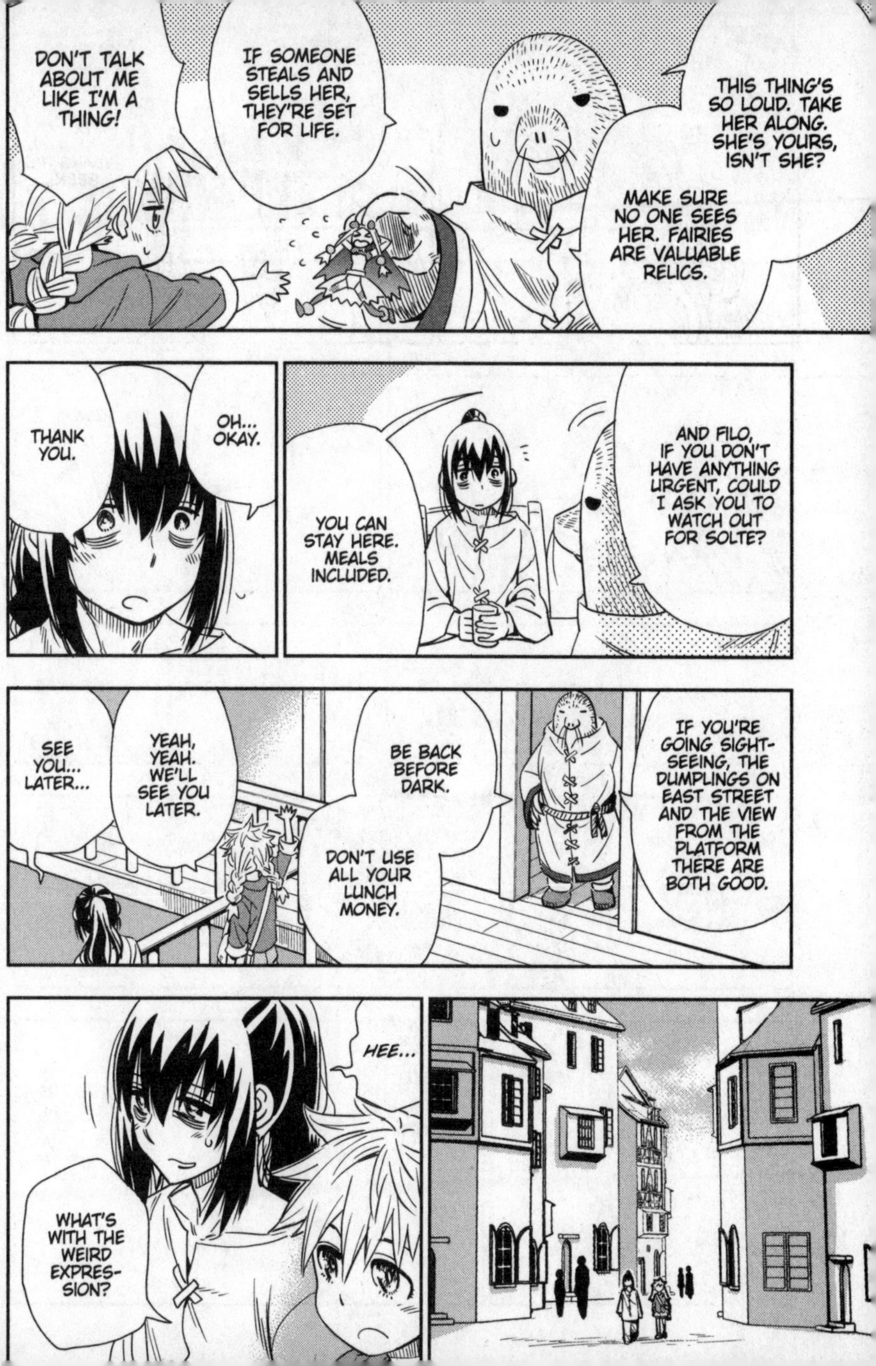
THIS THING'S SO LOUD. TAKE HER ALONG. SHE'S YOURS, ISN'T SHE?
MAKE SURE NO ONE SEES HER. FAIRIES ARE VALUABLE RELICS.
IF SOMEONE STEALS AND SELLS HER, THEY'RE SET FOR LIFE.
DON'T TALK ABOUT ME LIKE I'M A THING!
AND FILO, IF YOU DON'T HAVE ANYTHING URGENT, COULD I ASK YOU TO WATCH OUT FOR SOLTE?
YOU CAN STAY HERE. MEALS INCLUDED.
OH... OKAY.
THANK YOU.
IF YOU'RE GOING SIGHT-SEEING, THE DUMPLINGS ON EAST STREET AND THE VIEW FROM THE PLATFORM THERE ARE BOTH GOOD.
BE BACK BEFORE DARK.
DON'T USE ALL YOUR LUNCH MONEY.
YEAH, YEAH. WE'LL SEE YOU LATER.
SEE YOU... LATER...
HEE...
WHAT'S WITH THE WEIRD EXPRESSION?

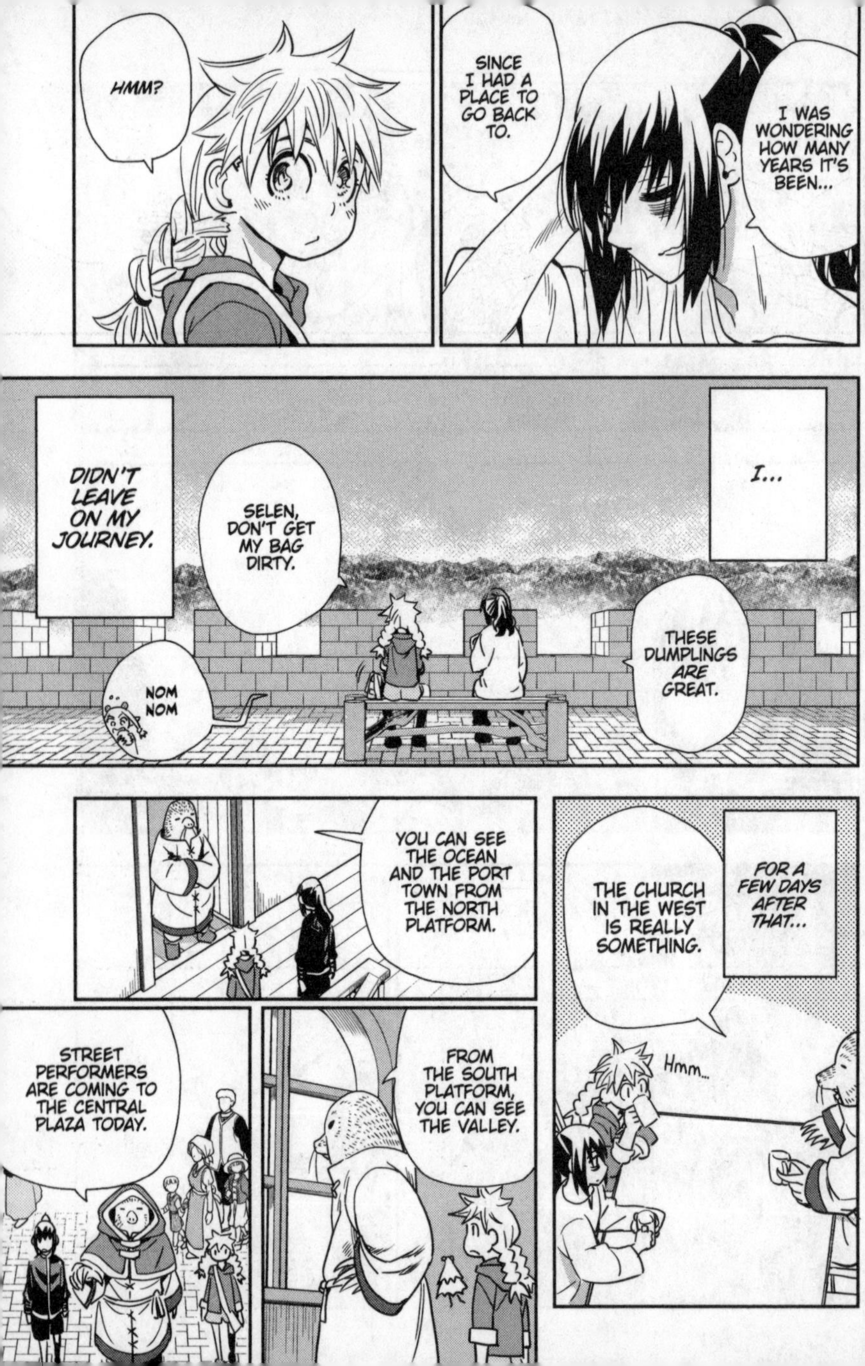
I WAS WONDERING HOW MANY YEARS IT'S BEEN...
SINCE I HAD A PLACE TO GO BACK TO.
HMM?
I...
THESE DUMPLINGS ARE GREAT.
SELEN, DON'T GET MY BAG DIRTY.
DIDN'T LEAVE ON MY JOURNEY.
NOM NOM
FOR A FEW DAYS AFTER THAT...
THE CHURCH IN THE WEST IS REALLY SOMETHING.
Hmm...
YOU CAN SEE THE OCEAN AND THE PORT TOWN FROM THE NORTH PLATFORM.
FROM THE SOUTH PLATFORM, YOU CAN SEE THE VALLEY.
STREET PERFORMERS ARE COMING TO THE CENTRAL PLAZA TODAY.

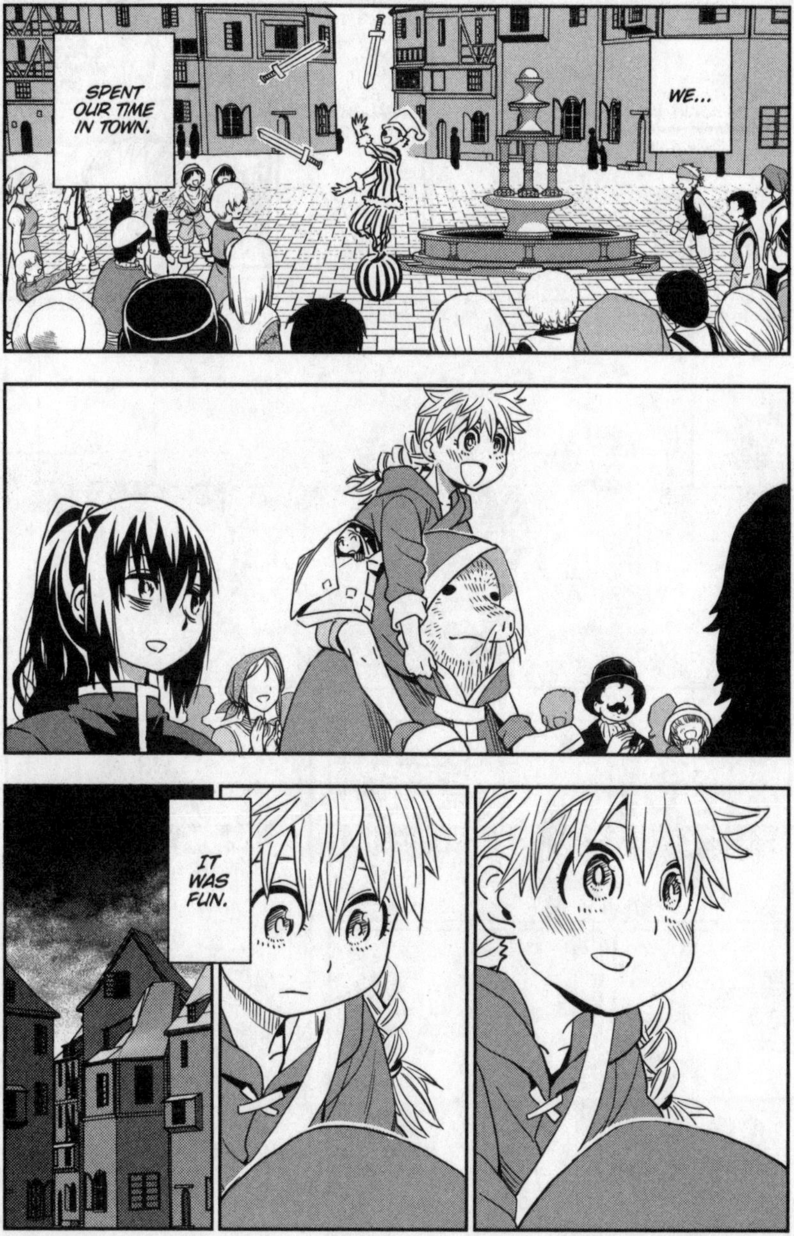
WE...
SPENT OUR TIME IN TOWN.
IT WAS FUN.

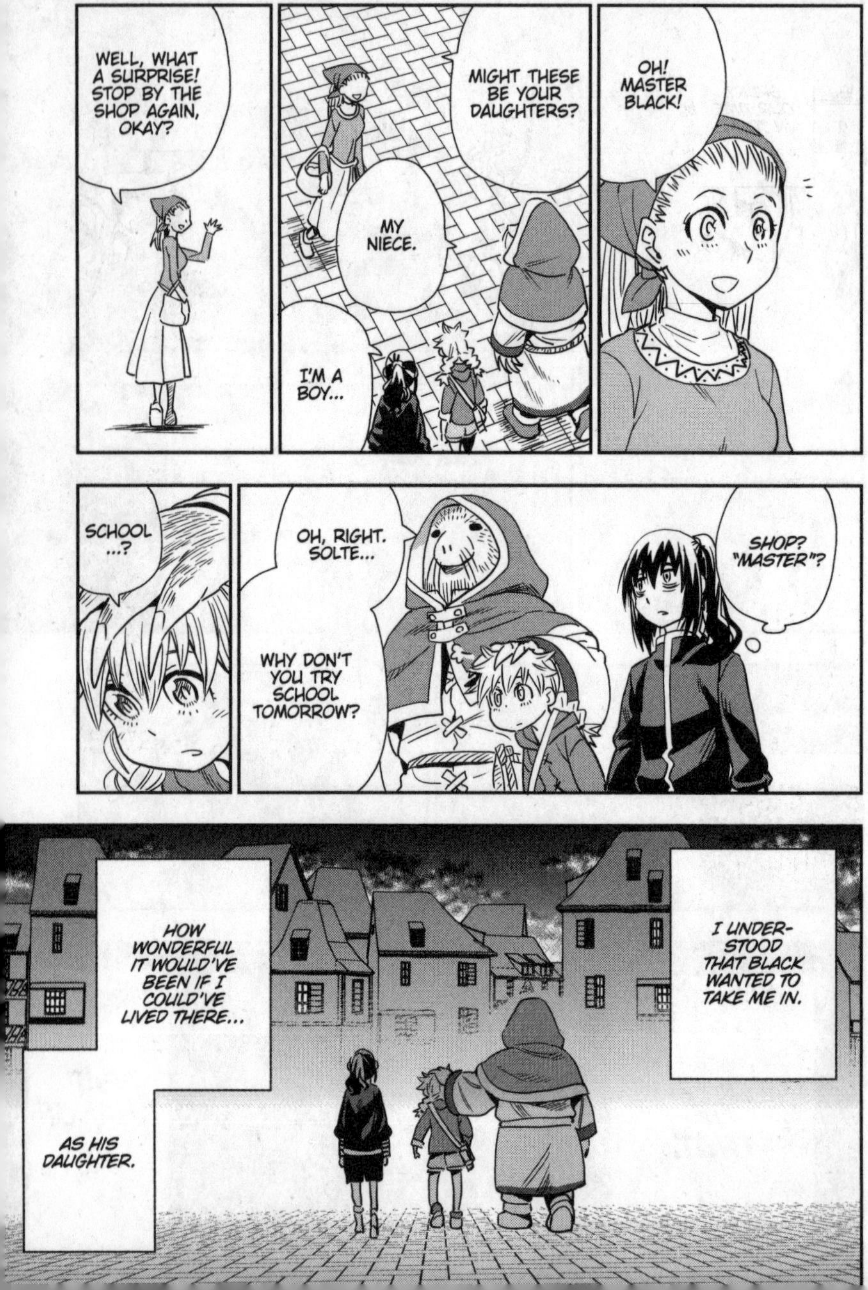
OH! MASTER BLACK!
MIGHT THESE BE YOUR DAUGHTERS?
MY NIECE.
I'M A BOY...
WELL, WHAT A SURPRISE! STOP BY THE SHOP AGAIN, OKAY?
SHOP? "MASTER"?
OH, RIGHT. SOLTE...
WHY DON'T YOU TRY SCHOOL TOMORROW?
SCHOOL ...?
I UNDERSTOOD THAT BLACK WANTED TO TAKE ME IN.
HOW WONDERFUL IT WOULD'VE BEEN IF I COULD'VE LIVED THERE...
AS HIS DAUGHTER.

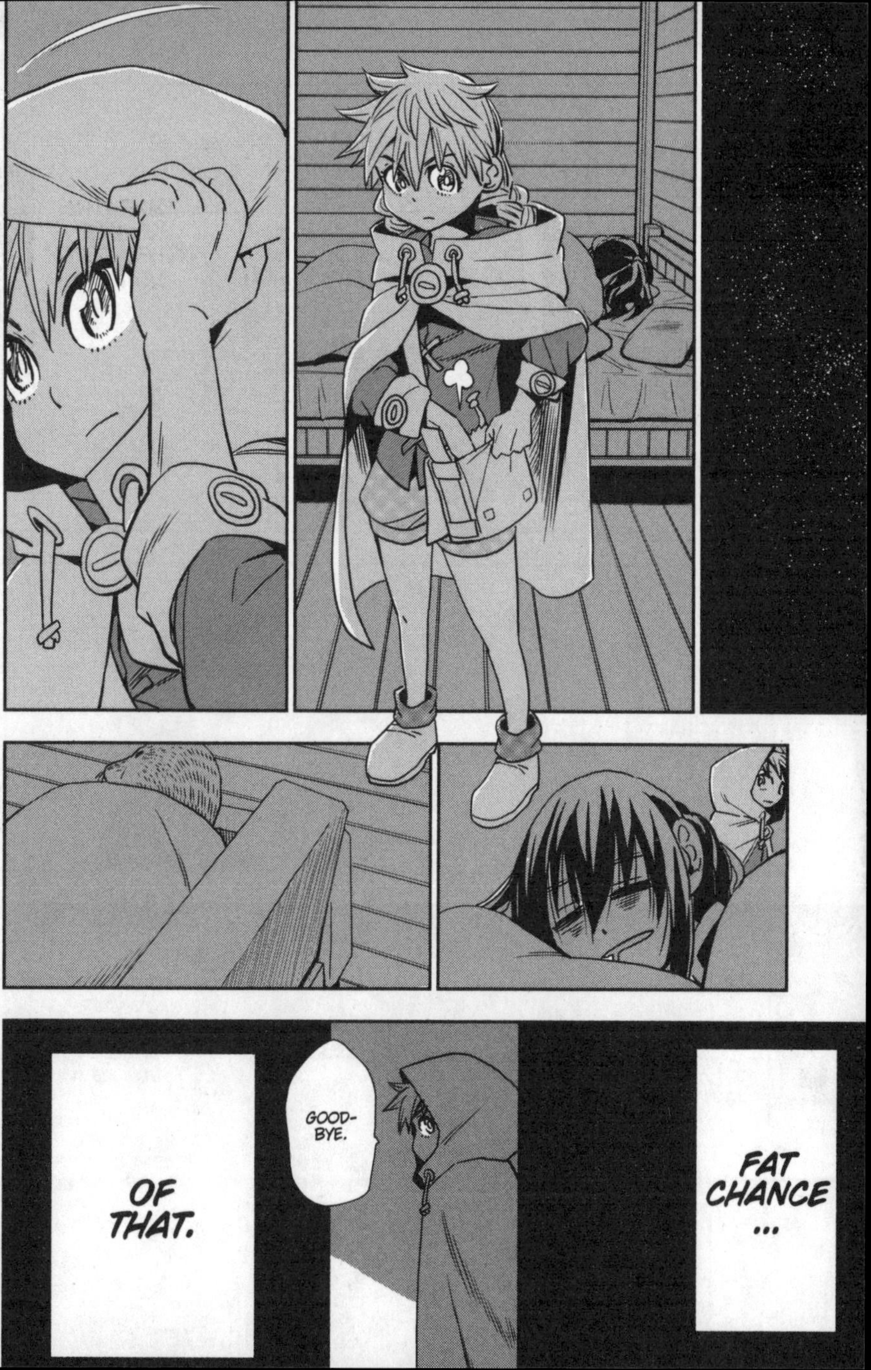
FAT CHANCE ...
GOOD-BYE.
OF THAT.

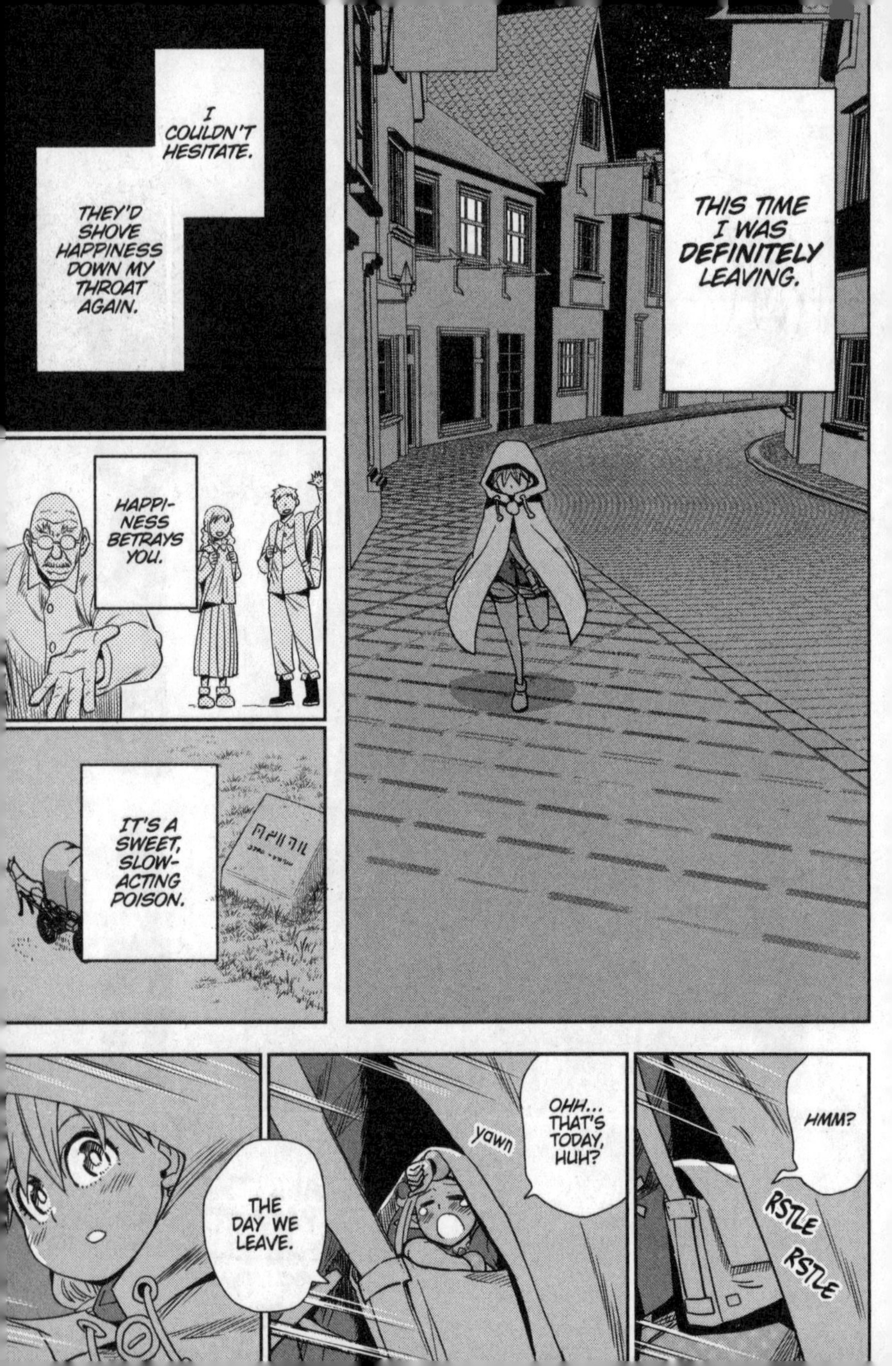
THIS TIME I WAS DEFINITELY LEAVING.
I COULDN'T HESITATE.
THEY'D SHOVE HAPPINESS DOWN MY THROAT AGAIN.
HAPPI-NESS BETRAYS YOU.
IT'S A SWEET, SLOW-ACTING POISON.
HMM?
RSTLE
RSTLE
OHH... THAT'S TODAY, HUH?
yawn
THE DAY WE LEAVE.

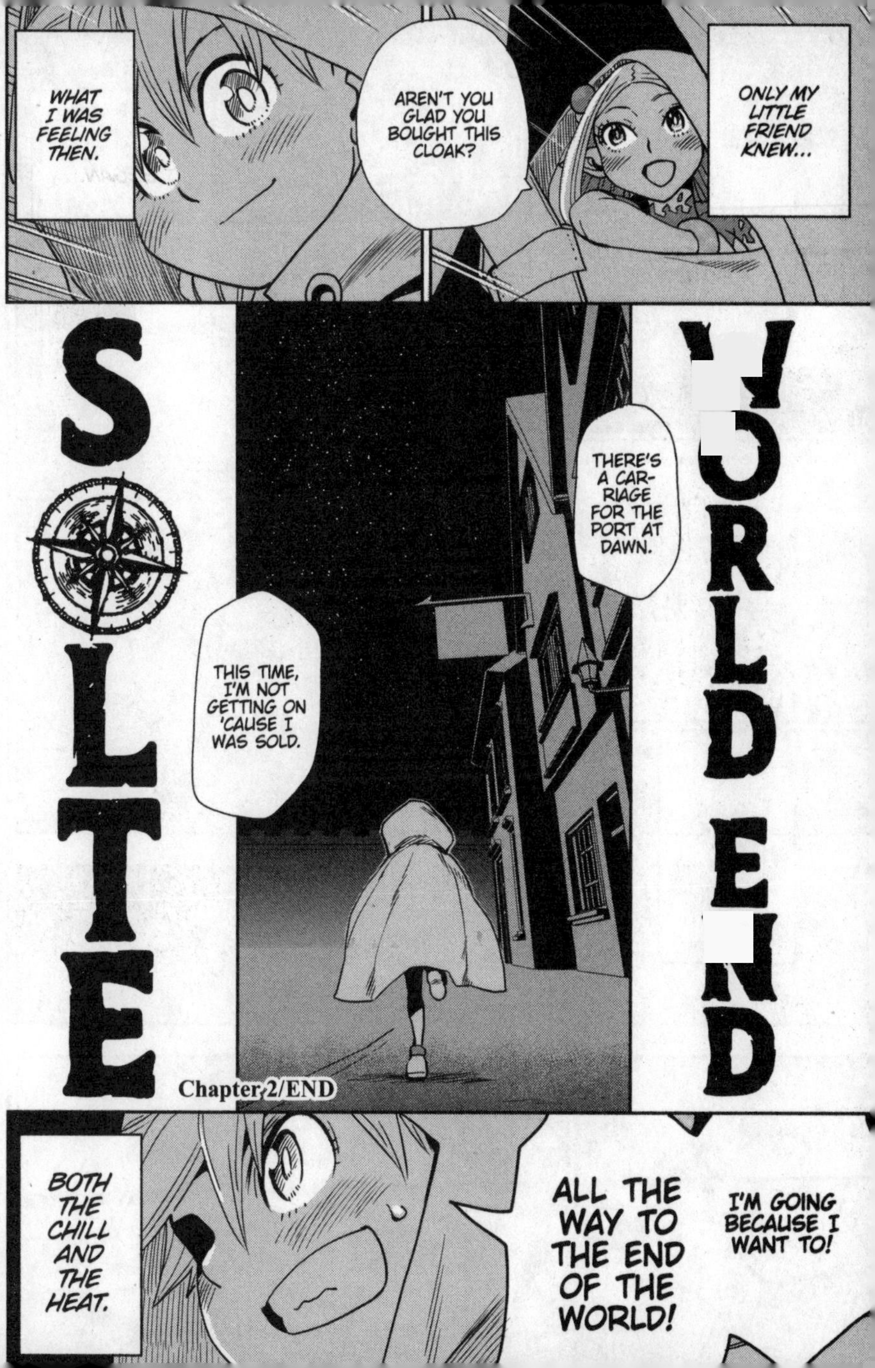
ONLY MY LITTLE FRIEND KNEW...
AREN'T YOU GLAD YOU BOUGHT THIS CLOAK?
WHAT I WAS FEELING THEN.
THERE'S A CAR-RIAGE FOR THE PORT AT DAWN.
THIS TIME, I'M NOT GETTING ON 'CAUSE I WAS SOLD.
SOLTE
Chapter 2/END
I'M GOING BECAUSE I WANT TO!
ALL THE WAY TO THE END OF THE WORLD!
BOTH THE CHILL AND THE HEAT.

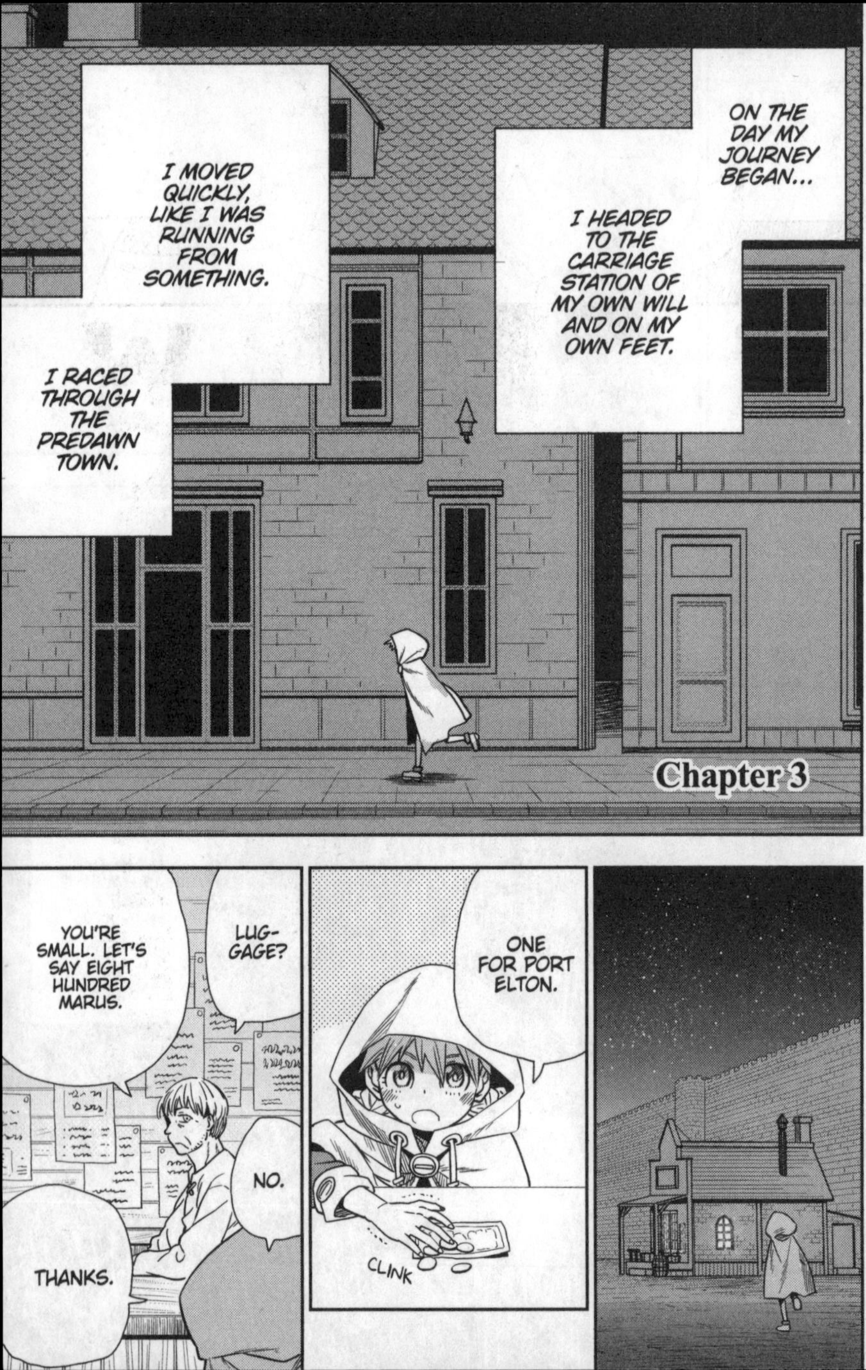
ON THE DAY MY JOURNEY BEGAN...
I HEADED TO THE CARRIAGE STATION OF MY OWN WILL AND ON MY OWN FEET.
I MOVED QUICKLY, LIKE I WAS RUNNING FROM SOMETHING.
I RACED THROUGH THE PREDAWN TOWN.
Chapter 3
ONE FOR PORT ELTON.
CLINK
LUG-GAGE?
YOU'RE SMALL. LET'S SAY EIGHT HUNDRED MARUS.
NO.
THANKS.

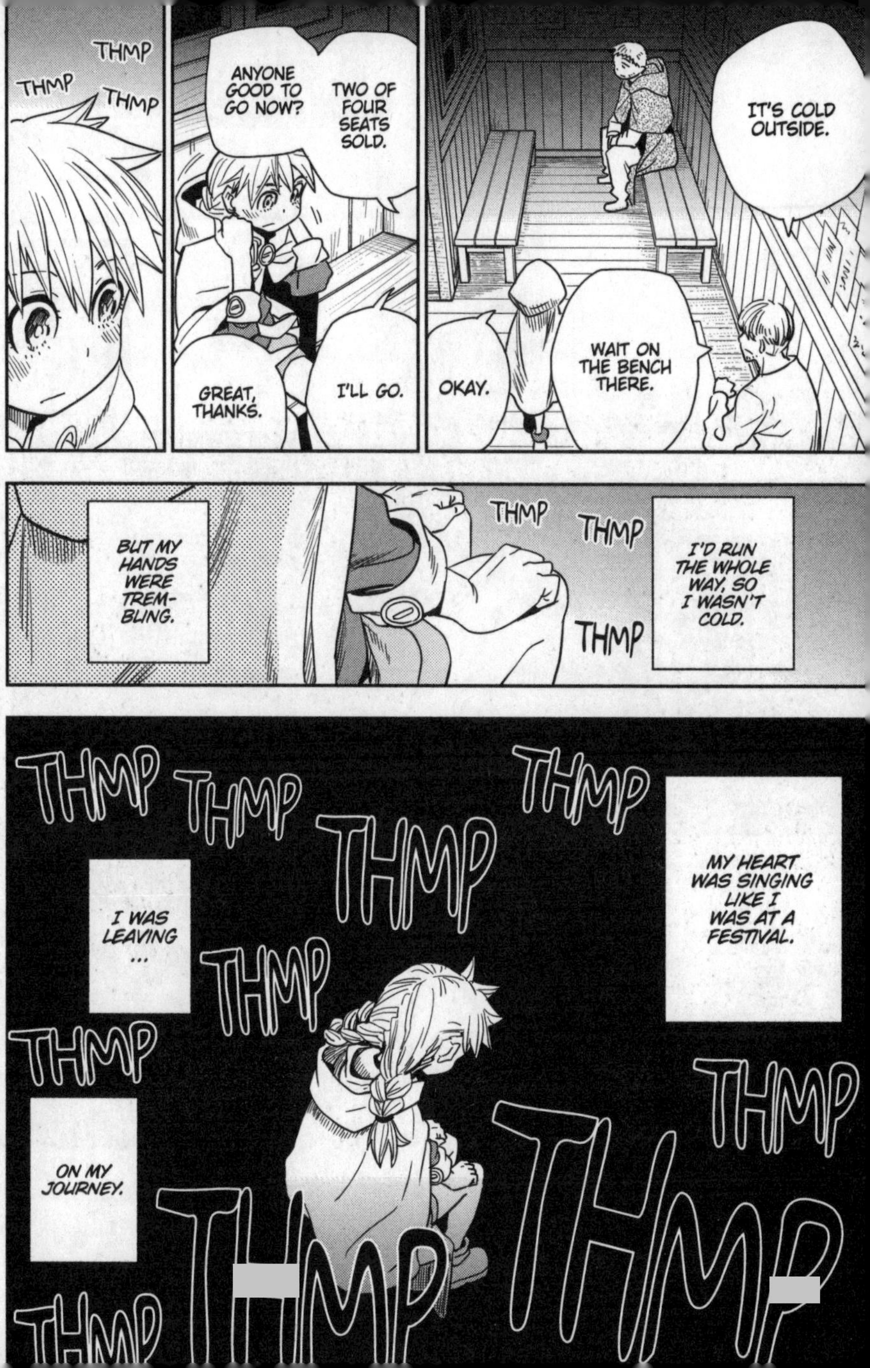
IT'S COLD OUTSIDE.
WAIT ON THE BENCH THERE.
OKAY.
TWO OF FOUR SEATS SOLD.
ANYONE GOOD TO GO NOW?
I'LL GO.
GREAT, THANKS.
THMP
THMP
THMP
I'D RUN THE WHOLE WAY, SO I WASN'T COLD.
THMP
THMP
THMP
BUT MY HANDS WERE TREMBLING.
MY HEART WAS SINGING LIKE I WAS AT A FESTIVAL.
THMP
THMP
THMP
THMP
I WAS LEAVING ...
THMP
THMP
THMP
THMP
ON MY JOURNEY.
THMP

Chapter 3: Fiends

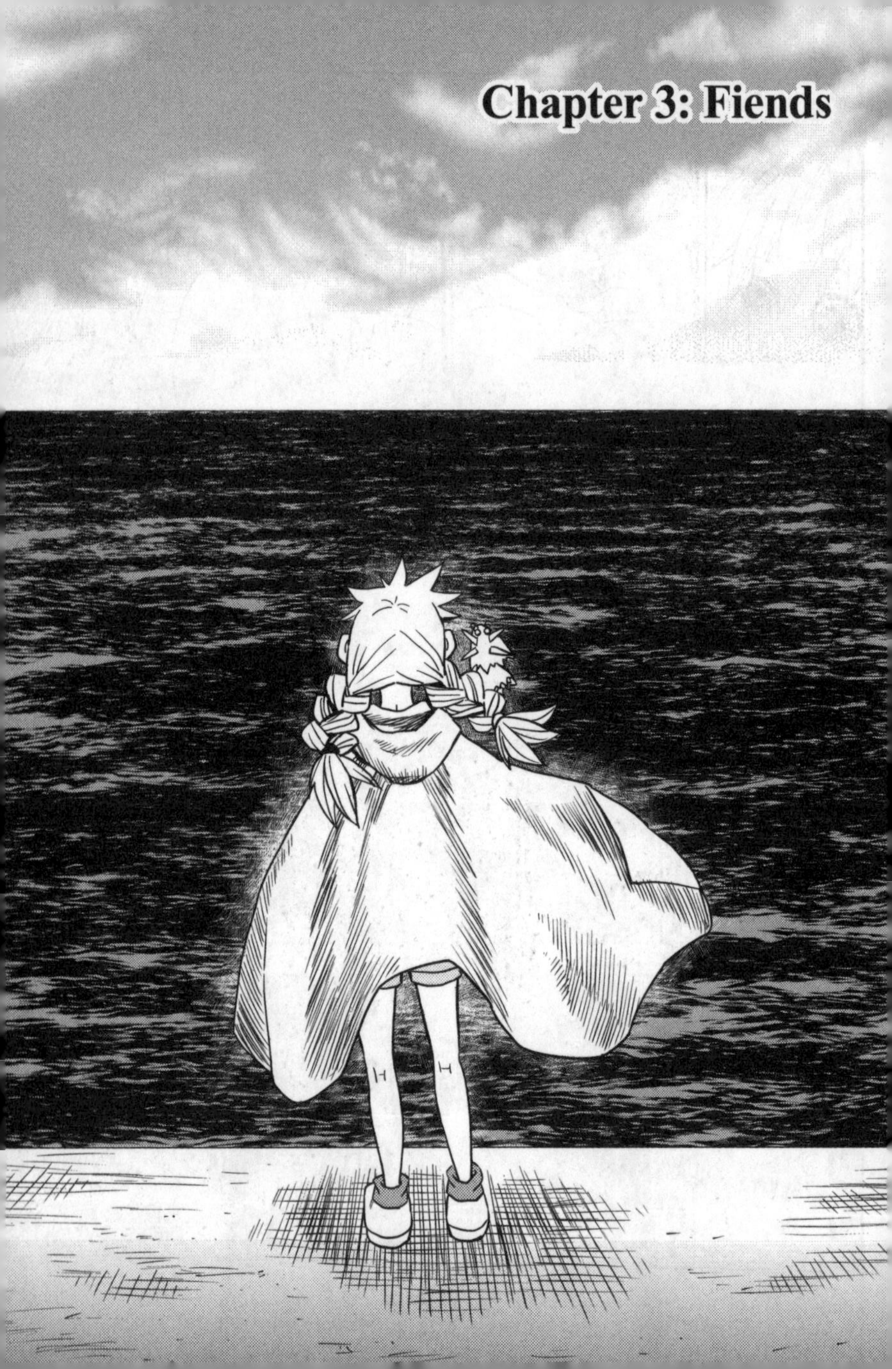

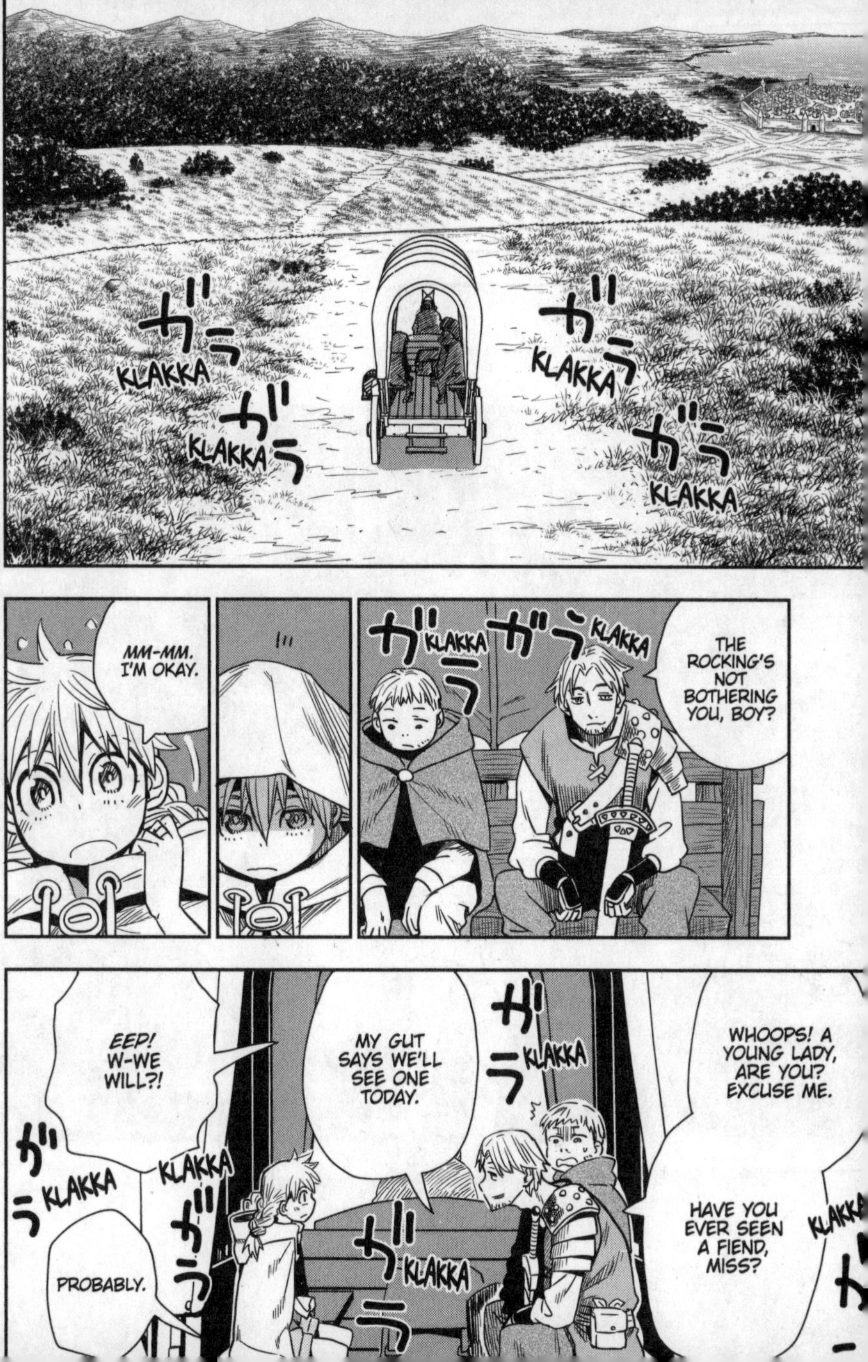
ガラ
KLAKKA
ガラ
KLAKKA
ガラ
KLAKKA
ガラ
KLAKKA
ガラ
KLAKKA
ガラ
KLAKKA
THE ROCKING'S NOT BOTHERING YOU, BOY?
MM-MM. I'M OKAY.
WHOOPS! A YOUNG LADY, ARE YOU? EXCUSE ME.
HAVE YOU EVER SEEN A FIEND, MISS?
KLAKKA
ガラ
KLAKKA
MY GUT SAYS WE'LL SEE ONE TODAY.
ガラ
KLAKKA
EEP! W-WE WILL?!
PROBABLY.
KLAKKA
ガラ
ガラ
KLAKKA

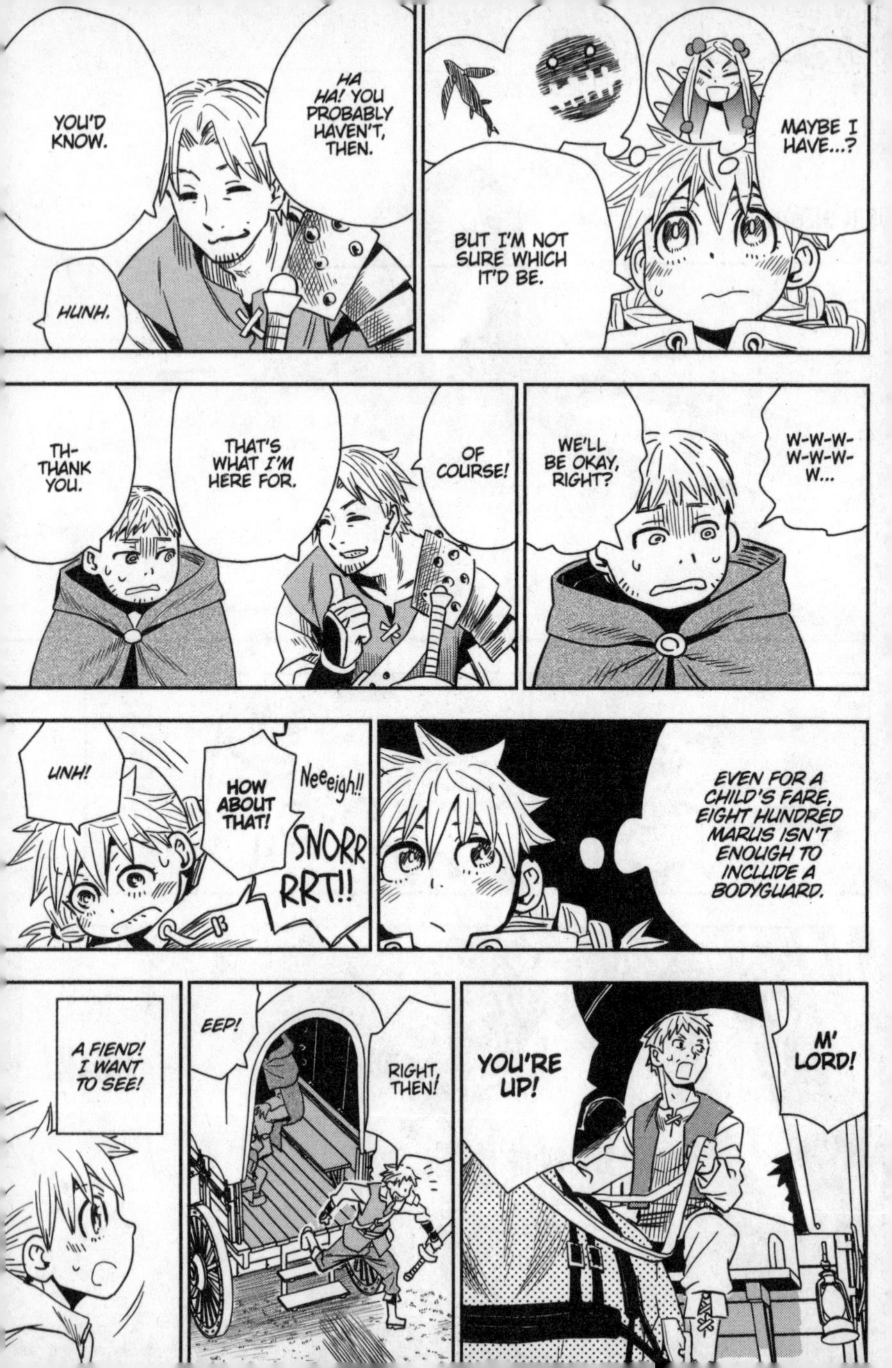
MAYBE I HAVE...?
BUT I'M NOT SURE WHICH IT'D BE.
HA HA! YOU PROBABLY HAVEN'T, THEN.
YOU'D KNOW.
HUNH.
W-W-W-W-W-W-W...
WE'LL BE OKAY, RIGHT?
OF COURSE!
THAT'S WHAT I'M HERE FOR.
TH-THANK YOU.
EVEN FOR A CHILD'S FARE, EIGHT HUNDRED MARUS ISN'T ENOUGH TO INCLUDE A BODYGUARD.
Neeeigh!!
SNORRRRT!!
HOW ABOUT THAT!
UNH!
M' LORD!
YOU'RE UP!
RIGHT, THEN!
EEP!
A FIEND! I WANT TO SEE!

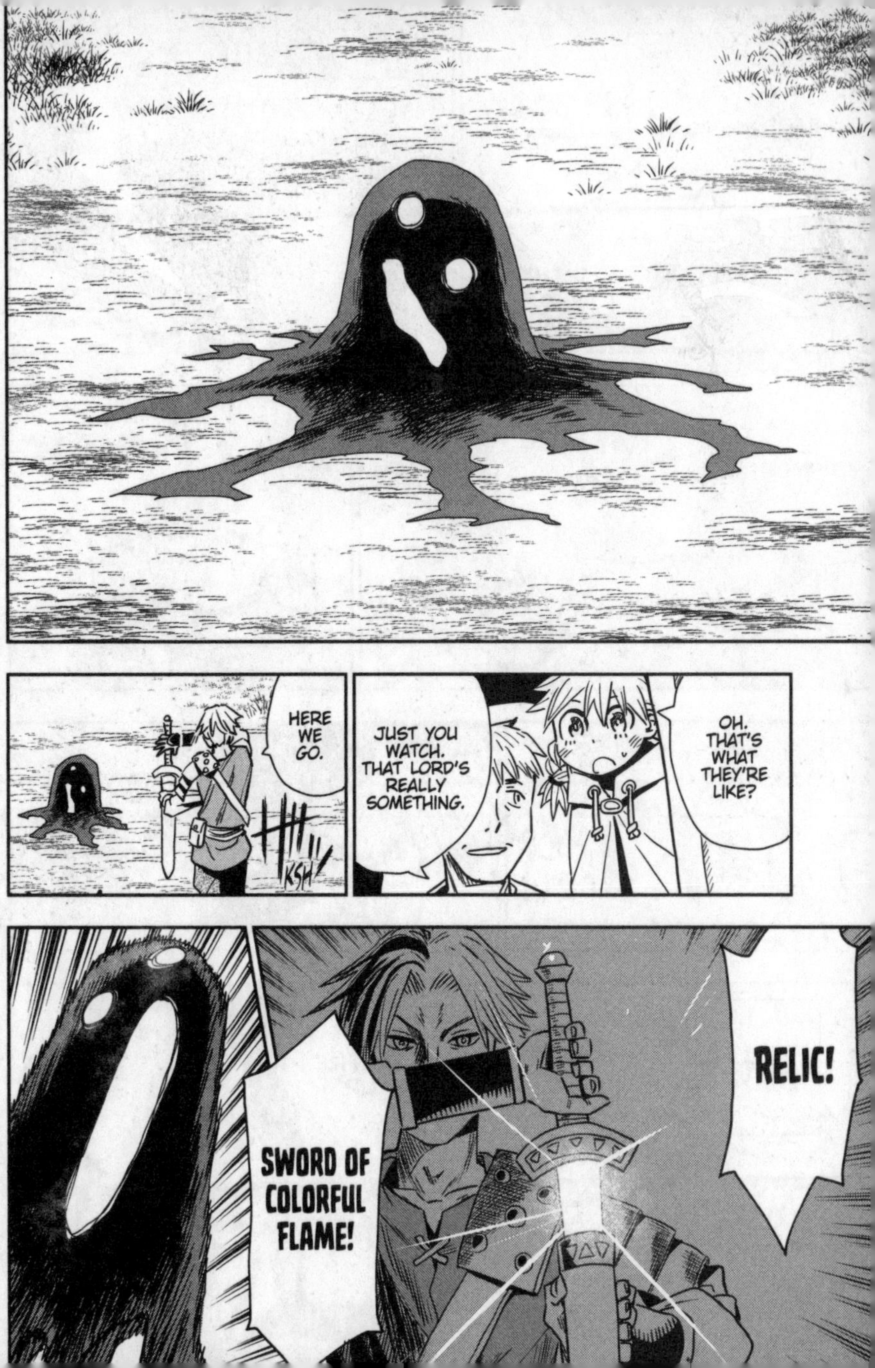
OH. THAT'S WHAT THEY'RE LIKE?
JUST YOU WATCH. THAT LORD'S REALLY SOMETHING.
HERE WE GO.
KSH
RELIC!
SWORD OF COLORFUL FLAME!

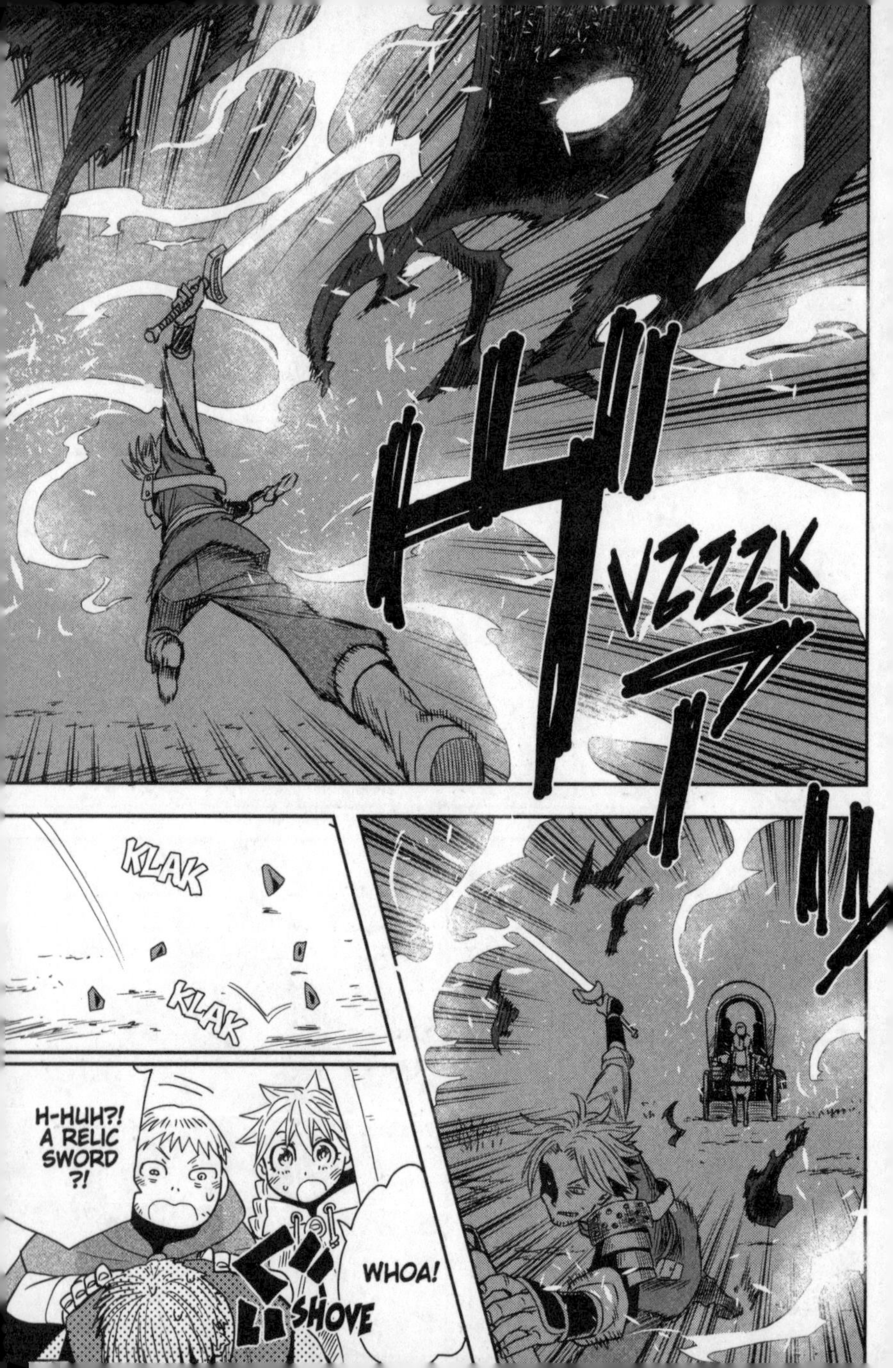
VZZZK
KLAK
KLAK
H-HUH?! A RELIC SWORD ?!
WHOA!
SHOVE

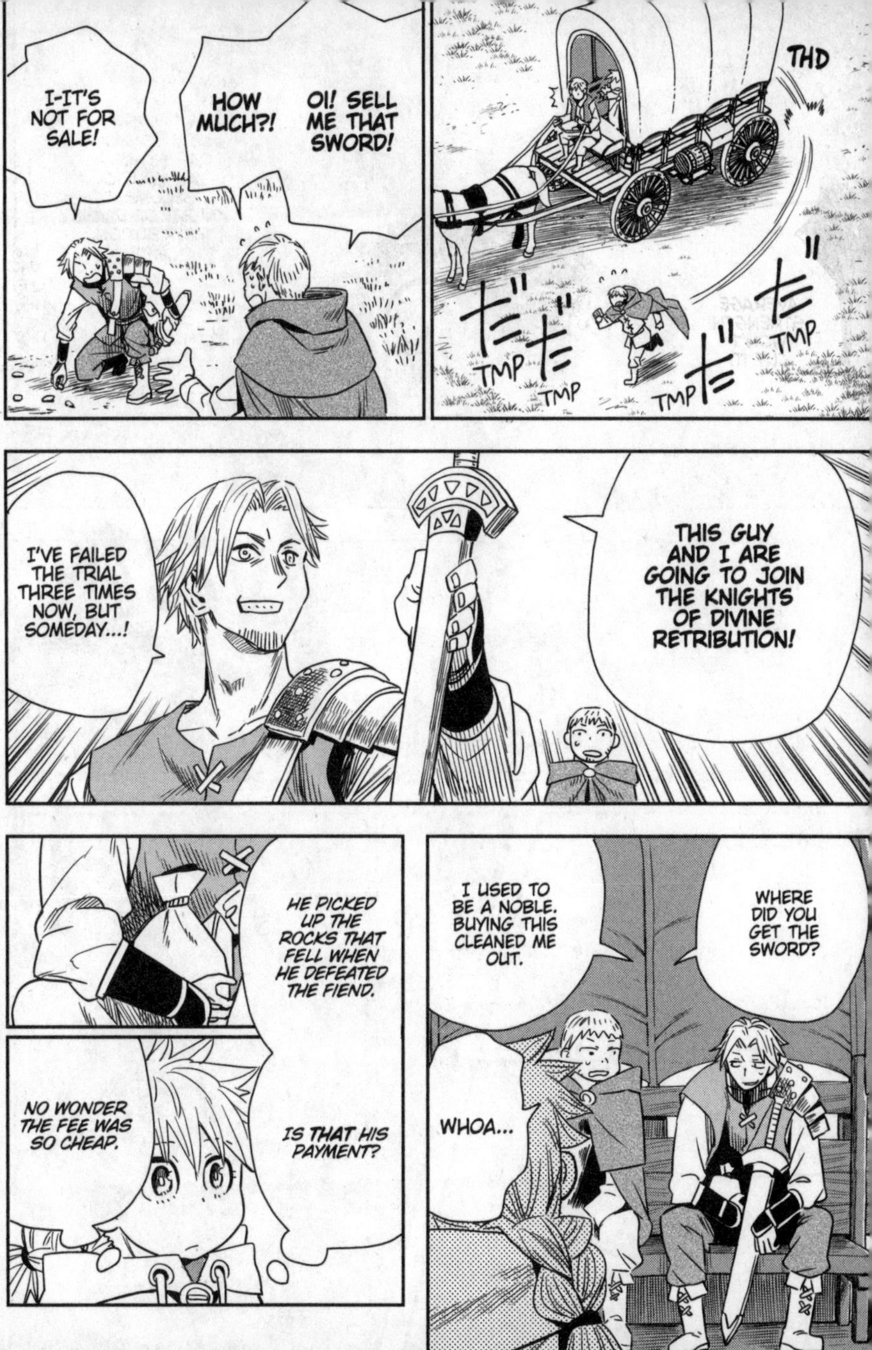
THD
TMP
TMP
TMP
TMP
OI! SELL ME THAT SWORD!
HOW MUCH?!
I-IT'S NOT FOR SALE!
THIS GUY AND I ARE GOING TO JOIN THE KNIGHTS OF DIVINE RETRIBUTION!
I'VE FAILED THE TRIAL THREE TIMES NOW, BUT SOMEDAY...!
WHERE DID YOU GET THE SWORD?
I USED TO BE A NOBLE. BUYING THIS CLEANED ME OUT.
WHOA...
HE PICKED UP THE ROCKS THAT FELL WHEN HE DEFEATED THE FIEND.
IS THAT HIS PAYMENT?
NO WONDER THE FEE WAS SO CHEAP.

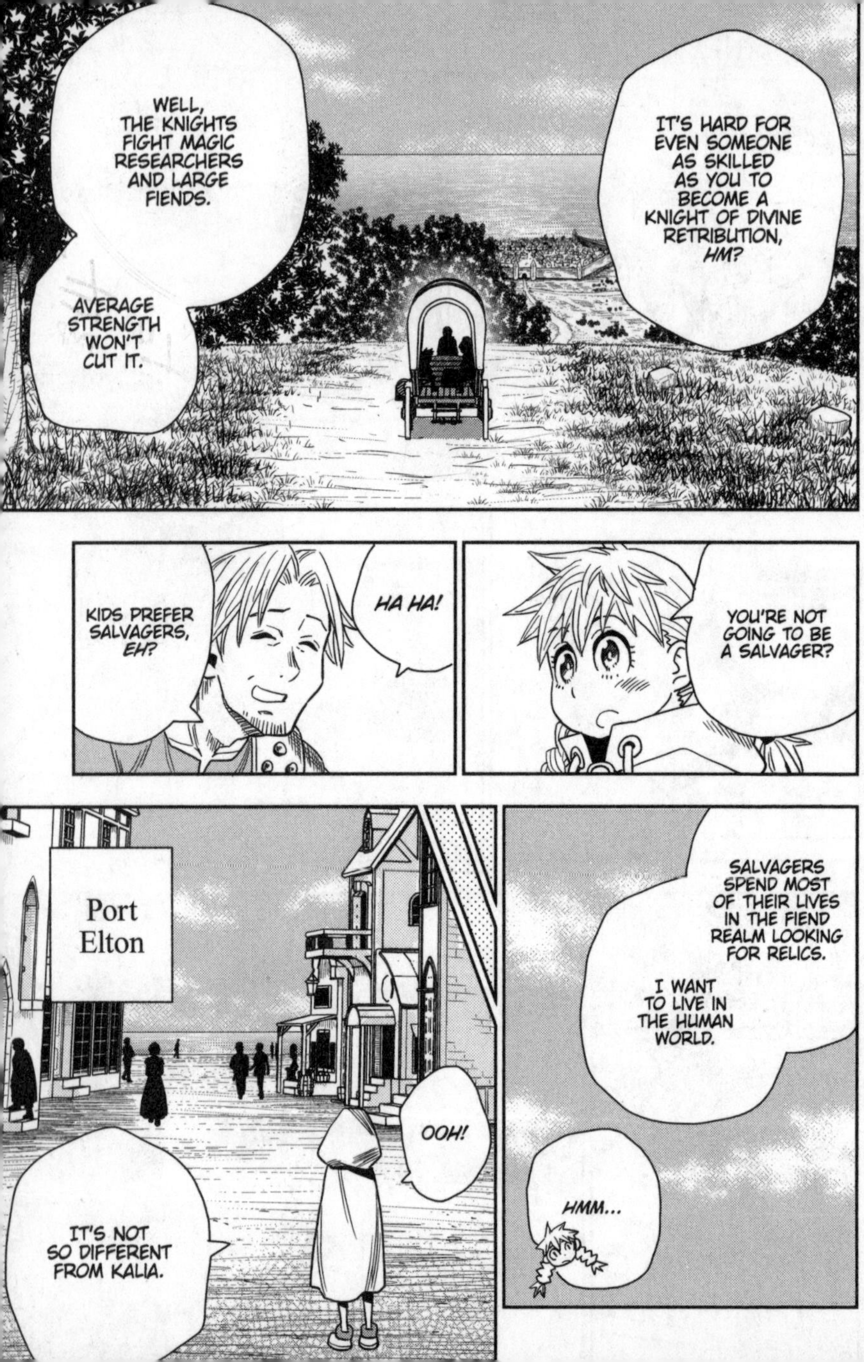
IT'S HARD FOR EVEN SOMEONE AS SKILLED AS YOU TO BECOME A KNIGHT OF DIVINE RETRIBUTION, *HM?*
WELL, THE KNIGHTS FIGHT MAGIC RESEARCHERS AND LARGE FIENDS.
AVERAGE STRENGTH WON'T CUT IT.
YOU'RE NOT GOING TO BE A SALVAGER?
HA HA!
KIDS PREFER SALVAGERS, *EH?*
SALVAGERS SPEND MOST OF THEIR LIVES IN THE FIEND REALM LOOKING FOR RELICS.
I WANT TO LIVE IN THE HUMAN WORLD.
HMM...
Port Elton
OOH!
IT'S NOT SO DIFFERENT FROM KALIA.

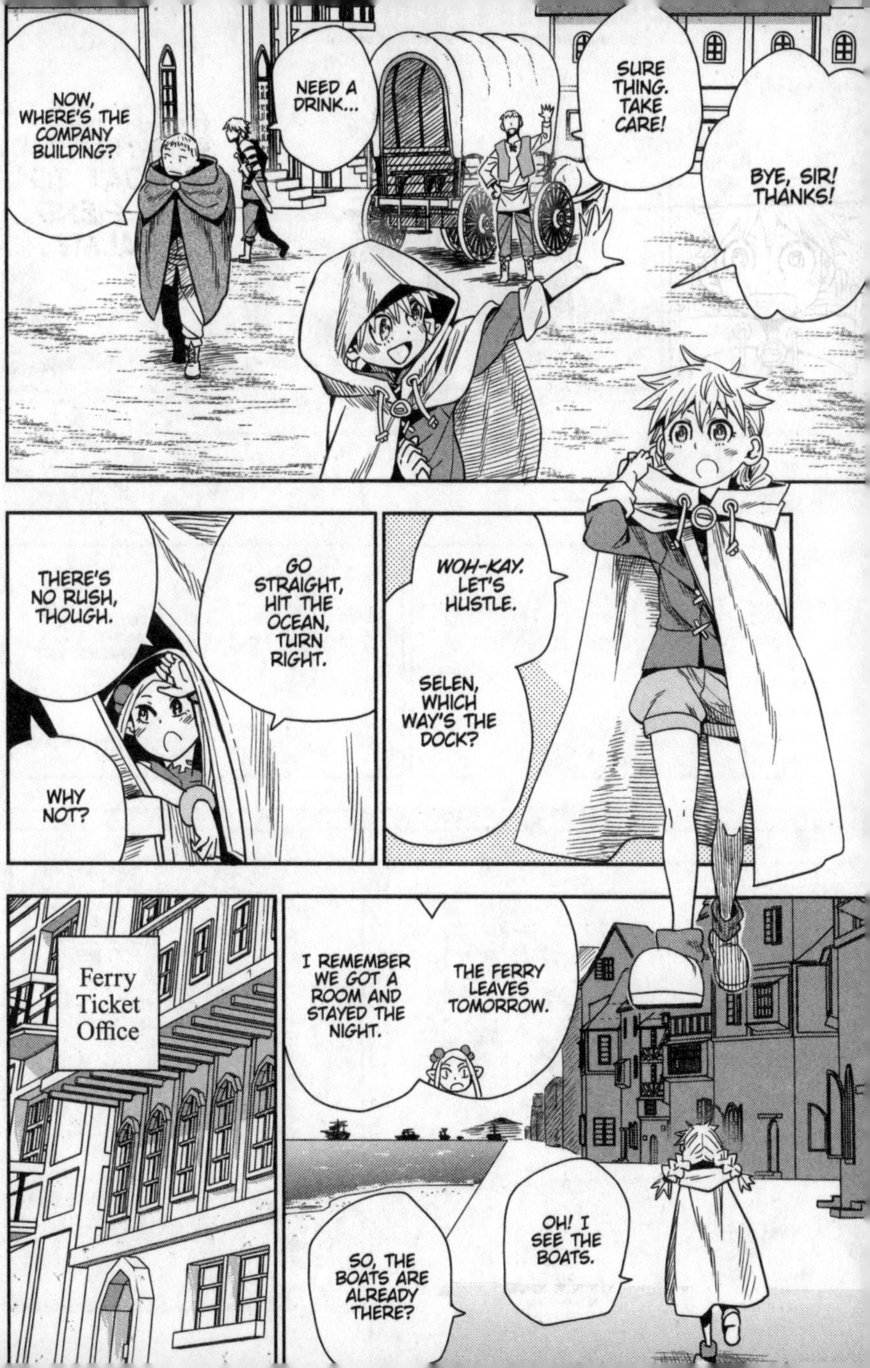
BYE, SIR! THANKS!
SURE THING. TAKE CARE!
NEED A DRINK...
NOW, WHERE'S THE COMPANY BUILDING?
WOH-KAY. LET'S HUSTLE.
SELEN, WHICH WAY'S THE DOCK?
GO STRAIGHT, HIT THE OCEAN, TURN RIGHT.
THERE'S NO RUSH, THOUGH.
WHY NOT?
THE FERRY LEAVES TOMORROW.
I REMEMBER WE GOT A ROOM AND STAYED THE NIGHT.
OH! I SEE THE BOATS.
SO, THE BOATS ARE ALREADY THERE?
Ferry Ticket Office

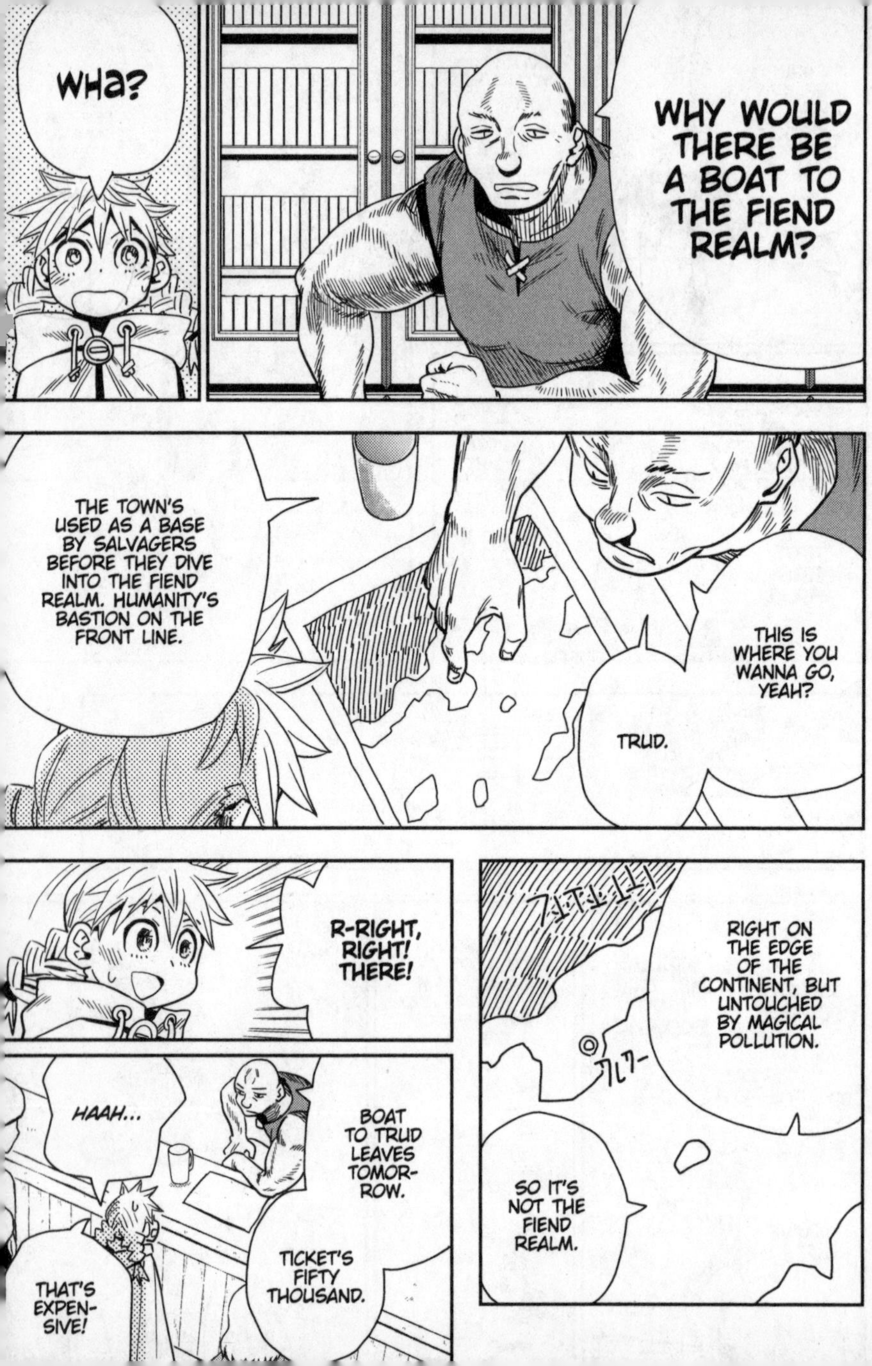
WHY WOULD THERE BE A BOAT TO THE FIEND REALM?
WHA?
THIS IS WHERE YOU WANNA GO, YEAH?
TRUD.
THE TOWN'S USED AS A BASE BY SALVAGERS BEFORE THEY DIVE INTO THE FIEND REALM. HUMANITY'S BASTION ON THE FRONT LINE.
RIGHT ON THE EDGE OF THE CONTINENT, BUT UNTOUCHED BY MAGICAL POLLUTION.
SO IT'S NOT THE FIEND REALM.
R-RIGHT, RIGHT! THERE!
BOAT TO TRUD LEAVES TOMORROW.
TICKET'S FIFTY THOUSAND.
HAAH...
THAT'S EXPENSIVE!

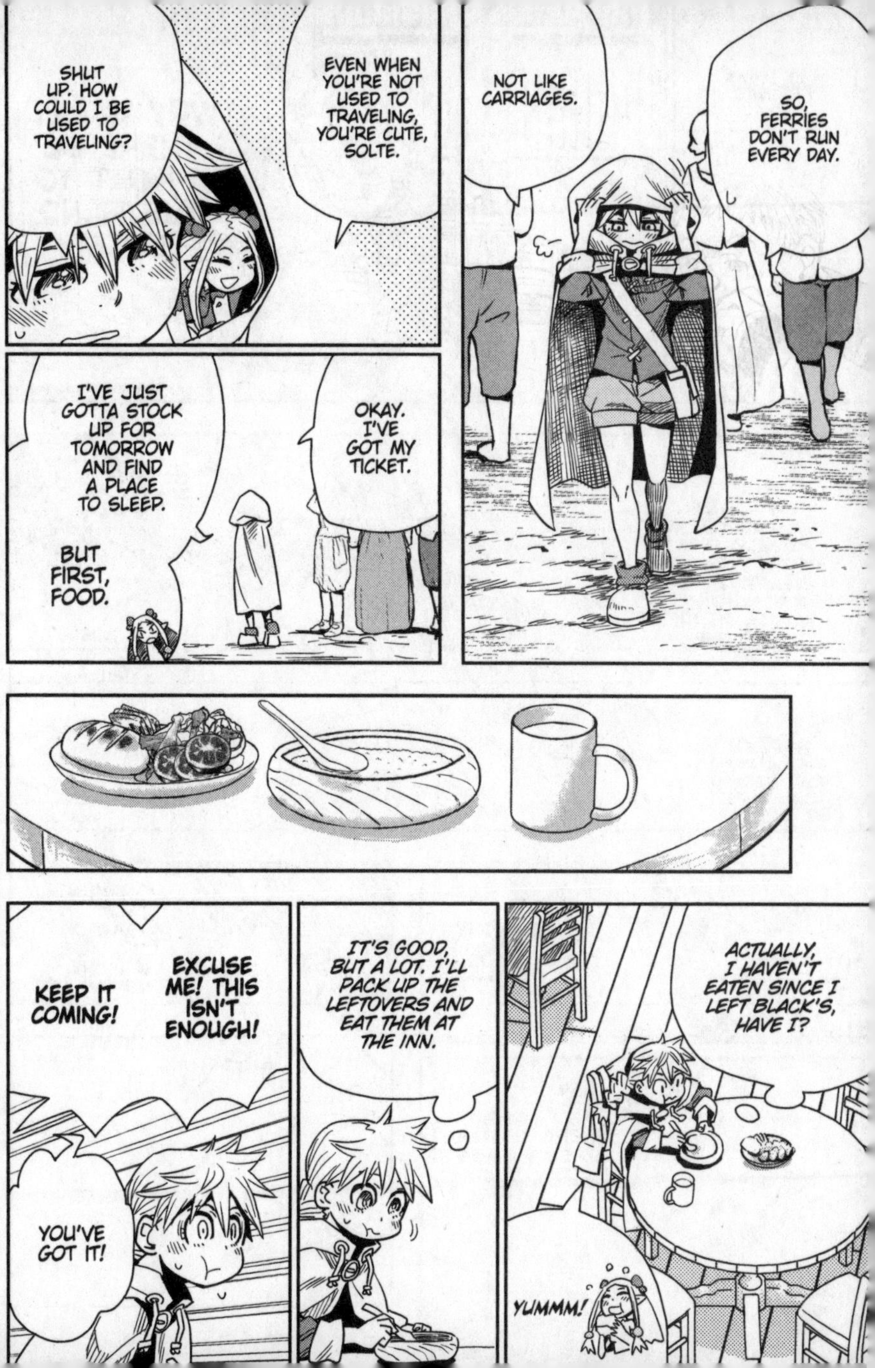
SO, FERRIES DON'T RUN EVERY DAY.
NOT LIKE CARRIAGES.
EVEN WHEN YOU'RE NOT USED TO TRAVELING, YOU'RE CUTE, SOLTE.
SHUT UP. HOW COULD I BE USED TO TRAVELING?
OKAY. I'VE GOT MY TICKET.
I'VE JUST GOTTA STOCK UP FOR TOMORROW AND FIND A PLACE TO SLEEP.
BUT FIRST, FOOD.
ACTUALLY, I HAVEN'T EATEN SINCE I LEFT BLACK'S, HAVE I?
YUMMM!
IT'S GOOD, BUT A LOT. I'LL PACK UP THE LEFTOVERS AND EAT THEM AT THE INN.
EXCUSE ME! THIS ISN'T ENOUGH!
KEEP IT COMING!
YOU'VE GOT IT!

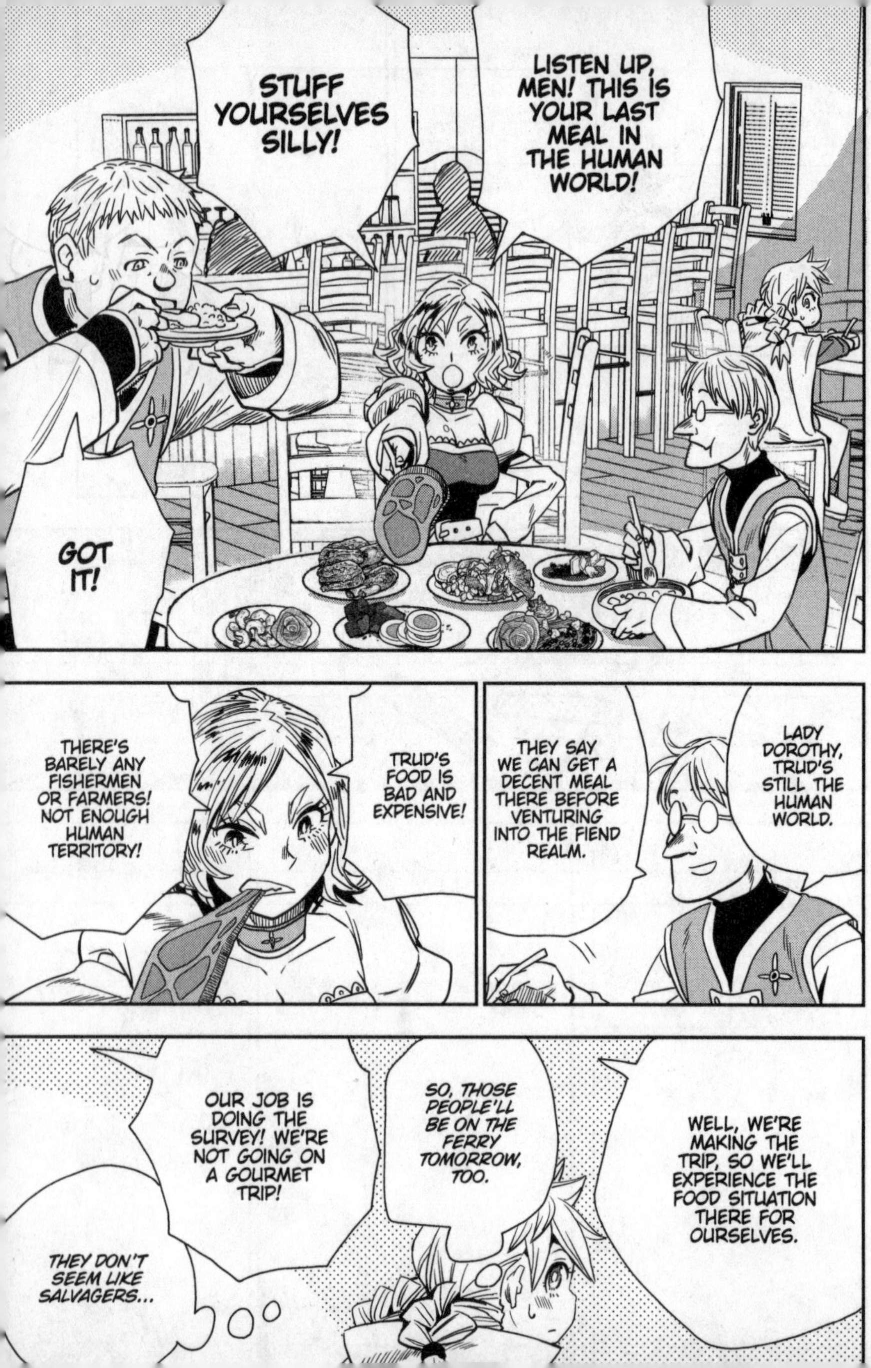
LISTEN UP, MEN! THIS IS YOUR LAST MEAL IN THE HUMAN WORLD!
STUFF YOURSELVES SILLY!
GOT IT!
LADY DOROTHY, TRUD'S STILL THE HUMAN WORLD.
THEY SAY WE CAN GET A DECENT MEAL THERE BEFORE VENTURING INTO THE FIEND REALM.
TRUD'S FOOD IS BAD AND EXPENSIVE!
THERE'S BARELY ANY FISHERMEN OR FARMERS! NOT ENOUGH HUMAN TERRITORY!
WELL, WE'RE MAKING THE TRIP, SO WE'LL EXPERIENCE THE FOOD SITUATION THERE FOR OURSELVES.
SO, THOSE PEOPLE'LL BE ON THE FERRY TOMORROW, TOO.
OUR JOB IS DOING THE SURVEY! WE'RE NOT GOING ON A GOURMET TRIP!
THEY DON'T SEEM LIKE SALVAGERS...

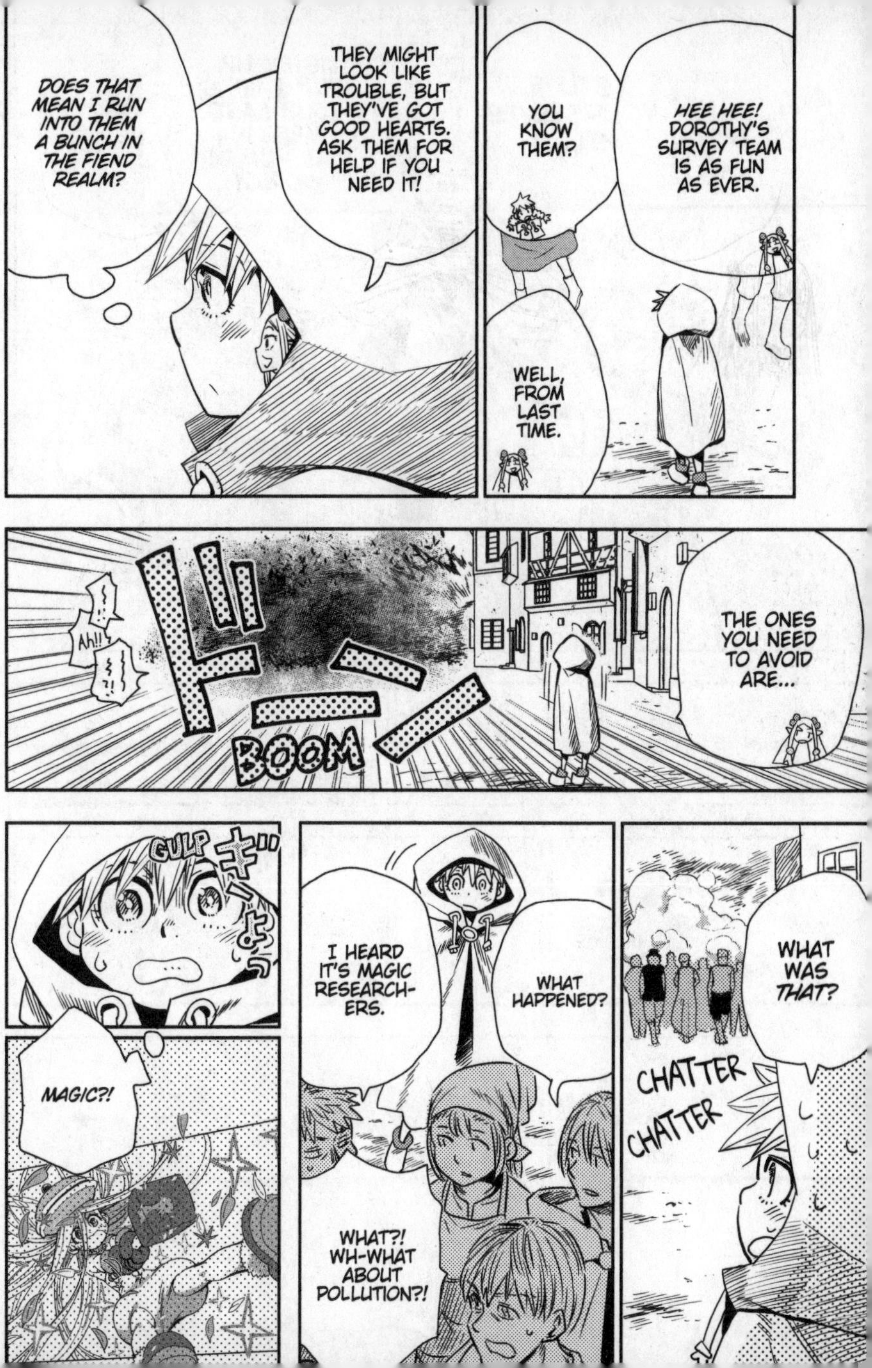
HEE HEE! DOROTHY'S SURVEY TEAM IS AS FUN AS EVER.
YOU KNOW THEM?
WELL, FROM LAST TIME.
THEY MIGHT LOOK LIKE TROUBLE, BUT THEY'VE GOT GOOD HEARTS. ASK THEM FOR HELP IF YOU NEED IT!
DOES THAT MEAN I RUN INTO THEM A BUNCH IN THE FIEND REALM?
THE ONES YOU NEED TO AVOID ARE...
BOOM
Ah!!
WHAT WAS THAT?
CHATTER
CHATTER
WHAT HAPPENED?
I HEARD IT'S MAGIC RESEARCHERS.
WHAT?! WH-WHAT ABOUT POLLUTION?!
GULP
MAGIC?!

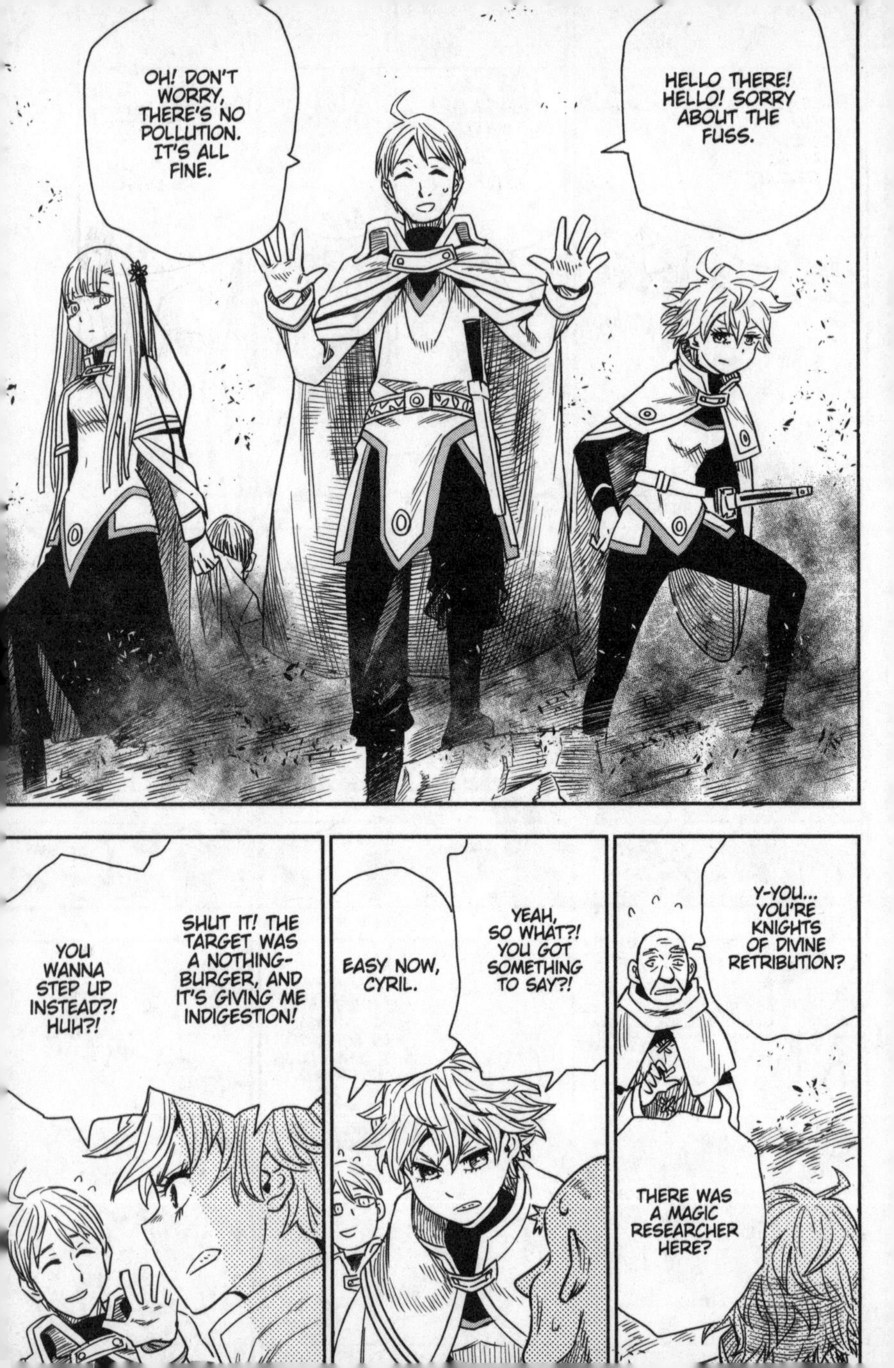
HELLO THERE! HELLO! SORRY ABOUT THE FUSS.
OH! DON'T WORRY, THERE'S NO POLLUTION. IT'S ALL FINE.
Y-YOU... YOU'RE KNIGHTS OF DIVINE RETRIBUTION?
THERE WAS A MAGIC RESEARCHER HERE?
YEAH, SO WHAT?! YOU GOT SOMETHING TO SAY?!
EASY NOW, CYRIL.
SHUT IT! THE TARGET WAS A NOTHING-BURGER, AND IT'S GIVING ME INDIGESTION!
YOU WANNA STEP UP INSTEAD?! HUH?!

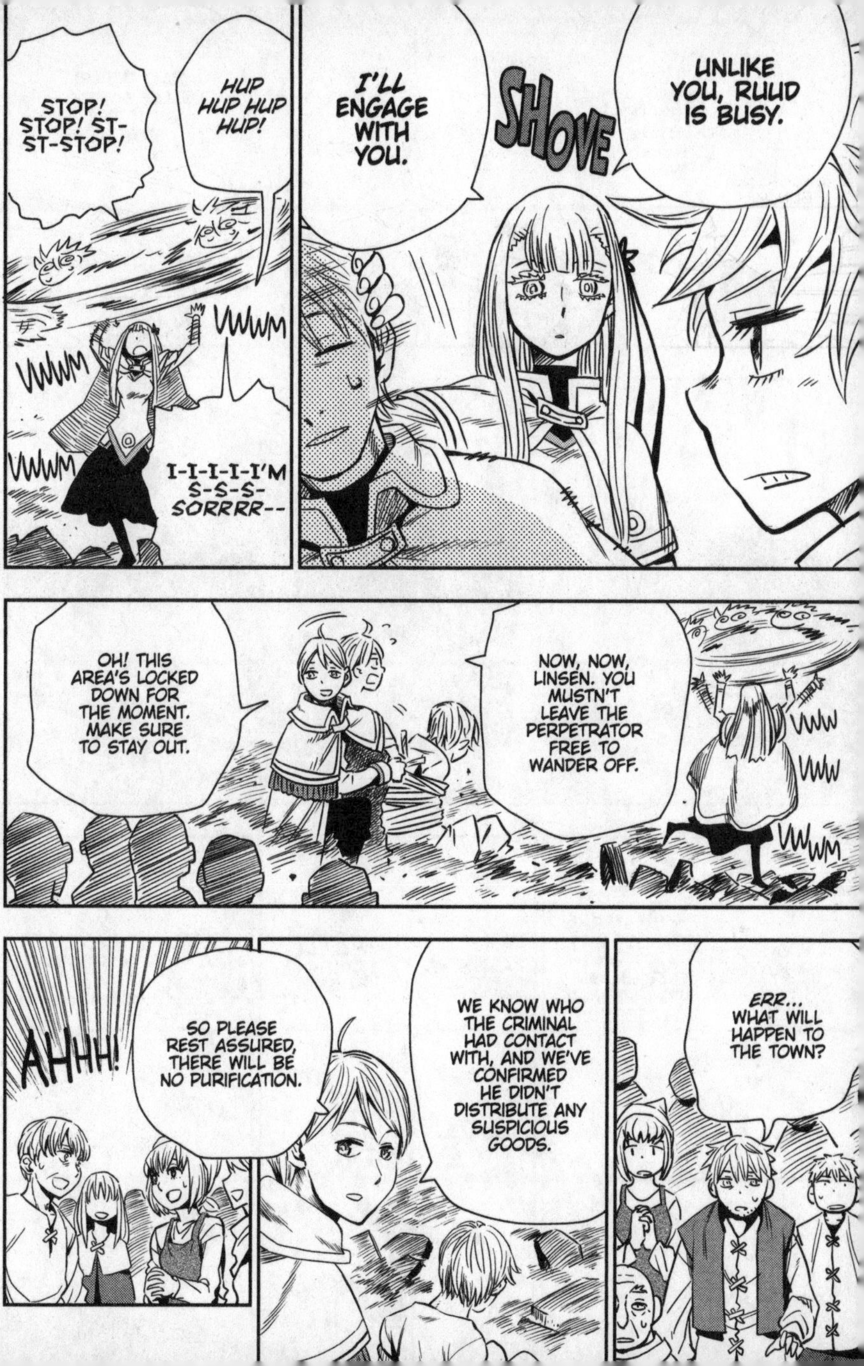
UNLIKE YOU, RUUD IS BUSY.
SHOVE
I'LL ENGAGE WITH YOU.
HUP HUP HUP HUP!
STOP! STOP! ST-ST-STOP!
VWWM
VWWM
VWWM
I-I-I-I-I'M S-S-S-SORRRR--
VWW
VWW
VWWM
NOW, NOW, LINSEN. YOU MUSTN'T LEAVE THE PERPETRATOR FREE TO WANDER OFF.
OH! THIS AREA'S LOCKED DOWN FOR THE MOMENT. MAKE SURE TO STAY OUT.
ERR... WHAT WILL HAPPEN TO THE TOWN?
WE KNOW WHO THE CRIMINAL HAD CONTACT WITH, AND WE'VE CONFIRMED HE DIDN'T DISTRIBUTE ANY SUSPICIOUS GOODS.
SO PLEASE REST ASSURED, THERE WILL BE NO PURIFICATION.
AHHH!

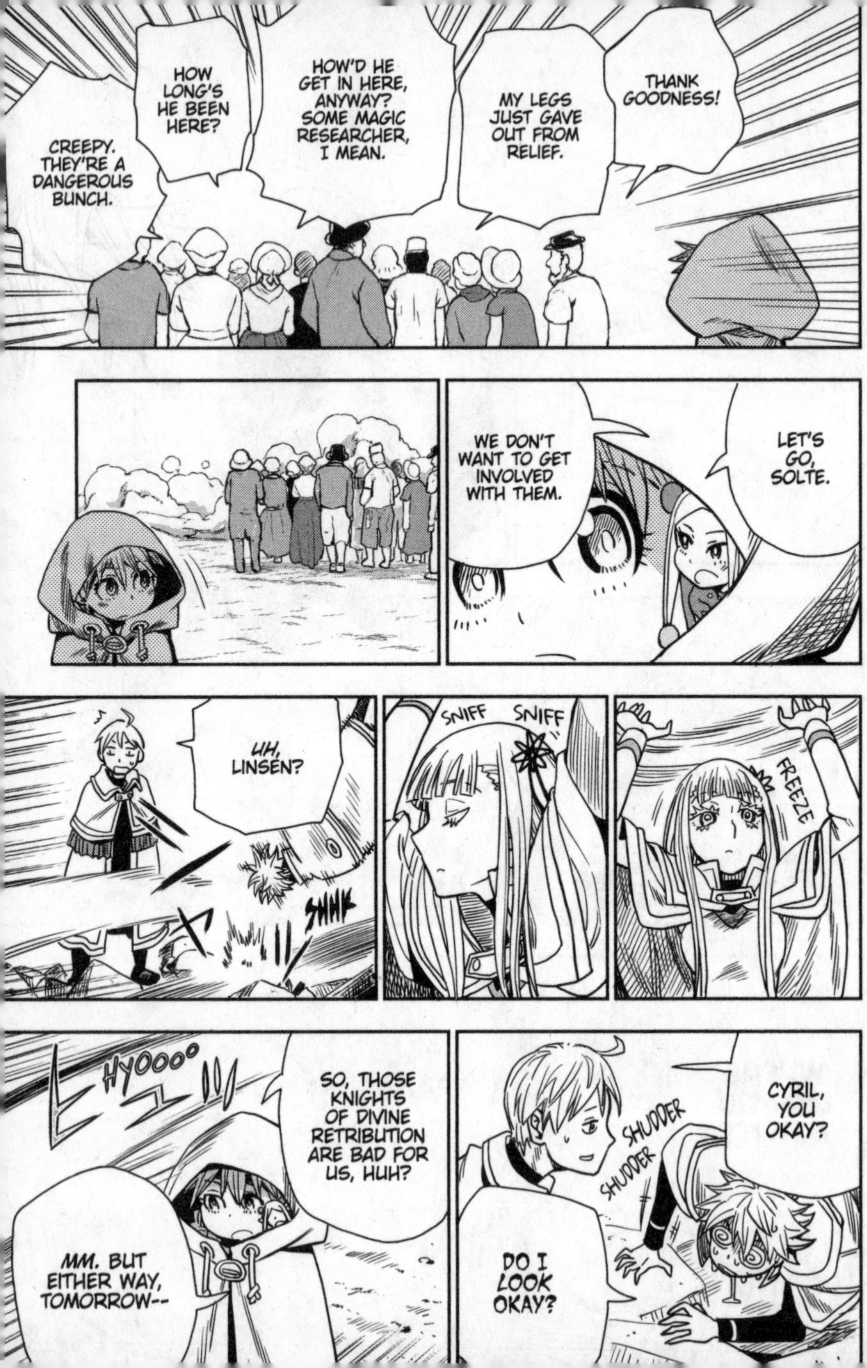
THANK GOODNESS!
MY LEGS JUST GAVE OUT FROM RELIEF.
HOW'D HE GET IN HERE, ANYWAY? SOME MAGIC RESEARCHER, I MEAN.
HOW LONG'S HE BEEN HERE?
CREEPY. THEY'RE A DANGEROUS BUNCH.
LET'S GO, SOLTE.
WE DON'T WANT TO GET INVOLVED WITH THEM.
FREEZE
SNIFF SNIFF
UH, LINSEN?
SHHK
CYRIL, YOU OKAY?
SHUDDER SHUDDER
DO I LOOK OKAY?
SO, THOSE KNIGHTS OF DIVINE RETRIBUTION ARE BAD FOR US, HUH?
HYOOOO
MM. BUT EITHER WAY, TOMORROW--

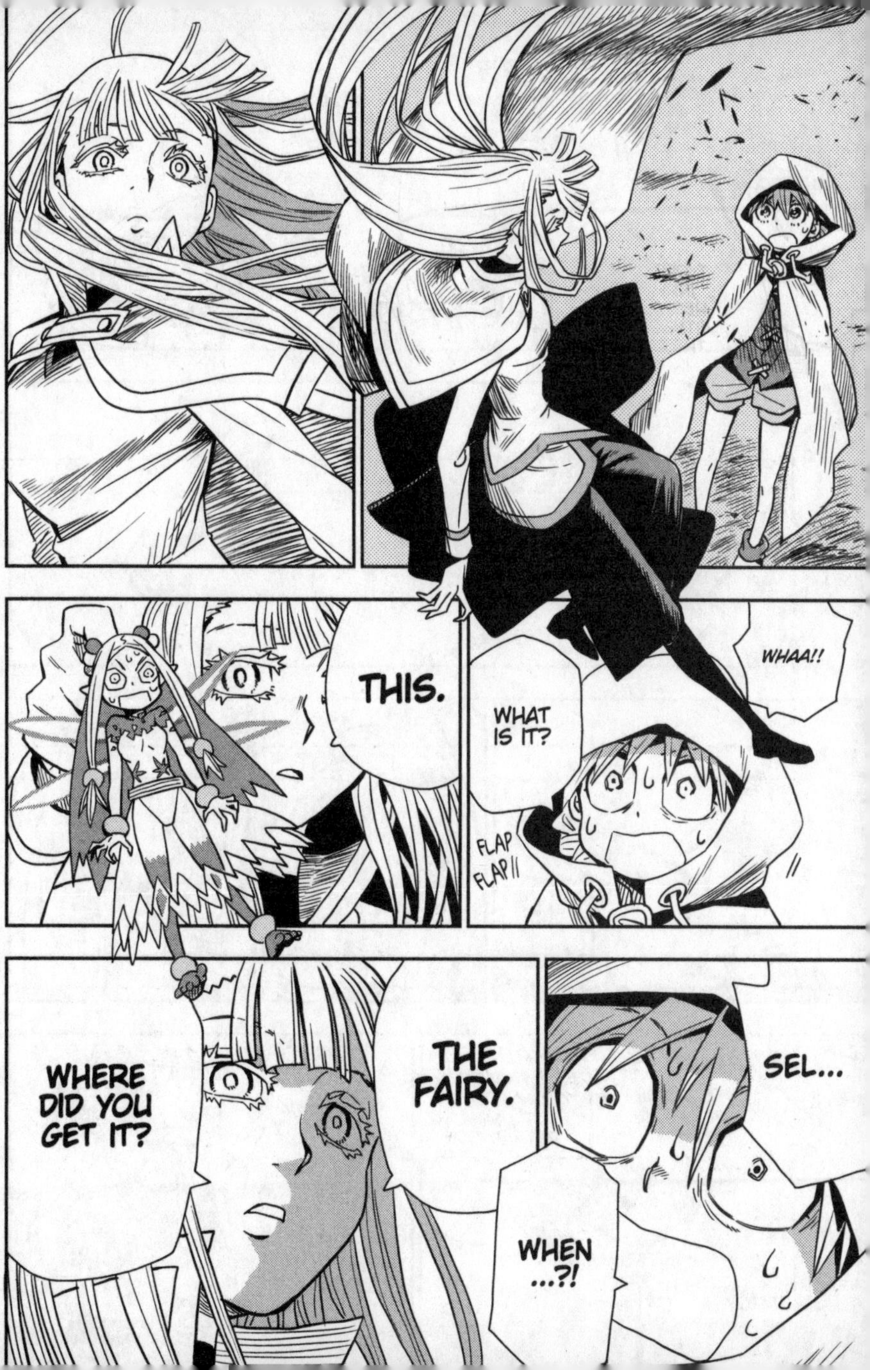
WHAA!!
WHAT IS IT?
FLAP FLAP!!
THIS.
SEL...
WHEN ...?!
THE FAIRY.
WHERE DID YOU GET IT?

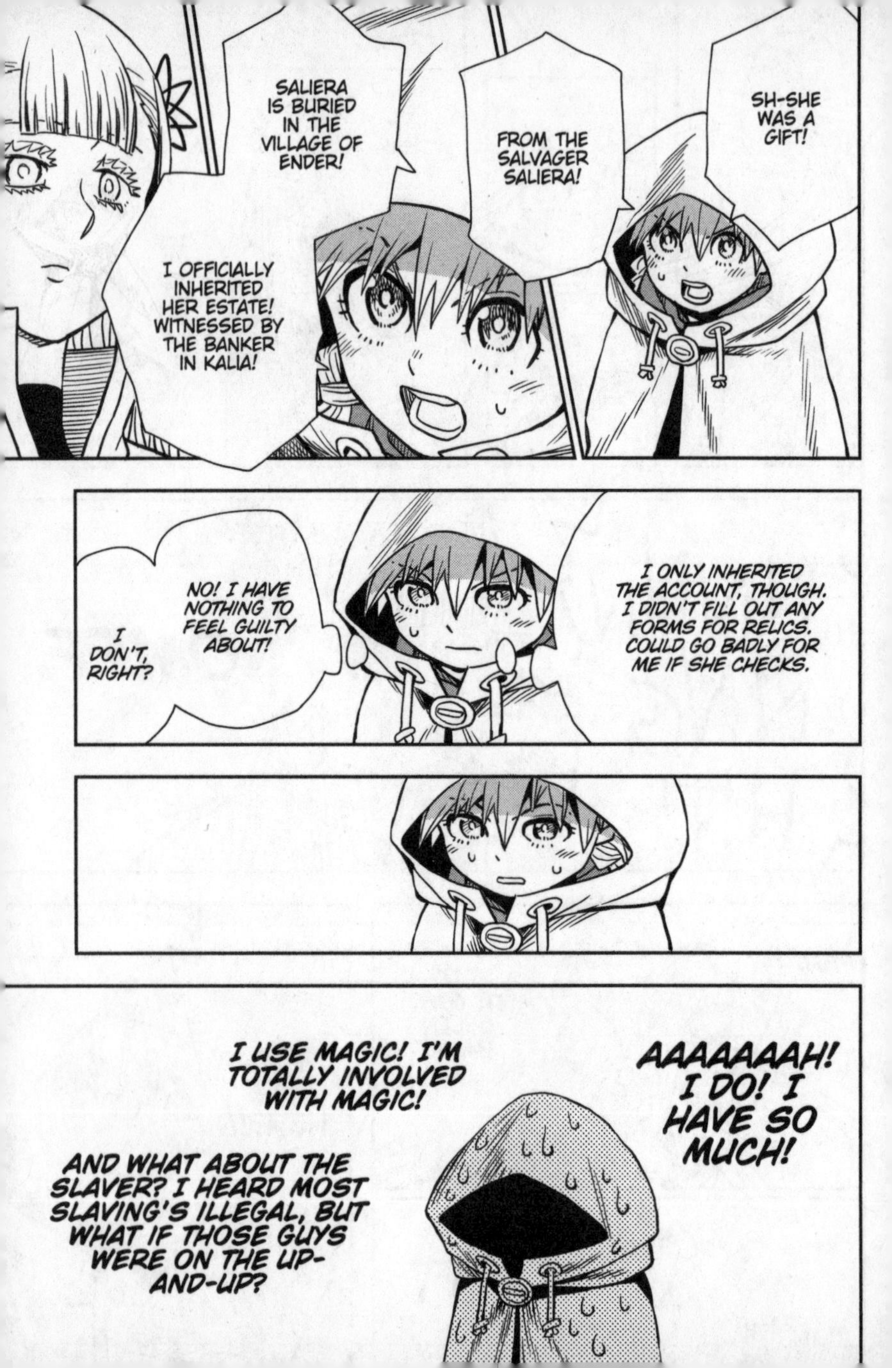
SH-SHE WAS A GIFT!
FROM THE SALVAGER SALIERA!
SALIERA IS BURIED IN THE VILLAGE OF ENDER!
I OFFICIALLY INHERITED HER ESTATE! WITNESSED BY THE BANKER IN KALIA!
I ONLY INHERITED THE ACCOUNT, THOUGH. I DIDN'T FILL OUT ANY FORMS FOR RELICS. COULD GO BADLY FOR ME IF SHE CHECKS.
NO! I HAVE NOTHING TO FEEL GUILTY ABOUT!
I DON'T, RIGHT?
AAAAAAAH! I DO! I HAVE SO MUCH!
I USE MAGIC! I'M TOTALLY INVOLVED WITH MAGIC!
AND WHAT ABOUT THE SLAVER? I HEARD MOST SLAVING'S ILLEGAL, BUT WHAT IF THOSE GUYS WERE ON THE UP-AND-UP?

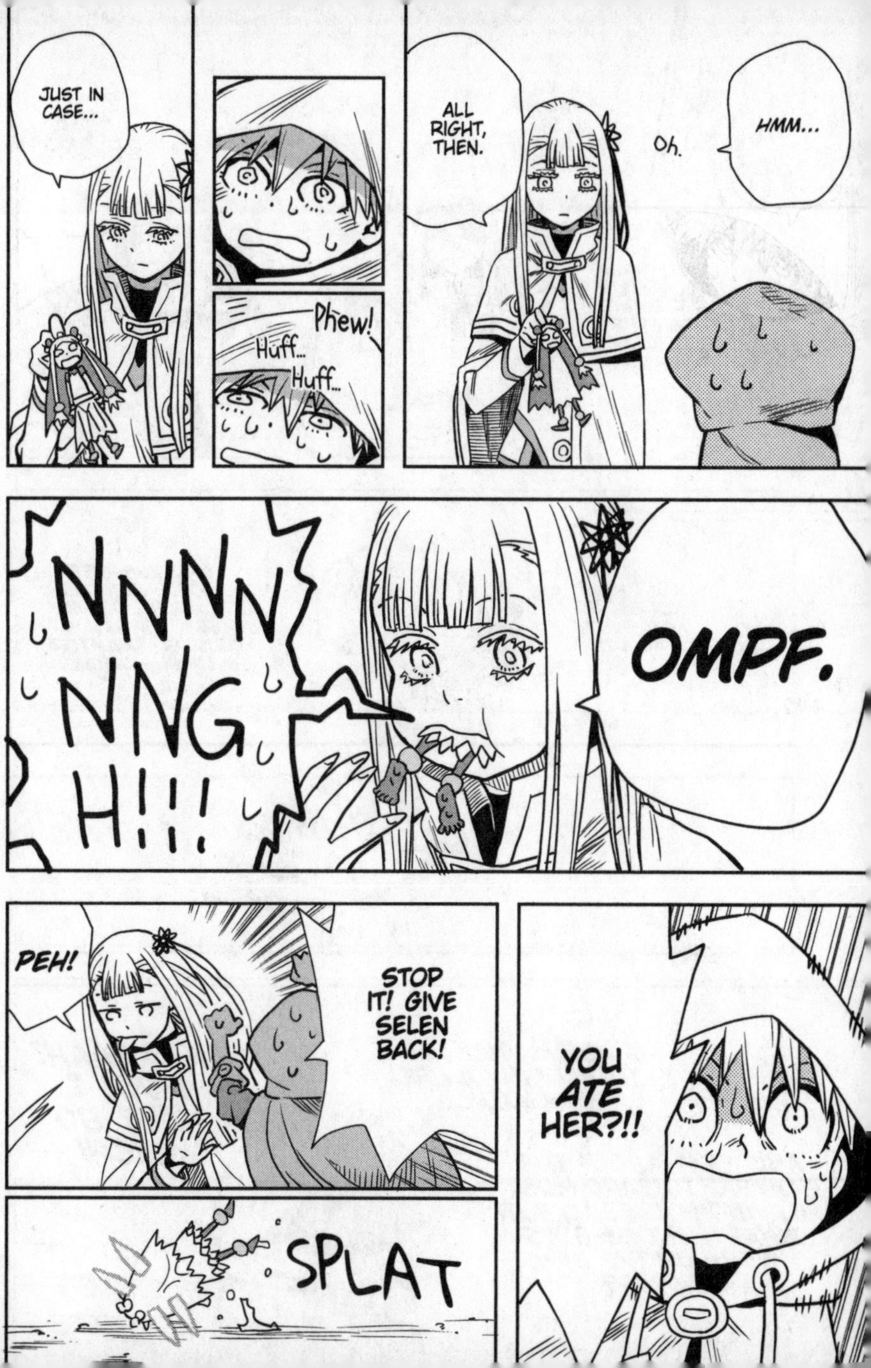
HMM...
Oh.
ALL RIGHT, THEN.
Phew!
Huff... Huff...
JUST IN CASE...
OMPF.
NNNNNNGH!!!
YOU ATE HER?!!
STOP IT! GIVE SELEN BACK!
PEH!
SPLAT

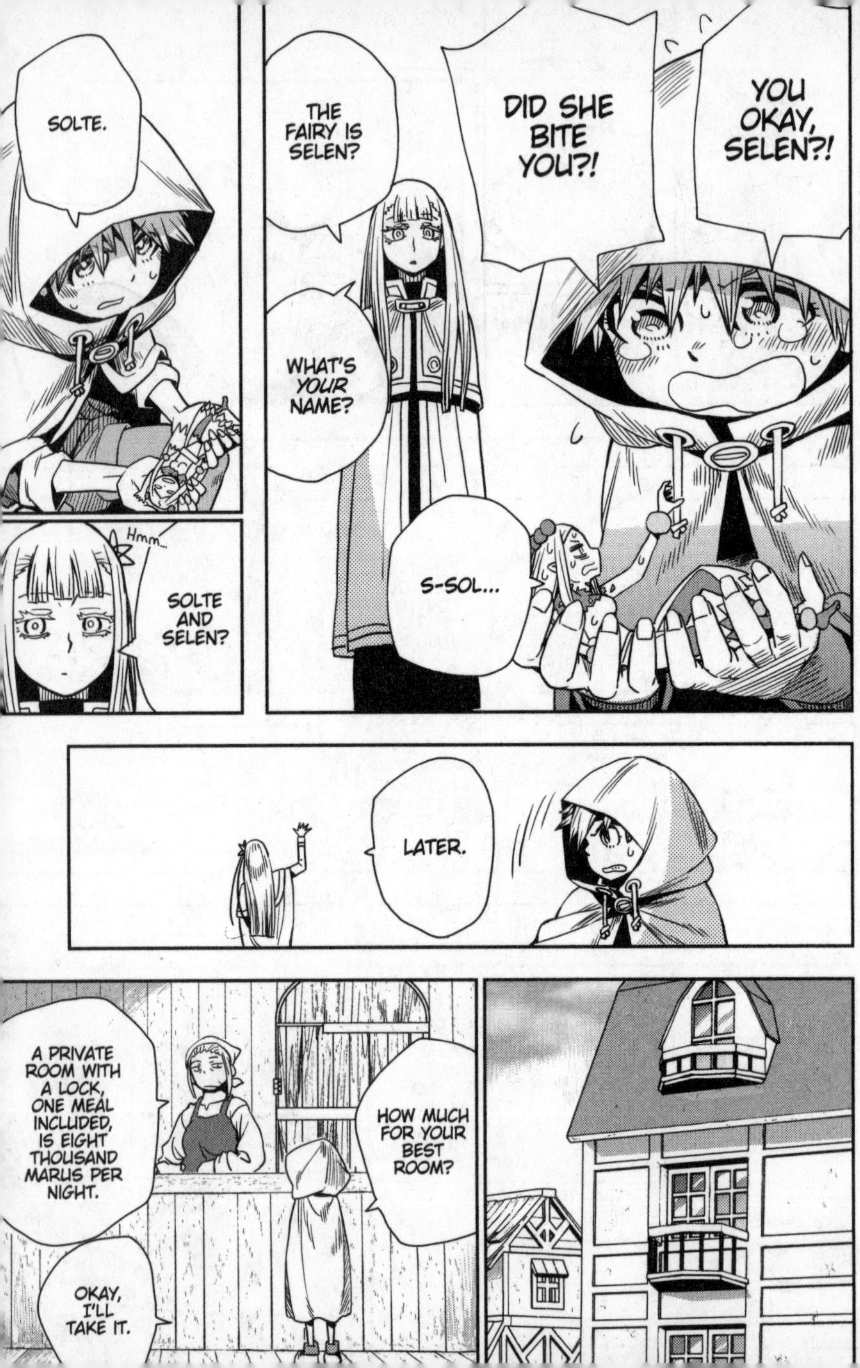
YOU OKAY, SELEN?!
DID SHE BITE YOU?!
S-SOL...
THE FAIRY IS SELEN?
WHAT'S YOUR NAME?
SOLTE.
Hmm...
SOLTE AND SELEN?
LATER.
HOW MUCH FOR YOUR BEST ROOM?
A PRIVATE ROOM WITH A LOCK, ONE MEAL INCLUDED, IS EIGHT THOUSAND MARUS PER NIGHT.
OKAY, I'LL TAKE IT.

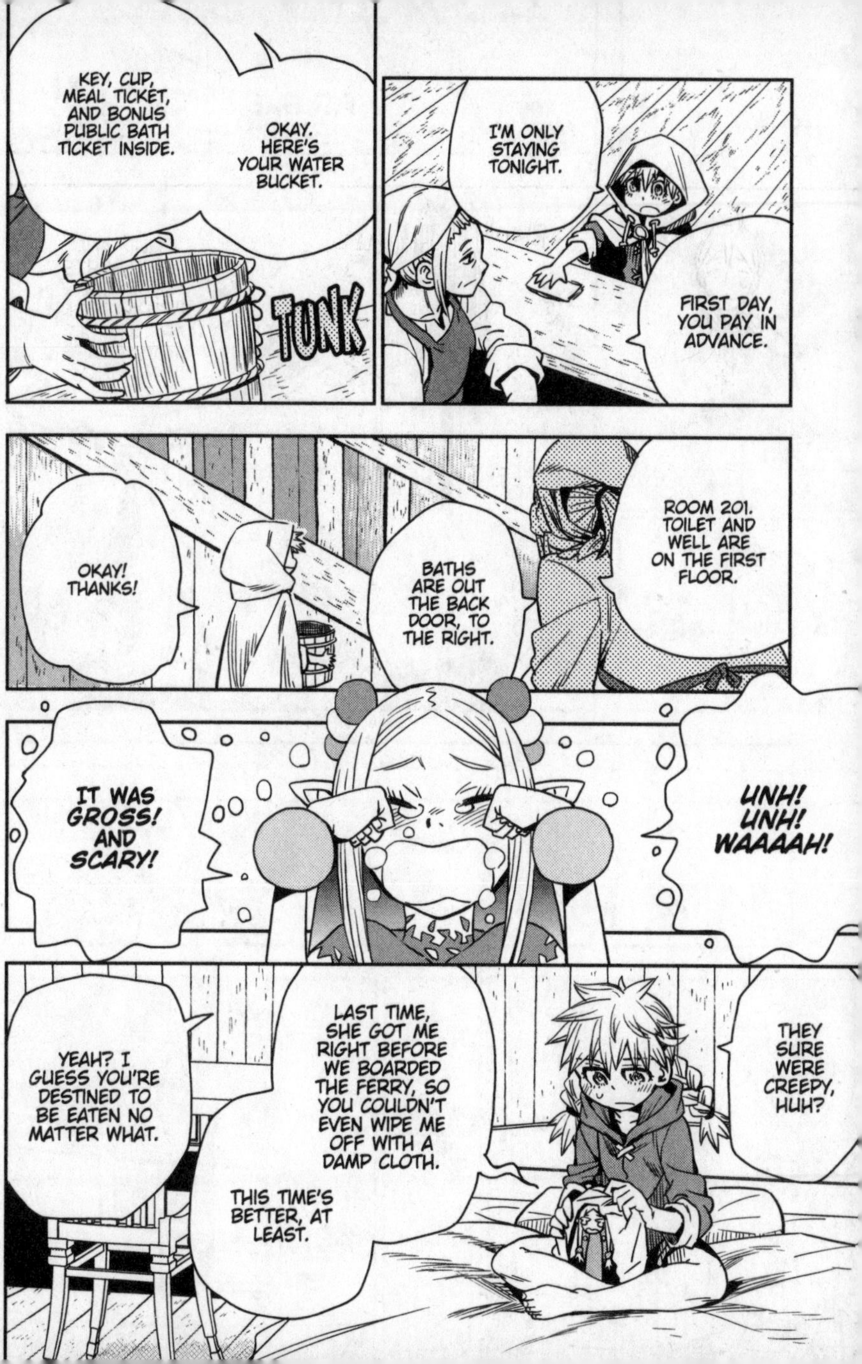
I'M ONLY STAYING TONIGHT.
FIRST DAY, YOU PAY IN ADVANCE.
OKAY. HERE'S YOUR WATER BUCKET.
KEY, CUP, MEAL TICKET, AND BONUS PUBLIC BATH TICKET INSIDE.
TUNK
ROOM 201. TOILET AND WELL ARE ON THE FIRST FLOOR.
BATHS ARE OUT THE BACK DOOR, TO THE RIGHT.
OKAY! THANKS!
UNH! UNH! WAAAAH!
IT WAS GROSS! AND SCARY!
THEY SURE WERE CREEPY, HUH?
LAST TIME, SHE GOT ME RIGHT BEFORE WE BOARDED THE FERRY, SO YOU COULDN'T EVEN WIPE ME OFF WITH A DAMP CLOTH.
THIS TIME'S BETTER, AT LEAST.
YEAH? I GUESS YOU'RE DESTINED TO BE EATEN NO MATTER WHAT.

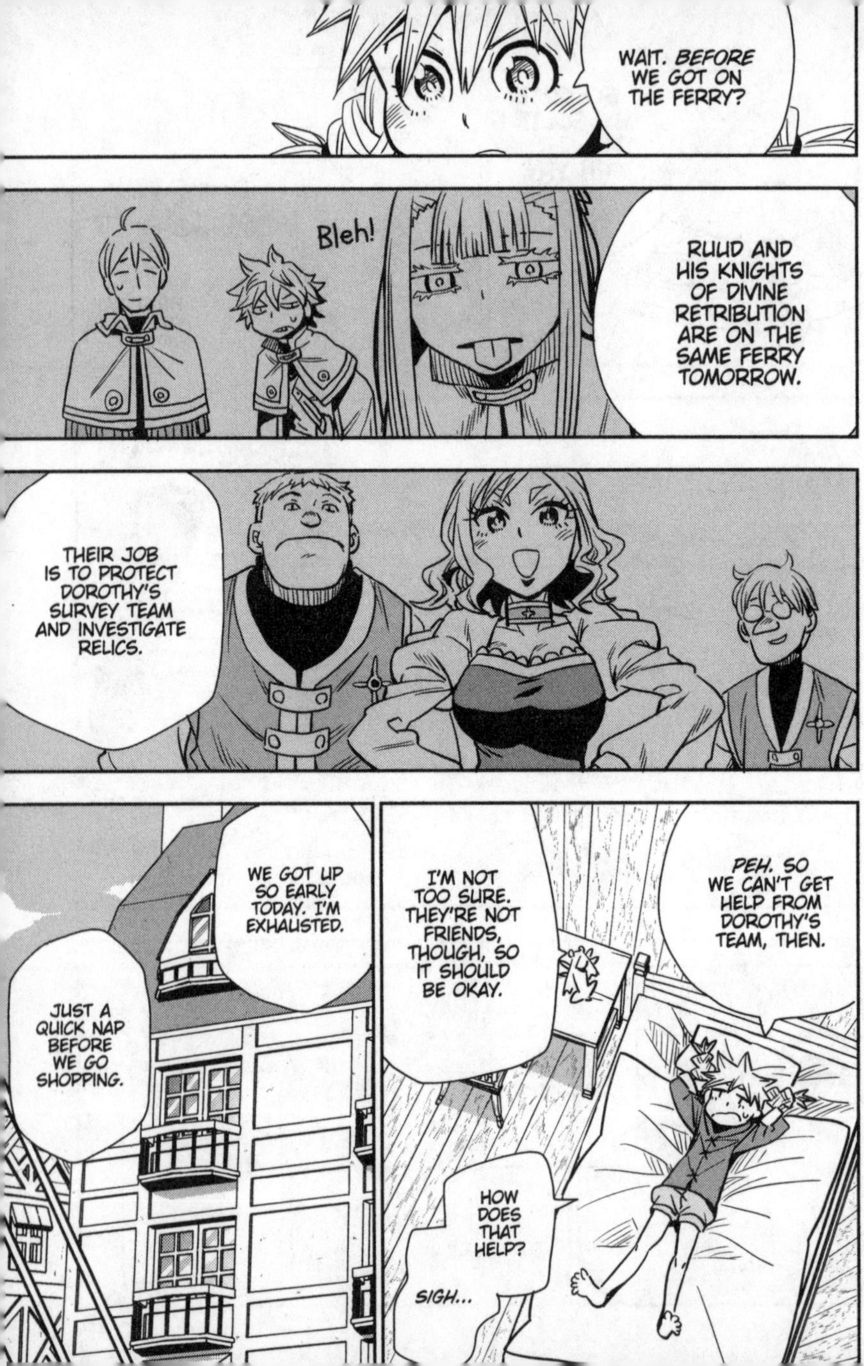
WAIT. *BEFORE* WE GOT ON THE FERRY?
RUUD AND HIS KNIGHTS OF DIVINE RETRIBUTION ARE ON THE SAME FERRY TOMORROW.
Bleh!
THEIR JOB IS TO PROTECT DOROTHY'S SURVEY TEAM AND INVESTIGATE RELICS.
PEH. SO WE CAN'T GET HELP FROM DOROTHY'S TEAM, THEN.
I'M NOT TOO SURE. THEY'RE NOT FRIENDS, THOUGH, SO IT SHOULD BE OKAY.
HOW DOES THAT HELP?
SIGH...
WE GOT UP SO EARLY TODAY. I'M EXHAUSTED.
JUST A QUICK NAP BEFORE WE GO SHOPPING.

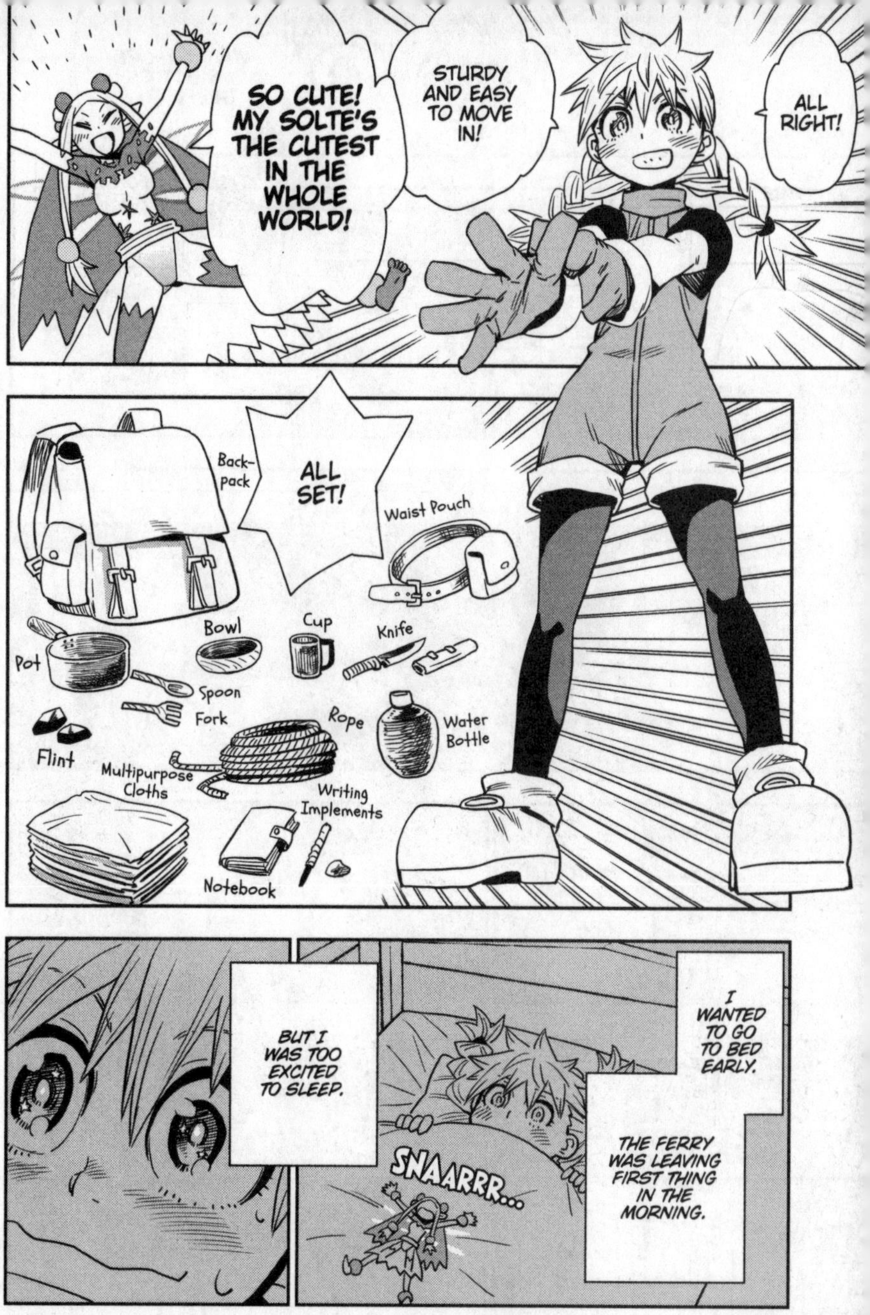
ALL RIGHT!
STURDY AND EASY TO MOVE IN!
SO CUTE! MY SOLTE'S THE CUTEST IN THE WHOLE WORLD!
ALL SET!
Back-pack
Waist Pouch
Bowl
Cup
Knife
Pot
Spoon
Fork
Flint
Rope
Water Bottle
Multipurpose Cloths
Writing Implements
Notebook
I WANTED TO GO TO BED EARLY.
THE FERRY WAS LEAVING FIRST THING IN THE MORNING.
SNAARRR...
BUT I WAS TOO EXCITED TO SLEEP.

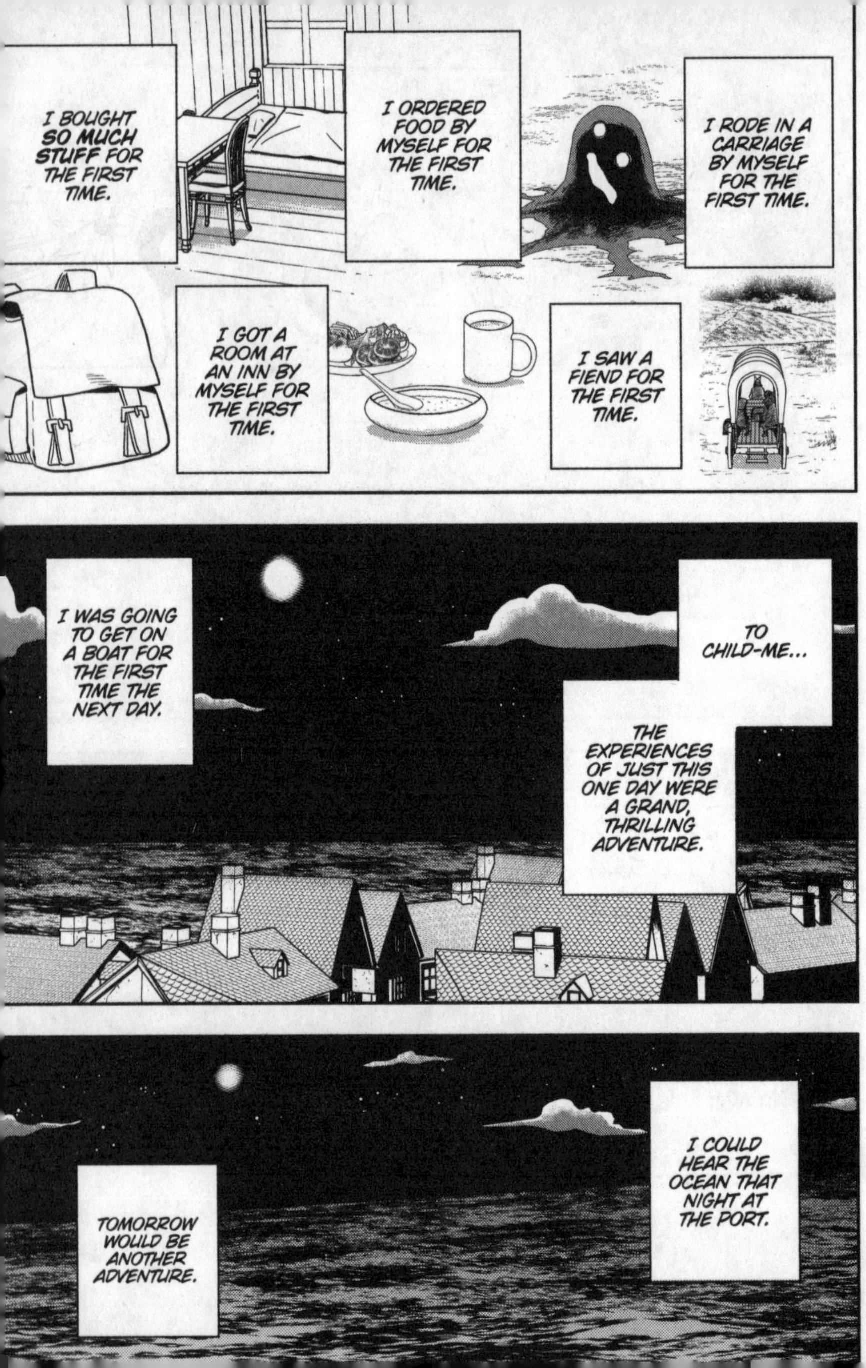
I RODE IN A CARRIAGE BY MYSELF FOR THE FIRST TIME.
I ORDERED FOOD BY MYSELF FOR THE FIRST TIME.
I BOUGHT SO MUCH STUFF FOR THE FIRST TIME.
I SAW A FIEND FOR THE FIRST TIME.
I GOT A ROOM AT AN INN BY MYSELF FOR THE FIRST TIME.
TO CHILD-ME...
THE EXPERIENCES OF JUST THIS ONE DAY WERE A GRAND, THRILLING ADVENTURE.
I WAS GOING TO GET ON A BOAT FOR THE FIRST TIME THE NEXT DAY.
I COULD HEAR THE OCEAN THAT NIGHT AT THE PORT.
TOMORROW WOULD BE ANOTHER ADVENTURE.

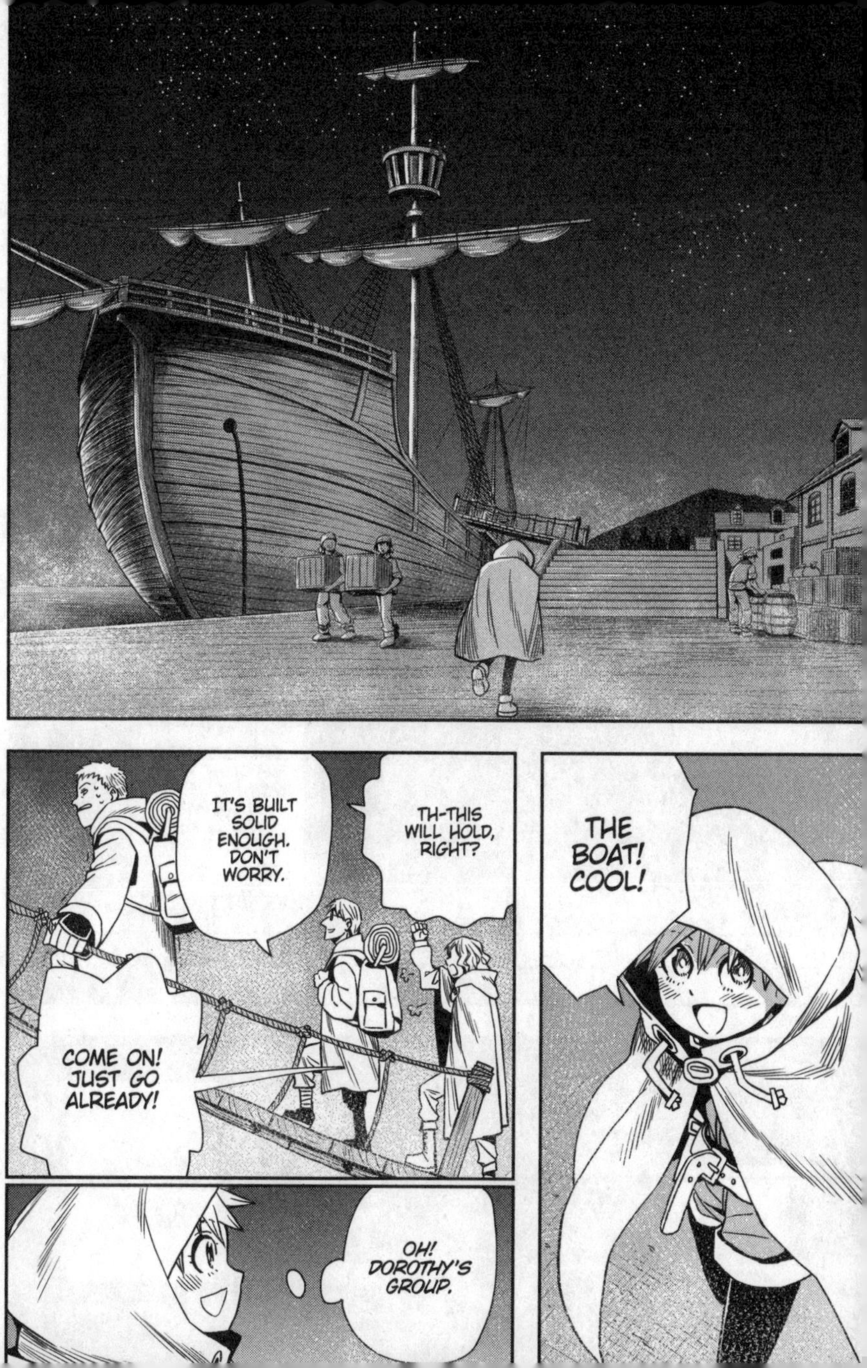
THE BOAT! COOL!
TH-THIS WILL HOLD, RIGHT?
IT'S BUILT SOLID ENOUGH. DON'T WORRY.
COME ON! JUST GO ALREADY!
OH! DOROTHY'S GROUP.

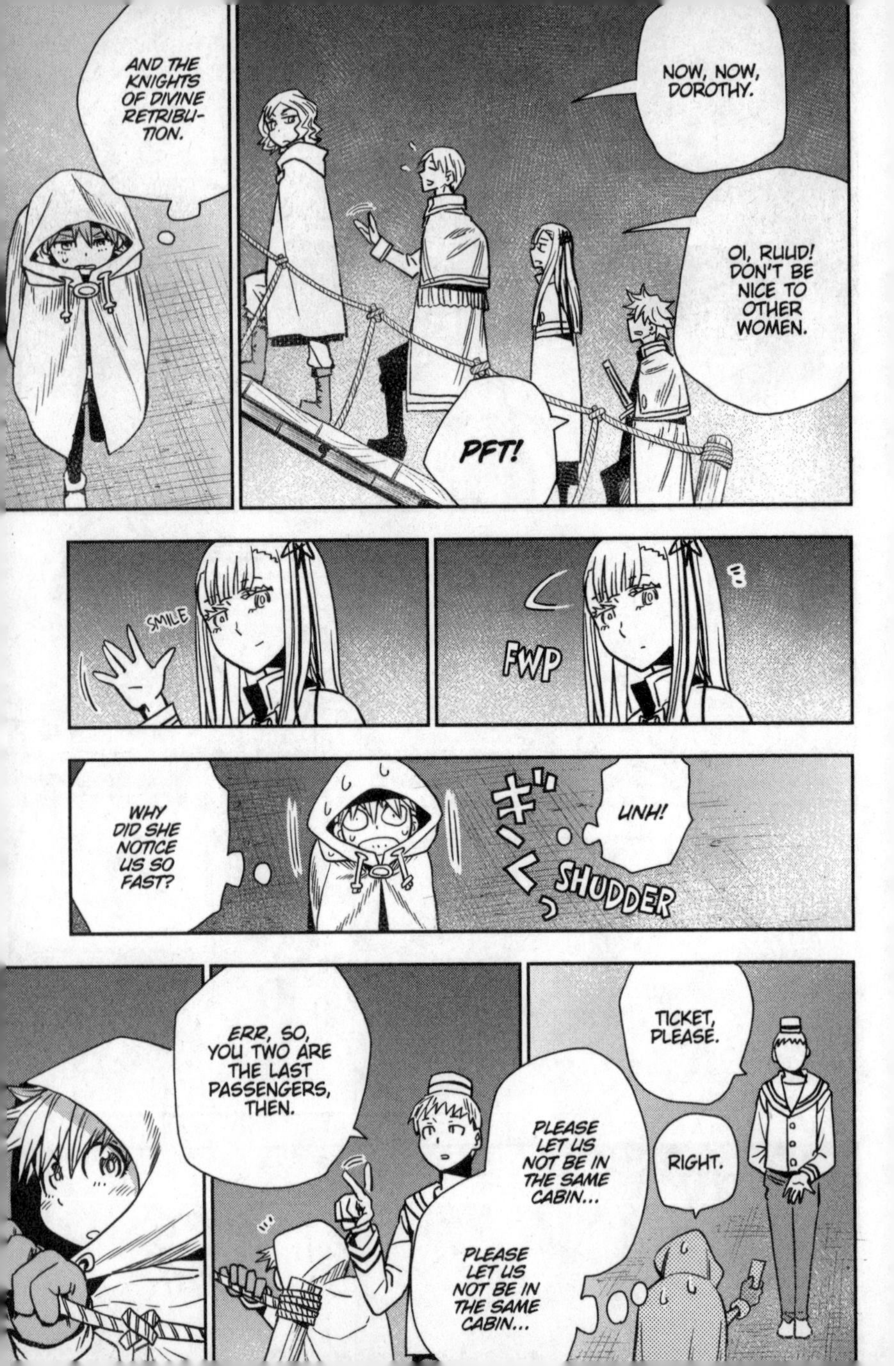
NOW, NOW, DOROTHY.
OI, RUUD! DON'T BE NICE TO OTHER WOMEN.
PFT!
AND THE KNIGHTS OF DIVINE RETRIBUTION.
FWP
SMILE
UNH!
ギくっ
SHUDDER
WHY DID SHE NOTICE US SO FAST?
TICKET, PLEASE.
RIGHT.
ERR, SO, YOU TWO ARE THE LAST PASSENGERS, THEN.
PLEASE LET US NOT BE IN THE SAME CABIN...
PLEASE LET US NOT BE IN THE SAME CABIN...

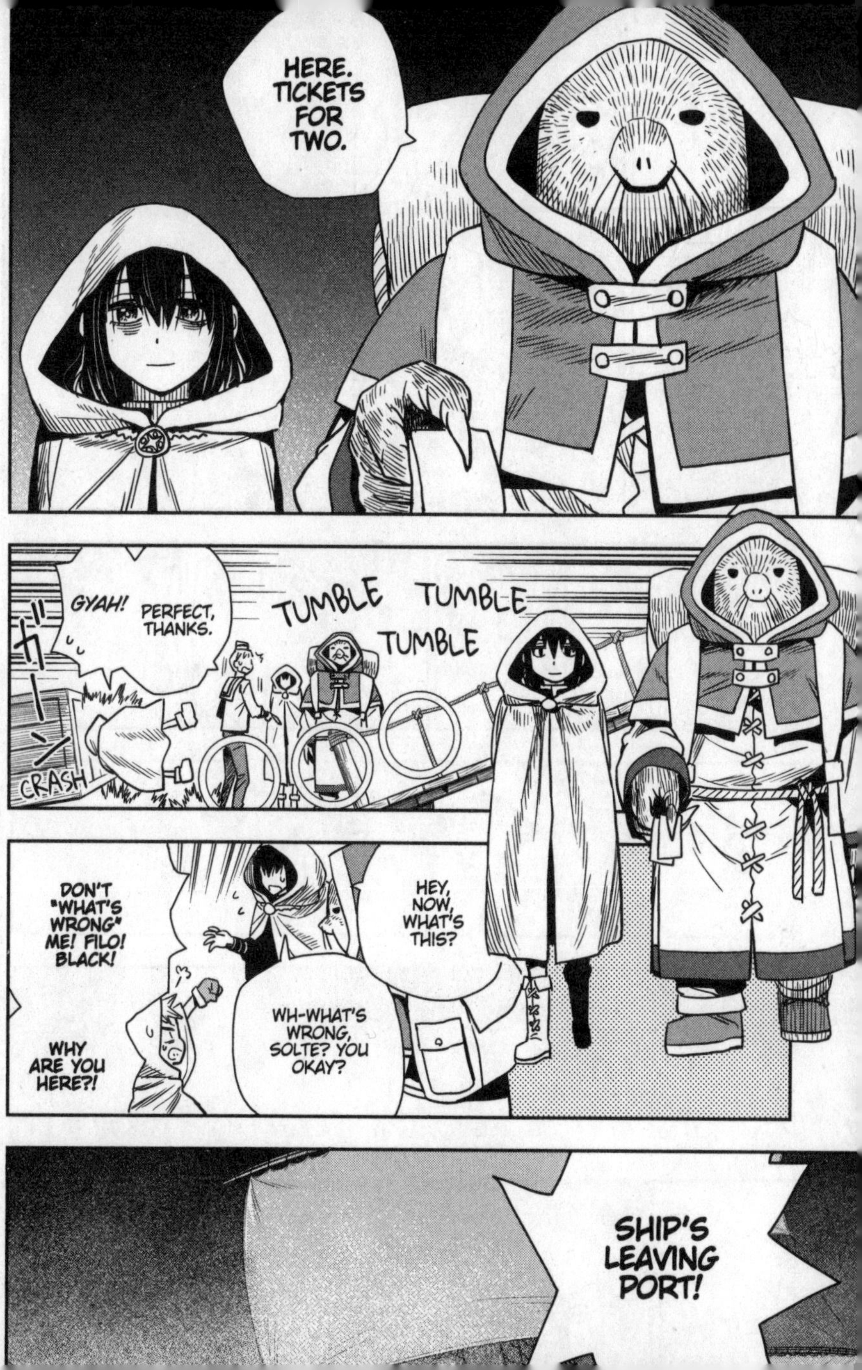
HERE. TICKETS FOR TWO.
TUMBLE TUMBLE TUMBLE
PERFECT, THANKS.
GYAH!
ガーン
CRASH
HEY, NOW, WHAT'S THIS?
WH-WHAT'S WRONG, SOLTE? YOU OKAY?
DON'T "WHAT'S WRONG" ME! FILO! BLACK!
WHY ARE YOU HERE?!
SHIP'S LEAVING PORT!

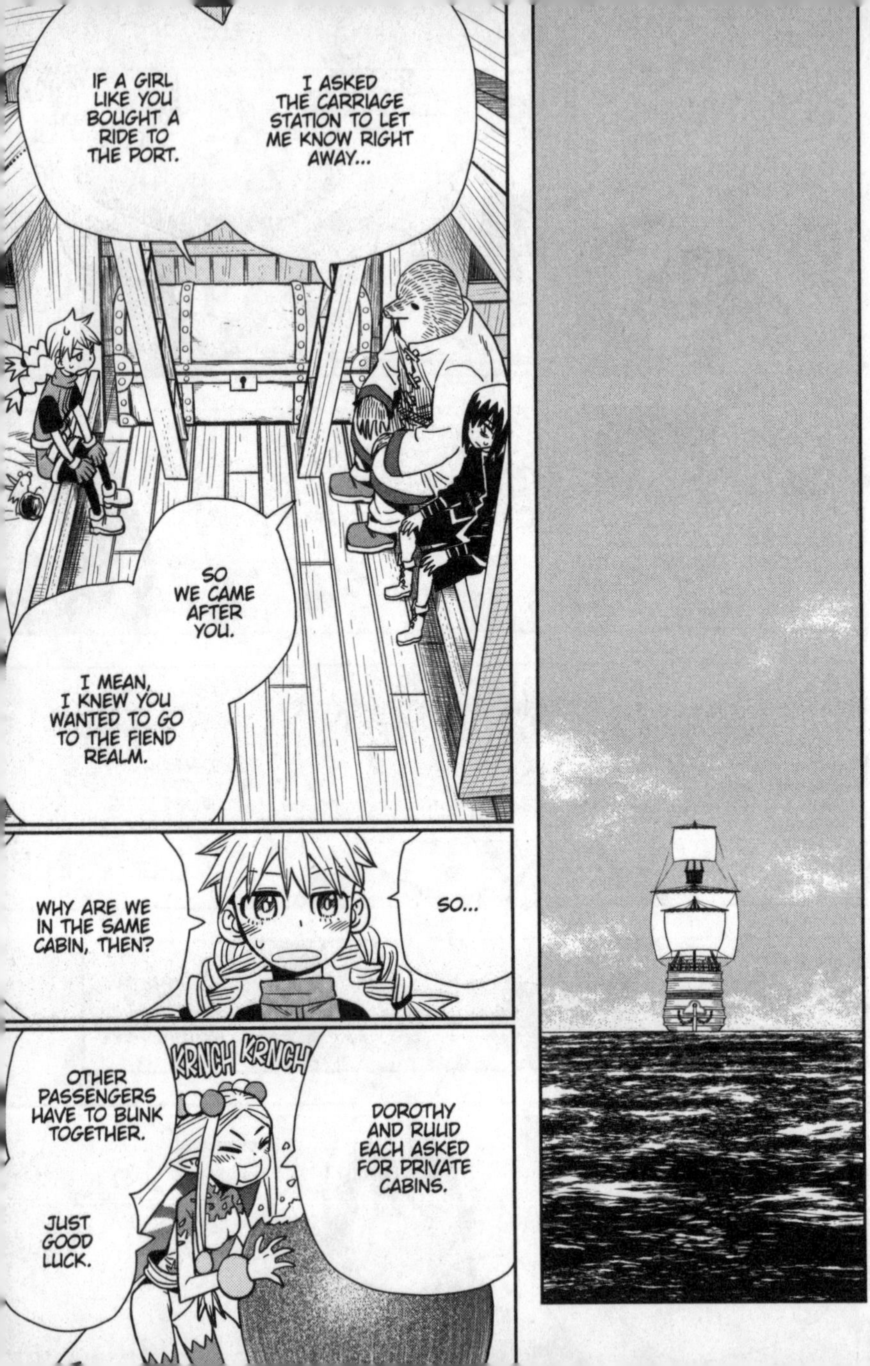
I ASKED THE CARRIAGE STATION TO LET ME KNOW RIGHT AWAY...
IF A GIRL LIKE YOU BOUGHT A RIDE TO THE PORT.
SO WE CAME AFTER YOU.
I MEAN, I KNEW YOU WANTED TO GO TO THE FIEND REALM.
SO...
WHY ARE WE IN THE SAME CABIN, THEN?
KRNCH KRNCH
DOROTHY AND RUUD EACH ASKED FOR PRIVATE CABINS.
OTHER PASSENGERS HAVE TO BUNK TOGETHER.
JUST GOOD LUCK.

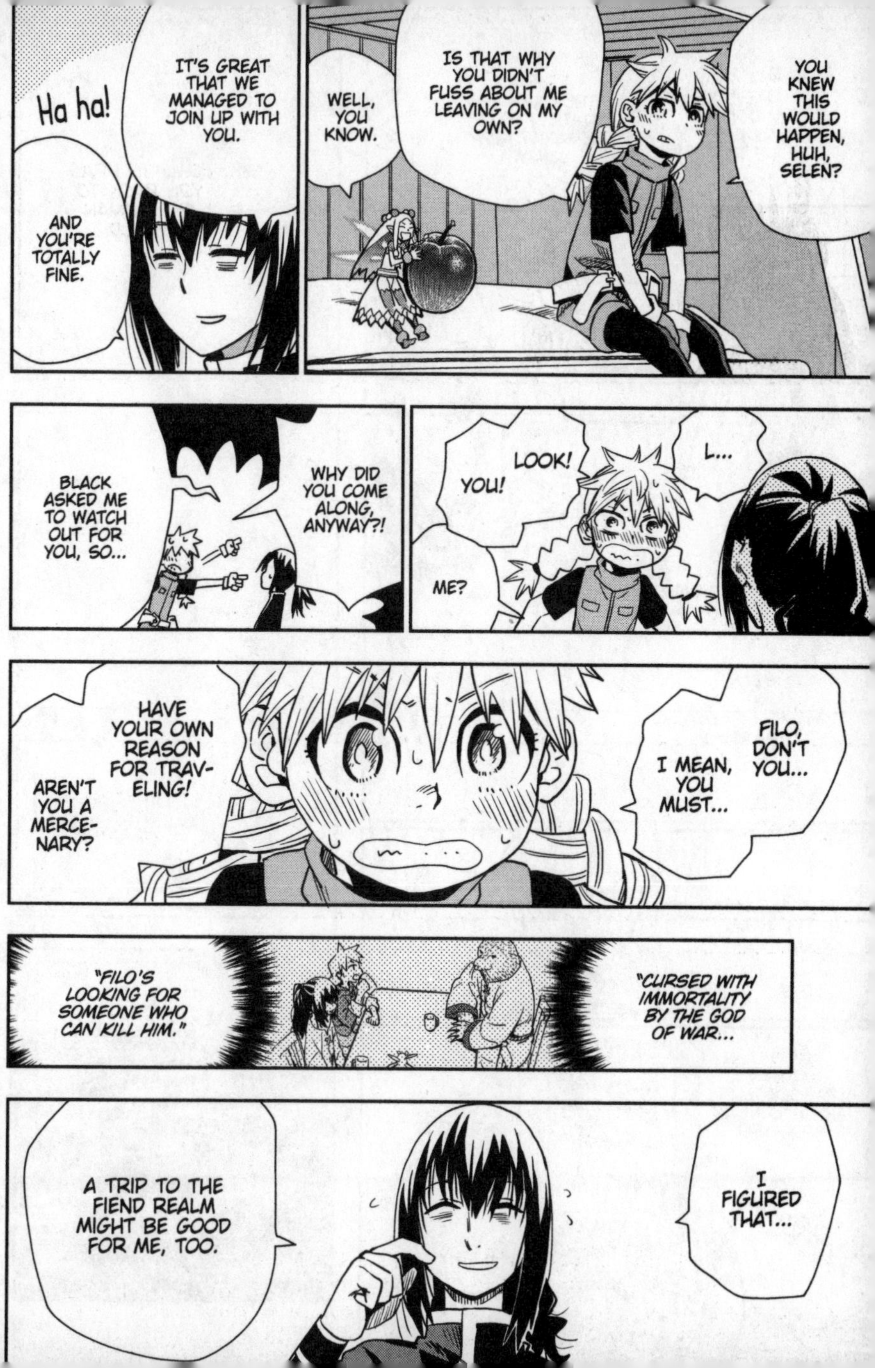
YOU KNEW THIS WOULD HAPPEN, HUH, SELEN?
IS THAT WHY YOU DIDN'T FUSS ABOUT ME LEAVING ON MY OWN?
WELL, YOU KNOW.
IT'S GREAT THAT WE MANAGED TO JOIN UP WITH YOU.
Ha ha!
AND YOU'RE TOTALLY FINE.
L...
LOOK!
YOU!
ME?
WHY DID YOU COME ALONG, ANYWAY?!
BLACK ASKED ME TO WATCH OUT FOR YOU, SO...
FILO, DON'T YOU...
I MEAN, YOU MUST...
HAVE YOUR OWN REASON FOR TRAVELING!
AREN'T YOU A MERCENARY?
"CURSED WITH IMMORTALITY BY THE GOD OF WAR...
"FILO'S LOOKING FOR SOMEONE WHO CAN KILL HIM."
I FIGURED THAT...
A TRIP TO THE FIEND REALM MIGHT BE GOOD FOR ME, TOO.

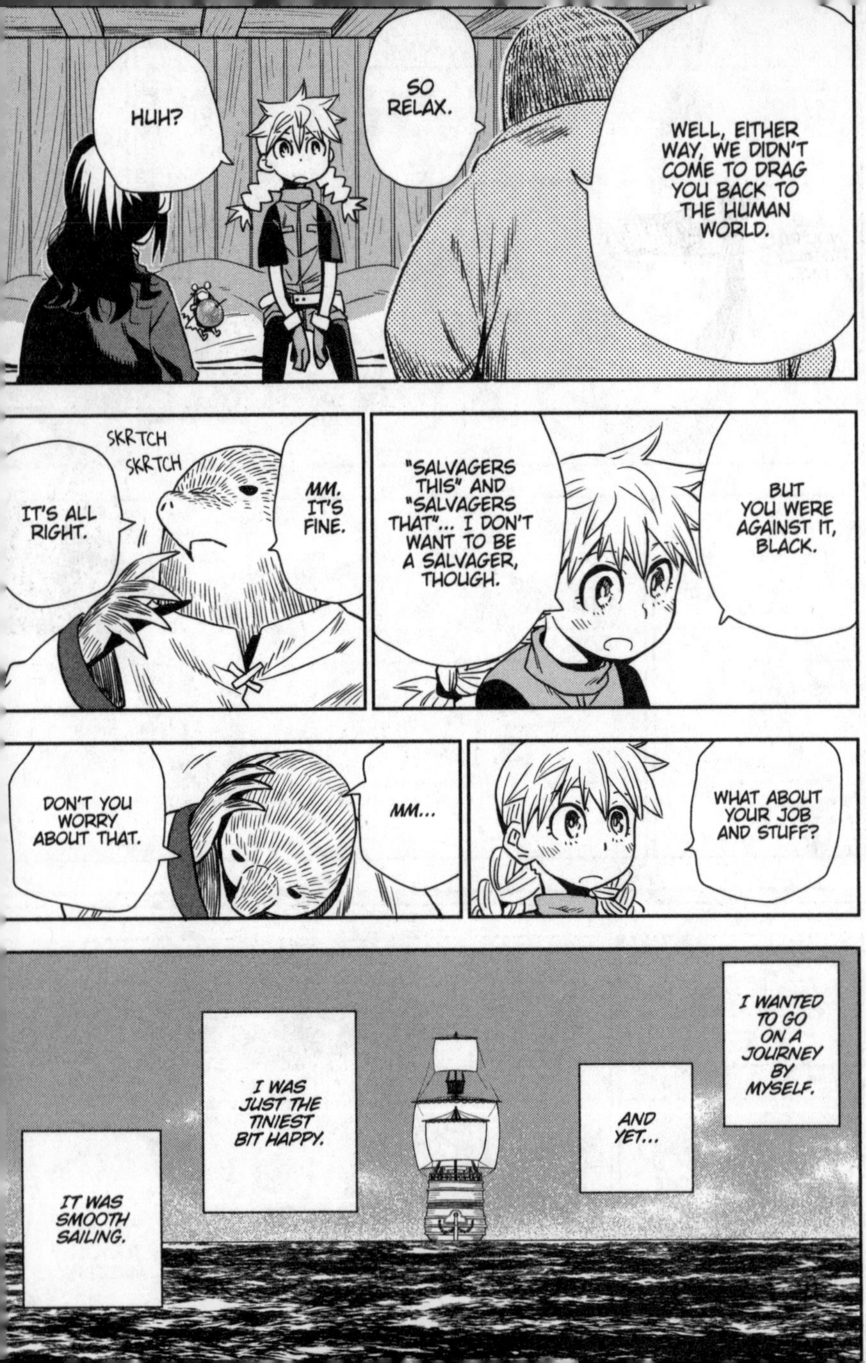
WELL, EITHER WAY, WE DIDN'T COME TO DRAG YOU BACK TO THE HUMAN WORLD.
SO RELAX.
HUH?
BUT YOU WERE AGAINST IT, BLACK.
"SALVAGERS THIS" AND "SALVAGERS THAT"... I DON'T WANT TO BE A SALVAGER, THOUGH.
MM. IT'S FINE.
SKRTCH
SKRTCH
IT'S ALL RIGHT.
WHAT ABOUT YOUR JOB AND STUFF?
MM...
DON'T YOU WORRY ABOUT THAT.
I WANTED TO GO ON A JOURNEY BY MYSELF.
AND YET...
I WAS JUST THE TINIEST BIT HAPPY.
IT WAS SMOOTH SAILING.

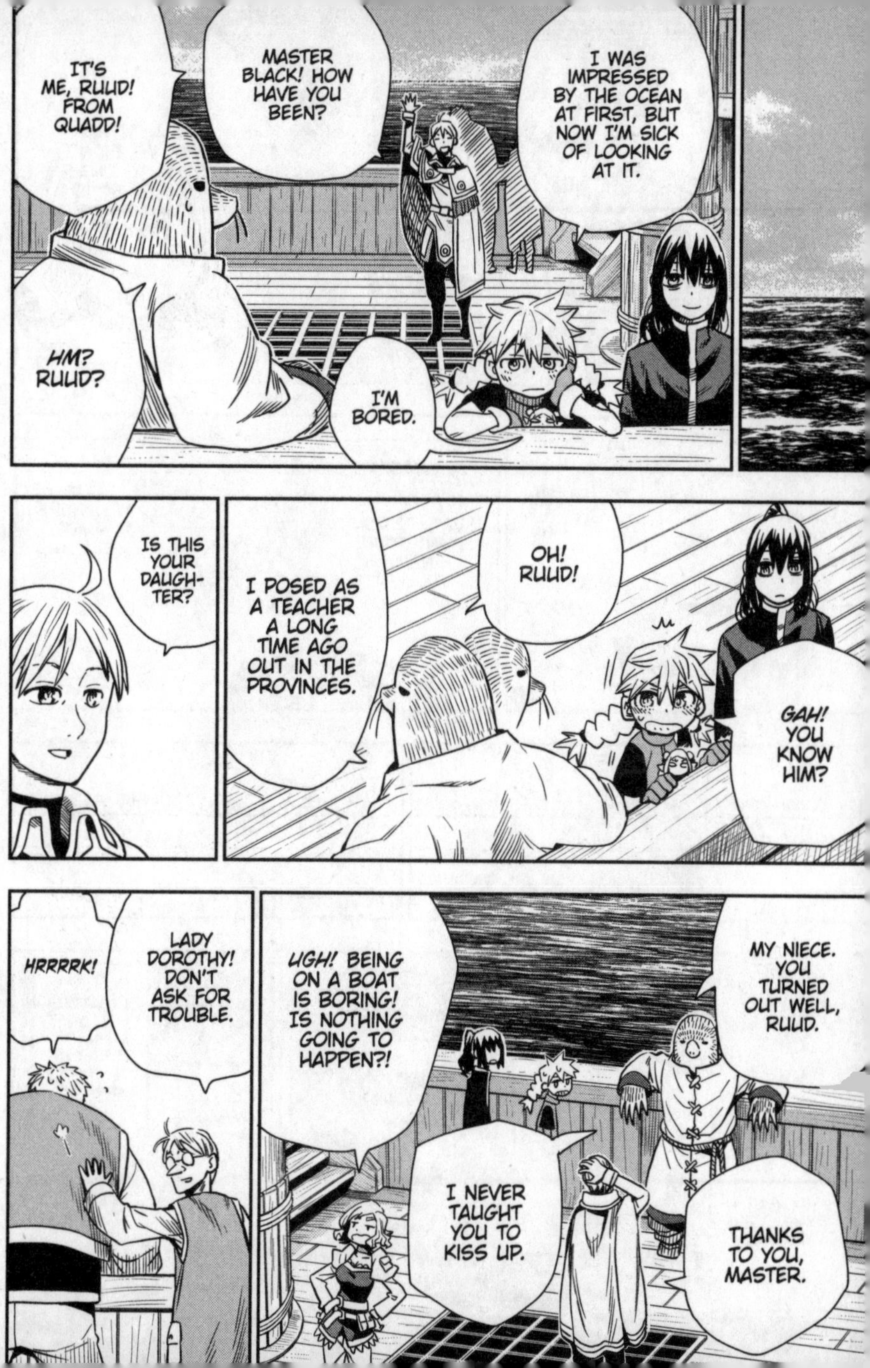
I WAS IMPRESSED BY THE OCEAN AT FIRST, BUT NOW I'M SICK OF LOOKING AT IT.
MASTER BLACK! HOW HAVE YOU BEEN?
IT'S ME, RUUD! FROM QUADD!
I'M BORED.
HM? RUUD?
OH! RUUD!
GAH! YOU KNOW HIM?
I POSED AS A TEACHER A LONG TIME AGO OUT IN THE PROVINCES.
IS THIS YOUR DAUGHTER?
MY NIECE. YOU TURNED OUT WELL, RUUD.
UGH! BEING ON A BOAT IS BORING! IS NOTHING GOING TO HAPPEN?!
I NEVER TAUGHT YOU TO KISS UP.
THANKS TO YOU, MASTER.
LADY DOROTHY! DON'T ASK FOR TROUBLE.
HRRRRK!

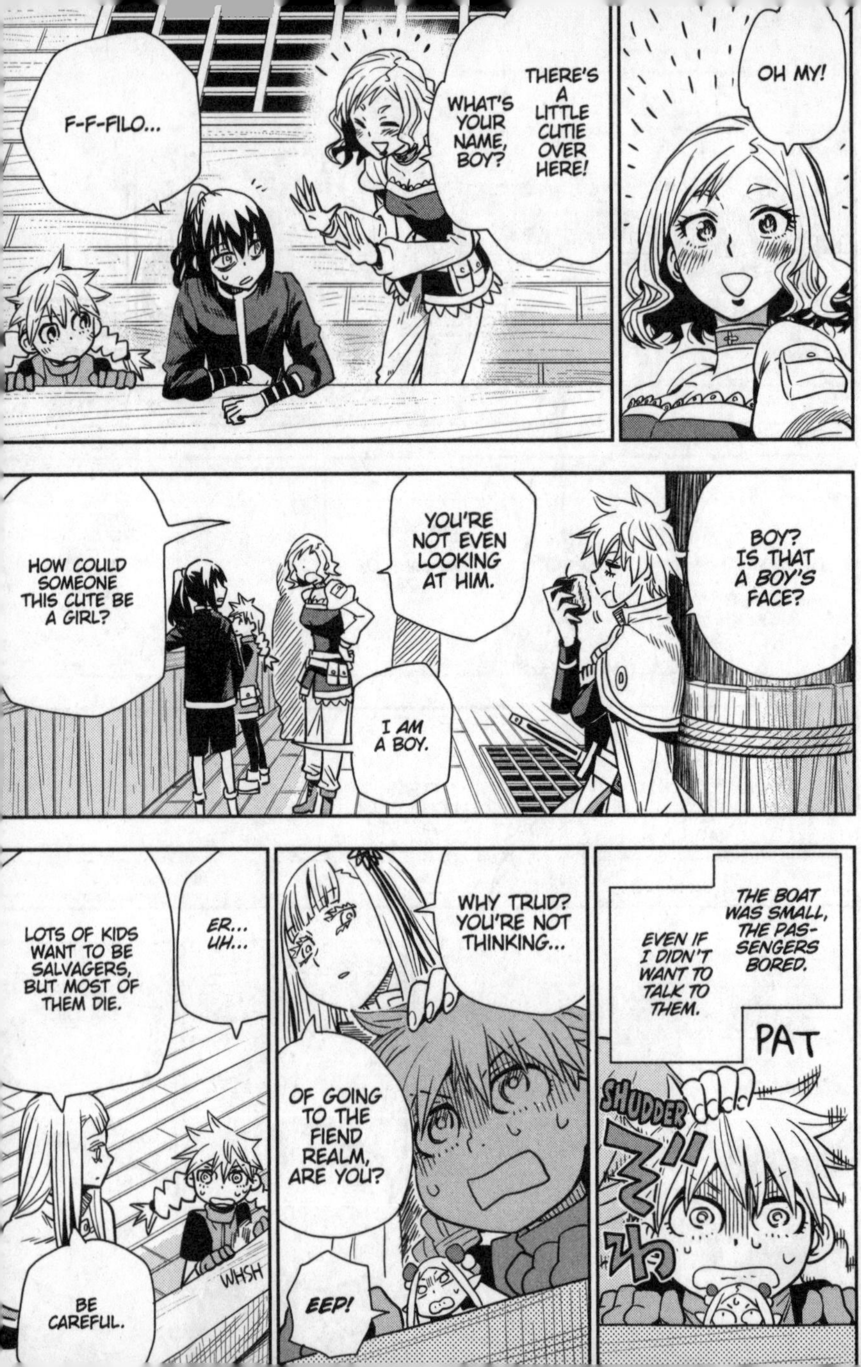
OH MY!
THERE'S A LITTLE CUTIE OVER HERE!
WHAT'S YOUR NAME, BOY?
F-F-FILO...
BOY? IS THAT A BOY'S FACE?
YOU'RE NOT EVEN LOOKING AT HIM.
HOW COULD SOMEONE THIS CUTE BE A GIRL?
I AM A BOY.
THE BOAT WAS SMALL, THE PASSENGERS BORED.
EVEN IF I DIDN'T WANT TO TALK TO THEM.
PAT
SHUDDER
WHY TRUD? YOU'RE NOT THINKING...
OF GOING TO THE FIEND REALM, ARE YOU?
EEP!
ER... UH...
LOTS OF KIDS WANT TO BE SALVAGERS, BUT MOST OF THEM DIE.
WHSH
BE CAREFUL.

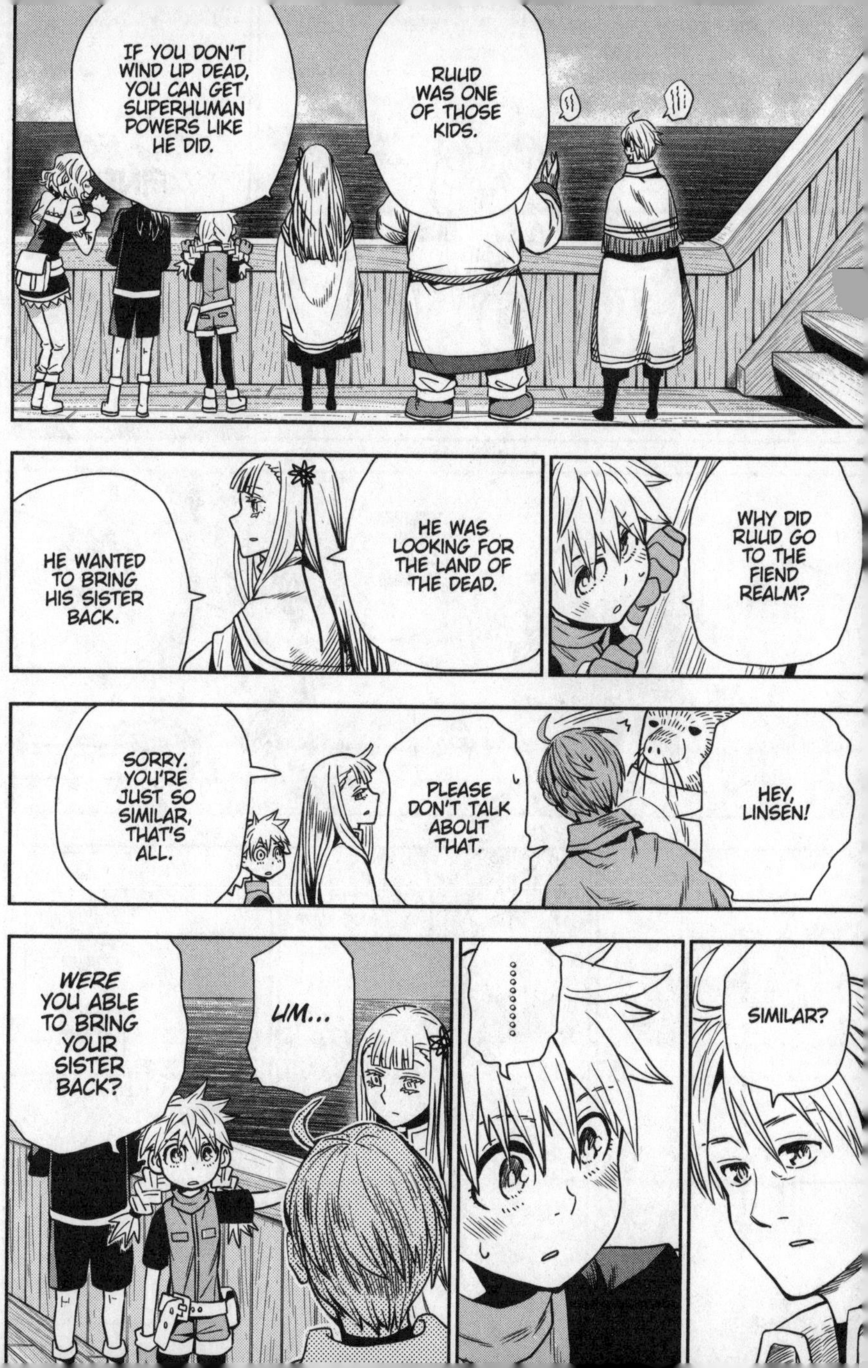
RUUD WAS ONE OF THOSE KIDS.
IF YOU DON'T WIND UP DEAD, YOU CAN GET SUPERHUMAN POWERS LIKE HE DID.
WHY DID RUUD GO TO THE FIEND REALM?
HE WAS LOOKING FOR THE LAND OF THE DEAD.
HE WANTED TO BRING HIS SISTER BACK.
HEY, LINSEN!
PLEASE DON'T TALK ABOUT THAT.
SORRY. YOU'RE JUST SO SIMILAR, THAT'S ALL.
SIMILAR?
....
WERE YOU ABLE TO BRING YOUR SISTER BACK?
UM...

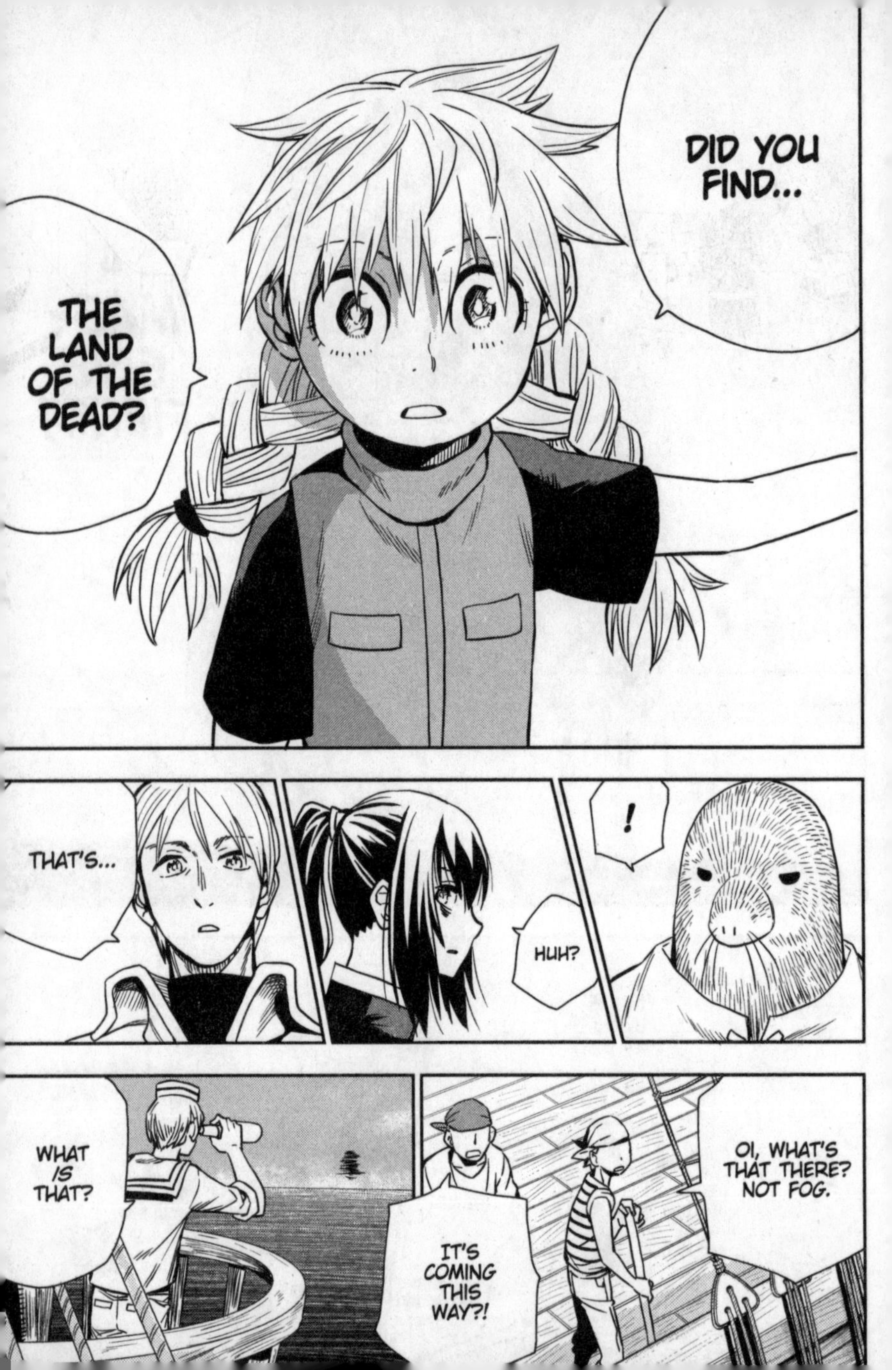
DID YOU FIND...
THE LAND OF THE DEAD?
!
HUH?
THAT'S...
OI, WHAT'S THAT THERE? NOT FOG.
IT'S COMING THIS WAY?!
WHAT *IS* THAT?

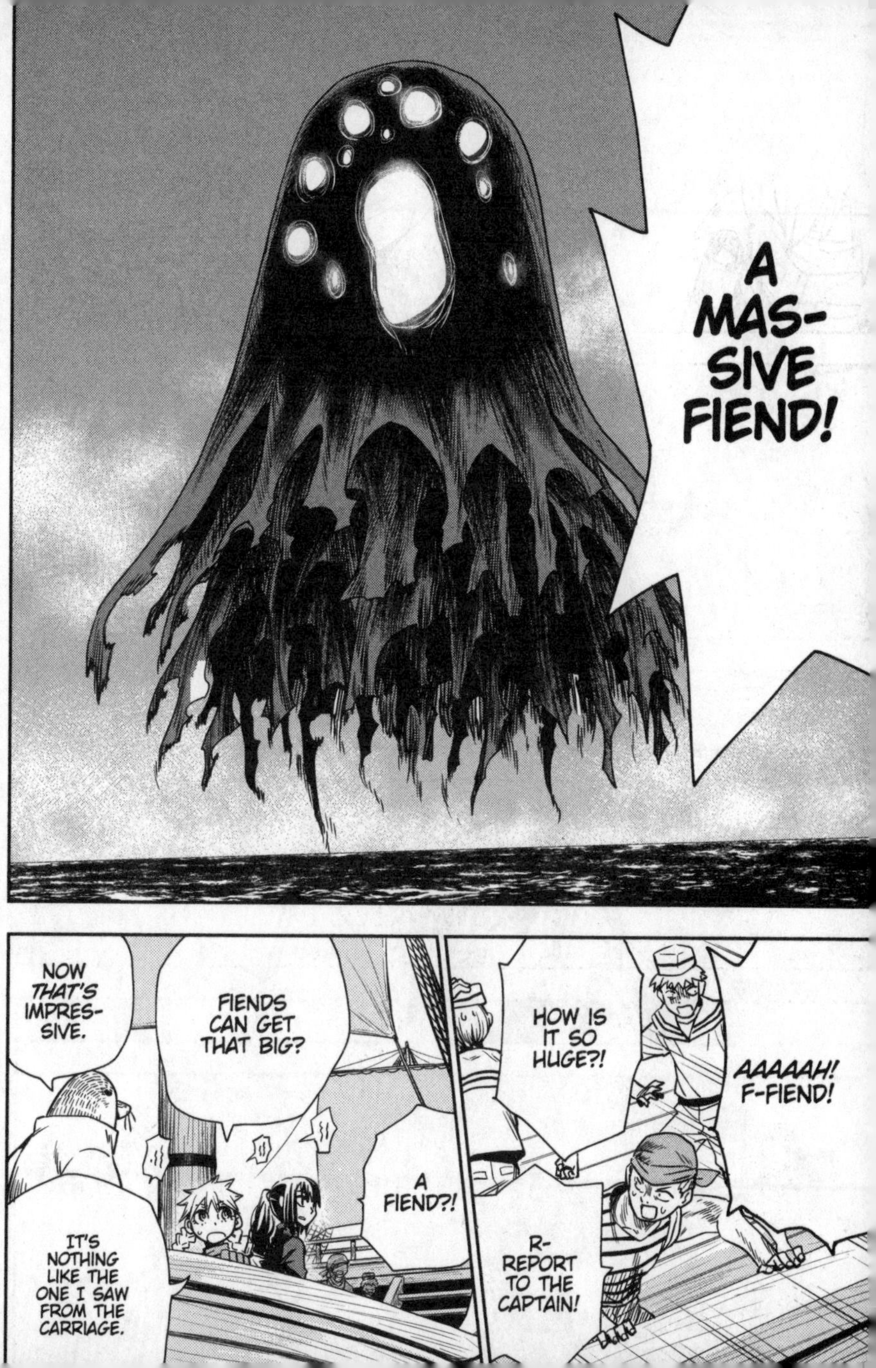
A MAS-
SIVE
FIEND!
AAAAAH! F-FIEND!
HOW IS IT SO HUGE?!
R- REPORT TO THE CAPTAIN!
FIENDS CAN GET THAT BIG?
NOW *THAT'S* IMPRES-SIVE.
A FIEND?!
IT'S NOTHING LIKE THE ONE I SAW FROM THE CARRIAGE.

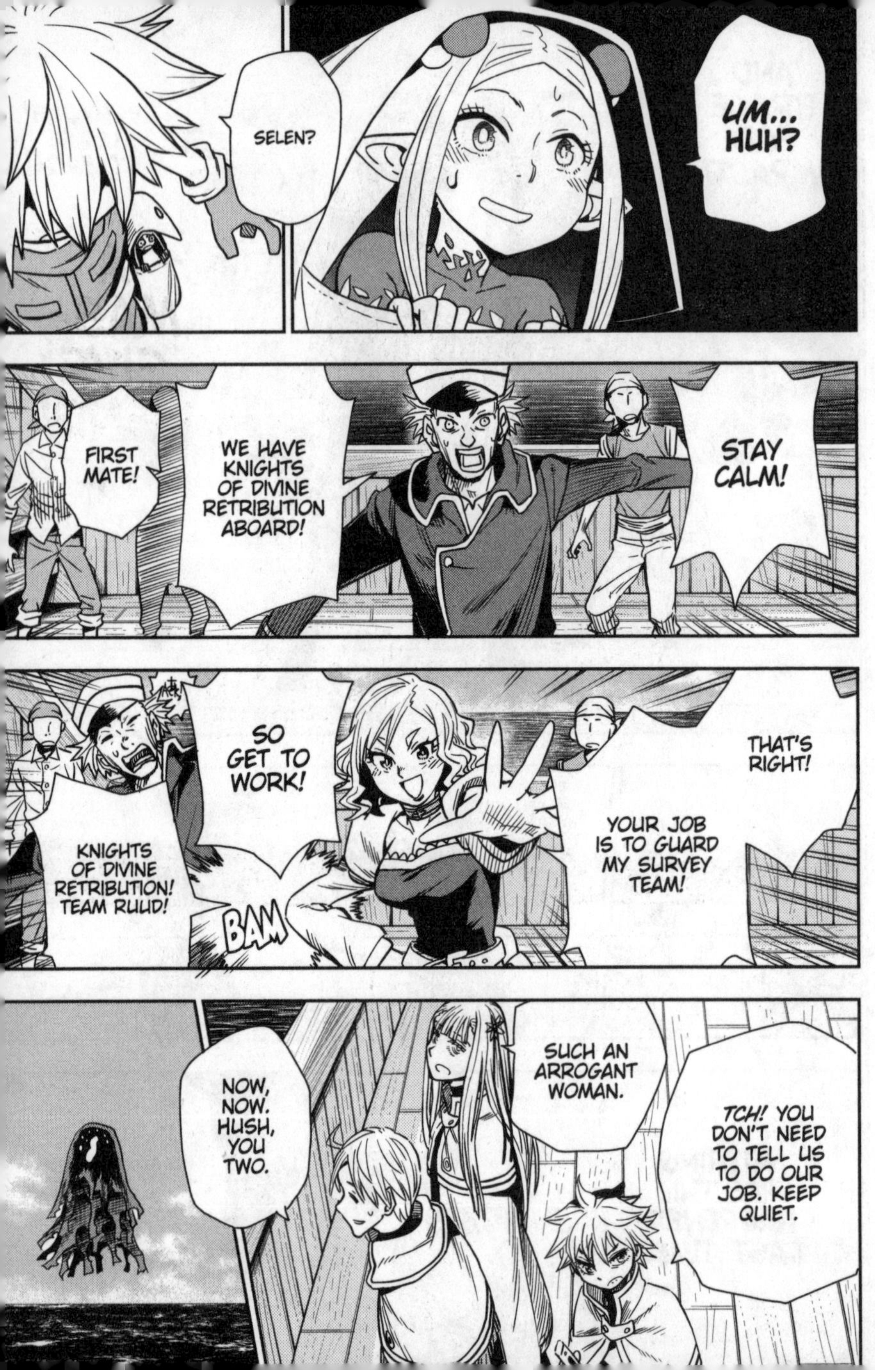
UM... HUH?
SELEN?
STAY CALM!
WE HAVE KNIGHTS OF DIVINE RETRIBUTION ABOARD!
FIRST MATE!
THAT'S RIGHT!
YOUR JOB IS TO GUARD MY SURVEY TEAM!
SO GET TO WORK!
KNIGHTS OF DIVINE RETRIBUTION! TEAM RUUD!
BAM
TCH! YOU DON'T NEED TO TELL US TO DO OUR JOB. KEEP QUIET.
SUCH AN ARROGANT WOMAN.
NOW, NOW. HUSH, YOU TWO.

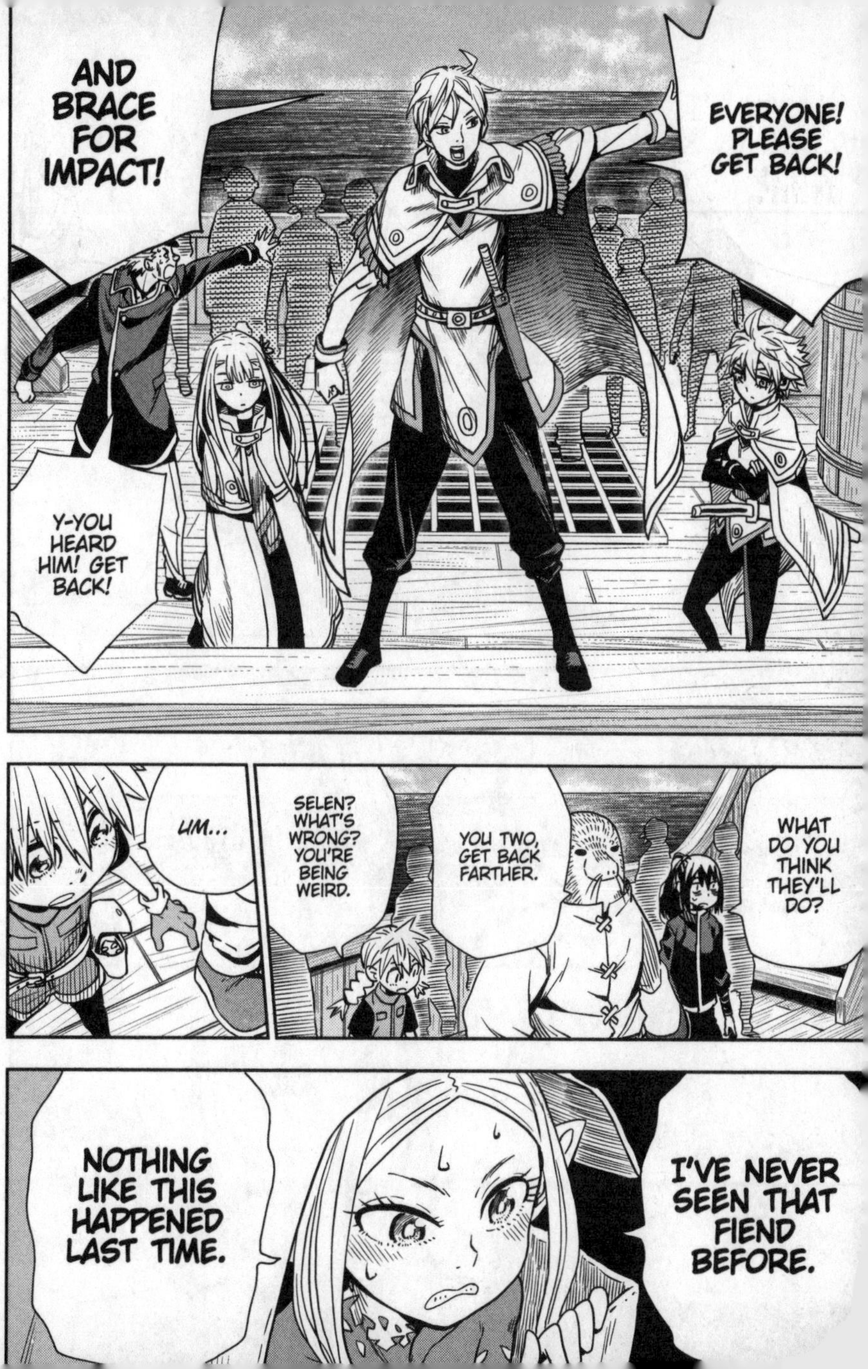
EVERYONE! PLEASE GET BACK!
AND BRACE FOR IMPACT!
Y-YOU HEARD HIM! GET BACK!
WHAT DO YOU THINK THEY'LL DO?
YOU TWO, GET BACK FARTHER.
SELEN? WHAT'S WRONG? YOU'RE BEING WEIRD.
UM...
I'VE NEVER SEEN THAT FIEND BEFORE.
NOTHING LIKE THIS HAPPENED LAST TIME.

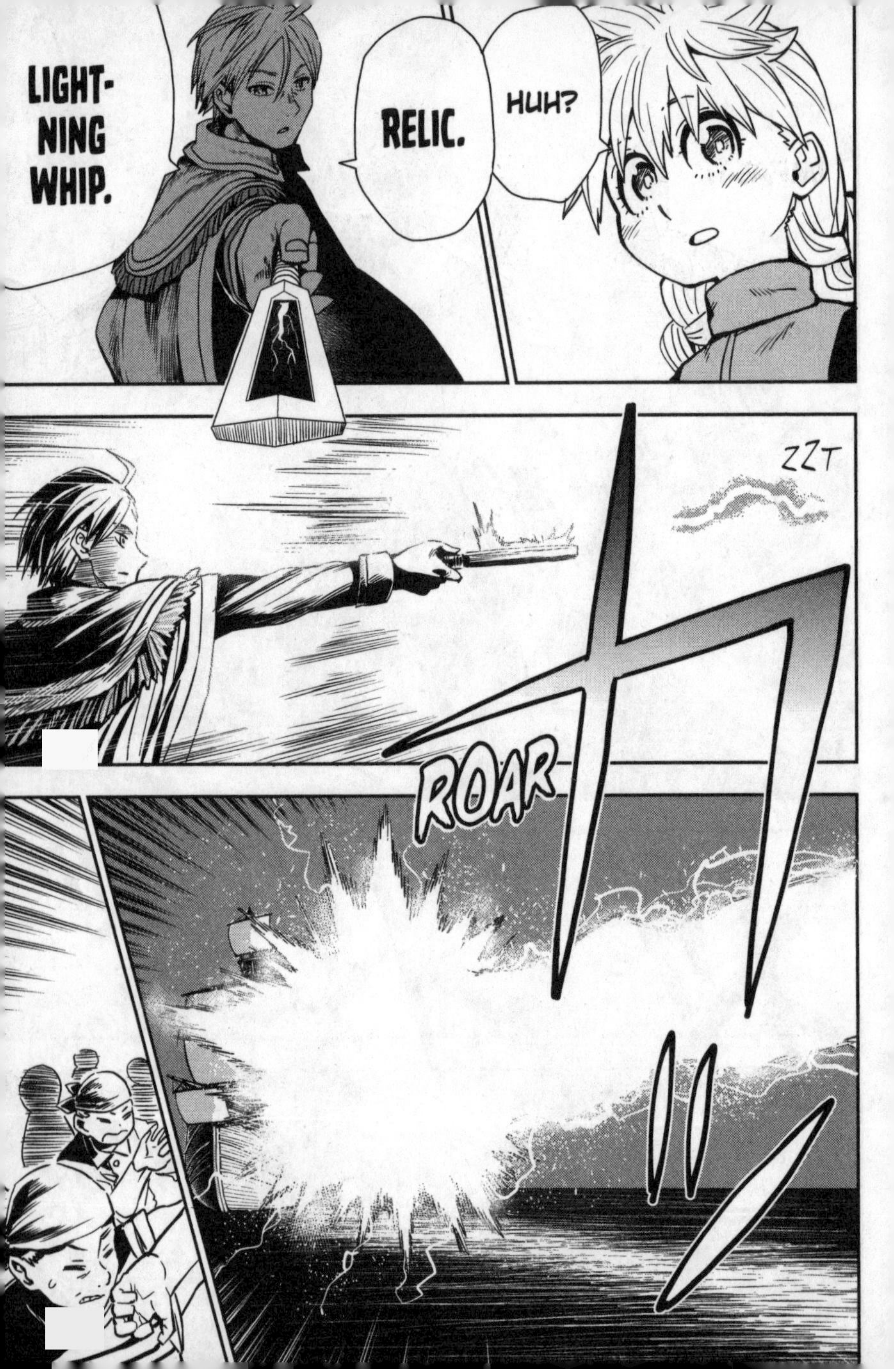
HUH?
RELIC.
LIGHT-NING WHIP.
ZZT
ROAR

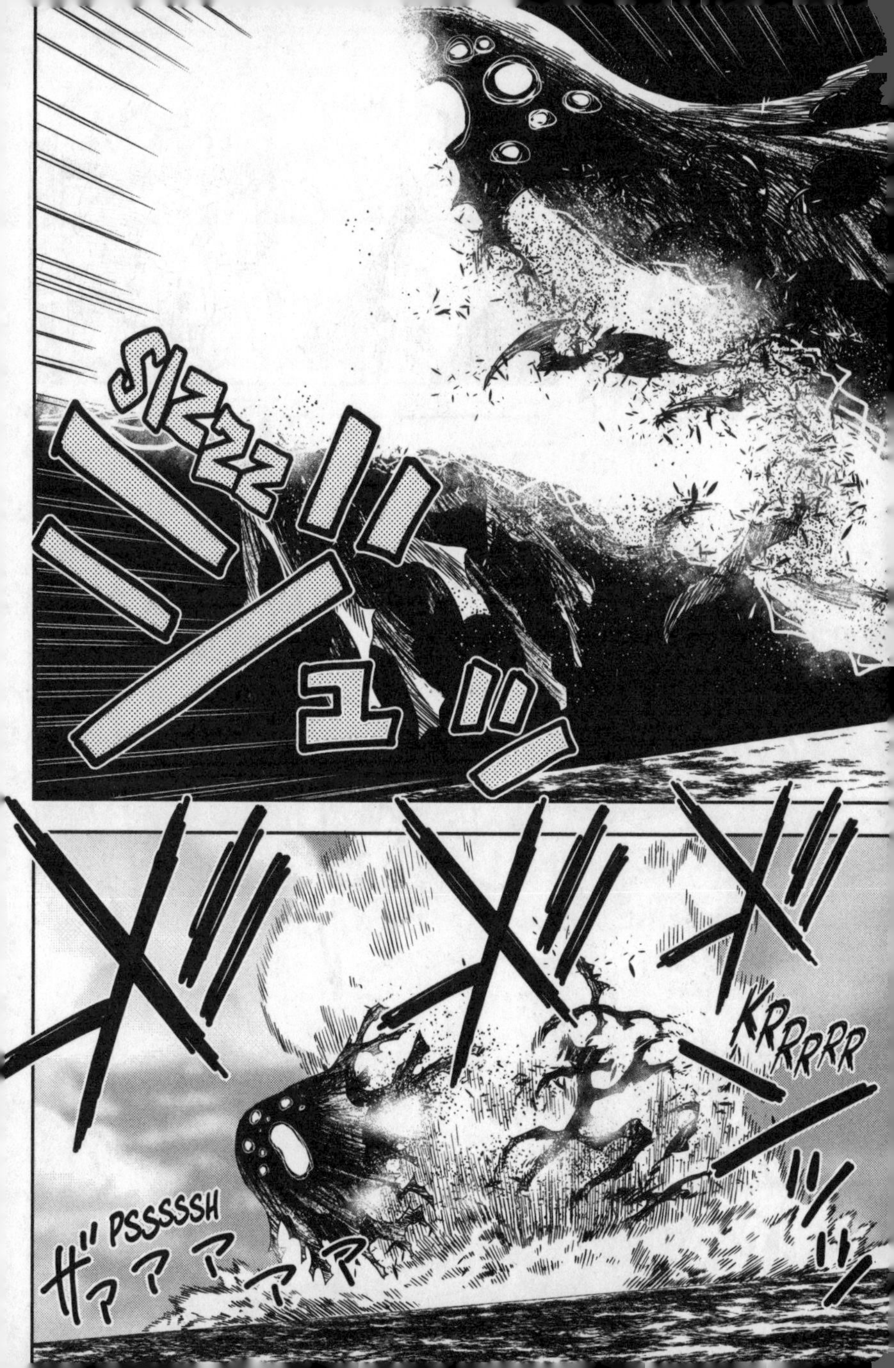
SIZZZ
KRRRRR
PSSSSSH

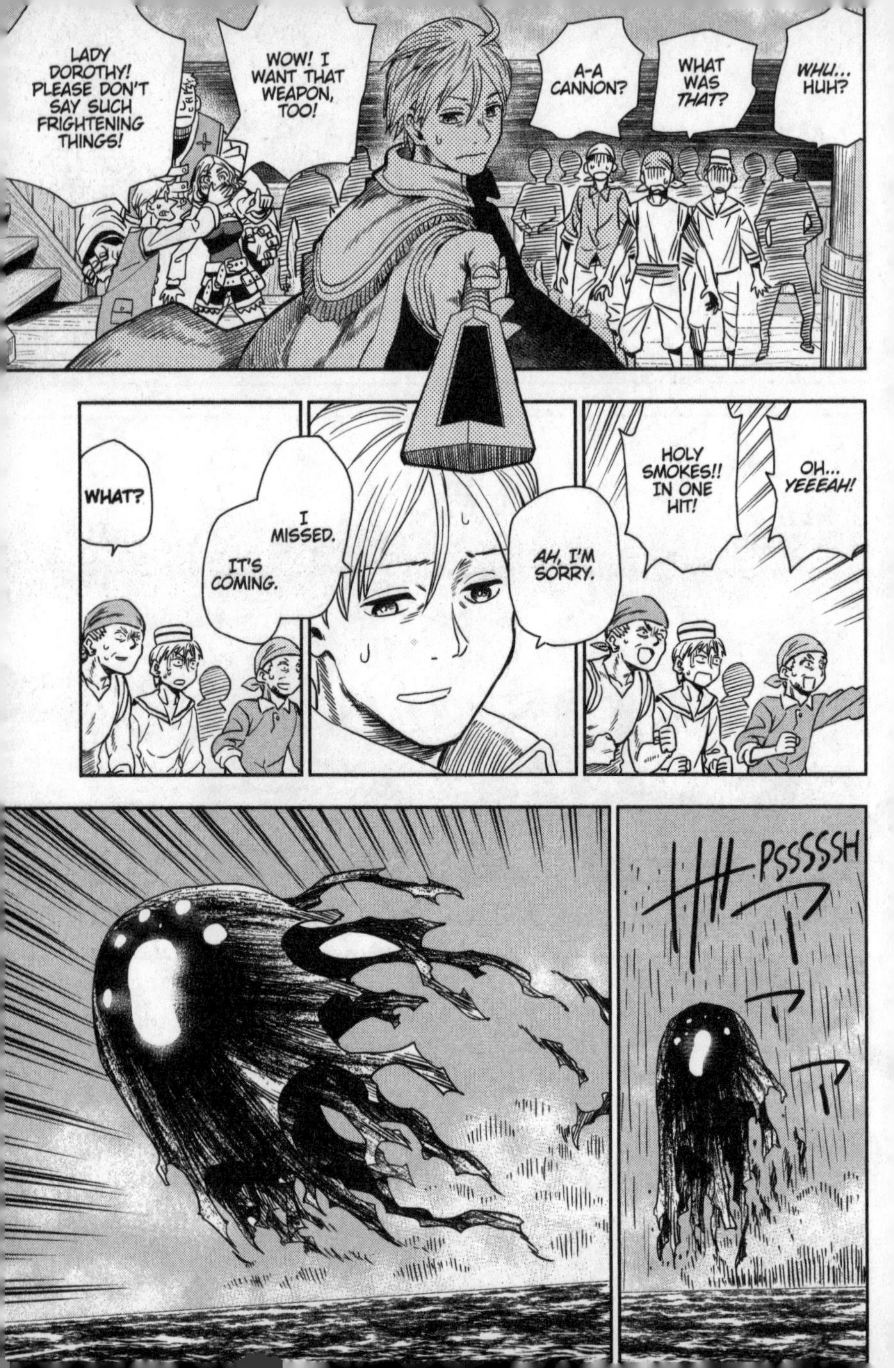
WHU... HUH?
WHAT WAS *THAT*?
A-A CANNON?
WOW! I WANT THAT WEAPON, TOO!
LADY DOROTHY! PLEASE DON'T SAY SUCH FRIGHTENING THINGS!
OH... YEEEAH!
HOLY SMOKES!! IN ONE HIT!
AH, I'M SORRY.
I MISSED.
IT'S COMING.
WHAT?
PSSSSSH

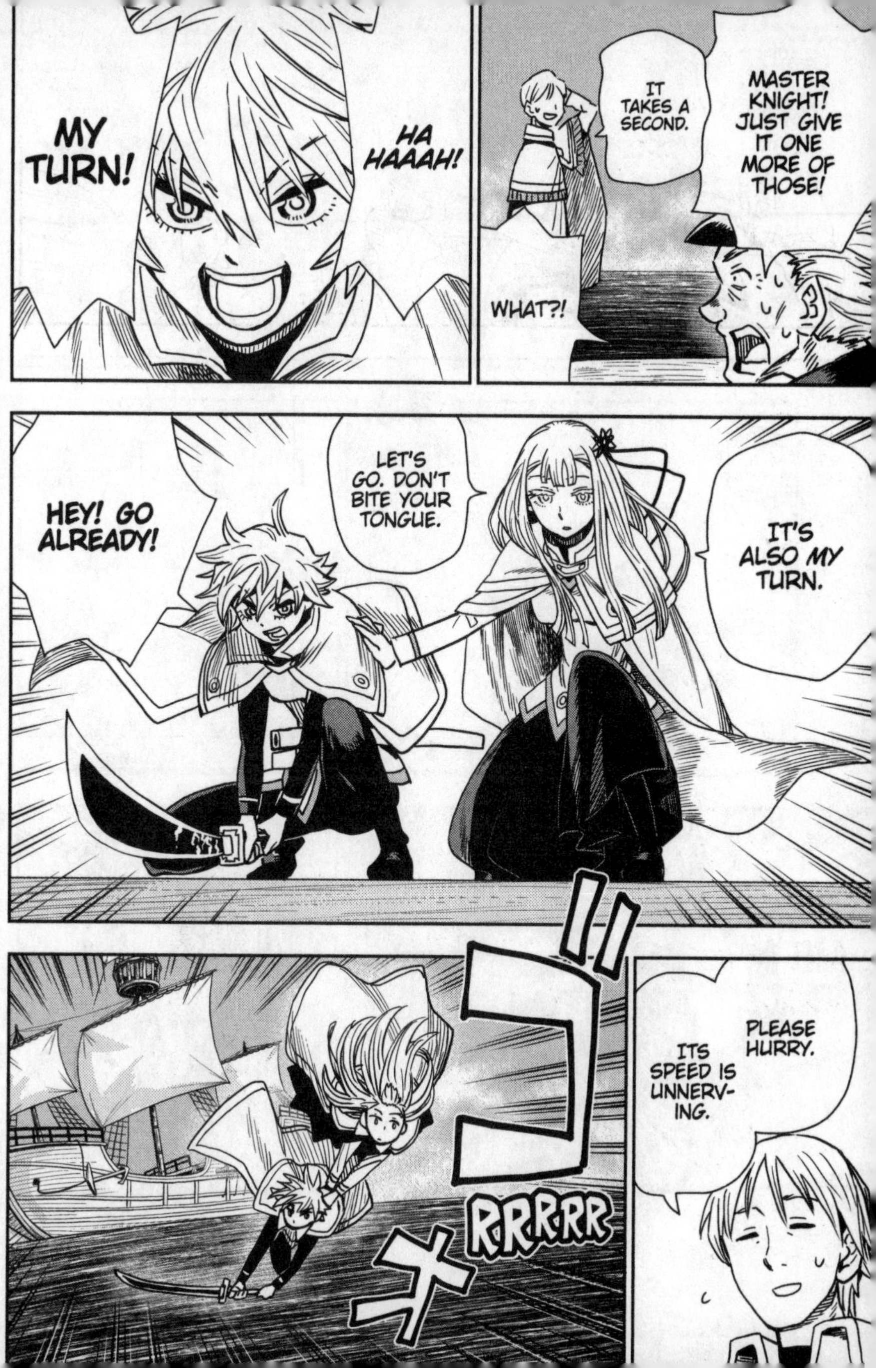
MASTER KNIGHT! JUST GIVE IT ONE MORE OF THOSE!
IT TAKES A SECOND.
WHAT?!
HA HAAAH!
MY TURN!
IT'S ALSO *MY* TURN.
LET'S GO. DON'T BITE YOUR TONGUE.
HEY! GO ALREADY!
PLEASE HURRY.
ITS SPEED IS UNNERV-ING.
ゴ
RRRRR
オ

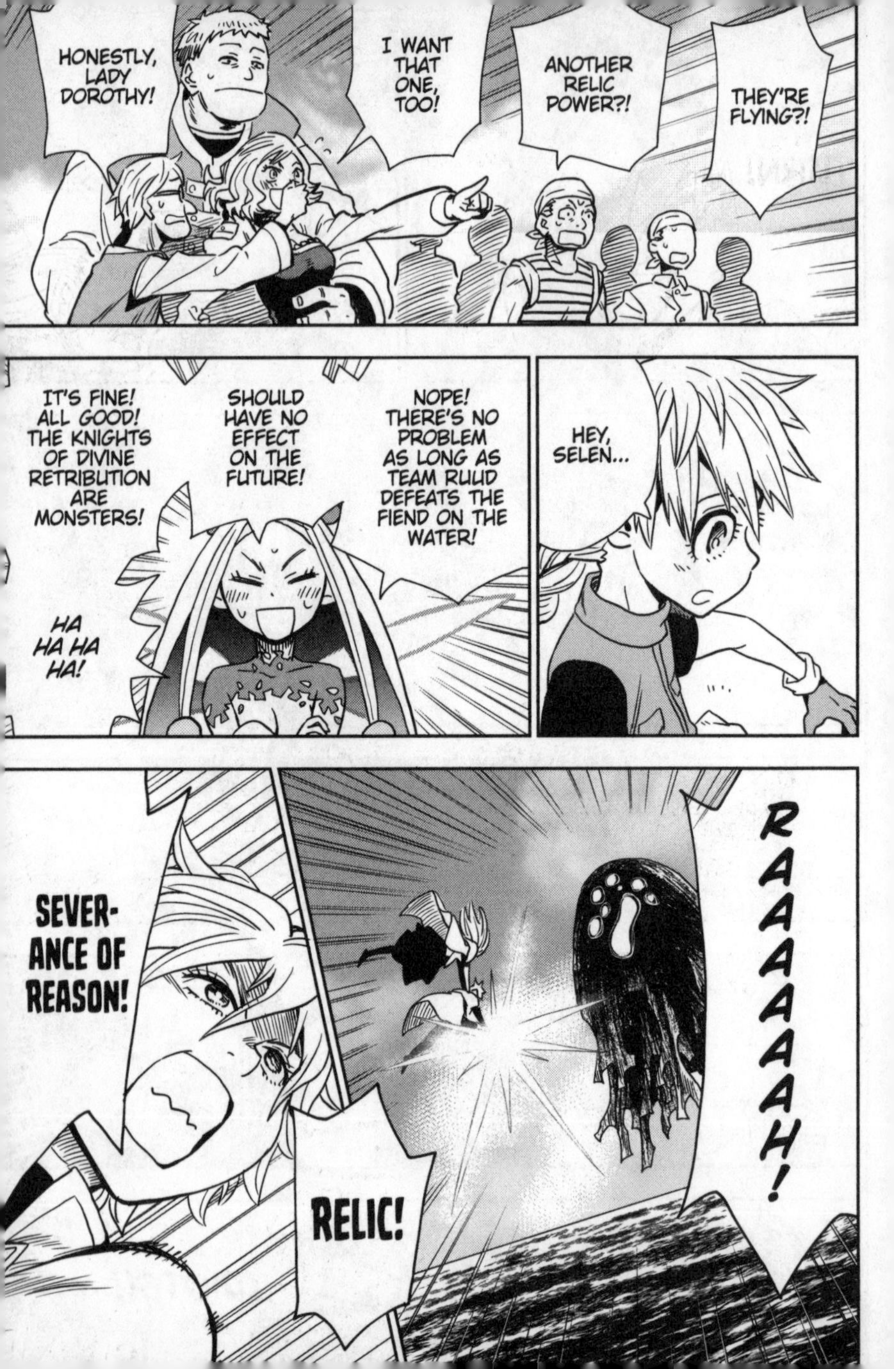
THEY'RE FLYING?!
ANOTHER RELIC POWER?!
I WANT THAT ONE, TOO!
HONESTLY, LADY DOROTHY!
HEY, SELEN...
NOPE! THERE'S NO PROBLEM AS LONG AS TEAM RUUD DEFEATS THE FIEND ON THE WATER!
SHOULD HAVE NO EFFECT ON THE FUTURE!
IT'S FINE! ALL GOOD! THE KNIGHTS OF DIVINE RETRIBUTION ARE MONSTERS!
HA HA HA HA!
RAAAAAAAH!
SEVER-ANCE OF REASON!
RELIC!

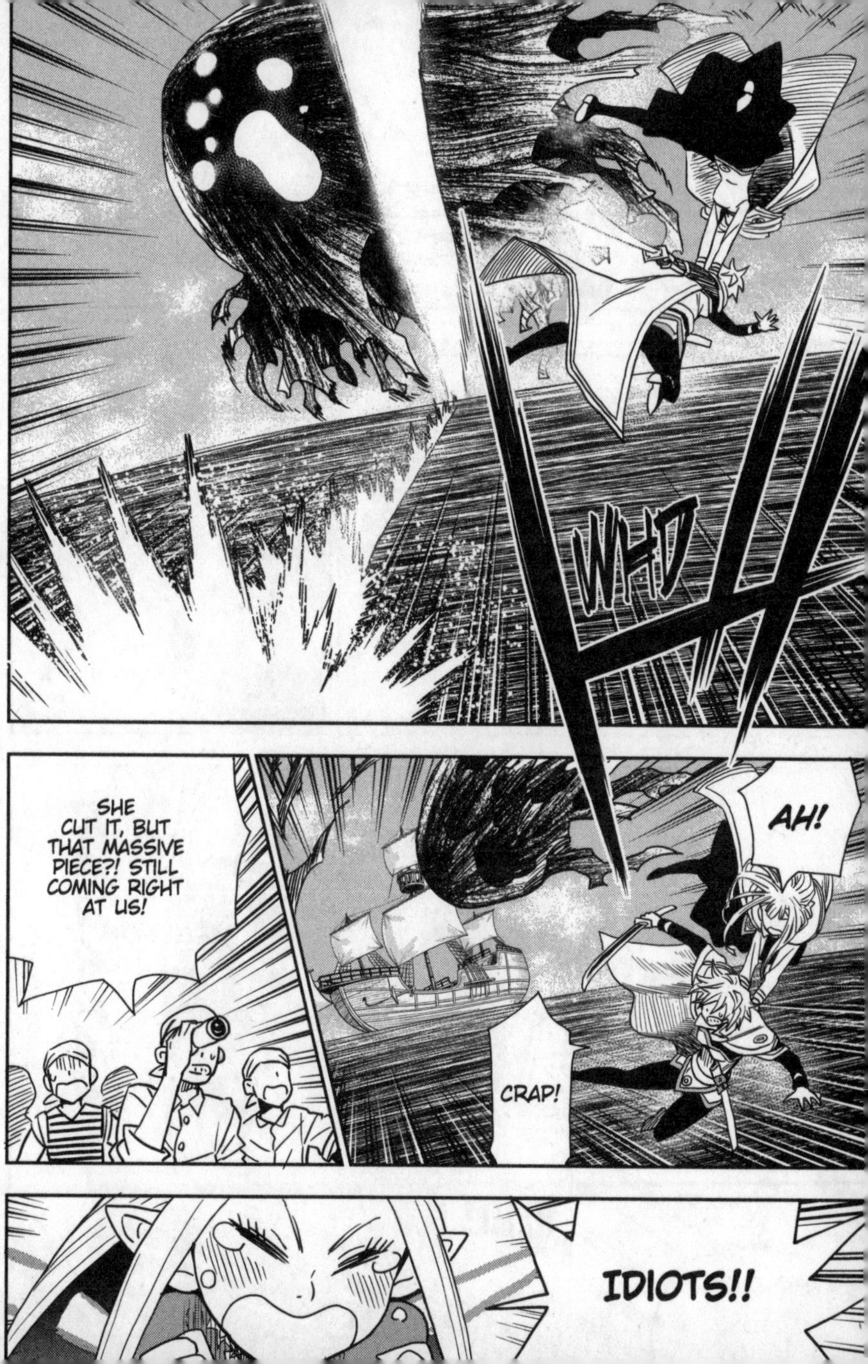
WHD
AH!
CRAP!
SHE CUT IT, BUT THAT MASSIVE PIECE?! STILL COMING RIGHT AT US!
IDIOTS!!

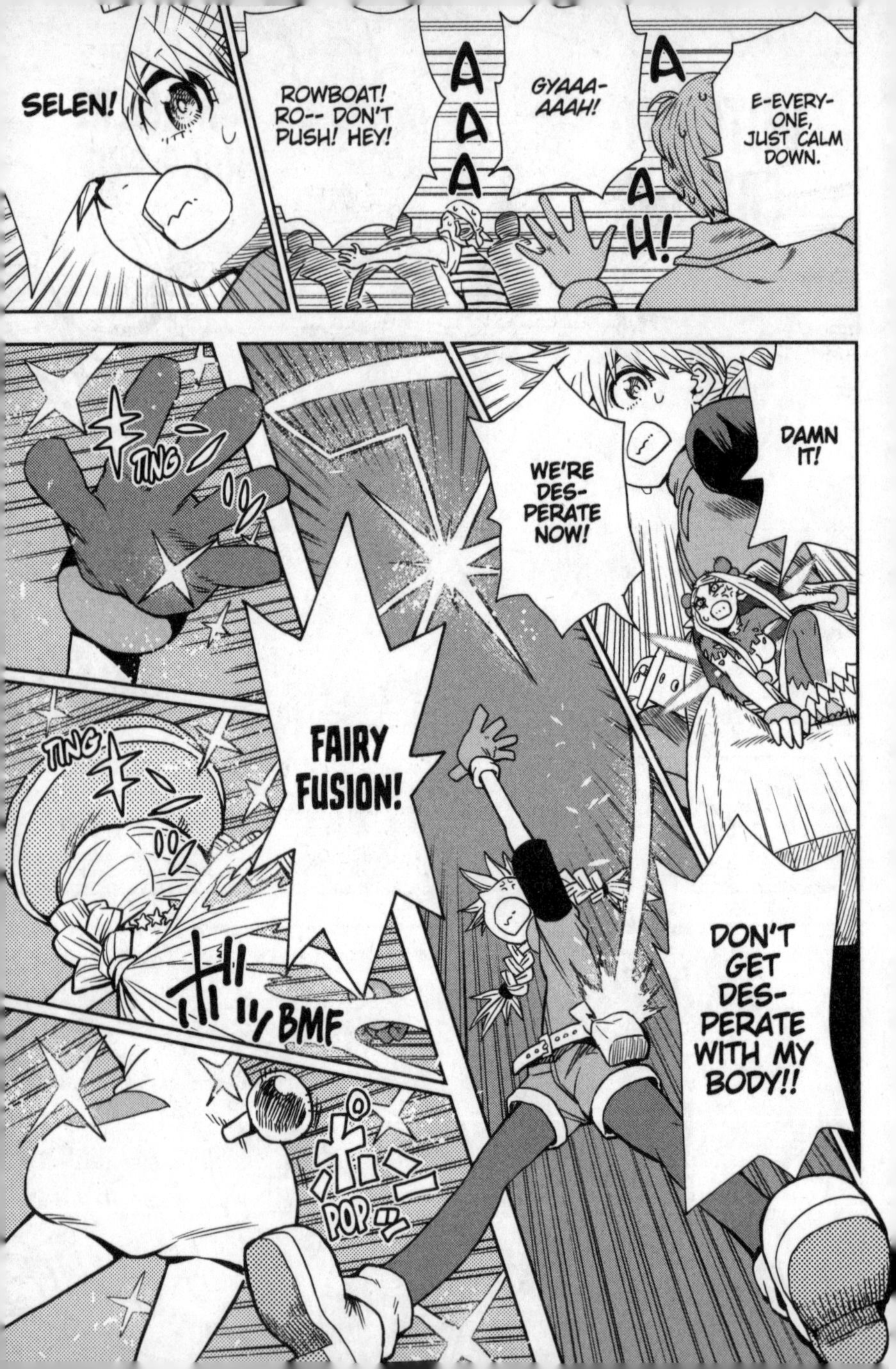
E-EVERY-ONE, JUST CALM DOWN.
AAH!
GYAAA-AAAH!
AAA
ROWBOAT! RO-- DON'T PUSH! HEY!
SELEN!
DAMN IT!
WE'RE DES-PERATE NOW!
DON'T GET DES-PERATE WITH MY BODY!!
FAIRY FUSION!
TING
TING
BMF
POP

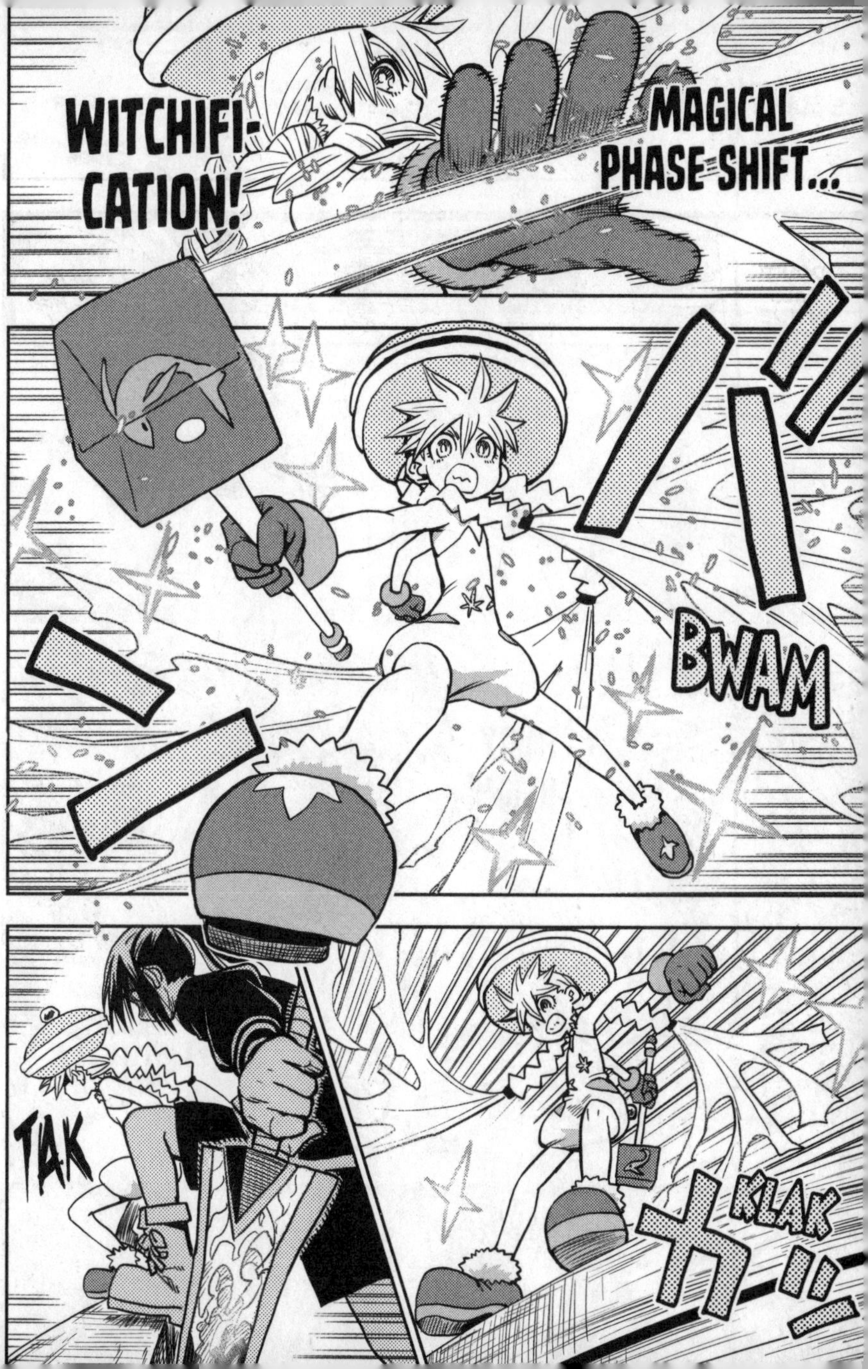
MAGICAL PHASE SHIFT...
WITCHIFI-CATION!
BWAM
KLAK
TAK

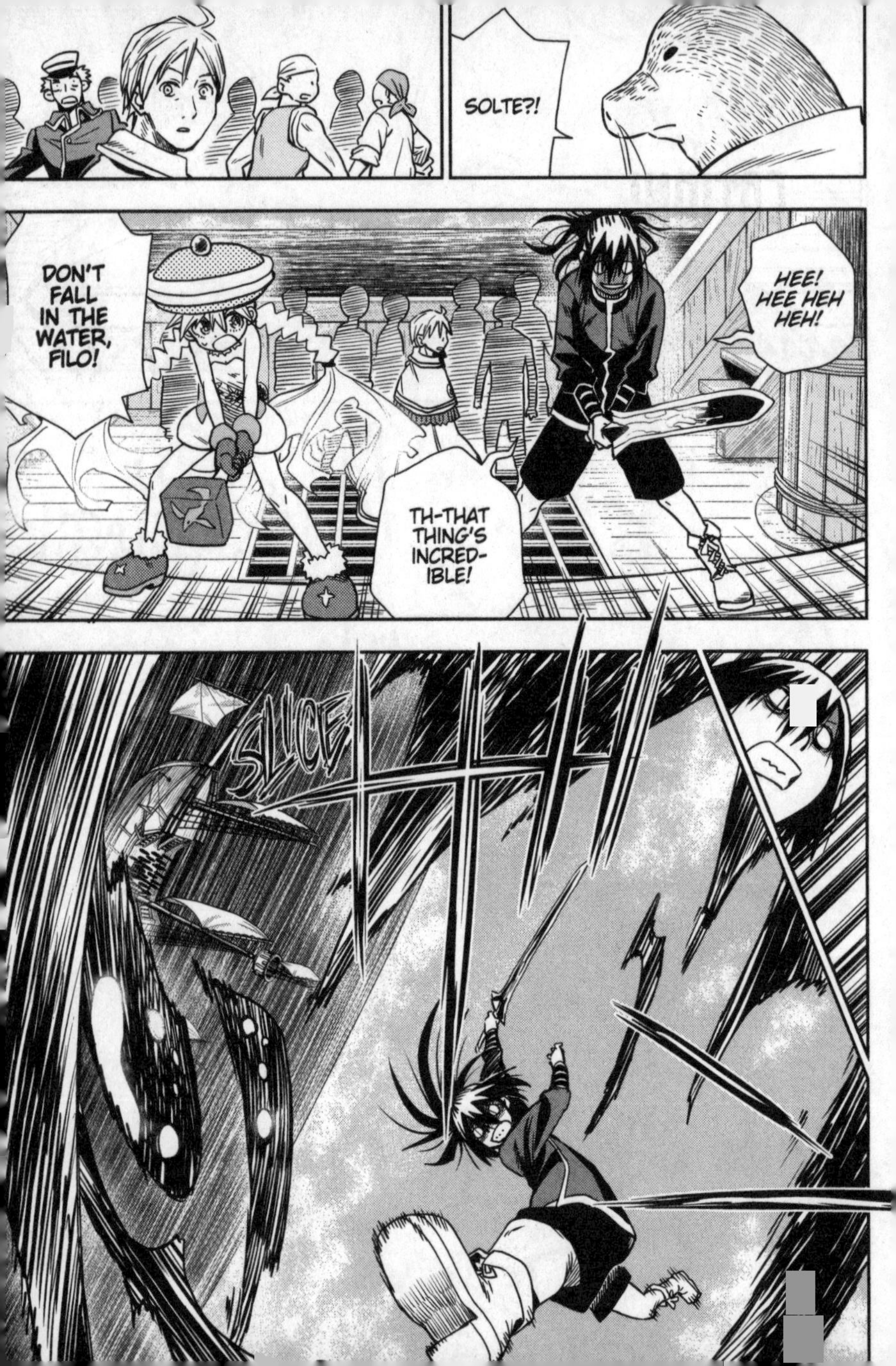
SOLTE?!
HEE! HEE HEH HEH!
TH-THAT THING'S INCREDIBLE!
DON'T FALL IN THE WATER, FILO!
SLICE

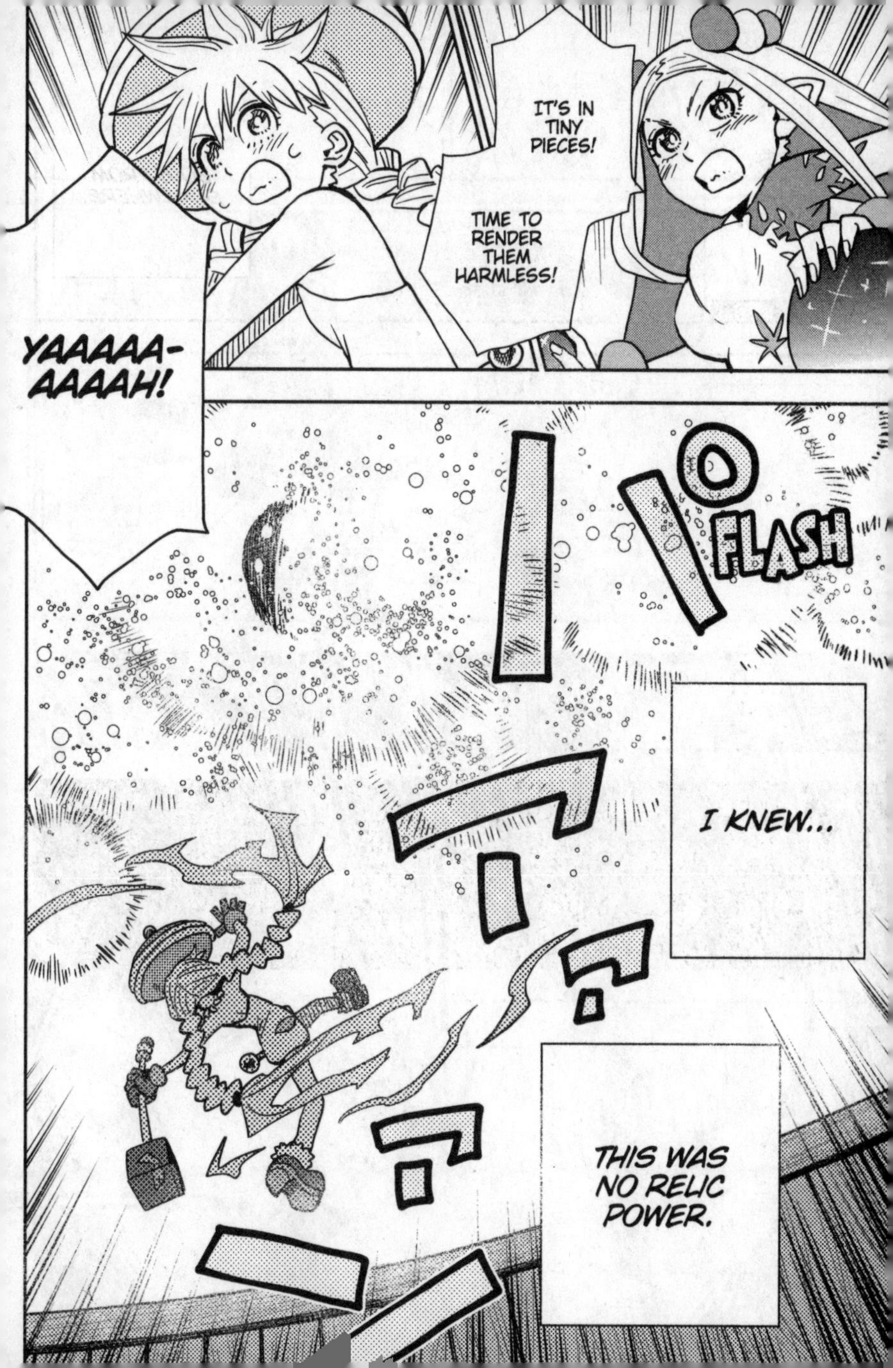
IT'S IN TINY PIECES!
TIME TO RENDER THEM HARMLESS!
YAAAAA-AAAAH!
FLASH
I KNEW...
THIS WAS NO RELIC POWER.

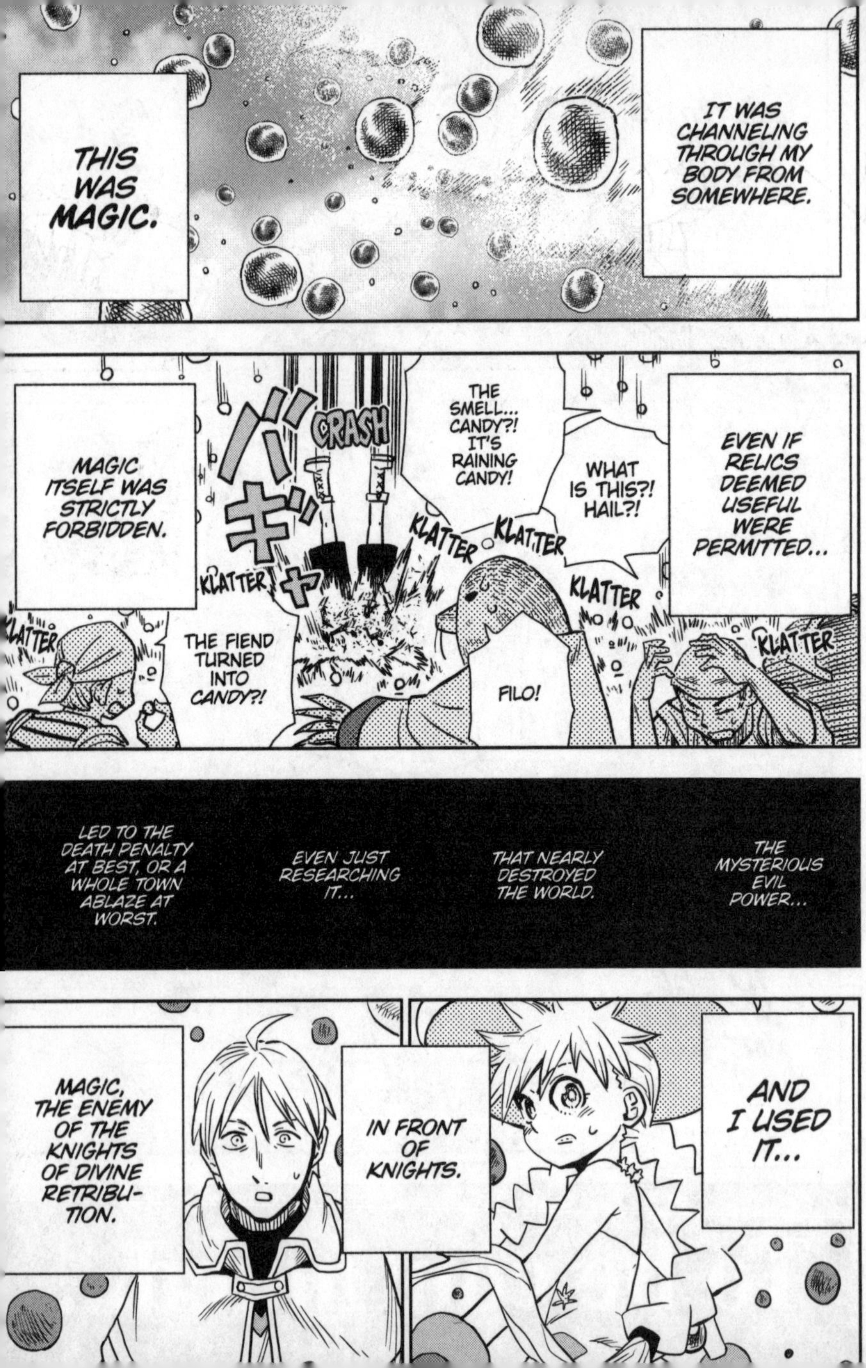
IT WAS CHANNELING THROUGH MY BODY FROM SOMEWHERE.
THIS WAS MAGIC.
EVEN IF RELICS DEEMED USEFUL WERE PERMITTED...
KLATTER
KLATTER
WHAT IS THIS?! HAIL?!
THE SMELL... CANDY?! IT'S RAINING CANDY!
KLATTER
KLATTER
FILO!
CRASH
バギャ
KLATTER
KLATTER
THE FIEND TURNED INTO CANDY?!
MAGIC ITSELF WAS STRICTLY FORBIDDEN.
THE MYSTERIOUS EVIL POWER...
THAT NEARLY DESTROYED THE WORLD.
EVEN JUST RESEARCHING IT...
LED TO THE DEATH PENALTY AT BEST, OR A WHOLE TOWN ABLAZE AT WORST.
AND I USED IT...
IN FRONT OF KNIGHTS.
MAGIC, THE ENEMY OF THE KNIGHTS OF DIVINE RETRIBU-TION.

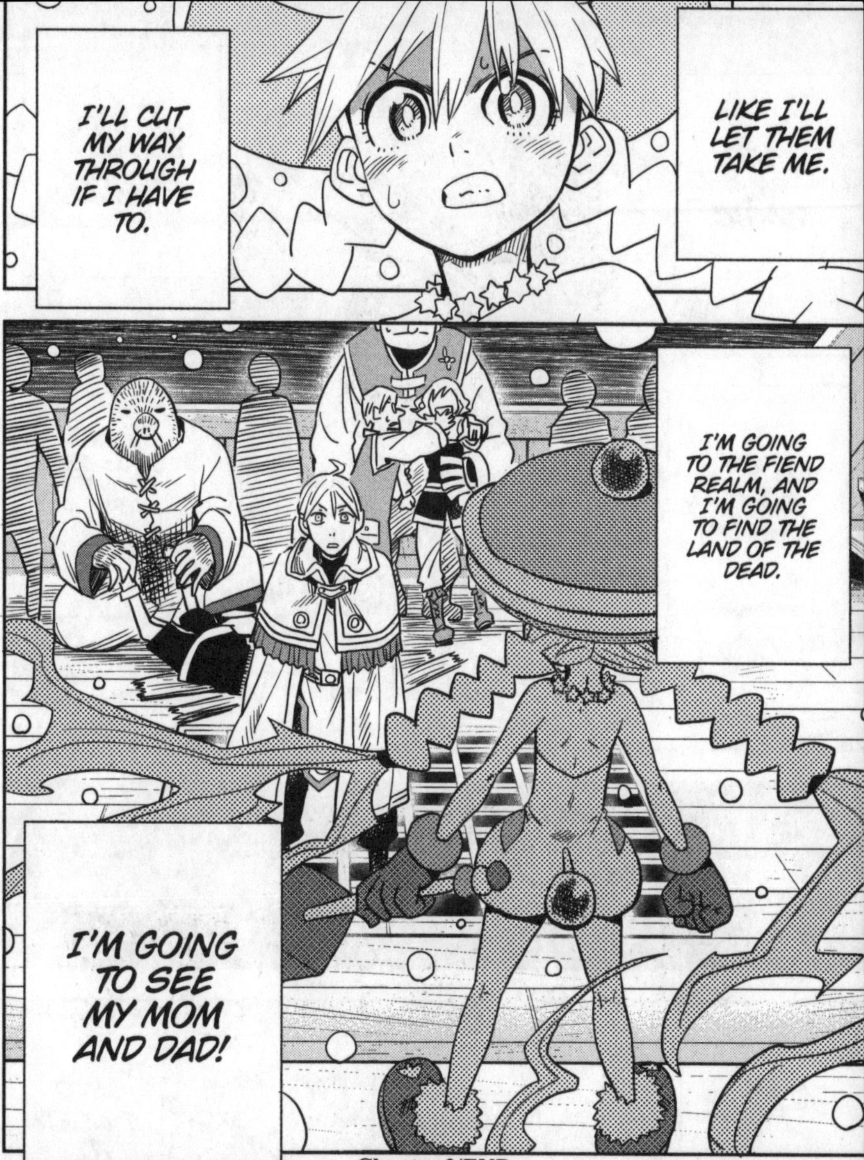
LIKE I'LL LET THEM TAKE ME.
I'LL CUT MY WAY THROUGH IF I HAVE TO.
I'M GOING TO THE FIEND REALM, AND I'M GOING TO FIND THE LAND OF THE DEAD.
I'M GOING TO SEE MY MOM AND DAD!

Chapter 3/END

To be continued...

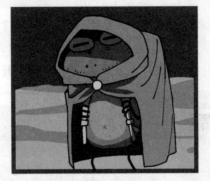

Satoshi Mizukami

Traveler...do you recall the
purpose of your journey?
Your very first objective. The
mission you were born with.
No? Nothing to fear if you've
forgotten. Remembering is a
journey in itself...

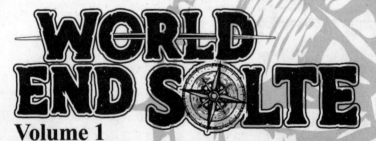

WORLD END SOLTE

Volume 1

Title Logo/Cover Design:
Takashi Kurosu
(Cross Media)

Staff:
Hitoshi Usui
Ichiri Seto
Tsubasa Shinonome

Supervising Editor:
Yukinori Miyamoto

SEVEN SEAS ENTERTAINMENT PRESENTS

WORLD END

story and art by **SATOSHI MIZUKAMI**

TRANSLATION
Jocelyne Allen

ADAPTATION
Ysabet Reinhardt MacFarlane

LETTERING
Lys Blakeslee

COVER DESIGN
H. Qi

PROOFREADER
Kurestin Armada

SENIOR EDITOR
Peter Adrian Behravesh

PRODUCTION DESIGNER
Christina McKenzie

PRODUCTION MANAGER
Lissa Pattillo

PREPRESS TECHNICIAN
Melanie Ujimori

PRINT MANAGER
Rhiannon Rasmussen-Silverstein

EDITOR-IN-CHIEF
Julie Davis

ASSOCIATE PUBLISHER
Adam Arnold

PUBLISHER
Jason DeAngelis

Seven Seas press and purchase enquiries can be sent to Marketing Manager Lianne Sentar at press@gomanga.com. Information regarding the distribution and purchase of digital editions is available from Digital Manager CK Russell at digital@gomanga.com.

ISBN: 978-1-63858-216-8
Printed in Canada
First Printing: July 2022
10 9 8 7 6 5 4 3 2 1

READING DIRECTIONS

This book reads from *right to left*, Japanese style. If this is your first time reading manga, you start reading from the top right panel on each page and take it from there. If you get lost, just follow the numbered diagram here. It may seem backwards at first, but you'll get the hang of it! Have fun!!

1
2
3
4
5
6
7
8
9

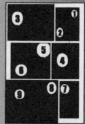

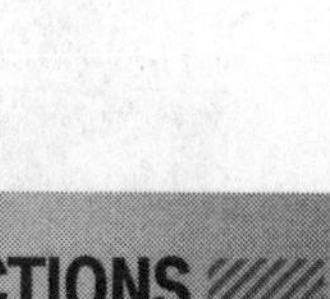

Follow us online: www.SevenSeasEntertainment.com